ESSAYS, LECTURES, ETC.

UPON

SELECT TOPICS

IN

REVEALED THEOLOGY.

BY

NATHANIEL W. TAYLOR, D.D.
LATE DWIGHT PROFESSOR OF DIDACTIC THEOLOGY
IN YALE COLLEGE.

"For I am not ashamed of the Gospel of Christ; for it is the power of God unto salvation to every one that believeth."

NEW YORK:
PUBLISHED BY CLARK, AUSTIN & SMITH,
3 PARK ROW & 3 ANN STREET.
1859.

Entered, according to Act of Congress, in the year 1859, by

NOAH PORTER, SAMUEL G. BUCKINGHAM, AND WALTER T. HATCH,

In the Clerk's Office of the District Court of the United States for the Southern District of New York.

RENNIE, SHEA & LINDSAY,
STEREOTYPERS AND ELECTROTYPERS,
81, 83, and 85 Centre-street,
NEW YORK.

PRINTED BY
C. A. ALVORD,
15 Vandewater-st.,
NEW YORK.

INTRODUCTION.

This volume, as its title imports, consists of Essays, &c., from the pen of Dr. Taylor upon various topics in Revealed Theology. Dr. Taylor did not leave a fully written system or course of Theological lectures. The notes and briefs from which he lectured are so full indeed, that it would not be difficult to give to the public his views in the form of a complete system of Revealed Theology. But this would involve the necessity of expanding, by another hand, the heads of argument which were sketched by him. In many of these views there is little that is original with him, except the arrangement and development of the reasoning. There seems therefore, to be no sufficient reason for publishing arguments with which theologians are already familiar. It would not however be just to the memory of the deceased, nor to the cause of truth, to withhold any discussions which may promise to throw light upon important scriptural doctrines, or to advance in any way the science of Christian Theology.

The volume contains papers on the Trinity, Human Sinfulness, Justification, Election, and Perseverance. The Essays on the Trinity were written after the discussions and controversy on this subject, which are not yet forgotten. The matter is somewhat different from that which Dr. Taylor was accustomed to read to his students in his earlier years. Whatever may be thought of the views expressed, they were carefully considered, and embody the results of earnest and honest thinking. It is to be regretted, that the Scriptural argument was so far unfinished that it is deemed unwise to publish any part of it. The papers on Human Sinfulness comprise all the lectures which the author was accustomed to read on this subject, with some additional matter. The Essays on Justification are but a fragment of an extended series of papers, upon which Dr. Taylor bestowed much earnest investigation and careful study for two or three of the last years of his life. But though they are a fragment, they treat *with great fullness* of one topic under this general head. Were there no other reason for publishing this fragment, one might be found in the earnestness with which the author prosecuted his inquiries, and the importance he attached to the discussion of the subject in the present state of theological opinion. The sermons on Election and Perseverance were prepared with great care, after the author had been for many years a theological instructor, and were always read in the place of lectures to his students, it being a favorite opinion with him that no truth of the Scriptures could be exhibited with so much effect by the preacher as the doctrine of Election; and that in no truth, when rightly exhibited, was the gospel made so glorious as "the power of God unto salvation." The sermon "What is Truth" is a condensed summary of his views upon the principal doctrines of Theology,—unfolding them also in their practical relations. It is to be regretted that the lectures of Dr. Taylor on the Atonement were in so fragmentary and unfinished a state as to make it unadvisable to publish them. His views on its necessity and nature can be gathered from the lectures on Moral Government, the appendix on Justice, and from section third of the Essay on the Trinity in the present volume.

N. P.

YALE COLLEGE, July, 1859.

CONTENTS.

I. THE TRINITY.

I.—THE IMPORT OF THE DOCTRINE.

II.—THE POSSIBILITY OF ONE GOD IN THREE PERSONS.

III.—NO PRESUMPTION AGAINST, BUT RATHER A PRESUMPTION FOR THE TRUTH OF THE DOCTRINE.

IV.—THE MANNER IN WHICH LANGUAGE IS USED IN THE SCRIPTURES RESPECTING THE MODE OF THE DIVINE SUBSISTENCE AND THE PERSON OF CHRIST.

III. JUSTIFICATION.

IV. ELECTION.

V. PERSEVERANCE

VI. WHAT IS TRUTH?

DOCTRINES OF REVELATION.

I.

THE TRINITY.

I.—THE IMPORT OF THE DOCTRINE.

Not presumptuous to attempt to define the doctrine.—Prevalence of the opposite view.—We may believe an unintelligible proposition to be true; but what we do believe, we understand.—The proposition *that there are three persons in one God*, in the ordinary signification of the terms, is absurd.—The meaning of the words may be limited.—Different statements of the doctrine.—Remarks upon them.—The Scriptural doctrine stated.—Plan of the discussion in five divisions.—1. The import of the doctrine does not involve the use of the words *being* and *person* in the same meaning.—The peculiar meaning of each defined.—General form in which Trinitarians hold their doctrine.—More particular form may be authorized by the Scriptures.

What is the doctrine of the Trinity?

By some this would be deemed, if not an irreverent, at least a presumptuous inquiry. The doctrine of the Trinity has so often been called a mystery, that he who claims to understand and explain it, can hardly expect a hearing, even on the part of many who profess to receive it as an essential doctrine of Christianity. Explain the doctrine of the Trinity—this profoundest of all mysteries! What presumption! Presumption—folly—though it be, I must be permitted to profess to understand what I believe, and to hope that, guided by the oracles of God, I may lead others to understand and believe also. Otherwise, I should feel myself to be in the awkward and disgraceful position of professing to teach what I am convinced I do not understand, and therefore cannot teach. Besides, what do they mean who characterize a doctrine of *revelation*—a doctrine *revealed to faith*—a *revealed* doctrine—as a mystery? A revealed doctrine, if it is any thing, is a truth taught by divine revelation—a truth intelligibly presented to the human mind, for its apprehension and assent. Be this truth more or less comprehensive, general or particular, so far as it is revealed, it is taught; so far as it is taught, it can be understood and believed; and so far as it can be understood and believed, it constitutes the revealed doctrine, and no farther. A doctrine announced in words which cannot be interpreted or understood, is not a *revealed* doctrine. To say *that God is one being in three persons*, is to express some meaning, or it is not. If it expresses no meaning, why say it, or why pretend to believe it? If it expresses some meaning, what is it? This meaning may be more or less. If it be real, it can be understood and believed; and we are bound, if it be a doctrine of divine revelation, to understand and believe it. It is true that a divine revelation must have a limit, for man cannot know all that God knows. There must be some point where the curtain is not lifted, and beyond which all is darkness. But so far as revelation goes, so far there is light; so far, and no farther, truth, be it little or much, is revealed, and therefore may be understood and believed. What then, I ask, is *a revealed* truth or doctrine which is *a mystery?*—what but a *revealed* doctrine which is *not* revealed? Men who take such ground, who claim to believe mysteries—what they do not understand, —must expect to be charged with holding contradictions and absurdities, and must, I think, be quite aware of the justice of the charge.

It ought perhaps here to be said, that Trinitarians, when pressed with the absurdity of professing to believe a doctrine which they constantly denominate *a mystery*, often resort to a distinction between *a fact* and the *mode* or *manner* of a fact; as, for example, *the fact* of the general resurrection, and the *mode* of the fact. This distinction is obvious. What is revealed—what is the fact—what is the *doctrine?* Plainly the resurrection of the body. "Behold, says the apostle, "I will show you a mystery." But this is *no mystery* when shown, but a fact, as easily comprehended as that man exists or lives before he dies. The mystery is not in that which is revealed—not in *the fact* which constitutes the doctrine to be believed—but in *the mode or manner* of the resurrection, which is not explained, and which of course is no part of the revealed doctrine, and in no respect the object of faith. So in the present case, the fact of one God in three persons, in some peculiar sense of the language, is the doctrine revealed and the doctrine to be believed. In respect to the mysterious, unrevealed *mode* of the fact, we are to have no faith. Now the error on the part of Trinitarians is, that they so constantly speak of *the doctrine* of the Trinity—the *fact revealed* to faith as *a mystery*—when after all and by their own showing, the fact which constitutes the doctrine is not a mystery, but only the mode or manner of the fact. So long as they confound this distinction, and call the doctrine (the truth revealed to faith) *a mystery*, what can they expect but to be charged with the absurdity of believing what they do not understand, or of teaching that what is revealed is not revealed?

It is true that one may believe an *unintelligible* proposition to be a *true* one, but he cannot believe the truth expressed in such a proposition. One who does not understand Greek, may be told that 'Eν ἀρχῆ ἦν ὁ λόγος is a true proposition, and, on the ground of sufficient testimony, may believe it to be; but he does not understand, and therefore cannot believe, the truth which it expresses. The proposition which he believes is one which he understands, viz., that the proposition in Greek is true; but not understanding its import, he no more believes it—no more assents to the truth which it expresses, than he assents to its converse. Let us then no longer pretend to believe what we do not understand, and when charged with it, exult in this self-stultification, as if we thereby honored God and God's revelation. This revelation, in requiring faith of men, proceeds on another principle. It limits its requirement to what is revealed, and of course to what can be understood. Without then, making the least claim to omniscience, or pretending to know all that concerning God which he knows concerning himself—without claiming to know what any one else may not know—I do claim to know what God has *revealed* concerning himself AS ONE GOD IN THREE PERSONS.

Let us then now look the difficulty directly in the face, that we may see what it is and all that it is.

It is admitted then, that there is only one living and true God; that is, that whatever God is as A BEING, there is *one and only one* such being. Now the word *person*, as does each of the pronouns *I*, *thou*, *he*, implies in its ordinary use and application, a being—a distinct being; and the word *being* denotes or implies the existence of one substance with one nature, or with one class or set of attributes or properties. Hence to say, in the *ordinary use and meaning of these terms*, that there is *one God in three persons*, or *three persons in one God*, is a plain contradiction. It is the absurdity of saying that one being is three beings—one God is three Gods; or that three beings are one being—three Gods are one God.

I have no desire to deny or conceal this absurdity; but to charge Trinitarians with maintaining, or the Scriptures with teaching it, is a shameless misrepresentation. Who does not know that Trinitarians claim, in the statement of their doctrine, to use the terms *being* and *person* not in their ordinary, but in a peculiar meaning, demanded by the nature of the subject? This, whatever else it may involve, does not necessarily involve the absurdity which results from the ordinary use of these terms. It is further claimed, that in using these and equivalent terms in a peculiar and unusual meaning in their present application, Trinitarians conform to the example of the sacred writers, and that they, in using the terms in question in a peculiar and unusual meaning, were led to do so *by those laws of usage* which decisively control the use of language in such cases.

It is undeniable that the words *God*, *being*, *person*, either of the personal pronouns *I*, *thou*, *he*—indeed, any word—may be properly used in a more extended or a more limited meaning than its ordinary one, provided there is good and sufficient reason for such a use, and good and sufficient evidence that it is so used. On this principle, we claim to vindicate the peculiar use of the words specified, when employed in relation to the doctrine of the Trinity. What the meaning of any of these words is when thus employed, we propose to show hereafter. I only say now, that if there is that eternal, self-existent, infinite Being whom we call God, there is a reasonable presumption that the mode of his subsistence and the constituent elements of his being should differ, at least in some respects, from those of creatures; and that, should it become necessary for the purposes of his goodness and mercy, to reveal this difference to any extent to the human mind through the medium of human language, it would become necessary also to change the terms used from the meaning they had acquired in their ordinary application. This is indeed the great law of usage which has ever prevailed when new truths are to be made known in the use of ordinary terms. When such truths are to be communicated to the popular mind, the natural and common mode of communication is not to invent new, but to employ old words, in more or less of their former meaning, and to rely on the known nature of the subject, or other evidence, to determine the new and changed import of the terms employed.

To recur to our leading inquiry—

What is the doctrine of the Trinity?

This question may be understood to refer to what the defenders of the doctrine have meant by it, or to the doctrine which is supposed to be taught in the Scriptures.

To pursue the inquiry in reference to all the varieties of opinion which have been propounded by the advocates of the doctrine, would take us beyond our prescribed limits. At the same time, it is important to our main purpose to examine some of the most prominent opinions on this controverted subject. The general and more common statement of the doctrine of the Trinity is, that there is one God in three persons,—the Father, the Son, and the Holy Ghost. Very different meanings however, have been given to the word *person* in this application. By the Sabellians, the phrase "three persons" was used to denote three relations of God; viz., that of Creator, that of Redeemer, and that of Sanctifier. "This," says Dr. Wallis, "is what we mean, and all we mean, when we say God is three persons." "If, among us, one man may sustain three persons (as when Tully says, '*Sustineo unus tres personas; meam, adversarii, judicis*'), without being three men, why should it be thought incredible that three divine persons may be one God, as well as those three other persons be one man?"—*Letters on the Trinity*, pp. 68, 69.

Says Bishop Bull: "The unanimous sense of the Catholic doctors of the Church, for the first three ages of Christianity, is—

"I. That there are in the Godhead three (not mere names or modes, but) really distinct hypostases or persons,—the Father, the Son or Word of God, and the Holy Ghost.

"II. That these three persons are one God, which they thus explain:

"1. There is but one fountain or principle of Divinity: God the Father, who only is αὐτόθεος—God of and from himself; the Son and Holy Ghost, deriving their divinity from him; the Son immediately from the Father; the Holy Ghost from the Father and the Son, or from the Father by the Son.

"2. The Son and Holy Ghost are so derived from the Fountain of the Divinity, as that they are not separate or separable from it, but do still exist in it, and are most intimately united to it."—*Works*, vol. iii., p. 829.

Says Waterland: "By person, I certainly mean a *real* person, an hypostasis; no mode, attribute, or property. Each divine person is an individual, intelligent agent; but as subsisting in one undivided substance, they are all together, in that respect, but one undivided, intelligent agent. The Church never professed three *hypostases* in any other sense but as they meant three persons."—*Vind. of Christ's Divinity*, pp. 350, 351.

Sherlock maintains that the word *person* signifies being, and considers the Father, Son, and Spirit as three distinct minds or beings, and yet maintains that these are inseparably one God. "It is plain," says he, "the persons are perfectly distinct. A person is an intelligent being; and to say there are three divine persons, and not three distinct infinite minds, is both heresy and nonsense."—*Vind. of the Trinity*, sec. iv., p. 76.

John Howe is more cautious, and without affirming three distinct substances, i. e., three distinct minds or spirits, asserts *the possibility* that there should be three spirits so united as to be one *thing*, and yet continuing distinct.—*Works*, p. 140.

Bishop Horsley says: "I hold that the Father's faculties are not exerted on external things, otherwise than through the Son and the Holy Ghost; that the Scriptures, by discovering a Trinity, teach clearly that the metaphysical unity of the divine nature is not a unity of persons; but that they do not teach such a separation and independence of these persons as amounts to Tritheism. I maintain that the three persons are *one being*,—one by mutual relation, indissoluble connection, and gradual subordination; so strictly one, that any individual thing in the whole world of matter and of spirit presents but a faint shadow of their unity. I maintain that each person by himself is God, because *each possesses fully every attribute of the divine nature*. But I maintain that these three persons are all included in the very idea of God."

Dr. Emmons, by three persons in the Godhead, means that "God exists in such a manner, that there is a proper foundation in his nature to speak of himself in the first, second, and third persons, and to say *I*, *thou*, and *he*, meaning only himself."

Dr. Worcester's view of the three persons in the Godhead seems to differ from that of Dr. Emmons, chiefly in being more particular. He speaks of three divine *agents* united in one God, and of each as possessing divine attributes, and affirms that his understanding of the term *person*, thus used, is as clear as when applied to angels or to men. How these agents, each possessing divine attributes, can be one God, he pretends not to understand. His proposition declares nothing of the *mode* of the union, and concerning this he believes nothing.

Professor Stuart, by the word *person*, intends that which, in some respect or other, corresponds to persons as applied to men, that is, *some distinction;* not that we attach to it the meaning of three beings with a separate consciousness, will, omnipotence, omniscience, &c. He says: "We undertake *not* at all to describe affirmatively the distinction of the Godhead." And yet he has done it to a certain extent. Thus he says, "There is a distinction which affords ground for the appellations of the Father, Son, and Holy Ghost, which lays a foundation for the application of the personal pronouns I, thou, he, which renders it proper to speak of sending, and being sent," &c. The same writer, in a letter to the Christian Spectator, 1821, p. 435, pronounces the distinction between essence and attributes a chimera; asserts that numerical unity—which he explains to be one instance of the union of divine attributes—is the only unity which can be predicated of the Deity. He rejects a distinction in divine attributes, and on the ground that the distinction of persons can be applied to neither essence nor attributes, supposes *other properties*, which are neither essence nor attributes, of which the distinction is predicable. And yet in his letters to Dr. Channing, he has virtually contradicted this by saying in respect to *numerical unity*, "How does this prove that there may not be, or that there *are* not, distinctions in the Godhead, either *in regard to attributes or essence*, the nature of which is unknown to us?" &c. How many incongruities there are in these statements I will not decide.

With respect to that view of the doctrine of the Trinity which supposes it to respect the three relations of God as Creator, Redeemer, and Sanctifier, I shall hope to show hereafter, that it contradicts the whole tenor of the word of God.

With respect to that view of the doctrine which considers the word *person* as equivalent to the word *being*, it is obvious, that if the word *being* is understood in its ordinary import, and if it be said that God is one being in three persons, this view is self-contradictory. This however, is not perhaps reasonably supposed.

With respect to that view which makes the distinction in the Godhead a proper ground for applying the personal pronouns to denote it, and yet maintains that the word *person* and the pronouns in this use have not their ordinary meaning, this, though a common view of the doctrine, is attended with one serious difficulty,—it is using language which conveys no definite meaning beyond the fact of a mere distinction. To say that there is a distinction in the Godhead which renders proper the application of the personal pronouns to denote it, is saying nothing, unless it be told what is meant by the pronouns when thus applied. Their import may be, as thus used, more or less extensive. To say that they are *not* used in their ordinary sense and no more, is simply saying what they do not mean. These terms, as used in the Scriptures, are designed to convey, and do unavoidably convey a meaning, and it becomes us to say what that meaning is. Otherwise there can be no reason for their use, and any other words, or no words, might as well be used as these.

With respect to that view of the doctrine which affirms a threefold distinction in the Godhead and disclaims any affirmative description of that distinction, and yet to a certain extent professedly gives such a description, it is difficult to say any thing positively. If the writer means that there is a distinction which is the ground of applying the pronouns *I*, *thou*, *he*, without any part of their ordinary meaning, his doctrine is the same as that last considered, and is liable to the same objections. If the pronouns retain a part of their ordinary meaning, the question is, how much and what? Unless this be told, who will be the wiser for such a use of words? Be these things however, as they may, the positions of this writer seem to justify the remark, that writers, in attempting to define or explain this doctrine, are liable to say too little as well as too much. On the one hand he seems to have said too much. When he pronounces the distinction between essence and attributes a chimera, he asserts more than he knows or can prove to be true. The same remark applies to his affirmation, that *numerical* unity, or one instance of the union of divine attributes, is the *only* unity that can be predicated of the Deity. When he supposes that other properties pertain to the Deity which are neither essence nor attributes, and of which the distinctions in the Godhead are to be predicated, he contradicts another supposition that he makes, viz., that there *are* distinctions in regard to either essence or attributes. On the other hand he asserts too little, when he simply says that there is a distinction in the Godhead which is the foundation of applying the personal pronouns *I*, *thou*, *he*. For to say this and nothing more, except to deny, as he does, the ordinary meaning of the words when thus applied, is to say nothing, or at the best, to assert the fact of a distinction which might as well be denoted by any three letters of the alphabet as by the personal pronouns. Besides, to predicate other properties of God, which are neither essence nor attributes, seems like predicating other properties than all which are essential to his Deity.

If the preceding remarks are just, we have arrived at no very satisfactory conclusion from examining the views of others respecting the doctrine of the Trinity. It ought however, to be remarked, that none of the statements which we have noticed are liable to the charge of Tritheism.

I now proceed to the inquiry—

What is the doctrine of the Trinity as taught in the Scriptures?

This doctrine respects the *peculiar mode* of the divine subsistence—the peculiar elements which constitute the being whom the Scriptures call God. On the one hand some suppose that in the exhibition which the Scriptures make of God, there is nothing peculiar in respect to *the mode* of his subsistence, but on the contrary, that they authorize and require us to form the same general conception of his being as consisting of one substance and one phenomenal nature (or, as this may be and is, for convenient conception and speech, subdivided into particular attributes, by which he is constituted the divine Being or God), that we form of the being of a man or of an angel, as consisting of one substance and one phenomenal nature (which may be subdivided and classified in like manner), and by which he is constituted a man or an angel. On the other hand, it is now maintained, that in the scriptural exhibition of God is involved a peculiar *mode* of subsistence, and that the Scriptures employ such peculiarity of language on this subject, as to oblige us to form a very different conception of what constitutes God the being that he is, from our ordinary conception of what constitutes man or an angel the being that he is. To express then, my own views of the subject, I now proceed to say, that—

The Scriptural doctrine of the Trinity, in some peculiar and authorized import of the language, is, that—

There is one God in three persons; or, *that God is one being in three persons;* or, *that God is one divine being in three divine persons.*

Here I will briefly state what I mean "by a peculiar and authorized import of the language." If the mode in which God subsists be peculiar and diverse from that of his creatures; if the revelation of this peculiarity to men was demanded by the designs of his wisdom and goodness, and could be expressed for his purposes, in the best way possible, by adopting terms already in familiar use, modifying their ordinary import by extending and restricting that import, according to usage in such cases; and if according to these principles the best form of announcing the truth were to say, God is one being in three persons, or to say the same thing in any other equivalent forms of speech, this would be using language in *a peculiar* yet *authorized* import.

I now propose to discuss, in several lectures, the subject under consideration in the following method:

I. To explain the import of the foregoing statement of the doctrine of the Trinity, in this general, and also in a more particular form of presenting it;

II. To show the possibility, in opposition to the alleged impossibility, of its truth in both forms of statement;

III. To show that there is no presumption against, but rather a presumption for, the truth of the doctrine;

IV. To consider the manner in which the language of the Scriptures on the subject is used;

V. To show that this language of the Scriptures, according to a just interpretation, teaches the doctrine of the Trinity as now explained.*

I propose—

I. To explain the import of this doctrine.

---

* The discussion of the last of these positions was not finished by Dr. Taylor.

Here I remark at the outset, that the very statement of the doctrine, though in general and unexplained terms, ought to be sufficient security against the charge of using the words *being* and *person* in the same meaning. Indeed this or any equivalent statement, made by men of ordinary intellectual capacity, and especially by a large class of distinguished scholars and divines, creates a strong presumption that they turn these words, as is common in the case of other words when the exigency demands it, from their ordinary meaning —that they intend not the same thing by *being* and *person*, but things so diverse as to exempt the proposition from self-contradiction, and that these words are the best for the purpose which language affords. Should one have occasion to say of some particular thing that it is one and three, or one thing in three things, the fair construction of his language would be, that he did not use the word *thing* in the phrase *one thing* in precisely the same specific meaning in which he used it in the phrase *three things*, and should he produce a threefold cord as the example and proof of the truth of his proposition, every honest mind would so interpret his proposition as to give it an obvious and consistent meaning. So in the present case. Though from the words merely, one might not be able to say precisely what Trinitarians do mean, it would be a gross violation of propriety and fair dealing, to assume that they intend the same thing by both words, and to affirm that, in this sense, they maintain that one being is three beings, or that three persons are one person. And yet when will such unfair and unauthorized representations of the doctrine of the Trinity cease to be made?

The words *being* and *person* then, in their present application, are not used in their precise ordinary import, but in a somewhat peculiar meaning demanded by the exigency of the case.

What then is this peculiar meaning? The answer to this question must be determined by those laws or principles of interpretation which are applicable to the language which the sacred writers employ on the subject. As my present object is merely to explain my own view of the doctrine of the Trinity, this is not the place fully to unfold those principles of interpretation by which I suppose this view of the doctrine to be established. And yet it will be of obvious advantage for the purpose of explanation, so far to refer to some of these principles as to unfold, to some extent, the process by which I am led to adopt that view of the doctrine now to be presented.

To the question then, concerning the peculiar meaning of the words *being* and *person*, when I say that *God is one being in three persons*, I answer first, that in the most general meaning, the word *being*, in its present application, is used to denote one substance with such other constituting elements denoted by the word *persons*, as the exigency of the case requires—meaning by this, that which arises from the known nature of the subject, and the facts of revelation. When I speak of the import *required* by this exigency, I mean such a conception of God as one being, as shall not be inconsistent with what, in some peculiar sense of the language, is called his *tri-personality*, or with three persons in the Godhead, and such a conception of his *tri-personality* as shall not be inconsistent with what is called his oneness of being. In this most general import of the doctrine of the Trinity, Trinitarians would agree, however they may differ in respect to more particular statements of that which constitutes and determines the oneness of the being and his tri-personality. I mean to say, that all Trinitarians, properly so called, or with exceptions which need not be noticed, maintain that God is one substance with such other constituting elements, that in some consistent, peculiar, and yet authorized import of the language, he is, in view of the exigency of the case, truly and *properly* said to be *one God in three persons.*

Again: in accordance with this general answer to the question proposed, I now give a somewhat more particular answer.

I remark then, first, in respect to the word *being*, that in its present application it is used in a more extended than its ordinary meaning. In its ordinary meaning, it is sufficient for the present purpose to say, that the word *being* denotes *one substance with a phenomenal nature—understanding by substance simply a something as opposed to nothing, to which a phenomenal nature pertains, and by a phenomenal nature, that nature which directly and proximately manifests itself in phenomena, and which, in its relations to different phenomena, is commonly called the attributes or properties, or the essential attributes or properties of a being.* This conception, in the ordinary use of the word *being*, may be said, so far as our present purpose is concerned, to constitute the entire meaning of the word.

Nothing less than the object of this conception can be properly called a being, even in its most restricted meaning. The moment we drop either of these elementary conceptions, we necessarily drop the other, and so both. The only possible conception without these, must be of that which can have no subsistence, for it must be either one which is a mere object of thought—as of a geometric point—or it must be a conception of that which can have no existence, except what depends, while it exists, on something as its cause—as the conception of a thought or volition. Hence, as it will be admitted that the conception of a being is the conception of a real subsistence—i. e., of that which, having existence, subsists of itself—it follows that the word *being*, when applied to God, however it may be extended beyond its ordinary meaning, must include at least one substance with one phenomenal nature—which nature, in its relations to different phenomena, is commonly called the attributes or properties, or the essential attributes or properties of the being. But the word *being*, in its present application, must also from the exigency of the case, have a more *extended* than its *ordinary* meaning; that is, its ordinary meaning, in view of the facts of revelation, must be so extended as to include, in some use of the language, the scriptural fact of the tri-personality of the being—the fact, in some sense, of three persons in one being. In determining the import of the word *being* in this application, we must adhere to the universal necessary conception of a being, so far as to include in it this import; that is, we must include in our conception of the being, *at least* one substance with one phenomenal nature. Without this conception, we can conceive of nothing which can be properly called a being. With this conception, though under the scriptural exigency, or in view of the scriptural evidence of the tri-personality of the being, it be extended and modified in any manner within the limits of possibility, we may with entire truth and propriety speak of him as one being. Facts known, or ascertained by sufficient evidence, do and must always control and determine the meaning of words. Hence new or peculiar facts, ascertained in the form of knowledge or faith, in respect to any thing or kind of a thing—in respect to any being or kind of a being—always change or modify, by extending or limiting the ordinary meaning of words. Accordingly, let it be thus ascertained that

God, or any other being, consists not only of one substance and one phenomenal nature, but one substance and of three phenomenal natures of the same kind, or of three phenomenal natures of the same kind, each having its own peculiar substance, and the whole united in one common substance, and all men, with such a conception in the form of knowledge or belief, would still with entire propriety speak of him as one being, so changing the language from its ordinary meaning, that it should express the new or peculiar conception of the object. It is true that while this would include our ordinary conception of a being, it would also include more; and there being evidence of more, it would necessarily include more.

The word *person*, in its present application, cannot be employed in more than its ordinary meaning, but must be used either in its whole ordinary meaning, or in such a part of it as the nature of the subject and the facts of revelation require, or as the scriptural use of the personal pronouns, when applied to distinguish the Father, and the Son, and the Holy Ghost, and the fact that God is one being, require. The word *person*, in its ordinary meaning, is not strictly synonymous with the word *being*, for although every person is a being, every being is not a person.

Now the use of the word *persons*, by Trinitarians, in affirming the existence of one God in three persons, is authorized *solely* by the scriptural use of the *personal pronouns* as applied to the Father, the Son, and the Holy Spirit; and no one of these pronouns can be used in any case, either literally or metaphorically, either in its full, ordinary meaning, or in a part of it, without implying, in the subject or the person to whom it is applied, capacity or qualification for action, in distinction from another person, or other persons, or both. If we drop from our conception the idea of this distinct capacity or qualification for diversity of action in the use of either of these pronouns, we necessarily drop from our conception the idea of any object to which either of them can be properly applied, according to any principles of extending or limiting the ordinary meaning of words. In such a case, it is obvious that there could be no more propriety in using a personal pronoun, than in using any other word. Even in any supposed case of personification by the use of a personal pronoun, the design must be to express an imaginary conception of the distinct qualification for action in the subject. It is plain therefore, that whatever else may be true of the personal pronouns when applied in the Scriptures to the Father, the Son, and the Holy Ghost, they must be employed either literally or metaphorically in personification, to express distinct qualification for distinct personal action in each of the subjects to which they are applied.

If now we suppose the Trinitarian, when affirming that *God is one being in three persons*, to use the language in its full, ordinary meaning, and to understand the personal pronouns to be so used in the Scriptures when applied to the Father, Son, and Holy Spirit,—he would not indeed fall into Tritheism any more than into Unitarianism, since he would assert oneness of being as well as tri-personality, in the ordinary sense of the language; but he would fall into self-contradiction and absurdity. If we suppose him to mean, by the above statement of his doctrine, three persons in the full, ordinary meaning of the language, and so including three beings in the ordinary meaning of the language, united by some common substance so as to constitute *one being* in an unusual and peculiar sense, though in this he may assert nothing which is known to be self-contradictory or impossible in the nature of things, still he may go beyond what the scriptural exigency requires or warrants him positively to affirm. Again, if we suppose the Trinitarian to use the phrase *three persons*, in the statement of his doctrine, to denote simply the most general idea of a threefold distinction, or three distinctions in the Godhead, which might as well be denoted by the letters x, y, z, as by the word persons, or by the personal pronouns, then he falls short of the Scriptures, which, in this use of these pronouns, clearly and undeniably exhibit, not merely an unknown threefold distinction in the Godhead, but a threefold distinction which these pronouns, compared with any other terms in human language, are peculiarly and well fitted to express; that is, a threefold personal distinction, in some restricted import of these pronouns, in which more or less of their ordinary meaning is retained. The question then is, in how much of the ordinary meaning of the word *persons* must the Trinitarian use it in his statement that *God is one being in three persons*, to express the meaning of the personal pronouns as they are applied to the Father, Son, and Holy Spirit, in the Scriptures? I answer, according to what has been already said, in no more of it than shall harmonize with the fact, in some peculiar sense of the language, that God is *one being*,—and in so much of it as shall involve a threefold distinction in the Godhead, or in the whole nature of the Deity, which is a threefold qualification for performing, in a corresponding limited sense, distinct, divine, personal, phenomenal acts, or distinct, divine, phenomenal acts of the so-called distinct persons. In this view of the subject, God is not only *one being* in the ordinary meaning of this language, inasmuch as he consists of one substance with at least one phenomenal nature, but as one being, he is more—he is one tri-personal being, or one being in three persons, inasmuch as he is qualified by the peculiar constitution of his Godhead or whole nature, i. e., by his tri-personality, for performing distinct, divine, phenomenal acts in each person,—which acts are not distinct in every respect as the acts of three beings are distinct, but in another and peculiar respect—distinct as may easily be conceived to be the acts of a being of one substance, either with a threefold phenomenal nature, or some other peculiarity of his entire nature, qualifying for the performance of three distinct forms of divine, personal, phenomenal action.

Thus it is believed that all Trinitarians, properly so called, maintain *that God is one divine being in three divine persons*—conceiving that sameness and community of substance, with at least one phenomenal nature, are essential to the oneness of God as a being, and that though they may differ in their more particular views of his tri-personality, they still maintain that it consists in some threefold qualification of the Godhead, for threefold, distinct, divine, and thus, in some sense, *personal* forms of *phenomenal* action. This too, it is believed, is the scriptural doctrine of the Trinity. It is, according to what has now been said, in its most general form, and in some peculiar yet authorized import of the language, that GOD IS ONE DIVINE BEING IN THREE DIVINE PERSONS; or, as now explained, that *God is one being, in such a modified sense of the terms as to include three persons in such a modified sense of the terms, that, by his tri-personality, or by the three persons of his Godhead, he is qualified, in a corresponding modified sense, for three distinct, personal, divine forms of phenomenal action;* or thus: *God, in a modified use of the language, is one being in three persons, qualified by the three persons of his Godhead for three distinct, divine, personal forms of phenomenal action.*

This, and nothing less than this, it is believed, is that doctrine of the Trinity which is an essential part of substantial Christianity, and which not only the Christian Church, but all men under the light of divine revelation, are bound to receive and maintain.

I now inquire whether the Scriptures authorize any more particular statement of the doctrine of the Trinity, than that which has now been given. This question I shall not positively decide. While I maintain that the scriptural doctrine of the Trinity, in that general form in which it is revealed to the faith of all men, is, in some peculiar yet authorized import of the language, *that God is one being in three divine persons*, it would not in my view, be strange, should a more particular statement of the doctrine be fully authorized by a more extended and thorough investigation of the Scriptures, than can be expected of the great portion of their readers. This, it is believed, is true in respect to other important doctrines. The great truths of revelation are, for the most part, presented in some general forms, as distinguished from particular or minutely full forms of statement. This is a signal excellence of the sacred writings, as designed for the instruction of the popular mind, which is almost exclusively conversant with general forms of truth.

The same general doctrine or truth is however, often presented by different writers, and by the same writer, under very different aspects and in very different connections. Not unfrequently also, some one element of a complex truth is presented, as necessarily involving yet another element, which is not expressed in the general statement of that truth. Hence, by a thorough comparative investigation, it will often be found, that under general forms of truth, other more particular truths are included; and we may justly, and with more or less confidence, infer more than is formally announced in general statements of the doctrine under consideration. In this way, I cannot but think it possible at least, that candid and thorough investigation might authorize a more particular statement of the doctrine of the Trinity than that which has now been made, viz., *that God is a being of one substance, with a threefold divine nature*, or, as already explained, *with three classes of divine attributes;* and that, in this sense, *God is one divine being in three divine persons.*

Let me not be understood to affirm that this is the scriptural doctrine of the Trinity, nor that it can be even justly inferred from the Scriptures as true; but that possibly, by comparing scripture with scripture, it may be found to be authorized as an inference more or less plausible. The use, and only use, which I would make of it in the argument, is that of a theory or an hypothesis—a mere supposition of a possible truth—and as such, sufficient to set aside the Unitarian assumption, that the doctrine of one God in three persons, in every possible conception of it, is an absurdity and a contradiction.

After what I have said of the foregoing hypothetical statement, I will here briefly intimate some considerations which have led me to say, that possibly, by a thorough investigation directed to this specific topic, it may be found that the Scriptures authorize, as an inference more or less plausible, what is now proposed as a mere hypothesis.

These considerations—assuming, as I must for my present purpose, the truth of the general statement of the doctrine of the Trinity—I will briefly present. That part of the statement then, which asserts that God is a being of one substance, will not be called in question. The inquiry respects the predicate of *three persons* in one God. The three persons are exhibited in the Scriptures as performing distinct divine *acts*, and in all our ordinary conceptions, distinct acts imply distinct natures, or distinct classes of attributes. Is it not difficult at least to conceive that the Father, the first person in the Godhead, sent the Son, the second person, into the world—and that the Son came voluntarily, or by an act of will, to do the will of the Father that sent him—without conceiving of distinct acts which imply distinct powers of acting, that is, distinct attributes? Not to specify other acts ascribed to each person, which are equally distinct and which seem to carry with them the same conception of distinct natures or attributes, I ask, is there not here some ground for inferring distinct attributes, unless there are other considerations which decisively forbid it? I might further say, that divine attributes are ascribed to each of the three persons, and ask whether the natural and fair implication is not that these are distinct, unless there is some decisive evidence to the contrary? I do not say that the inference is or is not authorized by the premises, nor that there is not decisive evidence against the inference; neither am I satisfied that there is such evidence, but merely regard it as probable that there should be none.

Another consideration is, that the statement as a theory or hypothesis, appears to account for the peculiar facts in the case. These may be comprised in the uncommon use of language on this peculiar subject. The subject is the mode of the divine subsistence; and the language is as peculiar as the subject. Thus, while the Scriptures teach that God is one being—which involves at least one substance of one divine nature or class of divine attributes—they speak of this one being as the Father, the Son, and the Holy Ghost, under one name; they also ascribe to each divine name the name of God, and teach that each is a divine person, by the use of the personal pronouns, and by ascribing to each, distinct, divine, personal acts, if not also distinct, divine, personal attributes. This use of language is so peculiar, that the writers cannot be vindicated from the imputation either of insanity, or of a mental imbecility, or perversion, not less incredible, except on the ground that the uncommon nature of the subject created the exigency. How, for example, could any sane man of ordinary capacity, use such a combination of terms as the apostle John employs in the first verse of his gospel, on any common subject? How could he say, in the beginning was Peter, and Peter was with James, and Peter was James? How could he speak of a person by whom all things are made, as made flesh or becoming a human being, &c., and expect the confidence or respect of those for whom he wrote? Surely his vindication in respect to mental sanity must be founded, if not in his inspiration and the singular nature of the subject, at least in the latter and his peculiar information respecting it. On these grounds, if on any, his readers must award to the writer their confidence and respect; on these also they must regard him as attempting, and as authorized to attempt, to impart knowledge to them on a peculiar subject; and this, so far as the peculiar nature of the subject would allow, according to the established use of the language he uses—a subject so peculiar however, and with conceptions of it so peculiar, that it is utterly impossible to express these conceptions in that ordinary use of language which accords with the ordinary conceptions of ordinary things. Hence the further conclusion that, in such an exigency, the writer must select such terms and adopt such forms of combination as shall involve, not only a departure from prior usage on ordinary subjects, but as shall, according to strict grammatical construction, involve absurdity or nonsense, provided that even in this way he can convey to his readers, as they will be led to interpret his language, the conceptions which he wishes to convey. Hence again, his readers, justifying on the grounds specified, all that is peculiar, and unheard and unthought of in his use of language, would, for the purpose of apprehending his meaning, feel the obligation, not indeed to separate from ordinary terms all their ordinary meaning, but by restricting, and modifying, and extending that meaning into another, made up if possible, of harmonious and true conceptions; and when these were arrived at, would rest in the assurance that the designed meaning was attained. Now, in view of these principles of using and interpreting the language of the Scriptures on this peculiar subject—*the existence of one God in three persons*—I apprehend that there is not a text, to which, in accordance with the theory which supposes God to be one being with a threefold divine nature, or with three classes of divine attributes, an intelligible, obvious, and consistent meaning may not be given,—no text in which the language of the writer would not appear the most natural and the best for his purpose which could be employed in the case. To illustrate in a few particulars: If we suppose a revelation to be made to us in respect to some one man, as consisting of one substance and of three human natures, like that now supposed of three divine natures united in one substance and constituting one God, what would be the effect on the use and interpretation of our language in respect to such a being? Can there be a doubt that it would be employed in substantially the same manner as that in which the sacred writers employ language on the subject now under consideration, and its meaning be determined in accordance with our conceptions of the nature of the subject and the manner of use in each instance? The common people, we may safely say, would not coin new terms in familiar and ordinary discourse, but would, at least for the most part, employ those already in use—relying on the connection and manner of speaking to show their meaning. Thus probably, as it seems to me, the word *man* in some cases would be applied to the whole being when there was no occasion to recognize his tri-personality; then again, when the occasion occurred for speaking of either person as a being, and not as a person, he would still, as before the revelation, be called *man;* and then, when it was necessary to distinguish the personal acts of either or of each of the persons, the personal pronouns would best answer the purpose; and so in all other predicates, affirmations, and negations, the words already in use, modified in import according to the exigency of the case, would be employed, and would be understood as so employed; and all this would be done by the common people, without a suspicion of any better or any other possible mode of using language as the vehicle of their conceptions. If these things would be so in the case now supposed, why are they not in the case under consideration—that is, if we suppose God to be a being of one substance, with a threefold divine nature? And if this, on this supposition, would be the mode of using language, then I ask again, what passage of Scripture which speaks of God as one being, or of the three persons of the Godhead, or of either of these persons, may not, according to the true principles of interpretation, be correctly and satisfactorily interpreted in accordance with the hypothesis *that God is a being of one substance, with a threefold divine nature, and in this sense one God in three persons?*

THE TRINITY.

II.—THE POSSIBILITY OF ONE GOD IN THREE PERSONS.

The real question at issue between the Unitarian and the Trinitarian.—Opinions of philosophers in respect to the definition of Being.—The opinions of common men, and their authority.—Rules for interpreting the words *Being* and *Person*.—The ordinary conception denoted by the word Being.—Is it possible that God, in some authorized use of the language, should exist in three persons?—(I.) Is it possible in the nature of things?—The terms are used in a modified meaning, and ought so to be understood.—So understood, they involve no contradiction, even when used by those who cannot define the sense in which they use the terms.—(II.) Is it possible, stated in its particular form, argued by showing (1.) that several modes of the divine subsistence are possible, which are not self-contradictory.—Various modes supposed.—(*A*) The doctrine of Spinoza.—(*B*) The doctrines of Sherlock and Howe.—(*C*) That of Leibnitz.—(*D*) The doctrine of one nature and three forms of action.—(*E*) The doctrine of three self-active natures in one substance.—No necessary self-contradiction in these theories.—Prop. II. argued still further, by showing (2.) the human mind cannot know that this mode of subsistence is impossible.—Various suppositions for illustration.—The subject-matter is such, that knowledge *a priori* is impossible.—What we do know, considered.—The assumption that more than this is impossible, constantly made by the Unitarian.

WE all believe that there is but one God, or that whatever God is as a being, there is not another such being. In respect to this doctrine, properly called the doctrine of the unity of God, there is no controversy between Trinitarians and Unitarians. Both believe that there is one, and but one God. The question between them is—*whether this one God is, in any peculiar and authorized sense of language, tri-personal, or whether the being whom we call God is, in some peculiar sense of the language authorized by the peculiarity of the subject, one being in three persons?*

This, it is obvious, is a question concerning what the one God is as a being, or what constitutes him the being that he is. It carries us into the investigation of the constituent elements of his being; and yet it is a question which every one who believes that God is a being—the Unitarian as well as the Trinitarian—must decide. Both actually decide it, though differently, and each forms a conception of what God is as a being.

The Trinitarian readily concedes that in the ordinary meaning of the words *being* and *person*, to say that God is one being in three persons is a plain contradiction, and that such a mode of subsistence is inconceivable and impossible in the nature of things. And yet, while making this full and undisguised concession, the Trinitarian strenuously maintains that God, in some peculiar yet authorized import of the language, is a being tri-personal, or that God is one being in three persons. This the Unitarian denies, and maintains that—according to the only authorized conception of a being, and of course of God as a being—it is impossible to conceive of God as one being in three persons. He ever insists, as the strength of his cause—as his grand and decisive argument against the doctrine of the Trinity—that the true and only idea of God as one being—the only conception of what is commonly called the unity of God, authorized by reason and by the Scriptures, necessarily excludes the conception of his tri-personality—renders the conception of one God in three persons a self-contradiction, and thus shows the existence of such a being to be impossible in the nature of things; as impossible as that one being should be three beings—one God three Gods.

Whether these things are so or not, most manifestly depends on *what is the only true and authorized conception of God as a being.*

It is undeniable that the Unitarian can form at his own pleasure, such a conception of God as one being as shall necessarily exclude the idea or conception of his tri-personality, or the conception of three persons in the Godhead. But it will not be pretended that any such idea or conception is arbitrarily formed—formed without reason or evidence, or against reason and evidençe—formed, perhaps, for the purpose of excluding the conception of his tri-personality; that it is the only authorized conception of God as a being, or is even authorized at all. There must be some other mode of determining what this authorized conception of God is as a being.

Shall we appeal to *philosophers* on the general question, *what constitutes a being*, in all other cases, and thus determine what is the only authorized conception of God as a being? But with philosophers of highest repute, this is an open or unsettled question. Mr. Locke, whose opinion, as most in accordance with common sense, seems to have been generally accepted, maintains that the idea of substance and properties, or one substance and one class of properties, or a subject and its properties, is the true and necessary idea of a being. Spinoza taught that there is but one substance in the universe with the different kinds of attributes or properties of matter and spirit, so that there is but one being in the universe, which is God, or so that God is all things. Bishop Berkeley denies substance altogether. Dr. Brown denies the distinction between substance and properties. Prof. Norton, of Cambridge, maintains that a being is one combination of attributes or properties without a substance; and Prof. Stuart, of Andover, affirms that the distinction between essence and attributes is a chimera. I might enlarge this specification of opinions on the part of philosophers. Now in view of this great diversity of opinion regarding the constituent elements of a being, it is manifest that the proposition, *God is a being*, or is one being, would have different meanings, or express different conceptions in the minds of these philosophers and divines. Nor could the meaning of either of them be determined with precision, without a previous knowledge of his conception of the subject. Though they should agree fully in the unity of God, or that whatever God is as a being, there is not another such being, there would be a diversity of opinion among them on the question, What constitutes God the being that he is? Differing thus widely on this, they would also on another question: whether this being—this one God—can be tri-personal, or one God in three persons? It is in vain then to appeal to the authority of philosophers, to determine what is the authorized conception of a being, and of course of God as a being.

Shall we then appeal to the idea or conception of a being, which is formed in all ordinary cases, by common sense? By this I mean, that conception which the competent, unperverted mind of mankind generally forms of a being in all cases except the present; which men form for the practical purposes of life; which prevails in all languages, in all ages, and in all countries, and has been recognized in all the conduct of men since the world began. This I shall call the *ordinary*, or *common* conception of a being. Shall we then appeal to this as the sure criterion of determining what is the authorized idea of God as a being? I answer, that in some respect we must appeal to, and to some extent be governed by it. How else can we understand—how else take a single step in interpreting the language which the Scriptures employ to convey the idea of

God as a being? If we have no idea or conception whatever of a being, to what purpose are we told, in any ordinary forms of language, that God is a being? And if we have such an idea, what is it but the ordinary notion which the word *being*, or equivalent language in common use, has been employed to express? Plainly, it can be no other. But then is this ordinary conception of a being, absolutely to control and determine our authorized conception of God as a being? Not of necessity, by any means. I admit indeed, that if properly used, it must as applied to God, be used in *some* of its ordinary meanings. But nothing is more common, or more abundantly sanctioned by the laws of usage, than to turn words from their ordinary meaning, and to employ them to express, according to the exigency of the subject, in different cases, either more or less, good and sufficient evidence being furnished of the change. This brings us to a main question—How are we to be governed by our ordinary conception of a being, in determining the authorized conception of God as a being? I answer, *that we are required to adopt its ordinary meaning, provided there is no good and sufficient evidence of any modification of its ordinary meaning, either by extending or restricting it;* and *that, provided there is good and sufficient evidence of some modification of its ordinary meaning, either by extending or restricting it, then we are required to modify that meaning, either by extending or restricting it, according to such evidence.*

It is important to add, that what has now been said in respect to the interpretation of the word *being*, or any equivalent term, is applicable to the interpretation of the word *person* or any equivalent term. Indeed, to deny the correctness of these principles in the interpretation of language, is to deny that we are to be governed by evidence in deciding its import. Nor do I suppose that the correctness of the above principles will be denied or doubted by the Unitarian. On the contrary, I should expect him to hail this announcement of them, as a full concession of the very principles which sustain his own interpretation of the scriptural language concerning God as a being.

Further, for the sake of narrowing the ground of debate, I here fully concede that there is no good and sufficient reason for *restricting* or limiting the ordinary idea or conception of a

2

being, when it is said that God is a being. Whether there is good and sufficient reason for *extending* or *enlarging* this conception of a being as applied to God, by the addition of some other elementary conception or conceptions, is another question. How this is, we may see hereafter. I now admit and affirm, that at least the full, ordinary conception of a being is included in the just scriptural conception of God as a being.

With these things in view, it is manifestly a material question, *What is the ordinary conception of a being?* And here I shall not appeal to philosophers nor to philosophic divines; for the conception is that of common sense, the notion of a being formed by mankind generally, in all ages and countries, and evinced clearly in all human languages and all human conduct. And further, the conception of a being concerning which I now inquire, is that which the unperverted intellect or reason of mankind generally forms in view of phenomena, and not the conception of being as modified or in any degree determined by revelation, or any supernatural information. The human mind, in forming or giving this conception of a being, is and must be originally guided and governed by phenomena, by effects which fall under the eye of its own observation. It is on condition of phenomena or effects, that the mind necessarily gives its conceptions or ideas of their cause. By these it graduates and determines these conceptions or ideas, and all that are thus given are to be received as true conceptions. In this way, and in this way only—supposing no revelation—it gives its ideas of all the beings that come within the limits of its knowledge. From these conceptions of individual beings, it forms the general abstract idea of a being which is common to every individual as conceived and known merely by phenomena, and which, for distinction's sake, may be called the *phenomenal* conception of a being, or the general conception of a being as conditioned on and determined by phenomena.

This is the conception of which we now seek a definition. It is the only ordinary or usual one which can be supposed by Unitarians to control or influence the interpretation of those scriptural passages which teach that God is a being. In answer to the question, What is this conception? I deem it sufficiently particular and precise to say, that *it is the conception of a substance of a nature which qualifies it to produce phenomena.*

This general conception the mind necessarily gives at first in the knowledge of itself. To man, as a spiritual being, we ascribe intellect, susceptibility, and will. In similar forms of language we ascribe the same to God, and also creative power, comprising in these all conceivable power in absolute perfection. Thus a spiritual being is conceived as a substance with a self-active nature—a being of that nature which we call *power*. A self-active nature, differ as it may in different beings, both in kind and degree, is that which we call *power*, and it is this nature of a substance, which in the convenient language of common life, we speak of in its relations to different phenomena, and call its essential properties or attributes; that is, all that can with truth be meant when this common form of language is used, is the nature of a substance, which is its power or self-active nature in its relations to different phenomena. This self-active nature of a substance may be called its *phenomenal* nature, in distinction from its whole nature—meaning by *phenomenal* nature, that particular element of its whole nature which qualifies it by acting proximately to produce phenomena.

Such is the necessary and authorized conception of a being which the mind gives on condition of mere phenomena, viz., *the conception of a substance with a phenomenal nature*, or more particularly, *the conception of a something to which a self-active nature belongs, qualifying it by acting proximately to produce phenomena.* This is the ordinary conception of a being, which I shall take the liberty to call the *phenomenal conception*, in distinction from that unusual and peculiar conception which, as I claim, we are bound to form of God as a being by other evidence than that of mere phenomena, even by his own revelation of the mode of his subsistence. This may be called the Biblical conception of God as a being.

It is readily conceded that this *phenomenal conception* of a being consisting of one substance and of one *phenomenal nature*, is one which the mind necessarily gives on condition of certain known phenomena; that it is a conception, which so far as it extends, is truly formed of every species or kind of a being, and that without evidence of any thing more, it is the only general conception of a being which we are authorized to form. It is still further conceded, that if this *phenomenal* conception of a being is the only one possible—or rather, if it be known to be impossible, in the nature of things, that any thing more should be true, or be known to be true of a being, and of course of the divine being, than what is necessarily, on condition of mere phenomena, known to be true—then it would be impossible, that even in any peculiar yet authorized use of language, there should be one God in three persons.

But is this known to be impossible in the nature of things? Is our knowledge of beings by phenomena, the measure and limit of all possible knowledge concerning them? Can nothing more be true, and nothing more be known to be true of any being, even of the eternal self-existent Being, than is revealed to us by mere phenomena? Can God know nothing more of himself—can he make known to us nothing more of the constituting elements of his being, or of the mode of his subsistence, than is revealed to us merely by his works of creation and providence? This brings us to a more particular and also fundamental question in the present controversy, viz.:

Is it possible in the nature of things, that God, in some peculiar and yet authorized import of the language, should subsist as one being in three persons?

Keeping in mind, that by a peculiar and yet authorized meaning of the language, is meant that import in which words are turned from their ordinary meaning on account of the peculiarity of the subject to which they are applied, I propose to consider the present inquiry concerning what is possible in the nature of things, *in the first place*, in respect to the general statement of the doctrine of the Trinity,—viz., *that God is one being in three persons;* and *in the second place*, in respect to the same statement of the doctrine in the somewhat more particular form in which I have explained it.

In the first place then, is it possible in the nature of things, that God in some peculiar and yet authorized import of the language, should subsist as *one being in three persons?*

In this general form of the doctrine,—viz., *that God is one being in three persons*, in some peculiar import of the language, it may be safely assumed that Trinitarians, as a class of Christians, would agree. Now there can be no question, that if the words *being* and *persons* in this proposition, by being changed more or less from their ordinary meaning, but still retaining some part of it, express as well, and even better than any other terms which language furnishes, the mode of the divine subsistence, they are used in a peculiar, yet in an *authorized* import. It is not uncommon thus to alter the meaning of words in cases of similar exigency, and therefore the change now supposed cannot be improper or unauthorized. The only question then must be, whether by such a change in the meaning of the words *being* and *persons*, they can be used to express any which will be free from self-contradiction; or to express any thing which can be true in the nature of things. What is now claimed is, that they can be; and that the only fair presumption is, that Trinitarians, in this use of the words *being* and *persons*, turn them from their ordinary import and employ them in one which is peculiar, on account of the nature of the subject, so modifying the import of each as to avoid all inconsistency or contradiction in their conceptions of oneness of being and of tri-personality, and still retaining in the use of each term some part of its ordinary meaning. I say that this is the only fair presumption. For in all cases in which words are used by men of common intelligence and principle, in such a manner that if understood in their ordinary meaning they involve manifest contradiction and absurdity, this fact is *prima facie* evidence that the words are turned more or less from their usual import, and throws the responsibility on the interpreter of judging and deciding whether the words by being thus turned, may not and do not express a meaning free from all contradiction or absurdity. If this may be so, there is a strong presumption that it is; and the charge of uttering contradiction or absurdity is absolutely forbidden. There is no law of interpretation more just, and none more imperiously binding on the interpreter, than that now stated. That the language, for aught that can be shown to the contrary, may be used in a meaning which is free from contradiction and absurdity, is quite sufficient to prevent the charge of contradiction. Until therefore, every possible meaning of the language thus employed—every one which is possible according to any law of usage in such cases, by changing or modifying the terms in relation to the exigency of the case—is ascertained and specified, and shown to be inconsistent or self-contradictory, the speaker may, for aught that appears to the contrary, use it in a consistent meaning, and the charge of self-contradiction is nothing better than slander. Besides, the only contradiction charged in the present case, is that involved in conceiving *one being to be three beings*, or *one God to be three Gods*. But the

Trinitarian disclaims and denies altogether this or any conception which involves it, and avows what he claims to be a very different conception of God,—the idea of God as one being in three persons, in a peculiar import of the words *being* and *persons*;—a conception which, as he claims, can be better expressed in some modified use of these than any other terms. The Unitarian then, in charging contradiction on this statement of the Trinitarian, does so in defiance of the only fair and honorable presumption, that the latter so employs the terms of it as to avoid the alleged contradiction; he does so without attempting to show that contradiction is necessarily involved in every possible meaning which can be authorized in the case; he does so in the face of the Trinitarian's declaration, that he does not use the language in the meaning charged. Such is the evidence then, of unjust and calumnious interpretation on the part of the Unitarian. Does he say that the Trinitarian gives no explanation of his statement to show that it does not involve the self-contradiction charged? Be it so; but he gives other evidence enough on this point without explanation,—evidence which, as we have seen, absolutely forbids the charge of self-contradiction;—*prima facie* evidence of no contradiction. It is not his concern to show that he is not guilty, because another is pleased, without evidence or the shadow of it, to say that he is guilty. The accuser must either make good his charge or retract it. If he does neither, what is he but a calumniator? But it may be asked, why not give such explanation as shall reveal the consistency of the doctrine? I answer, by readily conceding that the great majority of those who form this general conception of one God in three persons, may so form it that it shall involve no contradiction, and yet be unable so to define and specify by reflective analysis each elementary conception involved in the complex conception, as to show the consistency of the two conceptions of oneness of being and of tri-personality. Who, without peculiar habits of reflection, is able to define with logical precision even his commonest notions, and to show in all cases not only that things which are not the same are different, but in what the difference consists? But this inability is surely no proof that such conceptions as actually exist in the mind are inconsistent or self-contradictory. It may be well here to give an illustration.

Suppose the supernatural influence called inspiration, causing the human mind to *remember*, as in the case of the apostles, should be said to be impossible, on the ground that acts of memory, and all other mental states, must be caused by the mind itself, and therefore cannot, in the nature of things, be caused by an external supernatural agency, since this would imply that a man's own act is not his own act. Now if one who believes in the inspiration of the apostles, is unable by reflective analysis and logical definition, so to unfold and define the elementary conceptions involved in the complex conception of an inspired act of memory, as to exempt it from the supposed charge of contradiction to the satisfaction of him who makes the charge, does this justify the charge, or prove the fact of contradiction? Is this logical disqualification of uneducated believers in the doctrine of the inspiration of the sacred writers, proof that the doctrine is self-contradictory and absurd, and the fact, as conceived and asserted, is impossible in the nature of things? Take another example. One asserts that a man cannot think without thinking of something. Another denies the proposition, and claims to prove that it involves an absurdity by the following syllogism: A man cannot think without thinking of something: a man can think of nothing; therefore nothing is something, and something is nothing. Now if the former should be unable to expose the sophistry of this syllogism by showing the ambiguity of the terms, and giving to each a precise definition, would it follow that in his conception of the first proposition a real absurdity is involved? So in the present case, if the Trinitarian is not qualified by habits of mental analysis and logical definition to unfold the elements of his complex conception of one God in three persons, it is no proof that the conception as it exists in his own mind is self-contradictory, as involving either the contradiction of conceding that one being is three beings, which he wholly disclaims, or any other contradiction. The Trinitarian claims to form another and very different conception of one God in three persons, from that which the words denote in their ordinary use—from that of one being in three beings, one God in three Gods; to form a peculiar conception of the mode of the divine subsistence, and to use common terms to express this conception in a peculiar sense, as the best terms which he can use. And yet the Unitarian, with abundant evidence of the peculiarity of the conception, and without ascertaining what it is, charges self-contradiction on that which he knows, or ought to know, is not his conception. And further, it is utterly incredible that the Trinitarian should not clearly apprehend the inconsistency which the Unitarian so abundantly and superabundantly charges, viz., the inconsistency of conceiving that one being is three beings in the same sense of the word *being*. He does clearly apprehend it—admits it to be a contradiction, and with a clear apprehension of it as such, disclaims the conceptions and the belief which involve it. Now if this clearly apprehended contradiction actually pertains to his conception of one God in three persons, it is incredible that he should not perceive it; and if he perceives that it actually pertains to his conception, it is absolutely impossible that he should admit the truth of that which is contradictory. The mind may indeed, without reflection, believe that which involves a contradiction without perceiving it; but it is impossible from the very nature of the mind, that it should so reflect as to see and know the contradiction, and at the same time believe that which it knows involves it. Just so much evidence as there is that the Trinitarian perceives that the alleged contradiction pertains to his conception, so much evidence is there that he does not believe the conception to be true. If then we assume—and who can doubt?—that if the Trinitarian's conception involves the contradiction of one being in three beings, he sees and knows that it involves it, he cannot, in the nature of things, believe it to be true, and the charge of believing it, or that which involves it, must be false. Should it here be said, that they who adopt the language under consideration can affix no ideas to the terms which they employ to express their faith—be it so. Then what becomes of the charge of contradiction between ideas or conceptions which have no existence? Besides, on this supposition they can believe nothing, for there can be no belief of that of which the mind has no ideas. The only alternative therefore, for the Unitarian, is to say, either that Trinitarians believe what they intuitively and reflectively see and know, and deliberately and positively affirm, to be self-contradictory and false, which it is impossible, in the nature of things, that any mind should do; or, that they actually believe that of which they have no idea or conception, which is equally impossible. In either case he charges that which cannot, in the nature of things, be true, but is necessarily false. Should the Unitarian abandon the standing charge of contradiction, and simply say that Trinitarians have no belief—nothing which can be called faith in the doctrine of one God in three persons—then how do Trinitarians differ on the subject from Unitarians? Plainly, the parties are agreed in this: neither believes in the doctrine of the Trinity. The difference is, that while one openly professes to believe or disbelieve the doctrine, the other, without believing it, with the absolute reflective knowledge of the self-contradiction involved in it, with this knowledge familiarized to the mind, and constantly and openly avowed, and therefore, when under an absolute necessity of not believing but of disbelieving it, does with the most arrant hypocrisy—hypocrisy fully and perfectly known to themselves—profess to believe that there is one God in three persons. Let then this charge be substituted for that of believing contradiction and absurdity. Every charge of *contradiction* made by Unitarians on the belief of Trinitarians is, in the circumstances of the case, necessarily false. If Trinitarians must be reproached, let it be with arrant hypocrisy, which may have at least the semblance of possible truth. But can the charge be sustained? Will it, in view of the fact that so many of the wise and good, in every age since Christianity blessed the world, have avowed their belief of one God in three persons, be regarded as in the lowest degree credible? And why can it not be sustained? Because it may be true that the human mind can and often does form the conception of one God in three persons, in some peculiar import of the language, which involves no contradiction or absurdity; because, by changing the ordinary conceptions of oneness of being and of tri-personality, it can exclude from each the elementary ideas that result in contradiction, as formed into one complex idea or conception of one being in three persons.

Having thus attempted to show how entirely groundless and unauthorized is the Unitarian's charge of contradiction on the general form of the doctrine of the Trinity, as before stated, I now proceed as I proposed—

In the second place, to show the same thing in respect to the more particular form of the doctrine in which it has now been explained.

The doctrine of the Trinity then is, that *God is one being in such an extended sense of the terms, as to involve three persons in such a restricted sense of the terms, that by his tri-personality, or by the three persons of his Godhead, he is qualified, in a corresponding restricted sense, for three distinct, personal, divine forms of phenomenal action.*

That this doctrine involves no known contradiction, is manifest from the very general and very limited conception which the human mind ordinarily forms of the constituting elements of a being. This is what I call the phenomenal conception—that idea of a being simply, which the mind forms on condition of mere phenomena. It is complex, consisting of two elementary conceptions—that of a substance and that of a self-active phenomenal nature. This elementary conception of a *substance*, in the present use of the word, is merely the idea of a something as opposed to nothing, which is the subject or support of the self-active phenomenal nature; and the elementary conception of this self-active phenomenal nature is simply the conception of something as opposed to nothing, by which the being is qualified to produce phenomena. How very limited then is our conception of these elements of a being, and of course our knowledge of these elements, as this knowledge depends merely on phenomena. I admit and maintain, that what the mind thus gives, it gives necessarily; and that what it necessarily gives in the form of conception and knowledge, is true. But then how many more things may be true of both the substance and of the phenomenal nature of the substance, than enter into our merely phenomenal conception of either! How many of which we have formed no conception, as observers of mere phenomena, may be conceived and known to be true of the constituting elements of a being, by that Mind which knew how to give existence to beings from absolute nothing! And especially how many things of which we can form no conception from mere phenomena, may be true of that eternal, self-existent Being himself, which he, if he pleased, could make known to us by a revelation!

What a being is, in his whole nature,—in all that which he is as a being,—does not necessarily depend merely on what his phenomenal nature is, or on that nature which is evinced to our minds by phenomena. Particularly what the nature of his substance is in all respects as a substance,—whether it be something more than what it is manifested to be by mere phenomena,—viz., a mere substratum or support of its self-active nature or phenomenal properties, and if more than this, what more; what other relations, by virtue of its own peculiar nature as a substance, it may sustain to its self-active phenomenal nature besides the relation of a mere subject of that nature; in what different ways or modes it may be qualified by its own nature as a substance to control, direct, employ its self-active nature in the production of phenomena; whether as a substance it can be the subject of only one self-active nature, or of more than one of the same kind, or of different kinds; what its self-active nature may be besides that which qualifies the being to act and to produce phenomena; of what diversified modes of acting it may be capable, and what various effects it may produce; whether, if there be any such nature of a substance as qualifies it to sustain other relations to its self-active nature viewed as single or manifold, besides the relation of a mere subject of that nature, such nature of the substance can or cannot manifest itself to us by any possible phenomena, and whether it can be known to any other than the omniscient Being, and to those to whom he shall reveal it;—these are problems, the solution of which on *a priori* ground, lies entirely beyond the range of the human intellect. Yet on this ground must the Unitarian solve them, before he can know that the existence of one God in three persons, in some peculiar and authorized import of the language, is an impossibility in the nature of things. Are such decisions on the part of man any thing but those of presumptuous ignorance?

But the importance of this topic renders it worthy of a more particular investigation. I propose then to show from our limited conception and knowledge of the constituting elements of a being, and especially of the divine Being, that no contradiction or absurdity in the nature of things can be known to be involved in the doctrine of the Trinity as now explained; and this in two ways:

I. By showing that several particular modes of the divine subsistence may be supposed, which involve a plurality of persons in one being, without involving known self-contradiction; and,

II. By showing, that if this be not so, still there may be some other mode, which we may not be able to discern, or even to conjecture, in which a plurality of persons in one being involves no contradiction.

1. Several particular modes of the divine subsistence may be supposed, which involve a plurality of persons in one being without involving known self-contradiction. These supposable modes of the divine subsistence, I shall present in the following inquiries:

(A.) Is it, or is it not possible in the nature of things, that there should be, as Spinoza held, but one substance in the universe, with the different phenomenal natures, or attributes, or properties, of spirit and of matter, so that there is but *one being* in the universe, which is God; or so that God is all things and all things are God? I do not say that there is the shadow of a reason for believing the doctrine of this philosopher, nor that there is not abundant moral evidence, both from reason and the Scriptures, that it is false; but rather affirm that there is such evidence. But I ask, does any man *absolutely know* the doctrine to be false by knowing it to be *self-contradictory* and impossible in the nature of things? Plainly not. As I have said, the ordinary conception of a being is a very limited, complex conception, consisting of two which are elementary—the conception of a substance, and the conception of a self-active phenomenal nature pertaining to the substance. This conception of a substance is merely of a something to which the self-active phenomenal nature pertains. But who shall undertake to say on *a priori* ground, whether any thing more can or cannot be true of a substance; or, if more, what? Who shall in this manner decide how many phenomenal natures of the same kind, or of different kinds, a substance as such is capable of, or what diversity of effects, or diverse modes of acting and of producing effects, can or cannot depend on what the substance is as substance? Who, in this way, shall unfold the relations of the substance of the being man to his spiritual and corporeal nature, and so exhibit the interior structure and elementary constitution of the substance and the phenomenal natures of such a being, as to show us the mode of action and reaction between the spiritual and corporeal, and the ground of their continued union in life, and of their separation in death? And in respect to the self-active phenomenal nature of a substance, what is it but power to act, and by acting to produce effects or phenomena? Can there in the nature of things be only one such nature, or can there be many such in the substance? Can one phenomenal nature act in some one form of action as one nature, and also in other forms as several natures? Man as a spiritual being has what may be called an intellectual nature or mental power, but not creative power. God is a spirit, and possesses creative power. Is this communicable? If it is, and if it should be communicated to a created spirit, would it with his intellectual nature constitute one phenomenal nature of one substance, or a twofold phenomenal nature of one substance? If it is incommunicable, is it because in the nature of things it can pertain only to a self-existent substance; and if it be peculiar to such a substance, what must be the peculiarity of that substance by virtue of which it is capable of such power? Of what more is it or is it not capable in the nature of things? But not to multiply these questions. Who can so penetrate the constituting elements of a being of his substance and self-active phenomenal nature, that on the ground of *a priori* knowledge he can unfold these elements, and so determine what mutual relations, what unity and diversity of action, and what phenomenal effects, can and cannot in the nature of things be truly predicated of them, or of the being whose whole nature they constitute? If none can do this, then how limited must be man's *a priori* knowledge of the constituting elements of a being? If none can do this, who on the ground of his *a priori* knowledge will pronounce the doctrine of the philosopher of Amsterdam self-contradictory? The question is not, whether there is not proof enough that the doctrine is false, but who absolutely knows it to be false on *a priori* ground, and that it is impossible in the nature of things that there is but one substance in the universe, and that the only being, if oneness of substance is the criterion of oneness of being, is God? Who would pronounce this doctrine false, were it attested by a divine revelation? Thus attested, how would it, and how ought it, to change our conceptions of things, and with them the meaning and even the structure of language; especially the import of the word *being*, and of the personal pronouns.

In view of such *a priori* ignorance on the part of man in respect to this subject, I now proceed to propound some inquiries more directly related to the mode of the divine subsistence, which involves a trinity in the Godhead.

(B.) I ask, is it or is it not possible in the nature of things, that God should be—as Sherlock and Howe maintain—three beings, in the ordinary sense of the word being, and yet the three beings in this sense be so united in one by a common substance, as to be called in the most natural and appropriate words which language furnishes, one being; and the whole, one being in three *persons?* Who does not know, that were such a mode of the divine subsistence to be revealed in so many words or in equivalent phraseology, the meaning of the words *being* and *person* would, like other words in similar circumstances, be at once modified and changed according to the exigency of the case? I do not say that there is or is not any evidence, from the use of scriptural language, that God subsists as now supposed—one being in three persons. But I simply ask, who knows on *a priori* ground, that he does not so subsist? The question, be it remembered, is not what would be absurd or self-contradictory according to our present ordinary conceptions, or our common confident judgments or opinions, formed in view of phenomena; but what do we absolutely know on *a priori* ground, concerning possibility and impossibility in the nature of things? Do we know the impossibility of the mode of God's subsistence, now supposed, as we know the impossibility that two and two should be five?

(C.) I ask, is it or is it not possible in the nature of things, that God should be, as Leibnitz held, a being of several persons in an absolute substance, and that three persons are not as absolute substances as the whole? Who knows it to be impossible in the nature of things, that a being should consist of a threefold nature, or three phenomenal natures of the same kind, each being what may be called in some limited sense a *person*, or, as some say, *an agent*, and united with something called *its* substance, as peculiar to a divine, phenomenal nature,—and yet this substance different from that which is common to the whole being, as less absolute than the substance which unites the whole,—and so, with the three *persons*, constitutes one being? Who absolutely knows that such an existence involves a contradiction, and is therefore impossible in the nature of things?

(D.) I ask, is it or is it not possible that a being should consist of one substance and of one self-active phenomenal nature; and that while he is capable of one form of action in the exercise of his phenomenal nature, he is also, by virtue either of a peculiarity of substance or a peculiarity of a phenomenal nature, or of both, qualified so to act in three distinct forms of action, in the exercise of his one phenomenal nature, as to produce different phenomena, which a divine phenomenal nature only can produce? We have perhaps conceived and spoken, or heard others speak, of the same mind as carrying on at one and the same time, two distinct processes of thought—even as distinct as would be one process in moral reasoning and another in mathematical. Now the question is not one of fact, but respects what is and what is not possible in the nature of things. Is it then, or is it not possible, that there should be a being consisting, according to our present conception of a human mind, of one substance and one phenomenal nature, qualified as the human mind is to perform one complex mental action in thinking, feeling, and choosing, in the exercise of its entire phenomenal nature, and yet, unlike ourselves, capable, by some peculiar threefold qualification of its substance in relation to his phenomenal nature, of carrying on in other cases, two or three forms or processes of such mental action; not distinct in every respect,—not distinct or different as the acts of three phenomenal natures of three distinct substances; but still numerically different, and unlike in respect to their objects as the acts of any three beings are conceived to be different; and thus distinct by virtue of some peculiarity of one peculiar substance, in its relations to the acts of one peculiar phenomenal nature? Who knows enough of the nature of substance, and of the phenomenal nature of a substance, to decide the existence of such a being to be impossible?

(E.) Is it or is it not possible that three self-active phenomenal natures of the same kind, each conceived without a substance exclusively its own, should be combined in one common substance—for who can tell how many kinds of substances are possible *in rerum natura*—thus constituting one being with a threefold nature, or what, in the common use of language, may be called three classes of attributes or properties of the same kind; and that this one being, by virtue of the peculiarity of his one substance and of his threefold nature, should be capable of as many distinct acts—acts as distinct, so far as they depend on phenomenal natures, as the distinct acts of three beings? And here I further ask, in respect to the being now supposed, whether it is or is not possible, in the nature of things, that he should be capable also of acting in some cases as one being, in such a manner that his entire threefold phenomenal nature shall be in exercise in such action, while by virtue of his threefold nature he should be capable of acting in other cases, in three distinct forms of action?

These questions concerning what is and what is not possible in respect to the constituting elements of a being and the mode of his subsistence, are propounded as questions which, on *a priori* ground, no human intellect can decide. Am I then asked, why propound questions which no one can answer? I reply, because they are those which the Unitarian pretends to answer—thus deciding, with the confidence of infallible knowledge, that it is impossible in the nature of things, that, in any mode of conceiving of a being, or of the mode of his subsistence, such a one as the doctrine of the Trinity affirms should be conceived to exist; and that of course the existence of such a being is impossible, and cannot be taught even by a revelation from God. But if it be possible in the nature of things, for aught that any man knows to the contrary, that God should subsist in any one mode concerning the possibility of which I have inquired, then it is possible in the nature of things, for aught any man knows to the contrary, that God subsists, in some peculiar sense of the language, as *one being in three persons.* And if this be possible, what right or warrant has the Unitarian to assert that it is impossible in the nature of things? Does he know, in the form of absolute knowledge, that the mode of the divine subsistence supposed in each case of the foregoing inquiries, involves a contradiction, and is therefore impossible?

This question must be met by the direct and unqualified assertion of his absolute knowledge of the alleged contradiction and impossibility, and by making good the assertion. It is not to be evaded by some irrelevant and insufficient reply, founded in his preconceived opinions or judgments concerning the constituting elements of a being. Particularly, it is not enough for the Unitarian to say, that according to the ordinary conception or idea of a being, it is impossible that God should be, or be conceived to be, one being in three persons. This is readily admitted. The ordinary conception of a being is, as we have said, a phenomenal conception—a conception conditioned on and determined by phenomena only. It is the conception, in the most limited sense, of a being of one substance and one self-active nature—of a substance as the mere subject of one such nature, and capable of but one class of acts, and of whom nothing more is true. The impossibility that such a being should subsist as one being in three persons, is fully conceded. The present question does not respect such a being, but the known possibility or impossibility of a very different mode of subsistence from that which is the object of our ordinary conception. It respects something more in the constituting elements of a being than is evinced to our ordinary conception by mere phenomena—some nature or property which does not manifest itself merely by phenomena, and which must be made known by revelation, if at all. It is—what does the Unitarian know of this subject, or rather, whether he knows it to be impossible in the nature of things, that God should subsist in some one of the peculiar modes, concerning the possibility of which we have inquired? Does he then say that he has no other than the common or ordinary conception of a being? But how does this decide what is and what is not possible in the nature of things, in respect to the being whom we call God? If he has never allowed himself to form any other than the ordinary conception of the mode of a being's subsistence—a merely phenomenal conception—how does this show that no other can be formed, or that he is not required by the whole evidence in the case—even by a divine revelation—actually to form another, and a very different conception of the mode in which the divine being subsists? or how does it show that he knows any one of the modes of his subsistence, supposed in the foregoing inquiries to be impossible? Does he then say, that he *can* form no other than the ordinary conception of the mode of a being's subsistence, and that of course he can form none of those respecting the mode of the divine subsistence supposed in the foregoing interrogatories? This—admitting his ordinary intellectual capacity—we are constrained to deny. For if he can form the ordinary complex conception of the mode of a being's subsistence, he can—having the ordinary power of abstracting and compounding ideas—modify and change his ordinary conception by this process, and so form either of the supposed conceptions of the mode of the divine subsistence. If he can conceive of a substance to which one self-active nature pertains, he can conceive of a substance to which two or three self-active natures pertain.

If he can conceive that a substance with one self-active nature should perform one act, or one class of actions, he can conceive that a substance to which three self-active natures pertain, should perform three distinct acts, or three distinct classes of actions. In this way he can form any one of the conceptions of a being supposed in the foregoing interrogatories. At any rate, if he cannot form any one of these conceptions, then he cannot pronounce it self-contradictory, and the existence of its object impossible in the nature of things. Does he then say that the contradiction involved in each of the foregoing suppositions is, that one being is three beings, or three beings one being? I answer, that there is no pretense for such an assertion. For in each supposition the being is supposed to consist of one, and of but one absolute substance in three persons, in some peculiar or unusual sense of the language. According to each supposition, oneness of absolute substance is involved, to which the threefold distinction of three persons belongs. And surely oneness of substance—whatever nature, simple or complex, single or compound, be supposed to pertain to it—is the only criterion of oneness of being. Of course the word *persons*, in such a case, is manifestly used, as is claimed, not in its usual meaning—not even to imply, nor so that in any fairness of construction it can imply, three beings. On the contrary, it is plainly used in each supposition in such a restricted meaning as to imply at most, some threefold qualification for distinct personal acts or action, either in the peculiar substance or in the peculiar phenomenal nature—whether the latter be single or compound—or in both substance and phenomenal nature. How then is one such being three beings, by involving three such distinctions, called persons, in one being; or how are three such persons three beings, when each, as a person, is supposed not to be a being in the sense in which the whole subsistence is a being, but to be only one of the constituting elements of one entire being? Plainly, such a supposition, instead of implying that one being is three beings, or three beings one being, most expressly asserts the contrary. Neither of the three persons supposed to be included in one being, is supposed, as a person, to be identical with the entire being; but as a person, or divine person, is supposed to be not the entire being. How then can the supposed one being in three persons be, in one and the same sense, three beings?

Does the Unitarian now say that he cannot conceive *how* such a being can exist, as that concerning which we have hypothetically inquired? Such a reply would only show how entirely he mistakes, and thus evades the point now at issue. What if he cannot conceive *how* such a being can exist? Is the measure of his conception the measure of all possibility in the nature of things? Is nothing possible, unless he can conceive *how* it is possible? Can he conceive how mind or matter exists, or can be brought into being from nothing by the power of the Creator; how a man or an angel can be so constituted as to develop his nature in all the phenomena of intelligence and of action peculiar to each; ay, how the God and Maker of all should exist, and be what he is, and do what he does? Surely the question is not whether the Unitarian, or any one else, can or cannot conceive *how* a triune being can exist, or be what he is, or do what he does, supposing such a being to exist and to act; but it is, does the Unitarian, or any one else, absolutely know that it is impossible in the nature of things that such a being—in some one of the modes of subsistence, in respect to the possibility of which we have inquired—*can exist?* If he does, let him say he does, and make good his assertion; let him intelligibly state the contradiction in the conception which involves the impossibility alleged. My object in propounding the foregoing inquiries is not to affirm—nor have I occasion to do so—the possibility of such a being as I have made the subject of these hypothetical inquiries; but to ascertain whether the Unitarian knows as much concerning the possible constituting elements of a being—even of all that enters into the entire nature of the self-existent God—as he pretends to know; it is to challenge him to show the contradiction involved in each of the foregoing suppositions of one being in three persons, and thus compel him to fair reasoning, either by showing the contradiction which he asserts, or by retracting and never repeating what otherwise must be deemed an assertion entitled to no respect.

Having thus attempted to show that several particular modes of the divine subsistence may be supposed which involve a plurality of persons, or three persons in one God, as this doctrine has been explained, without involving any known contradiction, I now proceed to show—

2. That if it be not so—that is, if the human mind be unable to

suppose any particular mode of the divine subsistence including three persons in one being, which does not involve a contradiction—it is impossible that man should know that there cannot be such a mode of the divine subsistence.

What if neither Plato, nor Aristotle, nor any other human being has been able to devise a mode by which matter can be created from absolute nothing, does it follow that man can *know* that its creation from nothing does involve a contradiction? Because man can specify no mode in which matter can be thus created which would involve a contradiction, can there be no mode, and can God conceive no mode of creating matter from nothing which involves no contradiction? There is a plain difference between being *unable* to decide *a priori*, that a thing does not, and being *able* to decide that it does involve a contradiction. The human mind may be utterly unable to decide on *a priori* ground, that the creation of matter from nothing does not; but this is not being able to decide that it does. The mere fact, that the mind has not that full, comprehensive view of the subject which enables it to decide that it does not involve a contradiction, is not being able to decide that it does. It may be utterly unable to see *how* it can be done; but this is not seeing that it cannot be done. Or to take a more familiar case. What man is able to decide on *a priori* ground, that the supposition of a soul and body united in one being, either does or does not involve a contradiction? or whether the supposition that one portion of inert matter should possess power to attract another portion, does or does not involve a contradiction? And now what would be more preposterous than for one to infer, from his utter inability to decide such a question either way, his ability to decide it one way; that is, because he cannot decide, *a priori*, that the supposition of the creation of matter from nothing, or of the union of the soul and body in one being, or of the power of gravity in one portion of matter, either does or does not involve a contradiction, to infer that the supposition does involve a contradiction? So in the present case. Let it be granted for the sake of the argument, that no human mind can suppose any particular mode of the subsistence of one God in three persons, which does not involve a contradiction, and is therefore utterly unable to decide in this way, that the supposition of one God in three persons does or that it does not involve a contradiction, is it therefore able to decide that it does involve a contradiction? Plainly, though the human mind were wholly unable to suppose any particular mode of the divine subsistence including, according to the explanation given, three persons in one being, which does not involve a contradiction, this is not knowing that the doctrine of three persons in one God as now explained, does involve a contradiction. There may be for aught that appears to the contrary, some particular mode of the divine subsistence, in which God actually exists as one God in three persons. It is utterly impossible that man should know on *a priori* ground, that there cannot be. Unless the human mind can fully and perfectly comprehend all modes of subsistence which are possible in the nature of things—and in the present case, all the constituting elements which can enter into the whole nature of the Godhead, with the relation of each element to every other—it must be forever impossible for man to know or decide on *a priori* ground, that the doctrine of one God in three persons, as the language has now been explained, involves a contradiction.

Again: this topic may be presented in another light. The human mind necessarily conceives and knows that the supposition or assertion of some things—for example, that a part is equal to the whole, that two and two are five, that a thing is and is not—involves a contradiction; while it does not necessarily conceive and know, nor can it decide on *a priori* ground, that the supposition or assertion of some other things, either does or does not involve a contradiction; for example, that matter should be created from nothing, that a soul and body should be united as they are in one man, that fire should explode gunpowder, or burn the hand in contact with it. The former instances may be viewed as of two kinds. One is, when the proposition is an express contradiction of the plainest form, as, that what is, is not, or that one and the same thing is and is not. The other is, when the proposition can be reduced to an express contradiction, as when it is said that a part is equal to the whole; which is to say, that what is *not* equal to the whole, viz., a part, is equal to the whole. Now, when the proposition is of the former kind, or an express contradiction of the plainest form, then there can be no mistake. The mind that apprehends the meaning of the language, necessarily conceives and knows the contradiction to exist. When the proposition is of the latter kind—one which involves a contradiction without expressing it in the plainest form—it can be reduced to an express contradiction. If then, a proposition is not an express contradiction in the plainest form, and if it cannot be reduced to such, then no man can know or decide *a priori* that it is, or that it involves a contradiction. Now, in respect to the doctrine of the Trinity as we have explained it, I affirm that it is neither an express contradiction, nor can it be reduced to such. If then, the doctrine of the Trinity is not and cannot be the express contradiction of asserting that one being is three beings, in the ordinary use of language—if it cannot be reduced to this express contradiction, and therefore cannot be known to involve it—can it be known to involve any other?

On this question, it were perhaps sufficient to say, that in view of the facility—not to say the certainty—of detecting and exposing the contradiction of a proposition like this, could it be known to be of this character,—in view also of the intellectual strength which has been employed upon it for this very purpose, and of the fact that no other has ever been charged, except that which, as we have seen, is false,—in view of these things, it were sufficient and safe to say, that neither that contradiction which has been charged, nor any other, can be *known* to be involved in the doctrine.

But not to rest the question on this ground. The nature of the subject renders it impossible that the human mind should know on *a priori* ground, that the doctrine of the Trinity, as now explained, involves a contradiction. The inquiry respects the constitution of the Godhead—the constituting elements of an eternal, self-existent being; and there is nothing which falls more entirely without and beyond the range and grasp of the human intellect. It is true that man has a distinct, well defined, and even necessary conception, as far as it goes, of what he calls a being—of himself, of every other man, of an angel, of God. But what enters into the constitution even of a created being beyond a very narrow limit—what it is in all the elements, neither more nor less, which constitutes him the being that he is, as these are known to Omniscience, the mind of man, unperverted by philosophic speculation, does not attempt on *a priori* ground to determine. The inquiry at once associates with itself a consciousness of intellectual imbecility, and the mind falters in despair before entering on the investigation.

At the same time it necessarily forms a general limited conception of a being, and determines, not that more than it thus conceives is not true, but that what it thus necessarily conceives is true. From the nature of the mind as a knower, it is impossible that it should conceive and know a being, without conceiving and knowing him to consist at least of one substance and one phenomenal nature, or a nature qualifying him to produce phenomena. This conception of a substance and a phenomenal nature, may be said to be the common or ordinary conception of a being, and so much at least as is comprised in this we may be justly said to know of every being. But how little do we know, even of a created being, compared with Him who knew how to give him existence from nothing! How many things may be predicated of every being, for aught we know or can know to the contrary, on *a priori* ground, or from mere phenomena which, in the nature of things, would be credible, and which, supported by proper evidence, especially by God's declaration, would demand our unhesitating belief?

It is true that the idea of a substance is, of that to which a phenomenal nature, commonly conceived as a class of properties or attributes, belongs. Reason, the competent, unperverted intellect of man, necessarily gives the truth, that every subtance has a nature qualifying it for the production of all its diverse phenomena or effects. Hence the mind, forming this conception of a being from mere phenomena, and having no evidence of any thing more from mere phenomena than what is included in it, regards it in all such cases as a just and true conception of a being. Such it undoubtedly is. So much as this conception involves, is to be received as true in all cases; and on the ground of phenomena merely, and on the authority of reason merely, nothing more is to be received as true. But to return to the question, Can nothing more be true in the nature of things? Can nothing more be true of *the whole nature* of a being than is comprised in this limited conception, formed solely on the ground of phenomena? Can man absolutely know it to be impossible in the nature of things, that nothing more should be true? Were man omniscient, would he know more than he can know from mere phenomena? Could not God if he pleased, tell us something more than, in this manner, we now know—something which would greatly change and extend our conception beyond our ordinary phenomenal conception of a being—especially of himself?

Let us reflect carefully on the question, What then does mere reason, on the basis of phenomena merely, decide respecting the constituting elements of a being? I answer as before, that a being consists of that something, as opposed to nothing, to which a phenomenal nature pertains. But this is not deciding that nothing more can be true, nor that nothing more is true. What reason thus necessarily decides to be true, is true. But reason does not necessarily give, nor pretend to give us all truth. Reason is not omniscient. While therefore, on the authority of mere reason, it would be, for the want of evidence, in the highest degree irrational to believe that a being consists of any thing more than one substance and one phenomenal nature, as we have explained the language, still that nothing more can be true in the case, except what is comprised in this very limited conception,—nothing more, in respect to his substance and his phenomenal nature, except what qualifies him for one form of personal, phenomenal action, is not, as the Unitarian assumes, a judgment of reason, or a necessary decision of the human mind. The assumption of this is obviously THE FIRST AND GRAND ERROR OF THE UNITARIAN IN ALL HIS REASONING. He assumes, not only that reason necessarily gives the ordinary phenomenal conception of every being, but that it necessarily excludes from this conception that of *tri-personality*, or a threefold qualification for three distinct forms of personal, phenomenal action, as a false conception; in other words, he assumes that human reason necessarily decides that a being having one absolute substance and one phenomenal nature, qualifying him for one form of phenomenal action, cannot in the nature of things, either by any peculiarity of his substance or of his phenomenal nature, or of both, or in any mode of subsistence whatever, be qualified for three distinct personal forms of phenomenal action. This we say is an unauthorized, because a groundless assumption by human reason. I admit that reason necessarily conceives that every being consists at least of one substance and one phenomenal nature, qualifying him for at least one form of personal, phenomenal action. But reason does not necessarily decide either that more is or is not true of a being. It is true that, in all ordinary cases—even in all cases but one—there is an utter want of evidence of any thing more than is included in the ordinary conception of a being. This want of evidence requires us *not* to believe, or forbids us to believe, that there is any thing more; but does not require nor even authorize us *to believe*, and thus to assert, that there is *not* any thing more. The entire want of evidence of a fact or truth, forbids us to believe the fact or truth; but instead of authorizing us to *deny* the fact or truth, it forbids us to *disbelieve* it. The entire want of evidence that Saturn has more rings than one, forbids us to believe that it has more than one; but it does not authorize us to believe that it has *not* more than one. It forbids us to disbelieve that it has more than one, for evidence of more is quite supposable; and with evidence of more, we should be required to believe more. Besides, if it be granted that the want of all evidence that any being has a threefold nature in some sort, which qualification for distinct personal forms of phenomenal action authorizes the belief that he has not, still this is mere *belief*, and not knowledge—a mere inference, founded solely on the want of evidence. How then would it be if we had good and sufficient evidence, even God's declaration, that some particular being possesses this threefold qualification? If God should reveal on this subject something more of himself than human reason can discover from mere phenomena, would human reason be competent to contradict the revelation? Plainly, no man can know on *a priori* ground, and therefore no man can assert on this ground, that it is impossible in the nature of things that God should be one being in such a modified sense, as to include three persons in such a modified sense, that by his tri-personality he is qualified in a corresponding modified sense, for three distinct, divine, personal forms of phenomenal action.

In illustration of what has now been said, let us suppose as some philosophers and some Unitarians do, that the human mind consists simply of one phenomenal nature, or of one combination of mental properties, without a substance to which this nature or these properties belong. Let us now suppose any three such minds as we now conceive them to be, each to exhibit the same mental phenomena—the same distinct mental operations and states in its own consciousness—which any three minds now exhibit. If now God, in a well-attested revelation, should declare, contrary to the supposed conception in one respect, that these three minds were united by a common substance, would any man know the declaration to be false? Again, suppose that, in a well-attested revelation and in formal and express terms, God should announce to us that every three—every triplet of human beings—while they are three persons in respect to distinct qualifications for three distinct personal forms of mental action, as we now conceive them to be,—except that they are so combined in one and the same substance that they are as truly, though in a different respect, one being, as each of the three in our present conception is one being;—who is the man that knows so much of the elements of a being—even of himself as a being—of what is possible and impossible in the nature of things, as to be able to pronounce the revelation false? Who would do it with the same assurance that he pronounces the proposition that two and two are five, to be false? Who can absolutely know that the creation of such a being is beyond the power of the Almighty? If you say that it involves a contradiction, specify and make it manifest, or learn to be silent on the question of what is impossible to Omnipotence. "What is the soul?" said one to Marivaux. "I know nothing of it," he replied, "but that it is spiritual and immortal." "Well," said his friend, "let us ask Fontenelle, and he will tell us what it is." "No," said Marivaux, "ask anybody but Fontenelle, for he has too much good sense to know any thing more about it than we do."

Man then, has not that *a priori* knowledge of the constituting elements of any being, much less of one eternal and self-existent, which enables him to decide in all respects what can and what cannot be true in the nature of things, respecting the mode of his subsistence. In such inquiries the human mind is baffled, and falls back in despairing weakness; and so it must be, till man shall comprehend what God only knows. The vegetation of a blade of grass, the motions of an insect, the simplest organized being, the merest atom of inert matter, present mysteries which human reason cannot penetrate. In view then, of the greatness and incomprehensibleness of God, what known impossibility is there that he should subsist—what *a priori* presumption in the nature of things against supposing him to subsist in a very diverse *mode* from that of his creatures, even in that of one God in three persons, or of one divine being in such a modified and peculiar sense, as to include three persons in such a modified and peculiar sense, that by his tri-personality he is qualified in a corresponding modified sense, for three distinct, divine personal forms of phenomenal action? Surely, in respect to the constituting elements of that Being, who, himself uncaused, created mind and matter, men, angels, archangels, and all from absolute nothing, our feeble intellect may well consent to be enlightened by a revelation from himself, and to bow in humble, grateful adoration, before what he shall reveal concerning his eternal Godhead. What God reveals of himself, until it be absolutely *known* to be self-contradictory and impossible in the nature of things, is credible, and must be believed, or God must be made a liar.

I have thus attempted to show how entirely groundless and unauthorized is the charge of contradiction and impossibility, ever alleged and insisted on by Unitarians, against the doctrine of the Trinity. I have said the more on this topic, not because it would not be sufficient for the Trinitarian to meet the gratuitous charge with a simple denial, at least until the Unitarian shall specify some other contradiction than that which he does specify, but because, by a most unwarrantable assumption to which it is necessary to give prominence, and thus to call particular attention, he gives plausibility to this charge in his own mind, and often in the minds of others. This we claim to have shown to be entirely gratuitous, and even absolutely forbidden by the laws of rational belief. It is forbidden by these laws, even in respect to a created being. Man, though required to believe what he necessarily conceives to be true, and, though forbidden to believe any thing more, for want of evidence concerning the elements of his own being, is not *required to believe* that nothing more is true, but is *forbidden to believe* that nothing more is or can be true. To suppose otherwise is to suppose that man, in one set of circumstances may be required not merely *not to believe*, but *to disbelieve* that which, in an another set of circumstances, may be proved to be true. If then, it be gratuitous and unauthorized to believe that nothing more is or can be true of the elements of our own being than what is given by mere phenomena, how much more so is it to believe that nothing more can be true of the elements of God's being than is manifested merely by his works? It is this assumption in respect to God, which I consider the grand and fundamental error of the Unitarian in all his reasoning. When this shall be clearly seen, and not till then, will it be manifest how flagrantly gratuitous and unauthorized, not to say irreverent, is his charge of contradiction and absurdity, echoed and re-echoed against the doctrine of the Trinity.

THE TRINITY.

III.—NO PRESUMPTION AGAINST, BUT RATHER A PRESUMPTION FOR THE TRUTH OF THE DOCTRINE.

No such presumption in what man knows to be true of himself, nor in that we judge all other beings besides God to be like ourselves in this respect.—No presumption from divine revelation; none from the Unity of God.—The presumption for its truth is founded on the fact, that God is administering a Moral Government under an economy of grace.—This requires an Atonement.—An Atonement seems to be most easily furnished and explained on the supposition of this mode of the Divine subsistence.—Nature of the Atonement incidentally explained.—Temporary sufferings and death of the Divine-man a sufficient evil.

A PRESUMPTION, as the term is now used, may be said to be founded on evidence which the mind is authorized to *take*, though of a lower kind or degree than that which is called *full proof*. It may rest in it prior to the inquiry whether full proof exists or not. Such a presumption may be greater or less, stronger or weaker, at least in two respects,—either as that which furnishes it is sustained by more or less evidence, or as it is more or less fitted to support the proposition which it is alleged to support. Of course, if that which is alleged as furnishing the presumption has no existence, or if its existence is wholly without evidence, or if on the supposition of its existence, it is in no respect fitted to support the proposition, then there is no presumption.

The self-contradiction which Unitarians assert to be involved in the doctrine, if the allegation were true, would not be *a presumption* against the truth of the doctrine, but a full and unanswerable *proof* of its falsehood, giving an impossibility, which absolutely precludes all evidence of its truth.

But aside from all consideration of this contradiction, the assertion of which I claim to have shown is wholly groundless and absolutely forbidden by the laws of reasoning, there is in many minds a strong presumption against the truth of the doctrine of one God in three persons. This, so far as it exists in the view of those who receive it, is doubtless counteracted by abundant proof of its truth, while probably, in the view of the Unitarian, it is so strong as to be quite sufficient to prove that the doctrine is not revealed, and is not true.

My present design is to show—

I. That there is no presumption against the truth of the doctrine of the Trinity, as now explained; and,

II. That there is a strong presumption in favor of its truth.

I. There is no presumption against the truth of the doctrine.

Any presumption which may be asserted against its truth must be implied in the doctrine itself, or must arise from what the doctrine asserts respecting the mode in which one God or one Divine Being subsists; or, respecting the constituent elements of his being, when it is said, in the meaning in which the language has now been explained, that he is one God in three persons. What then is this doctrine? It is that God is one being in such a modified and extended sense of the language, as to include three persons in such a modified and restricted sense of the terms, that he is qualified, in a corresponding restricted sense, for three distinct divine personal forms of phenomenal action. Now what presumption is furnished by this doctrine against its truth? Does it assert that one God is three Gods, or that there are more Gods than one? It admits of no such construction, for it expressly affirms that there is but one God, and that the three persons, *as persons*, are not three beings or three Gods. Does the doctrine then, exclude from the conception of God the ordinary, necessary phenomenal conception of a being? So far from it, that in asserting that God is one being, it includes this conception. Does the doctrine then, include more in the conception of God as one being, than is comprised in the ordinary, necessary phenomenal conception of a being? But allowing this, what presumption does it afford against the truth of the doctrine? What shadow of evidence can the mind of man discover, that the eternal, self-existent God should not subsist in a mode peculiar to himself, and quite diverse from that of creatures? Rather, what evidence can man possess that nothing more enters into the full and true conception which is formed by his own infinite mind of himself, than is comprised in the ordinary, phenomenal, and very limited conception which man forms of the same being? What evidence has man or can he have, that this limited phenomenal conception of his own being comprises all that is true, and all that God, who made him, conceives and knows to be true? If there is nothing like evidence to his mind that more is not, in this respect, true of himself, what presumption can there be that more is not true of the self-existent God, even that which constitutes three persons in one God? More particularly, is any presumption against it furnished by either reason or revelation? Not by reason. Reason indeed, gives what I have called the ordinary phenomenal conception of a being—the conception of one substance and one phenomenal nature, and of nothing more. Here obviously, is the radical error of those who suppose that there is some reasonable presumption against the doctrine of the Trinity. They confidently but falsely assume, that because, when they have formed the ordinary conception of a being from phenomena merely, nothing more can be rationally believed to be true on this ground than what is included in the phenomenal conception, they are authorized to believe that nothing more is true. Whereas they are, by the laws of reasoning, absolutely forbidden in such a case to believe that nothing more is true, there being not the faintest shade of evidence that something more than is proved to be true by phenomena, is not true. What right does reason or logic give to any man to believe, or even to surmise, that his conception of the nature of any being is the exact limit and measure of all that is true?

But it may here be asked, Is not this phenomenal conception a true one, fully authorized and even required by reason and evidence, when formed of every other being but God? and is there not also some presumption arising from this fact, that it is also a true conception of God as a being? I answer, undeniably. But the question is not, whether this is a true conception of God and of every other being, nor whether there is not a presumption that it is a true conception, for there is the most *decisive proof* that it is; but does this true conception comprise all that is true, either of God as a being, or of any other being as a being? Is it said that every man knows in respect to himself, that he is what, in this phenomenal conception, he conceives himself to be? and that if more entered into the constitution of his being than what he thus conceives to be true, he would know that also? I answer, that nothing is plainer, than that if more pertained to his constitution as a being than he now conceives, he could not, if the phenomena of his mind being in his own consciousness exactly what they now are, know that any thing more pertained to it than he now conceives. Is it then said, that if more were true than is involved in his present conception, the phenomena of the mind would indicate the fact? I answer, this is gratuitously said. Who can adduce the slightest evidence to show, that he who has made any three men, cannot, by a common substance, so unite them, that they shall be even more properly said to be one being than three beings, and yet the mental operations and phenomena of each be exactly in the consciousness of each, what they now are? No such evidence can be adduced, and when there is no evidence there is no presumption. The error then is palpable. There is no presumption furnished by the phenomenal conception either of God or any being, and therefore none furnished by reason, that God is not one being in three persons.

Further, no presumption against the doctrine of the Trinity is furnished by divine revelation. The only one which can be supposed, must arise from the assumption, that the sacred writers, when they speak—as they confessedly do—of God as *a divine being*, or as *one divine* being, mean that he is *a being* in the *ordinary* or *usual* sense of the word. On this ground if on any, a presumption must be supposed against his tri-personality.

On this topic it is easy for the mind to mislead itself by indefinite conceptions and language. Different views of the manner in which the sacred writers use language may be entertained, any one of which may seem to authorize the presumption concerning which we now inquire. Some of these different views I propose to examine.

It may be said then, that the sacred writers in all cases when they speak of God, mean that he is a being in the *usual* sense of the word, and that this fact, considered in itself, furnishes a presumption that they do not speak of him as *a being* in any further meaning. It is readily admitted, and fully believed, that whenever they speak of God, they mean that he is *a being* in at least the full, *ordinary*, or *usual* meaning of the word. But this, considered simply in itself, by no means proves that they do not, at the same time and in all cases, conceive of and use the word *being* in more than its ordinary import. That it may be warrantably said that they do *not* use the language in a more extended meaning, there must be *evidence* that they do not; for it is supposable that there should be evidence to the contrary, and if it exists, then there is no evidence, or *presumption* even, that they do *not* use the language in a further meaning than its usual one. If it does not, then the evidence that they mean that God is a *being* in the ordinary use of the word, is all the evidence in the case. But this is simply evidence that they mean to say that God is a being in nothing more nor less than the *usual* meaning of the word. Indeed, without a revelation, asserting or evincing in some way the fact that God is *not* a being in a further than the ordinary meaning of the word, the sacred writers could have no warrant to mean *that he is not*, because they could have no evidence *that he is not*. The utter want of evidence of the fact is not the slightest proof against it. It is not so in respect to any supposed fact, except when evidence of the fact exists with it. But it will not be pretended that, if God as *a being* is something more than is involved in the *usual* meaning of the word, he would certainly furnish evidence of the fact. That the sacred writers then, according to the present supposition, speak of God as a *being*, in at least the usual meaning of the word, does not furnish the slightest *presumption* that they do *not*, in every such instance, conceive and speak, and intend to be understood as speaking of him as a being in a further than the ordinary sense, even as one being in three persons. To illustrate by an example: should one affirm that God is a being, or one being, in a case in which nothing more can be known or reasonably conjectured concerning his particular opinion, his assertion ought to be understood to mean that God is a *being* in the *usual* sense of the word, and nothing more. This is all that the language, thus considered in itself merely, can be justly said to express. In this meaning however, it furnishes not the slightest evidence that the conception of the speaker concerning the being of God, is that of the Unitarian, nor that of the Trinitarian, nor that it is the particular conception of either. If now we suppose the speaker, in connection with the supposed assertion, to be known as a Unitarian, then he is justly understood to mean, not only that God is a being in the ordinary sense of the word, but also that he is *not* a being in any further meaning, or at least in that which the Trinitarian maintains. On the other hand, if the speaker is known as a Trinitarian, then he is justly understood to mean that God is a being not only in the full, usual sense, but in a still further meaning of the word. Until some evidence besides the supposed assertion be adduced, that the speaker means to say that God is *not* a being in any further than the usual acceptation of the word, there can be no warrant for asserting that he does mean to say this. It is to assert that to be true of which there is no evidence, and when it is as likely to be false as to be true, there being no evidence or presumption either way. Let the Unitarian and all others see, in this view, the palpable injustice which would be done to the supposed speaker, were he a Trinitarian, by this interpretation of his language, and be sure to avoid the same injustice toward the sacred writers.

Again: it may be said that the sacred writers, by the language which they use in some cases, clearly mean that God is *a being* in the usual meaning of the word, without giving in those cases the least supposable intimation that he is a being in any extended meaning; and that hence a presumption arises, that they in no case speak of him as a being in any such. For the sake of the argument let it be admitted that, in those earlier periods of divine revelation, when the great design was to deny and subvert polytheism, that the sacred writers spoke of God as a being, or as one being only in the ordinary use of the language, and without giving the least intimation that he is a being in any further meaning. But if this be admitted, it furnishes no presumption against a further use of the same language, sustained by abundant proof, in some subsequent revelation. God, in his wisdom and goodness, has given to this world a progressive revelation. It is quite supposable therefore, that the only authorized conception of God in the time of Abraham and of Moses, was more limited than in the time of the later prophets, and in the time of the latter than in the time of Christ and of his apostles. If this were so, the word *God*, as denoting the Divine Being, would acquire a further or more extended meaning as the conception and knowledge of him should be extended. This is unavoidably true of all words in analogous cases. The time was when gold was not known to be soluble in aqua regia, nor common air to be heavy. Subsequent to such knowledge, and as its necessary consequence, these words acquired a further meaning than what they had before. In like manner, it is altogether credible, that when the time arrived to unfold in its full and final form the great work of this world's redemption, God should more fully reveal than before that grand peculiarity of the mode of his subsistence, on which this work, in its provisions for deliverance from the penalty and power of sin, is supposed by some to depend. And, on this supposition, what possible presumption could arise from speaking of God as a being, or as any being, only in the *usual* meaning of the word, during the period of a less perfect revelation, against conceiving and speaking of him in a further meaning of the language, under a fuller revelation, and with further knowledge of the mode of his subsistence? What possible presumption could be created by speaking of God as a being in the *usual* meaning of the word, that nothing more was or could be true of him than what is involved in this limited conception? Who that knows how to estimate evidence, will say that a subsequent revelation of a further meaning had to encounter the least presumption against its truth, or that God could not announce a certain degree of truth concerning himself, and subsequently announce more, without, by the latter annunciation, contradicting a belief which he had before authorized, and even required. The mere supposition that God, for highly important ends, might in his later revelations increase the knowledge of his mode of subsistence, precludes every presumption against the fact, arising from the prior limitation of such knowledge.

Is it then affirmed, that the sacred writers when they speak of God, mean *in all cases* that he is a being in the *usual* sense of the word, without deciding or intimating either that he is, or that he is not, a being in any that is more extended; and that hence a presumption arises, that God is not a being in any further meaning than the usual one? This view of the language of the sacred writers presents the strongest case in regard to the question under consideration, which can be supposed with any plausibility. There can however, be no pretense that they have by any logical definition, or by any philosophical explanation, in respect to his substance and properties, or essence and attributes, shut off all further conception of him as a being than what is included in the usual meaning of the word. For any distinct, accurately defined, philosophic import of their language on this subject, we shall look in vain to their writings. The most that can be pretended is, that they speak of God as a being, or as one being, in the usual sense of the word, without deciding or intimating that more is true, or that more is not true. Let it then be supposed, that such is the manner in which the sacred writers in all cases speak of God. On this supposition, I readily admit that nothing more than what is included in this ordinary conception of a being can be proved from the Scriptures to be true of God; and that of course no one can be authorized to believe or assert that more is true; or that God is one being in three persons. But it is equally obvious that there is in this case no evidence nor presumption that nothing more is true of God than what is comprised in the merely ordinary phenomenal conception of a being. There is a palpable difference between *no* evidence, or the utter want of evidence that a thing is, and evidence that it is *not.* Who then that pretends to reason can say, that the utter want of evidence that God, as a being, is any thing more than is comprised in the *usual* meaning of the word, is evidence even of the lowest kind, that he is not any thing more, even one being in three persons? Admitting the utmost that can be supposed with the least plausibility, in respect to the language of revelation concerning God, there is not from this source the slightest presumption against the doctrine of the Trinity.

But another thing is here to be said. To assume what is now supposed in respect to the language of revelation, is, in the present stage of inquiry, wholly gratuitous and forbidden by the laws of fair reasoning. No one can be authorized to assume that the sacred writers always speak of God in *merely the usual* meaning of the word *being*, until the question be first decided on independent grounds, whether they do not conceive and speak of Him in a more extended meaning of the word, even as one being in three persons. To assume that this is not so, until the contrary is shown to be true on its own independent grounds of argument, is to beg a main question in debate. It is to assume that the doctrine of the Trinity is not revealed in the Scriptures, and that of course there is no sufficient warrant to believe it. He who asserts that the Scriptures do not reveal this doctrine, is bound to prove it. Does he say no man can prove a negative proposition? If so, then he is forbidden to assert that it is a true proposition. Besides, if there is no evidence from the Scriptures that the doctrine is true, then we are bound simply not to believe, or forbidden to believe, that it is true. But this is not being bound to believe that it is *not* true. Besides, the question here is not whether the Scriptures do or do not reveal God as one being in three persons; but it is whether there is any *presumption*—any low degree of evidence from the Scriptures, that God is *not* one being in three persons, prior to the inquiry whether there is or is not *full proof* from the Scriptures that he is such a being. Without then, assuming what cannot be done without gross unfairness in the argument, that the Scriptures *always* speak of God as a being in *merely* the usual sense of the word, the only fact in the Scriptures which can be supposed to furnish a presumption against the tri-personality of God is, that they speak of him in some instances in the *usual* sense of the word being; a fact quite consistent with their speaking of him in other instances as a being in a further meaning, even as one God in three persons. The only supposable fact in the case cannot therefore furnish the least evidence or presumption that God is not such a being, nor that the Scriptures do not speak of him as such.

From what has now been said, it follows that there is *no presumption*, either from reason or revelation, that God is not a being in a more extended than the usual meaning of the word, even in any which involves no contradiction, and therefore that he is not one being in three persons. So far from there being any such presumption, the supposition of it must result solely from *falsely assuming*, that when there is not a particle of evidence either that a thing *is* or that *it is not*, there is evidence that *it is not* in the fact that there is no evidence that *it is*.

The Unitarian, supposing him as I now do, to abandon the charge of self-contradiction as involved in the doctrine of the Trinity, would, as I have said, *probably* consider the presumption against it arising from what he calls the Unity of God, so violent as to authorize the most confident *belief* that the doctrine is not true. I say *probably;* for who does not know that the Unitarians constantly deny the true reading and Orthodox interpretation of Trinitarian texts chiefly, and often solely on the ground of what they call the Unity of God? I suppose this fact will be admitted, at least to a great extent; and if it be so, I ask how is it possible that a Unitarian persuades himself that there is such a strong presumption from the Unity of God against the doctrine of the Trinity? I admit indeed, that the simple fact that God is a being in the ordinary meaning of the word, furnishes no evidence nor the least presumption that he is one being in three persons. But how does this simple fact furnish, in the view of the Unitarian, the strong presumption that God as a being is not something more, even one being in three persons? Evidence or proof both from reason and revelation merely to the simple fact that God is one being in the *usual* meaning of the word, is evidence or proof of the simple fact, and of nothing more. How then, can the Unitarian regard it as evidence that God is *not* a being, or one being in three persons? How is this possible, except that he falsely assumes that the utter want of evidence which requires us *not to believe* that a thing is, is equivalent to evidence which requires us to believe that *the thing is not?* Plainly, it is by this error in estimating evidence that he finds this strong presumption against the doctrine of the Trinity. Hence, with the falsehood of the doctrine confidently settled and assumed beforehand, he goes without one misgiving to the work of amending and interpreting the sacred text. What a basis is this for a Christian's faith!—that *the utter want of all evidence from the Unity of God for the tri-personality of God, is decisive proof that God is not tri-personal!*

If the Unitarian denies that this most unwarrantable assumption is the first and main premise of his best argument for the falsehood of the doctrine of the Trinity, then I ask him either to admit that no presumption against it arises from the doctrine of the divine Unity, or to show how such a one can arise from this doctrine, except it depend on the specified assumption. Dislodged, as I have a right to assume that he is, from his position that the doctrine of the Trinity is self-contradictory, if he admits that there is no presumption against its truth arising from the divine Unity, then he must admit that the doctrine of one God who is tri-personal, is as credible as the doctrine of one God who is not tri-personal. With this admission, with what success will he oppose the doctrine of the Trinity, or assail the scriptural arguments alleged in its support? If, on the other hand, he still maintains that this strong presumption from the divine Unity exists against the doctrine of the Trinity, then I repeat the challenge, and call on him to show how this presumption can arise, except from the monstrous assumption, that the utter want of evidence from the divine Unity that God is tri-personal, is decisive evidence that he is *not* tri-personal.

I have dwelt longer on this topic than the mere exigency of the argument requires, because it is difficult in many cases to hold the mind to the precise point at issue. In such cases there is a great want of reflection, resulting in indefinite and confused or rather vacillating ideas of the subject, by which the mind at most attains only a cloudy conception of something very like a Trinity of persons, and very nearly as incredible. To secure the mind from this vague and necessarily false mode of conceiving of this momentous subject, by giving precision to the conception of one God in three persons, by directing attention steadily to the import of the terms employed in stating the doctrine, and particularly by an examination of every plausible ground of a presumption against the truth of it, I have attempted to show that no such ground does or can exist, and that any and all such must depend on the false *assumption*, that the utter want of evidence from the divine Unity that God is tri-personal, is proof that he is *not* tri-personal; or, in the form of a general principle, that the utter want of evidence that a thing is, is proof that it *is not*, which is a palpable absurdity. There was a time when man was ignorant that the loadstone had the power of attraction, and another and later time when there was no knowledge of its attribute of polarity; but who will say that this want of evidence of these properties of the loadstone was evidence that it did *not* possess them? It is obvious that, on the principle of the Unitarian, our knowledge of God, supposing it to be limited and inadequate at one time, could never be extended or enlarged, even by a revelation from himself.

I only add, that it were enough to say that such are the greatness and incomprehensibleness of God, as to remove every presumption that he is not a being in a more extended sense than the *usual* meaning of the word,—a being in a mode of subsistence quite diverse from that of any of his creatures,—even one being in three persons. For who that asks *what God is as a being*,—who that in the attitude of this inquiry ventures to look up to such greatness and glory,—shall be incredulous in respect to any discovery which such a being can make of himself by his own revelation? Who that comes to the living oracles or consults his own reason, and so finds that the God of eternity is one being, shall hence decide or even *presume* that he is *not* one being in that peculiarly sublime and august mode of subsistence which qualifies him, in each of three distinct divine and personal forms of action, to express his whole Deity?

I now proceed to show—

II. That there is a presumption for the truth of the doctrine, that *God is one being in three persons.*

The facts from which this presumption is supposed to arise, may be summarily comprised in these:—that God is administering a perfect Moral Government over men under an economy of grace, with the design to reform, to pardon and reward sinful beings; that the accomplishment of this design renders necessary the two great provisions of an adequate Atonement for sin and an adequate reclaiming influence from its power; and that the mode of divine subsistence in the Trinity furnishes the most, if not the only satisfactory explanation of the adequacy of these provisions, which by the human mind is conceivable. With these things in view, it is now maintained that a presumption arises that the doctrine of the Trinity is true.

It is difficult however, to present to the apprehension of many minds the reality and intrinsic force of this presumption. The Moral Government of God over this world, as a part of natural theology, has been but imperfectly unfolded, or rather I may say, in its nature and fundamental principles, has scarcely been made a subject of investigation. Hence comparatively few minds, even among those which in many respects are well versed in theology, have formed any adequate views of the facts from which arises a presumption for the truth of the doctrine of a triune God, while by others, and especially by our Unitarian opponents, these facts, at least so far as they are supposed to furnish the presumption now maintained, are altogether denied. It is difficult therefore, not to say impossible, without a prolonged and labored discussion of the nature of God's Moral Government and of the principles of its administration under a system of grace—and thus turning aside too far from our present main design—to exhibit to the apprehension of many, especially of Unitarians, the grounds of the presumption which is now maintained. All therefore which I now propose, is a brief recapitulation of some facts and principles which I have already attempted to establish, respecting God's Moral Government over men. I shall also confine myself chiefly to showing a presumption for the distinct divine personality of the Son.

That we may better appreciate the kind of evidence which, it is claimed, exists in the present case, let us look at some examples in which it presents itself in a more familiar aspect.

Suppose then, that one who has long and in vain employed his invention on the construction of a watch, abandons the attempt in despair, being thwarted in his design by an utter inability to devise any expedient by which to adjust the relations of the spring and the balance-wheel. Suppose now, that he is informed that another has devised an expedient by which the difficulty which he encountered is surmounted, and has actually produced a watch of the most perfect structure. He naturally inquires how the difficulty, which appeared to him wholly insurmountable, had been overcome. His informant, without being able to answer the inquiry in respect to the method actually adopted, merely describes one which had been suggested to him by the maker of the watch, as a possible method which would be fully adequate to the purpose. This possible and perfect method of attaining the object carries with it its own evidence to the mind of the inquirer, and he no sooner apprehends its adaptation and adequacy to the end, than he regards it as affording a strong presumption that it is the very expedient by which the successful watchmaker has given perfection to the watch.

The same thing might be illustrated in cases innumerable. The principle is, that when we know another has accomplished an object or end, then, so far as we have evidence that there is one and only one expedient or means by which that object or end could be accomplished, so far we conclude, or at least, as the case may be, presume, that he adopted that expedient or means.

But is this principle as applicable to the doings of God as to the doings of men? Let us see. Suppose then, that one were well assured that God has given a revelation to this world, who as yet has never seen the Bible and knows nothing of its contents. Suppose now, he accidentally opens a book, and without a suspicion that it claims to be a revelation, reads the law promulged, the moral precepts inculcated, and the plan of divine mercy unfolded in the book which we call the Bible; that he closes the book and never sees it again nor learns any thing more of its contents;—could he now reflect on what he had read, and especially, with a knowledge of *the end* to be attained by a divine revelation, could he reflect on what he had read in its adaptation to accomplish that end, without regarding it as affording a strong presumption that this is the book which contains God's revelation to man? Let us take another example. It has often been said that there is a strong presumption, arising from the regularity of nature's laws, against miracles,—even a presumption too strong to be overcome by testimony to their reality. Now let it be admitted that there is this presumption against a miracle, when alleged as a simple insulated fact, without any connection with or relation to any other fact worthy of such divine interposition. But how is it when the miracle is alleged as the seal of God's testimony,—God's own proof of his own revelation given to a lost world to accomplish his chief design toward it, the design of his mercy? And especially how is it, when that system of truth, claiming to be his revelation, is once understood—the necessity of it to the end for which it is given, seen and admitted, and the obstacles to its reception on the part of those to whom it is given, duly appreciated? Does not all depend on its having, and being received as having, God's authority? Is there then, the shadow of a presumption, that God would not work miracles in attestation of the divine origin of such a system of truth? Surely, here is an object worthy of God's miraculous interposition. Miracles are his own peculiar signature and seal,—a manifestation of himself which cannot be mistaken. Miracles, so far as the human mind can conceive, are alone fitted to accomplish the end for which they are alleged to be wrought. Nor can any mind understand and appreciate the end to be accomplished by miracles, their adaptation to the end, and, so far as the human mind can see, their necessity for its accomplishment, without admitting that every presumption against the miracles of Christianity is removed, and that a strong presumption is furnished of their reality.

In like manner, assuming the fact that Christ has made a complete Atonement for sin, it is now maintained, that, as on the supposition of his divine personality, and on this supposition only, his Atonement is seen, and can be seen, in its complete adaptation and adequacy to its end, a presumption arises, that he is a divine person in the Godhead. By this I do not mean to imply that the human mind would ever, of itself, have originated the conception of the distinct divine personality of Christ; but I mean to say, that with this conception in the mind, be its origin what it may, and with the fact of an Atonement admitted, a complete adaptation and adequacy in the Atonement to its end is seen, which, without this conception, cannot be seen by the human mind, and that hence arises a presumption of the truth of this conception. To explain still further. Assuming the fact, and the necessity of an Atonement to the forgiveness of sin under the Moral Government of God, the human mind, once possessed of adequate views of this necessity, or of the obstacles to be surmounted that sin may be forgiven, finds itself utterly unable to devise or even to conjecture, under the light of nature, or without a revelation, any expedient adequate to this great exigency. *How shall sinful man be just with God*, is not only one of the most momentous of all problems, but one of the most intractable to all solution by the human mind. Man might know the fact of an Atonement, he might have full assurance of its adequacy as a ground of forgiveness, from the divine declaration, and still have no conception of its adequacy to this end, from any knowledge of the nature of the provision. I do not say that human confidence could not rest in the divine declaration of its adequacy. But I say that human confidence,—the confidence of a guilty mind, of a guilty world, in its sweetest repose, its richest joy, and intensest gratitude,—can find its perfect basis only when the full and godlike adequacy of the provision is unfolded in the nature of the provision. The Atonement of Christianity, to be seen in its perfect adequacy to its end, must also be seen in its perfect adaptation to its end. My object then, is to show, that as the adaptation of this Atonement, so its adequacy can be most satisfactorily seen only in view of the divine personality of Him by whom it was made; and hence to infer a presumption that he is a divine person in the Godhead.

I claim then to have shown, that God is administering a perfect Moral Government over men, as the best means of the best end, or as a system of influence which is dictated and demanded by infinite goodness; that in this high and august relation of the Moral Governor of creatures formed in his own image, he is under the necessity of establishing his authority or right to reign, in the view of his subjects, by decisive proof; that he cannot do this without proving his moral perfection or benevolence; that he cannot prove his benevolence, and so establish his authority, by any thing which he can do in his other relations, nor by any thing which he can do in this relation, without annexing to his law a penalty which shall express or manifest the highest disapprobation of disobedience which he can feel toward any object which can come into competition with it as an object of disapprobation; that he must inflict, in the form of penalty, the highest degree of natural evil on every transgressor, since otherwise he could not show higher disapprobation of his disobedience than of this degree of suffering; and that in case of transgression, he must either execute this penalty on the transgressor, as the manifestation of his highest disapprobation of his disobedience, or make an equivalent manifestation of his disapprobation by another measure or expedient—that of an Atonement.

In maintaining these principles, I claim to have shown, that if any thing is proved by moral reasoning, it is that God as a benevolent being, must feel, and must show himself to feel, a supreme abhorrence or hatred of sin, which in its true nature tends to the destruction of all happiness, and the production of all misery in God and his sentient creation. A more monstrous incongruity cannot be conceived, than that of a perfectly benevolent God, who does not feel this supreme hatred of sin, and who does not evince to his moral creation by what he does, the reality of this feeling. Not to feel thus, is to be, and not to show that he feels thus, is to show himself to be, a being of unqualified selfishness, even of infinite malignity. Indeed, form what views we may of God's government over this world and other worlds, one thing is most indubitable. If he would receive the homage, the love, the submission, the confidence, the gratitude of his moral creation, he must evince to them his goodness, and thus to evince his goodness, he must do it in the form of supreme, immutable, everlasting abhorrence of sin, the worst of evils. Not to do this, is to manifest indifference to that action on the part of his creatures, which is, in its true nature and tendency, the only and the sure means of the highest misery of all. Not to do this, is to show himself indifferent to the weal and woe, the life and death, of his own creation,—a being having no rectitude of principle; and who, for aught that appears, will sacrifice to self-will, to favoritism, to caprice, to selfishness in some form, every interest of every creature,—a being whose character can excite no love, awaken no hope, inspire no confidence; whose heart is untouched by pity, unmoved by woe,—a being, the bare thought of whom is enough to fill the soul with consternation and dismay. Such is the God—let sentimentalism think and say what it will of his goodness—such is the God, and such he proves himself to be, who does not feel, and show himself to feel, a supreme abhorrence of sin, compared with any possible evil that can come into competition with it as an object of his practical abhorrence.

Now this manifestation of his supreme abhorrence of sin can be made only in one of two ways: either by inflicting on every transgressor of law that degree of suffering which shall manifest or prove it, and thus prove his benevolence, and thus sustain his authority or right to reign; or, by an Atonement, that is, by some expedient which shall make an equal manifestation, or furnish an equally decisive proof of this abhorrence of sin.

The question then now to be examined, is, whether a manifestation or proof of God's supreme abhorrence of sin, equivalent to that which would be furnished by the infliction of the legal penalty on every transgressor, can be satisfactorily seen to be furnished by the Atonement of Christ, except in view of his divine personality?

In giving a negative answer to this question, let me not be understood to assert on *à priori* ground, that the divinity of Christ was absolutely necessary to an adequate Atonement for sin. What was possible or impossible with God in the nature of things, on such a subject, I pretend not to decide. If however, the fact of his divinity be revealed, it would seem altogether unreasonable to doubt its necessity to the perfection of his Atonement. Why should the second person of the Trinity become incarnate, and the great end of his incarnation be the redemption of a lost world by making an Atonement for sin, unless his divinity and incarnation were necessary to his making an Atonement? Indeed, who shall say, that had God not subsisted in the Trinity, the redemption of sinful beings would not have been impossible, and that therefore this world would not have been created? Whether however, these things are so or not, is not now the question. The question now is, whether the most satisfactory view—or the only satisfactory view—to the human mind, of the Atonement of Christ, in its adaptation and adequacy to its end, does not depend on viewing him as a divine person in the Godhead?

The end of an Atonement under the perfect Moral Government of God, is to furnish the same decisive proof of God's supreme abhorrence of sin as the transgression of law, and in this way, decisive proof of his justice as a lawgiver or Moral Governor, that is, of his benevolence in the form of a supreme regard for his law and authority, as the necessary means of the highest happiness of his moral kingdom, which he would furnish by the infliction of the legal penalty on a revolted world.

Assuming that an Atonement includes the infliction of suffering on an innocent or perfectly holy being, some minds find it difficult to conceive how it can express or prove displeasure for the sin of transgressors, and so manifest the justice and uphold the authority of a lawgiver. It involves rather, in their view, violence to every principle of equity and every sentiment of benevolence. They see—what is indeed, very obvious—that it cannot express on the part of the benevolent being who inflicts it, displeasure toward the innocent and holy sufferer. He is not merely faultless, but the object of unmingled complacency and love to him who inflicts the suffering. No fiction of law, no scheme of imputing or transferring the sins of the guilty to one who knew no sin, can transfer the abhorrence of infinite benevolence for the guilty perpetrators of sin to the immaculate victim. The motive to the infliction surely is not furnished by his character. The gross injustice, as well as the revolting absurdities of every such scheme, are too obvious and have been too often exposed, to require present consideration. How then can benevolence inflict suffering at all on one who is perfectly holy? and how, if inflicted on him, can it manifest or prove abhorrence of the sin of the guilty, and thus prove the justice and sustain the authority of the lawgiver?

In answering the first of these questions—how can benevolence inflict suffering at all on a perfectly holy being—I remark, in homely but sententious phrase, *that circumstances alter cases.* When the design of the supposed infliction is to prevent an immeasurable amount of suffering which must otherwise be endured, and to secure an immeasurable amount of happiness which must otherwise be lost; when this end can be attained by the supposed expedient, without sacrificing or impairing any necessary means of the highest conceivable happiness of the universe; and when the suffering is inflicted with the consent of the sufferer, then perfect benevolence can and will inflict the suffering.

But it is also asked, how can suffering, inflicted on a perfectly holy being, prove abhorrence of the sin of the guilty, and thus prove the benevolence in the form of justice, and sustain the authority of the lawgiver, even as decisively as would the execution of the penalty?* To give a satisfactory answer to this question, we must in the first place see how the execution of the legal penalty on transgressors proves the justice and thus sustains the authority of the lawgiver. This it does, as a full and decisive expression of his supreme abhorrence of transgression. The act of transgression not only tends directly in its own nature as action, to destroy all happiness and to produce unqualified misery, but utterly to subvert the authority of the Moral Governor. It is a direct, unequivocal, and decisive declaration or testimony, that the Moral Governor is unworthy of submission or obedience; and as such, if uncounteracted by opposing proof, establishes the fact, and thus as effectually subverts his authority or right to reign, as were he driven, an insulted and degraded exile, from his throne. The Moral Governor therefore, as a perfectly benevolent being, has reason to be more displeased with transgression than with the complete and endless misery of the transgressor,—and now, to prove his benevolence and show that he is worthy to reign, is under the necessity of expressing the degree of displeasure for transgression which as a benevolent being he must feel. Hence when transgression occurs, averse, as a perfectly benevolent being must be, to the infliction of such suffering, considered simply as suffering, the alternative is either to acquiesce in the uncounteracted contempt of the transgressor, and in the decisive proof furnished by the act of transgression that he does not abhor transgression as a benevolent being must abhor it, and thus forfeit his character for justice, that is, for benevolence, in the form of supreme regard for his law and for his kingdom, and of course his authority or right to reign; or he must inflict the full penalty of the law on every transgressor, and thus incur this immense evil, revolting as it is to his infinite benevolence, rather than permit unpunished transgression to disprove his supreme abhorrence of the evil of sin, and so disprove his be-

* Vide West on Atonement, chap. 7.

nevolence, his justice, and his authority or right to reign. There is no other way conceivable, in which, in the single relation of a lawgiver or Moral Governor, he can rescue his character, his law, his authority, his throne, from beneath the feet of rebellion. Immense as the evil is, and revolting as it must be to the heart of infinite benevolence to inflict it, it is made necessary for sin. *The evil* of inflicting the penalty *must be incurred*, or the means—the only means—of the great ends which infinite benevolence has proposed to accomplish, with these ends themselves, must be sacrificed and lost. By incurring such an evil, in the form of penalty, these means are safe; his character, his law, his authority, his throne, are established forever, and the great end of his eternal dominion is secured, in the highest perfection in which it can be by his infinite attributes.

Thus when transgression has occurred under the perfect Moral Government of God, it is only by incurring an immense evil, that a still greater, far greater evil, can be prevented, and the great ends of infinite benevolence be accomplished, in the highest perfection possible to him who reigns over all. Now if there be another evil than the execution of the legal penalty, by incurring which the Moral Governor can manifest or prove an equal abhorrence of sin, and show the reality and sincerity of his determination to punish it as a lawgiver; or more particularly, if by inflicting limited suffering on some perfectly holy being, with his consent, and for the purpose of exempting transgressors from the threatened penalty and of showing the degree of evil which he would incur as a lawgiver rather than exempt them from the penalty, he can manifest or prove his supreme abhorrence of sin, and thus prove his justice or supreme regard for his law, and thus his perfect benevolence, and thus his authority or right to reign, as decisively and impressively as by the execution of the penalty,—then can an Atonement for sin be made; for then one great end to be answered by inflicting the penalty can be answered by another expedient. But how it may be asked, can the supposed infliction of evil on a holy being prove the lawgiver's abhorrence of the sin of transgressors, even in the lowest degree? This is a vital question. God then cannot, as we have seen, either feel or manifest the slightest displeasure toward a being so pure and holy, either on account of his character, or by imputing or transferring to him the guilt of transgressors, or by considering him as guilty when he is not, or by his standing in their law-place, or for any other conceivable reason. Indeed, the magnitude of the evil incurred on the part of God in the infliction, must be measured by the degree of his love to the holy sufferer. Nor can God inflict evil on such a being without some benevolent design dictating and demanding the infliction; nor with such a design, without the strong and intense aversion which infinite benevolence must feel to the infliction of evil on the object of its highest complacency and love. How then can the infliction of evil on a holy being, manifest or prove the lawgiver's abhorrence of the sin of transgressors? I answer, *that it does so by being set forth as the criterion and measure of this abhorrence.*

The infliction of the penalty on the transgressors answers the same purpose, by sustaining the same relations or characteristics. It is presented to God's moral kingdom, not as a spectacle of malice or selfish revenge, but as an expression of his benevolence to his kingdom, as being the criterion and measure of his benevolence, and therefore just abhorrence of sin. Whether the evil be inflicted in the form of penalty on transgressors, or in the form of an Atonement on a holy being, it is done to prevent other and greater evils which would otherwise follow the transgression of law,—the evil of God's not manifesting or proving his benevolent and supreme abhorrence of transgression,—and with this, the evils of subverting his rightful authority and defeating the ends of his infinite benevolence. The evil inflicted in either form is designed as the known criterion and measure of his abhorrence of sin, to make manifest and evince beyond all denial or doubt the degree of his abhorrence. This is done by incurring—and can be done in no other conceivable way than by incurring—an immense evil to himself as a benevolent being. By inflicting the full penalty of his law on a world of transgressors, he would incur an immense evil to himself. By inflicting the supposed evil on a perfectly holy being, he also incurs an immense evil to himself. In either case the immense evil to himself is the measure of his abhorrence of the evil inflicted, and therefore the true criterion and measure of his abhorrence of that which is the cause of the necessity of his incurring such an evil. Sin, the transgression of law, is this cause. Sin cannot occur under the perfect Moral Government of God, and God as a Moral Governor, not be under an imperious, immutable necessity of incurring an immense evil to himself, for the purpose of showing the degreee of his abhorrence of sin. By incurring evil to himself in the form of inflicting the legal penalty on transgressors, as the criterion and measure of his abhorrence of sin on account of which it is inflicted, he would show himself as much displeased with sin as he is and must be as a perfectly benevolent being. In like manner, when for the purpose of exempting transgressors from the legal penalty, he incurs another immense evil to himself on account of sin and as the known criterion and measure of his abhorrence of sin,—the immense evil to him of inflicting intense though limited suffering on a perfectly holy being, and which, according to the supposition, is an evil to himself equivalent to that involved in the infliction of the legal penalty on transgressors,—he shows himself to be as much displeased with sin as he is and must be as a benevolent being—and of course as much displeased with sin as he would show himself to be by inflicting the legal penalty on transgressors.

Thus it is obvious *how it is* that God, by inflicting suffering on some perfectly holy being, may manifest or prove his abhorrence of the sin of transgressors, viz., *by setting forth or holding up to his moral kingdom this immense evil to himself, as the criterion and measure of this abhorrence.*

I may add in the way of inquiry, what other reason than that now supposed, can be assigned why God should incur such an immense evil as that of inflicting intense suffering and death on a perfectly holy being? What other end can be assigned for such an infliction than that now supposed, which would even authorize such an infliction? Aside from this peculiar end to be attained, it would involve, so far as the human mind can conceive, the most flagrant violation of the truth, the justice, and the benevolence of God, as a Moral Governor, toward an obedient subject of his law,—one who has an inviolable right to unmingled and perfect happiness from his king,—a right which, in any other case than the present, he cannot be supposed to relinquish, nor his king to violate. Did Christ die as a martyr? There is not the slightest intimation of the fact,—while the perfection of God's Moral Government has never been and never will be marred by the martyrdom of a perfectly obedient subject of his law. Did he suffer and die to manifest God's love and kindness to the erring and lost creatures of his power,—lost only by remaining sinful,—and thus to bring upon them this mighty influence to reclaim, and in this manner to save? But if there was no just, and therefore necessary exposure on their part to the penalty of law,—exposure with deliverance made absolutely hopeless by the demands of God's inexorable justice,—where were the love and kindness of God to men in inflicting suffering and death on his beloved Son? What interest, or benefit, or good on their part, could be the object of God's supposed love to them, manifested by this means? Their reformation? But the infliction of suffering and death on a perfectly holy being, for no other purpose or end except to reform sinful beings, were in the highest degree preposterous. It is easy to see how, on the principle that the goodness of God leadeth to repentance, that this infliction of sufferings and death on a perfectly holy being for the redemption of sinful beings from the penalty of sin, should possess a reclaiming influence; but viewed in any other light, how can it possess the least possible reclaiming influence or tendency? This point demands our careful consideration. Those there are who place the whole efficacy of the infliction of the sufferings and death of Christ in its reforming influence or tendency to reclaim men to duty. Can this be so? If the infliction has any tendency to reclaim sinful beings, it must have it as its own inherent tendency, that is, as a *direct* tendency of the nature of the act, or it must have it as an *indirect* tendency arising from it as an act of goodness to sinful beings, designed for their benefit, either in delivering them from the legal penalty or in some other respect. Has it then any such inherent tendency, any direct tendency in its own nature to reclaim sinful beings? The conception is impossible. No human mind can conceive of the least inherent direct tendency to reclaim sinful beings, in the simple naked act of putting to death a perfectly holy being. So far from it, that the act considered simply in itself or aside from its relations to other ends, can be viewed only as an act of palpable injustice and cruelty, fitted to dishonor its author, and to increase the alienation and disloyalty of every rebel. Is it still said that Christ died as a martyr—we reply, that on this supposition, his death could only confirm his *sincerity and devotion* to his work as a reformer by his doctrines;

so that at most the tendency of his death to reclaim would still be *indirect*, as so much evidence or proof of his earnest desire for their reformation, by the means he had employed for this purpose. But further: we say that Christ did *not* die as a martyr. The facts and principles of God's Moral Government over this world have settled this point—that none but sinners have died or shall die as martyrs. Christ's death too was, in every important and every essential respect, unlike that of a martyr. Not only was he forsaken of God and abandoned to the terrors of death without alleviation, while other and sinful martyrs have died in triumph, but he died without the alternative of escaping death by the renunciation of his doctrine—an alternative without which no man can die as a martyr, since his death can furnish no testimony of his sincerity. Since then the death of Christ could possess *no inherent direct* tendency to reclaim sinful men, and no *indirect* tendency to reclaim them as the death of a martyr, it could have no tendency to this end at all, except an *indirect tendency as an act of goodness to sinful beings.* But how or in what respect could it be an act of goodness to sinful beings, except as an act designed for their benefit in delivering them from the penalty of the law? I ask then why, for any other possible reason than that now supposed, should a benevolent God incur such an evil as that of inflicting intense suffering and death on a perfectly holy being? Such an evil, great as it is, he can be supposed to incur in the case under consideration, for the sake of making the necessary manifestation of his supreme abhorrence of sin, in providing redemption from its penalty. When sin exists, God must manifest supreme disapprobation of it, either by incurring the evil of inflicting the penalty, or by incurring an equivalent evil if the penalty be remitted. By incurring the latter for the remission of the penalty, he shows that, were it necessary to the full manifestation of his abhorrence of sin to incur the evil of inflicting the penalty, he would inflict it and incur the evil; for he incurs an equivalent evil to himself in providing for exemption from the penalty, and thus manifests the same degree of abhorrence for sin which he would manifest by inflicting the penalty on transgressors.

I have thus attempted to show how suffering inflicted on a perfectly holy being may express displeasure for the sin of transgressors, and that such suffering, by furnishing an equally decisive manifestation or proof of God's supreme abhorrence of sin as would be furnished by the execution of the legal penalty on transgressors themselves, would be an adequate Atonement for sin under God's perfect Moral Government, inasmuch as it would as fully manifest his justice or benevolent regard for his law, and thus as fully sustain his authority or right to reign.

I now recur to our present leading inquiry—whether a manifestation or proof of God's supreme abhorrence of sin, equivalent to that which would be furnished by the infliction of the legal penalty on every transgressor, can be satisfactorily seen to be furnished by the Atonement of Christ, except in view of his divine personality?

Here, that we may justly make the comparative estimate which is now to be formed, it is important to advert distinctly to the following considerations: First, that if Christ was not divine, he was merely a man, or at least merely a creature. Secondly, that his humiliation, sufferings, and death, in which, viewed as a comprehensive evil, his Atonement consisted, was an evil of short duration. Thirdly, that this comprehensive evil is not to be viewed as simply so much evil suffered by him who endured it, but also as an evil incurred especially by him who inflicted it on such a sufferer. Fourthly, that while it is not supposed that the second person of the Godhead as such suffered, much less died, such was the peculiar and intimate union between the second person of the Godhead and the man Christ Jesus, that the magnitude of the evil is to be estimated by this fact, and as immeasurably enhanced by it.

With these things in view I proceed to say, that the temporary sufferings of one who is merely a creature, however intense these sufferings, and however exalted in rank the creature who endures them, and still less, that any sufferings or evil endured by a mere man, should furnish the requisite manifestation and proof of God's supreme abhorrence of sin, cannot be conceived. Suffering or evil inflicted by the will, and virtually by the hand of a lawgiver on an obedient subject, that the transgression of another or of others might be pardoned, would doubtless express a greater or less degree of displeasure toward the transgressor or transgressors, according to the excellence and dignity of the sufferer, and as he should be the object of a greater or less degree of affection on the part of the lawgiver.

Now the present exigency requires in one form, a manifestation or proof of displeasure toward sin, equal in degree to that displeasure toward sin which would be manifested in another form. Accordingly, if we suppose an Atonement for an offending world to be made by the sufferings of a mere creature, and especially by his sufferings for a few hours, or even years, the expression or proof of the degree of God's displeasure toward sin compared with that which would be expressed by the unqualified and endless misery of our guilty race, is too faint and insignificant to be seen or felt to be at all adequate to the end to be accomplished by an Atonement. The mind decides at once without hesitation or doubt, that the degree of displeasure expressed and proved in one of these forms is as nothing compared with what is expressed and proved in the other. The temporary sufferings of the supposed victim furnish no manifestation or proof of that degree of displeasure toward sin on the part of the lawgiver, which would inflict the full penalty of God's violated law on a revolted world. No mind could rest in the entire sufficiency of such a manifestation to the end, which must be accomplished by an adequate Atonement. None could receive from it the same impression of God's goodness in its necessary abhorrence of sin, and of himself as the determined friend, patron, and benefactor of his moral creation through the medium of his perfect Moral Government, and therefore the determined and righteous avenger of sin, as would be derived from the full execution of the penalty of his law on all transgressors, or even on one. On the contrary, were the supposed sufferings of a mere creature to be presented and received as the criterion and measure of God's abhorrence of sin, they would show that he did not feel as a benevolent being must feel, and as a Moral Governor must show himself to feel toward sin, and thus disprove his moral perfection or goodness, and thus subvert his right to reign; or rather, they would prove his selfishness, and so reveal his malignity to his kingdom, and render him only an object of terror and dismay. There is therefore all the presumption, or rather all the *proof* against the fact of an Atonement made by the temporary sufferings of a mere creature, which there is of God's goodness or moral perfection, and that he is administering a perfect Moral Government over men under an economy of grace. It is obvious then, that on the supposition that

Christ was merely a creature, the adequacy of his humiliation, sufferings, and death, to the end of an Atonement for sin under God's perfect Moral Government, cannot be conceived by the human mind. So far from it, that such an evil incurred on the part of God, as the criterion and measure of his abhorrence of sin, would, at most, decisively show that low estimate of sin as an evil which none but a selfish being can form, and which, by utterly subverting his authority, would defeat the great and only end of an Atonement.

Let us now contemplate the Atonement of Christ on the supposition of his divine personality. Here our object is, not to assume or assert his divine personality, but merely to propound it as an hypothesis, or as a possible truth, and thus to present the Logos or second person of the Godhead as incarnate, or the human and divine natures of Christ united in one complex whole, as a fact on which depends the only satisfactory conception of the nature of his Atonement as adequate to its end.

Here then, on the present supposition, we have presented to human apprehension an object of thought altogether peculiar, and to which none other in the universe can be likened,—an object still, on the just conception of which, just and adequate views of the subject under consideration depend. Who then, or what, according to the present hypothesis, is Christ the Son of the living God, the Redeemer, Saviour of this lost world? I answer, that he is a man—a perfect man. He has a human body, and a human soul; he knew no sin, but is holy, undefiled, and separate from sinners. He is more; he is the Logos, who was in the beginning, who was with God, and was God. He is the second person in the Godhead, distinguished as such from the first and third persons, the Father and the Holy Ghost. Each person as a being is properly called God. Each is distinguished from the other by the personal pronouns. To each are ascribed divine attributes, divine works, and divine worship. Here is indeed a use of language which involves a plain departure from all prior usage of terms employed; but which, supposing the reality of the object, is authorized and required by the peculiar nature of the subject, and the laws of usage in such cases.

Further: according to the present hypothesis, the man Christ Jesus and the Logos, or second person of the Trinity, are one, by a most intimate and mysterious union. We speak in the ordinary use of language, of the oneness of two or more, in relation to certain results, purposes, or ends, which depend on or arise out of it; and we conceive of the intimacy of the union as greater or less *in degree*, as the results which depend on it approximate in a greater or less degree to those of the absolute oneness of an individual being, or of one self-subsisting being—one determinate reality, having his own strict personal identity. Thus we speak and conceive of partners in trade as one, of friends as one, of husband and wife as one—even as one flesh; of Christ and the Church as one—even as one body; and of a human soul and a human body even as one man.* Every one knows how, in such cases, our conceptions and our language are modified and changed, as divinity or oneness is the object of thought; and especially when the latter is the more prominent or even exclusive object of thought, how the inferior in our conception is exalted and honored by the superior, and the superior lowered or degraded by the inferior, and this in proportion to the intrinsic difference between them. For example, every one knows how in his own necessary conception and feelings, a human body, compared with the body of an animal, is exalted by its union with a human soul—a spirit bearing God's image. Yet the matter and the spirit which constitute the man or human being, are distinct substances; nor can we say that they constitute one being by virtue of a union in one of the same substance. The intimacy of the union is such, be the *mode* of it what it may, as to authorize, for all practical purposes, the full conception of the body and the soul as the man—one being; and to exalt our conception of a living, active human body when before us as a visible object, to the conception of a being bearing the image of his Maker. How much more exalted, in our necessary conceptions and feelings, would be a man whose very being was appointed and fixed permanent and immortal, in the closest union conceivable in the nature of things, with the most exalted spirit whom Omnipotence could create; and how much more still were that spirit, in all his attributes known to be divine, and the complex whole to be presented to us as a veritable object of contemplation and knowledge. Who could stand in his presence and not adore?

---

* Demoniacal Possession.

Now of the *mode* of the supposed union between the human and divine natures in Christ, we pretend to form no *direct, positive* conception, but to conceive of it only *relatively*, or *in its relations*. We say then, that according to the present supposition, the man Christ Jesus and the Logos, or second person of the Trinity, are united by a most intimate yet mysterious *mode* of union,—so united, not indeed as to become or constitute strictly one *being* or *person*, in the ordinary import of these terms, but as to render it *proper* and *true* to speak of the whole as a being or person, in a modified and peculiar meaning, because it is the best form of speaking of the object of the conception which common language furnishes when common language must be employed for the purpose of speaking of him as he is,—so united, *that by virtue of the union, so intimate and peculiar, the complex whole, in respect to all true, just, practical conceptions of him, of his relations to the Father, of the Father's supreme, intensest love for him, of his work as mediator between God and men, and especially of his humiliation, sufferings, and death, that is, of his sacrifice for sin, is all that he would be, as one self-subsisting being, one determinate reality, having his own strict personal identity.* In accordance with this view of the union of the divine and human natures in Christ, we further say, that according to the present supposition they are so united as to render it proper to affirm, in a modified, and in a most momentous and august import of the language, the Logos was made flesh and dwelt among us; that being in the form of God, he took on him the form of a servant, was made in the likeness of men, and found in fashion as a man; so united, that the complex whole is properly and truly called under the necessary modification of the terms, either the man Christ Jesus, or God manifest in the flesh,—a descendant of Israel, or God over all, blessed forever; so united, that all essential human attributes, as well as all divine phenomenal attributes, are properly and truly ascribed to him; that he is truly and properly said to be born of a woman, to increase in wisdom, not to know the day of judgment, and also to know all things, and to be the creator of all things; that he is truly and properly spoken of as the devout and humble worshiper of God, and himself the object of the same worship which is rendered to Him who sitteth on the throne, as made under and as obedient to the law, and also as the Lord and Lawgiver, Sovereign, and

Judge of all; so united, that the human nature of this complex whole has all the dignity, excellence, worth, value, which such a nature can derive from the most intimate possible union with the divine—an exaltation and worth by this peculiar union, not less than would result, were that possible, from a strict consubstantial union with the second person of the Godhead; so united, that the human nature serves not the less but the more in respect to manifestation and impression, by presenting the divine nature through the benignant design of the union, in the brightest splendors of its glory; so united, that while the divine nature is necessarily prominent to thought, the human nature qualifying for the suffering and death demanded by redemption, serves to call forth immeasurably higher affection on the part of the Father for the Son, than his own perfect benevolence can feel toward the guilty world to be redeemed, or toward any and every other object of affection; an object which, when revealed in heaven, awoke a song of joy from angels and archangels unheard and unthought of in that world before, and which will be the theme of every song in the eternal temple, while the glory of God doth lighten it, and while the Lamb is the light thereof. Such is the being—for so we must speak of him, if we use human language to say what he is—by whose humiliation, sufferings, and death, this world's Atonement has been made.

Shall we here be told, that after all, reason, philosophy decides that it is but a man—a creature—who suffers and dies; and that the amount of the evil is far inferior to the infliction of the penalty on every transgressor? This is readily admitted, at least for the sake of the argument. Without affirming or denying on the question whether the divine nature of Christ suffered, and maintaining only its extreme and unspeakable humiliation, we admit that it was but a man who suffered and died. But his sufferings were the most intense, his death the most ignominious and dreadful. His sufferings were not merely corporeal. To say nothing of the insult, the scorn, the reviling, the malignant cruelties he received, he endured the most intense mental anguish. In the garden of Gethsemane his soul was exceeding sorrowful, even unto death. Martyrs, who deserved only God's displeasure, through abundant mercy died in the triumphs of faith and with the foretaste of heaven; while this holy man—the object of perfect complacency to eternal love—died utterly forsaken of his God. His death, though simply considered, it consisted of the separation of a human body and human soul, yet how was it attended by every cause and circumstance of agony,—how it stands forth signalized by the miracles of God, in its nature and design, among all the events of earth and time! Jesus died. The vail of the temple was rent, and the Holy of Holies uncovered. The graves were opened, the dead were raised to life, the sun was darkened. Jesus died, and the God of Christianity is revealed. Jesus died, and on that death depend redemption—all that is great and good to a lost world—grace, mercy, peace, life, salvation with eternal glory—the most stupendous manifestation of the Deity—the brightest glories of God, the deliverance of guilty myriads from hell triumphing in heaven's purity and heaven's joys! That death, that blood—the price of all—is memorialized of God on earth while time shall last, and made the theme of praise to Him that sitteth on the throne and to the Lamb while immortality endures. We admit that it was a man who died. But is this the whole truth? Is it not, in more adequate language, A DIVINE MAN? Is it not the great miracle of omnipotent mercy—Divinity humanized to suffer, humanity deified to redeem? We suppose this, meaning, not that the Logos and the man became strictly identified as one being; not that the Divine Nature, as such, suffered; but that such was the peculiar union between the two natures, that there is no authorized use of language which so adequately expresses the true conception, as to say the Lord of glory was crucified, or that He who was equal with God became obedient unto death. In this sense, the sufferings and death of the man Christ Jesus have, in the true conception of them, all the magnitude and moment in respect to our redemption, which would pertain to the sufferings and death of the second person in the Godhead, had it been possible for him to suffer and to die. This is what we suppose. And now whose philosophy shall deny it?* Whose philosophy shall tell us the precise nature of the union between the man Christ Jesus and the divine Logos? Whose philosophy shall tell us how remote this supposed union of the human

---

* Nor is this, in words and in the strictest construction, further from philosophic accuracy or truth, than to say that a *man dies*, intending his body and not his soul.

and divine natures is from a strict identity of substance and of being? Whose philosophy shall measure and determine the exaltation and worth which can be given to a human soul, by such a union with the second person in the Godhead, as shall approximate the nearest possible point of identity in oneness of being? Whose philosophy shall decide that any forms of language can adequately express the former, except those which in common life would imply the latter, and that even those, instead of raising our conceptions above the reality, do not necessarily leave them below it?* We admit that the temporary sufferings and the cruel death of this holy man were not, as so much evil in itself, equal in amount to that involved in the infliction of the penalty of sin on a world of transgressors? Had they been, they had not been endured; for nothing, in respect to the diminution of evil or the increase of good to the universe, would have been gained. The question here is not, whether the amount of evil, as such, in the one case is equal to that in the other. It is, whether the evil incurred by the Moral Governor for the purpose of showing his displeasure for sin, of manifesting his justice and benevolence to his kingdom, and thus sustaining his authority or right to reign, is not equal to what he would have incurred for the same purpose by inflicting the penalty. And we ask again, whose philosophy shall decide that the sufferings and death of the man, exalted, and excellent, and worthy as he may be in the Divine estimation by the supposed union with the second person of the Godhead,—beloved and delighted in with the intensest affections of Divine benevolence,—may not be as great an evil to that benevolence, and be truly regarded by it with as much benevolent abhorrence, as would be the same evil, were the two natures conceived as constituting one being, or as would be the evil of inflicting the legal penalty on a revolted world? Whose philosophy shall measure the evil to infinite benevolence of inflicting such suffering as Christ endured, on so spotless, so perfect, so exalted, so holy a being? Aside from the consent of the sufferer, every principle of law, of justice, of truth and goodness, had been violated—the empire of righteousness forever sub-

* Leo the Great says, "that the effusion of the blood of Christ was so rich in price, that had a universe of captives believed in their Redeemer, no devil could have retained his chains."

verted. Whose philosophy shall decide that the evil incurred by divine benevolence in the sufferings and death of Christ, is not as great an evil in the estimation of that benevolence, as would have been the infliction of the legal penalty on this sinful world? We say it is not for human reason to resolve such an inquiry in the negative, by assumptions of what is impossible in the nature of things like these. We fall back then on our supposition, and affirm that there is no pretense, on the authority of reason or philosophy, to assert that the union between the divine and human natures of Christ is any thing less, in the mode of it, or in its relations and actual results, than we have now supposed it to be. While the supposed union would require us to admit a distinction of the two natures, and authorize, in some cases, a corresponding use of language, still it would involve an intimacy of connection between them in what, if it be called any thing, or distinguished as one thing, in the use of common terms, must be called a being or a person,—an intimacy of connection which authorizes the same forms of language, though in a somewhat modified sense, which the strictest identity of substance and being would authorize. Nor would this use of language,—as when it is said that he who is equal with God takes the form of a servant, and becomes obedient unto death,—raise too exalted a conception, and in this respect, a false one, of him who dies. What the interpreter of the language is required to do in such a case, is to avoid on the one hand, confounding the two natures, and to admit on the other, an intimacy of union between them which can be nothing less in all its supposed relations—especially in relation to the work of our redemption—than would be true were the two natures united as one being in one substance.

Language employed to denote the divine and human natures united, would necessitate in every mind that should contemplate the object, an engrossing conception and impression of the divine nature of Him who suffers and dies. He would not unnaturally be called *divine man*, or God-man, or by other phraseology which would present the magnitude of the sacrifice made for sin. On the present supposition, should we read that the Lord of glory was crucified, we should be obliged to conceive that something more than a mere creature had died. Or should we read of the Church of God (I know this is a disputed text) which he purchased with his own blood, we should feel constrained to admit that the ransom involved, so far as it could in the nature of things involve, Divinity as well as humanity in the sacrifice. Or should we read in the fuller and more precise form of didactic statement, that "Christ Jesus, being in the form of God, thought it not robbery to be equal with God; but made himself of no reputation, and took upon him the form of a servant, and was made in the likeness of men, and being found in fashion as a man, he humbled himself and became obedient unto death, even the death of the cross," we should hear the voice which saith, "Awake, O sword, against the man that is my fellow;"—we should look on Him "who is the brightness of the Father's glory and the express image of his person," as he bows his head, gives up the ghost, and exclaims, "It is finished!" and we should feel that there is nothing great besides.

Now we do not say that these views are scriptural—we do not allege that they are any thing more than the fictions of the imagination—we present them as a mere hypothesis concerning the nature of an Atonement for the sins of a lost world, in view of which the adequacy of an Atonement can be satisfactorily conceived by the human mind.

We have seen how entirely inadequate must be any temporary sufferings of a mere creature to the end of an Atonement under the perfect Moral Government of God. But contemplate as we may the greatness of the exigency arising from the obstacles to the pardon of sin,—and who can unduly magnify these obstacles and the exigency which they create under God's Moral Government—a government which ought to be, and will be upheld in all its stability and perfection, though rebellious worlds sink forever under his severest displeasure;—I say contemplate as we may the greatness of the exigency, yet the more we consider the greatness of the sacrifice which according to the present supposition has been made to meet it, the more we ponder the evil incurred by the eternal Father in not sparing his own Son, his well-beloved, his only-begotten Son—the worthiest object of his supreme love—and in delivering him up for us all—the evil incurred by the Son in emptying himself of equal divine glory, in assuming humanity, and dying on the cross,—the more the equivalency of this evil to that of inflicting the legal penalty will appear, the more the perfect adequacy of the former to the end of an Atonement will possess the mind, and the more the fitness of such an Atonement will be seen to impart unfaltering repose to the trust and confidence of the guilty world for whom it is made. Let the inquiry be put in any form;—let it be asked how a perfect God, feeling that supreme abhorrence of sin which he must feel, and with the intensity of infinite benevolence, becoming, as he must become, a sin-avenging God, can ever regard with forgiving mercy, complacent love, and rewarding kindness, the transgressions of his law,—how can a manifestation of an equal abhorrence of sin be made to that which would be given by turning a revolted world into hell? How can God show an equal regard for his law, his authority, his throne of moral dominion, as he would, by sacrificing for their preservation the rebellious hosts of earth in the consuming fire of his indignation; how can the holiness of God, who is of purer eyes than to behold iniquity, in its recoiling and withering abhorrence of sin, be displayed; how can the truth of God, which is as the great mountains, be vindicated; how can the justice of God, that column of royal majesty, be upheld, and yet the guilty, with the defied penalties of sin averted, be received to favor? Here all is mystery—utter darkness to the human intellect. Before this great problem, presented in any form, the mind of man retires baffled—confounded. No answer can be given—none be conceived. Christianity in its Orthodox interpretation, alone gives the solution. Christianity thus interpreted, reveals a triune God, and shows the throne of God upheld by the man that is his fellow, and a guilty world redeemed.

Thus is the great crisis met. Law is magnified and made honorable. The pillars of eternal justice stand unshaken, and the splendor of its throne is untarnished, while mercy lavishes all its riches on a guilty world. Thus we see the most impressive spectacle, the highest achievement of infinite goodness and grace, the fullest expression of God in the Atonement of Christ. No similar event can we suppose has occurred on the theater of the universe, or will ever again occur in a coming eternity. It has formed a new epoch in the moral administration of the Deity, and given birth to a new order of things throughout his moral creation. It stands amid the lapse of ages and the waste of worlds, a solitary monument, "to the intent, that now unto principalities and powers in heavenly places might be made known by the Church the manifold wisdom of God."—Vide Robert Hall's Works, vol. i. p. 265.

Christianity thus interpreted solves the problem which God alone can solve. On the most momentous inquiry to a lost world—how can man be just with God?—it removes all rational doubt, satisfies all rational inquiry, and gives all rational assurance. The vilest, the guiltiest, even a guilty world, can rest and be at peace, in view of the sacrifice of Calvary.

We say then, that if there be an adequate Atonement for sin (and this our present argument assumes), then the Atonement of Orthodox Christianity is the only Atonement whose adequacy can be satisfactorily conceived by the human mind. It is this Atonement, and this only, which, in view of its nature, can still the agitations of guilt, and bring relief to the laboring heart of man. I do not here affirm what indeed I fully believe, that in its nature and perfection it bears the impress of God as its author. But I ask, can man, reasoning from his necessities as a sinner against God, and admitting the fact of an Atonement for sin, deny the Atonement of Orthodox Christianity? Can he fail to see, in the perfect adaptation and adequacy of such an Atonement to its end, a strong presumption that it is the veritable Atonement which God has provided, and an equally strong presumption of the divine personality of Him who hath redeemed us to God by his blood!

THE TRINITY.

IV.—THE MANNER IN WHICH LANGUAGE IS USED IN THE SCRIPTURES RESPECTING THE MODE OF THE DIVINE SUBSISTENCE AND THE PERSON OF CHRIST.

Language of the Scriptures peculiar or self-contradictory.—The result of Unitarian and Trinitarian attempts to explain it.—The sacred writers give no indications of embarrassment.—Natural inference.—Positions stated.—(I.) Important to decide whether the language is peculiar.—Opinion of the Infidel.—Is the peculiarity unauthorized?—The first thing to be decided—before the question of inspiration.—Is the peculiarity authorized and proper?—If so, it should be settled beforehand.—Argued (1.) from known importance in analogous cases; (2.) from results of overlooking this; (3.) from the ease of ascertaining it.—(II.) The language of the Scriptures is marked by some peculiarity.—The contrary unsupported by evidence.—Primary and secondary import of terms.—Positive proof decisive.—The common meaning involves absurdity.—An uncommon and peculiar import gives a consistent and important meaning.

It must be confessed, that the language of the Scriptures respecting the mode of the divine subsistence and the person of Christ, is either replete with self-contradiction, or characterized by some authorized peculiarity. That the scriptural writers should teach so unequivocally as they do, that there is but one God, and yet employ such language concerning the Father, the Son, and the Holy Ghost, and that this language is to be interpreted in its literal, common import, cannot be supposed consistently with their divine authority. Hence Infidels with one consent, assuming that this language is in no respect peculiar on account of any necessity required by the subject, pronounce it self-contradictory, and utterly subversive of the claim of the writers to divine inspiration.*

It is in these circumstances that the defenders of divine revelation—both Trinitarians and Unitarians—are shut up to the necessity either of admitting the self-contradictions of the sacred writers, or of vindicating them from the charge, on the ground of some *authorized peculiarity* in their language, and on

---

* What sort of impostors, it may be asked, were those who invented and uttered such a palpable absurdity as the Infidel pretends, and yet expected the world to receive the *known* falsehood as truth taught by divine inspiration?

this, the methods of this vindication adopted by both Trinitarians and Unitarians, though widely different, may be said wholly to depend. The words now referred to are those of ordinary use, and have a primary or common and literal import. How, for example, can the word *God* and the word *man*, as they are applied to Christ,—how can the words *Father*, *Son*, and *Holy Ghost*, as they are used in the baptismal formula,—how can the language concerning the Logos, in the first chapter of John's Gospel,—be interpreted in any of the diverse meanings adopted by Unitarians, without supposing some peculiar use of them—some modification of their common literal meaning?

It is true, that Unitarians are not agreed among themselves in any one method of vindicating the language under consideration from absurdity, and in giving it what they regard as a consistent and authorized meaning. Every method however, to which they resort for the purpose specified, will be found on close examination, to imply some peculiarity in the use of the language. Thus, when the same words and forms of expression which are confessedly applied to the self-existent and eternal Being to distinguish him from all others, are also applied to Christ, the latter is supposed by some to teach that Christ is a subordinate Deity begotten of the Father, and as, under the self-existent God, creating, upholding, and governing the universe; by some, that he is a super-angelic being employed as an instrumental agent in the formation of the solar system, or at least of this world; by others, that he is a mere man or other creature, possessing a delegated omnipotence or creative power; by some that while he is a mere man, he is entitled on account of his exaltation to the right hand of the Father, to religious worship from angels and from men; and by some, that while he is a mere man, and not entitled to such worship, he is highly exalted above all creatures by his office as Messiah, or Mighty Prince, who reigns over this world, and whose dominion shall endure for many ages to come. Thus the language above specified, when applied to Christ, is supposed by Unitarians to be modified, and to be used in a sense more or less restricted, according to the *peculiar nature* of the subject in the view of the different interpreters. In like manner, when they resort to *personification* in the use of the word *Logos*, and the phrase *Holy Spirit*, they suppose a use of language which, compared with the primary, literal meaning of the words, is peculiar on account of the nature of the subject, not to say very peculiar also in other respects.

It is equally manifest, that the Trinitarian construction of the language under consideration, not less than the Unitarian, proceeds on the supposition of a *peculiar use* of ordinary terms, which results from the nature of the subject. Trinitarians maintain, that however the language is to be interpreted, the Scriptures, so far as words are concerned, assert that there is but one God, and also, that the Father, the Son, and the Holy Ghost are three divine persons, that each is God, that each possesses divine attributes, that each performs divine works and receives divine worship; that one of these persons was in the beginning, that he was with God and was God, that he was made flesh and dwelt among us, that he was in the world and that the world was made by him, that he was a man, that he increased in wisdom, that he was ignorant of the day of judgment and of the destruction of Jerusalem, that he was a descendant of Israel, that he knew all things, that he is omnipresent and omnipotent, that he is the final judge of the world, and God over all, blessed forever; that he was born of a virgin in Bethlehem of Judea, that he was before all things, that he had glory with the Father before the world was, and was loved of the Father before the foundation of the world; that he was equal with God, was made in the likeness of men, that he became obedient unto death, that he created all things, that he upholds all things by the word of his power, that he rendered divine worship to the Father, and was himself the object of divine worship; that he addressed God as his God, and was addressed by God himself saying, "Thy throne, O God, is forever and ever." The Trinitarian not only maintains that these things, so far as words are concerned, are asserted in the Scriptures, but is forward to admit that as many verbal contradictions, and that if the words be interpreted in their primary literal meaning, as many that are real, can be charged upon this use of language as the Unitarian and the Infidel are pleased to allege.

But while all this, on the present supposition of the primary literal use of the language, can be done to any assignable extent, the sacred writers themselves furnish not the slightest evidence that in their own view they occasion any embarrassment to their readers. The language is not characterized by the authorized obscurity of enigma, of allegory, of prophetic annunciation, or of typical or symbolic representation. It betrays no artistic plan, no dramatic or other contrivance for representing that to be real which is not real. It bears none of the peculiar marks of figurative or metaphorical language. Nor is it the unusual and often occult language of scientific refinement and analysis. It is accompanied by no logical definitions or explanations, nor employed as needing any to render it intelligible, nor with an indication of a suspicion that it would be unintelligible or absurd in the view of its readers. It is the language of plain men in practical life writing or speaking for the instruction of plain men,—the language of common life consisting of common words in common forms of combination ; language, the meaning of which, in all these respects, is fitted to the apprehension of the most ordinary capacity ; language which all men know how to interpret and understand, which the writers themselves obviously expected would be correctly interpreted and understood, and which, as we hope to show, aside from all perversion, would be so interpreted and understood, without exception, by all its readers. At the same time it is language, which if employed by men who could be supposed to be weak-minded, or ignorant, or beside themselves and maddened by a learned fanaticism,—men careless and reckless in the use of it, having sinister designs to accomplish, and conforming to any prevalent opinions and prejudices of others ; or by men liable from any cause to propound false, contradictory, and senseless propositions, and which, if interpreted as ordinary language in all ordinary cases ought to be and would be, must inevitably convict the writers of uttering the most palpable absurdities and nonsense. And yet these confused, incongruous, and inextricably perplexed and perplexing forms of expression—for such they are when considered as ordinary forms on an ordinary subject—are not of such rare occurrence that they can be accounted for as errors of transcription, or as corruptions of the original text ; but they are frequent—constantly, as it were, meeting the reader in the Old as really as in the New Testament, in inseparable alliance with the substantial truths of Christianity. On the part of the writers there is no studied design to avoid them—no stopping to explain or to vindicate, to reconcile or adjust—and especially no solicitude to prevent misapprehension ; but fearless alike of all misunderstanding or distortion of their actual meaning, either by uncandid dullness, captious criticism, or malignant perversion, they go on with clear, unqualified, unexplained statements of subject and predicate, as the exigency arising from the course of thought in each instance demands. Thus they calmly leave all to the honest simplicity of the reader, and to his professed submission to their divine authority, to gather from every sentence and every word the intended meaning, as truth coming through the proper and authorized forms of human language from the mouth of God himself.

With these things in view it is manifestly a fundamental inquiry in the present discussion, *whether there is any peculiarity, and especially any authorized and proper peculiarity in the use of the language under consideration; and if so, what this peculiarity is?*

The decision of this must lie at the foundation of the greater question, what is *truth* in respect to the mode of the divine subsistence; for until the former is decided, no satisfactory or even plausible attempt can be made to determine the principles of interpreting the language, nor of course to ascertain its meaning according to these principles. On its decision depends nothing less than whether the language has an absurd meaning, or none at all, or a consistent and true one—in short, nothing less than whether the Scriptures are a divine revelation or not. A peculiar importance also pertains to this inquiry, because, as it seems to me, both Trinitarians and Unitarians in the controversy between them, by unwarily overlooking the question, or by mistaking an unauthorized and improper use of language for an authorized and proper one, have often adopted an insufficient and unsatisfactory mode of reasoning on the main question.

I propose therefore to show—

I. The importance of deciding the preliminary inquiry—whether the language under consideration is characterized by any peculiarity, and especially by any authorized and proper peculiarity in its use; and if so, what is it?

II. The language is characterized by some peculiarity in its use.

III. It is erroneously assumed both by Trinitarians and Unitarians, as characterized in its use by an unauthorized peculiarity.

IV. It is characterized by a proper peculiarity in its use—one which is fully authorized and demanded by the nature of the subject, the tri-personality of one God—and by the facts and circumstances of the case.

I proceed then to show—

I. The importance of deciding the preliminary inquiry—whether the language under consideration is characterized by any peculiarity, and especially by any authorized and proper peculiarity in its use; and if so, by what?

It must then be admitted, either that there is no peculiarity in the use of the language as compared with the use of the same terms in their common literal meaning, or that if there is, it is either an authorized or an unauthorized peculiarity.

The Infidel maintains that there is no peculiarity in the use of the language either authorized or unauthorized, but strenuously insists that the language is that of the ordinary, literal use of the words, that it is therefore to be interpreted strictly, and to the letter, and that thus interpreted, it is in its actual meaning contradictory and absurd, and subversive of the inspiration of the writers. Nor if these premises be admitted, can the conclusion be denied. And yet who has shown by any legitimate process of reasoning, that these premises are not to be admitted? Here then is a preliminary question, which must be decided on its own independent grounds, before any attempt can be made to interpret the language with success. Until this be done, the question whether the scriptural writers do not abound in contradictions and absurdities in the use of the language, is also undecided. If it be settled in the affirmative, the charge of numerous contradictions and absurdities with their consequences, must be admitted; if in the negative, it involves a peculiarity in the use of the language, and this peculiarity is either *authorized* or *unauthorized*.

Shall we then suppose an *unauthorized* peculiarity? This renders the language incapable of any reliable interpretation, and all inquiry concerning its import nugatory and useless. On this supposition, no meaning can be authorized by any laws of interpretation applicable to the case, and therefore none in the lowest degree. Both the Trinitarian and Unitarian meanings on this supposition are wholly arbitrary and groundless, and equally remote from vindicating the inspiration of the writers. The language, being wholly without any reliable meaning, is neither less dishonorable to the writers, nor less useless to their readers, than contradictory and absurd. If then, the interpretation of the language by both Trinitarians and Unitarians, proceeds—as I shall have occasion to show hereafter—on the ground not merely of a peculiarity, as all just interpretation of it must, but of an *unauthorized* peculiarity in the use of the language, the consequence is, that the Infidel, unassailed by either party, is strong in his position respecting the ordinary use and consequent absurdity of the language, and that the truth, whether with the Trinitarian or Unitarian, is left undefended. The language, according to the present supposition, being incapable of any reliable interpretation or meaning, both the Trinitarian and Unitarian meanings are unworthy of respect, and the inspiration of the writers must be abandoned.

Every honest inquirer after truth, before he can consistently be either a Trinitarian or Unitarian, must decide in what manner the language of the Scriptures under consideration is employed. On the decision of this question depends that of another,—whether the language admits of any reliable interpretation and meaning or not. If he decides that the language is used in the primary, literal meaning of the words, or is characterized by no peculiarity in its use, the consequence, in view of its manifold contradictions and absurdities, is Infidelity. If he decides that the language is characterized in its use by an *unauthorized* and *improper* peculiarity, the consequence, in view of the language as nothing but a jargon of unmeaning sounds, is still Infidelity. Thus, on the supposition of either of these decisions, logical consistency shuts up the honest inquirer to the denial of the inspiration and divine authority of the Scriptures. It is only on the supposition that he decides that the language is characterized in its use by an authorized and proper peculiarity, and by just interpretation gives a meaning free from all absurdity, that he can avoid Infidelity as the true logical result.

I am aware that many suppose that the first question with the honest inquirer after truth is, were the writers of the book divinely inspired? I readily admit that their inspiration must be determined before we can decide on their divine authority that what they say, that is, that the meaning of their language is true. But before we can settle the question of their inspiration we must decide some others, particularly whether they use language in an unauthorized and improper manner; and if not, whether they use it in its primary, literal meaning,—that is, in a meaning which is replete with contradiction and absurdity. On the decision of these questions the proof of their inspiration depends, and they must therefore be settled before it can be known that there is not decisive evidence against their inspiration. The inspiration of the writers being justly assumed, they cannot be reasonably supposed to use language which, according to the laws of usage, can have no meaning. But how can their inspiration be justly assumed as proof that their language has any actual meaning according to such laws, when it is presumed to be used in an unauthorized and improper manner, which precludes all meaning according to such laws? For if the language, according to the laws of usage, is meaningless on the supposition that they are not inspired, it is equally so on the supposition that they are. The supposition of their inspiration in such a case is not only wholly admissible because the fact is disproved, but it cannot furnish the shadow of evidence as to what the meaning of the writers is, or that they have any. I further admit, that the inspiration of the writers being justly assumed, they cannot be supposed to utter contradiction. But how can their inspiration be justly assumed as the *proof* that they do not utter contradiction, when without this assumption, and according to the just laws of interpretation, the proof is decisive that they do utter contradiction? When the laws of interpretation convict them of uttering absurdity, how can the supposition of their inspiration exempt them from the charge? If it be said that there is as much evidence that the writers do not use either meaningless or contradictory language, as there is that they were inspired, and that this amounts to a strong *presumption* that they do not use the language in either of these modes, it may be fully admitted. But such a *presumption* cannot amount to *good proof* so long as it is or may be balanced or outweighed by opposing evidence. And who shall affirm the inspiration of the writers, unless it be first made to appear that they do not use language in a manner which involves them in abundant and irretrievable self-contradiction? Especially how can the Trinitarian or the Unitarian affirm it, while in interpreting their language, he proceeds on the assumption that it is used in that unauthorized and improper manner which necessarily deprives it of all meaning? If it be said that the evidence of their inspiration far outweighs the evidence either of an unauthorized use of the language, or of its absurd meaning, this, in the case as now supposed, that is, while the question concerning the manner of use is undecided, is more easily said than proved.

Besides, is it credible that God should hold men responsible for believing the inspiration of the scriptural writers, when their language must either be so interpreted as to be replete with contradiction and absurdity, or be assumed to be utterly incapable of any meaning according to the laws of usage? Must we thus divest the language of all truth to save the infallibility of the writers—destroy the revelation to preserve its divine authority? Such an expedient is as vain for the purpose, as it is unworthy of the cause which it is intended to subserve. We must admit the reality of the language as a vehicle of thought according to the laws of usage, nor shrink from a just application of these laws in its interpretation, be the consequences what they may.

It is in vain then that the Trinitarian and Unitarian appeal to the inspiration of the scriptural writers for the purpose of sustaining their respective meanings of the language under consideration, until the previous question concerning the manner in which the language is used, is decided on other grounds. That the Trinitarian and Unitarian should gratuitously assume that the writers were inspired, and that the one should arbitrarily give one meaning and the other a different one to the language of these writers, and thus both proceed on the gratuitous assumption of an unauthorized and improper use of the language, cannot satisfy any candid and enlightened inquirer after truth.

This brings me to consider *the third supposition* before stated, viz., that the language under consideration is characterized in its use by *an authorized and proper peculiarity.* If this be so—if the language, instead of being characterized by *no peculiarity*, or by one which is *unauthorized and improper*, is characterized by an *authorized* and *proper* peculiarity—then to ascertain the fact, and the nature of this peculiarity, is of essential importance in this discussion. This will appear from the following considerations:

(1.) From the well-known importance of ascertaining the

same general fact, and the nature of it in analogous cases. Every competent judge knows that authorized peculiarities in the use of language, compared with the common, primary, literal use of words, are not only frequent and almost constant, but to a great extent necessary to the ends of speaking and writing. It is equally undeniable, that language thus used, must be as truly subject to fixed laws in its use and interpretation as any other, and that otherwise it must utterly fail of the end for which language is employed. Who does not know this to be true in respect to much of the language of prophecy, of allegory, and of parable—all metaphorical and figurative language—all which is used in a secondary sense? These peculiar uses of language vary in different cases, and are authorized and required for different reasons. Hence the knowledge of these reasons, and of all the material facts and circumstances in each particular case, is indispensable to a correct interpretation of the language. The general nature of the subject—the character and condition of the writer, and of those for whom he writes—the more general or particular ends he has in view, and the means of accomplishing them which are available in the case, have a decisive influence in occasioning the peculiar use of language, and also in determining its meaning. It is in vain therefore, to attempt to interpret language when employed in a peculiar manner, without regard to these considerations and the nature of the peculiarity. What is thus true in all cases of this kind must of course, according to the supposition, be true of the present case.

(2.) If the language under consideration be characterized in its use by a proper peculiarity, the importance of recognizing the fact and the nature of the peculiarity, is obvious, from the natural and highly probable results of overlooking these things in the interpretation of the language. Even supposing, what I would by no means deny, that the actual meaning of the language has to no inconsiderable extent been obtained by the common-sense process, or when judged of for practical purposes, still if the speculative or scientific process of critics and interpreters has been in any respect erroneous and inconclusive, then the actual meaning is left without a full and thorough defense, and viewed in this respect, unworthy of reliance. On any other supposition than the present—that of an authorized peculiarity in the use of language, if this be the true one—the results, being obtained only by some arbitrary assumption, would themselves be wholly arbitrary. Infidels—assuming that there is *no peculiarity* in the use of the language, and having no respect for the good sense and integrity of the writers, much less for their inspiration—would of course find in it only contradictory and absurd meanings. Trinitarians and Unitarians, maintaining the inspiration of the writers, and proceeding by different processes of interpretation, might claim to vindicate the language from absurdity. Both processes however, depending not on the ground of an *authorized and proper*, but on the assumption of an *unauthorized and improper* peculiarity in the use of the language, would be wholly arbitrary, and their results alike exegetically invalid. And further—what diversity of meanings would different individuals of these parties in the controversy be likely to obtain, so that it would not be strange if neither, as a party, agree more with itself than each should agree with the other. Interpreting the language on the assumption of an unauthorized and improper use, they could be guided in its interpretation by no established principles. The process and results must be wholly arbitrary, having no other warrant or even plausibility, than such consistency as the ingenuity of the interpreters could give them. I do not affirm that such have been the actual results of both the Trinitarian and Unitarian interpretation of the language under consideration, but I ask, do they not show the entire absence of any of those fixed principles which control the authorized and proper use and interpretation of language? Have not a large class of interpreters, both Trinitarian and Unitarian, employed their ingenuity in arbitrarily obtaining a meaning which shall exempt the language from absurdity, rather than in showing that it is used in a peculiar and proper manner, and in determining its meaning as so used, whether it be absurd or not? Must not such a method greatly mar the defense of the meaning obtained by it, in the view of the enlightened inquirer after truth, and be deeply calamitous to the cause which it is designed to subserve? And can it be rationally expected that these and other evils of interpreting the language, as if it were not characterized by any authorized peculiarity in its use, will ever be prevented, without ascertaining its nature, and being guided by it in the interpretation of the language?

(3.) On the supposition of an *authorized and proper peculiarity* in the use of the language under consideration, its meaning may be easily and surely obtained, for language is subject to fixed and well-known laws of interpretation. Language used in the primary, literal meaning of the words, is not the only kind whose meaning can be determined by such laws. Metaphorical and figurative language—that which is used in a secondary sense—language turned from its primary meaning either by extending or restricting that meaning, and this, not only when it is thus turned or modified, but when the new meaning, as often happens, becomes by subsequent usage as established as the primary—in these cases and in all others, language, as the vehicle of thought, is subject to fixed laws of interpretation. Such changes are, to a vast extent, necessary to the existence and the ends of language, and are made according to certain laws or principles which control them, and determine their propriety; so that however novel or singular they may be, if made according to these laws, they are *proper*, being sanctioned by the laws of usage which control such changes. Thus a *peculiar* use of language becomes in many cases as *proper* a use as the common literal one; and the meaning of a word or a sentence when employed in a *peculiar* manner, is as easily and surely determined by the laws of interpretation applicable to the case, as when words are employed in their primary, literal meaning. Indeed almost no important words, those of the exact sciences excepted, reveal in their actual use, their own meaning. This, in cases innumerable, must be determined by circumstantial considerations, which, if the language be properly used, will decisively show that some one of two or more different meanings which the mere word will bear, is the meaning intended. Otherwise the writer is in fault, and his language is unauthorized and improper. The cases in which a peculiar use of language occurs, by turning words from their primary literal meaning, are very diverse. The *propriety* of such a change in any particular case does not depend on any previous use of the same words in the same manner. The peculiar use, if conformable to the general laws of change, is *proper* and fully authorized in the first instance, or in a single instance of change. Besides those cases of peculiar use which are familiar to all in what we call figurative language, there is another which may be called *secondary*.

Among the important cases of this kind there are two which deserve notice. One is, when a word in the first instance of change is used figuratively as opposed to literally, and when, by subsequent common usage in the same application, it loses its figurative character by losing its primary meaning in this application, and becomes in this limited, but secondary meaning, a literal word. This might be illustrated by such words as conception, perception, apprehension, stage-post, and a variety of others. Another case, and one to which we shall hereafter call particular attention, is, when the change in meaning has no connection with any figurative use of the word, but depends merely on some change in our knowledge or belief, or rather in our conception of the subject which is modified by this. Words change their meaning to correspond with our conceptions of things of which words are the signs. The words *heaven* and *earth* have, by the extension of our conceptions in some respects, and the restriction of them in others, greatly changed their meaning since Moses wrote, "In the beginning God created the heaven and the earth." Thus all the *peculiar* uses of words are *secondary*. Some however, are strictly figurative as well as secondary. Others, though at first figurative, by use lose their representative character and become in their secondary use literal terms; while others without being used figuratively, are employed in a secondary meaning as opposed to their primary, as our conceptions are modified by extension or restriction. Diverse however, as are the cases in which language is used in a peculiar manner, it is subject to fixed laws in respect to the use and interpretation of the words employed. The principles of interpreting such language are not, it is true, in all respects the same in all cases, much less are they the same as those of interpreting the same words when employed in their primary, literal sense. But they are the principles of interpreting such words when employed in the peculiar manner in which they are used in each particular instance, and as such are as familiarly known, and may be as successfully applied by mankind generally in each particular case, as other principles in any other case. Nor is this all. The peculiar use of language in most cases in which it is *authorized* and *proper*, and especially in those in which it results from a change in our conceptions of things, is the most natural, and for popular purposes the best. With these things in view, the supposed peculiarity in the use of the scriptural language under consideration can be no sufficient cause for surprise, even when the language is considered as designed to convey to the popular mind some peculiar truths concerning the mode of the divine subsistence and the person of Christ. On the contrary, it may be what was to be confidently expected as being what the peculiar nature of the subject, the circumstances of the case, and the ends to be accomplished, imperiously demanded. Indeed it may appear, with just views of the reasons for the supposed peculiar use of language in this case, that such a use should not be adopted, or that any other in its stead should be, would be not only surprising, but incredible. Nor would the supposed peculiarity in the use of the language occasion any demand for unusual skill in its interpretation; but being fully authorized and made proper by the exigencies of the case, the meaning of the language would be as easily and surely obtained as that of language used in any other manner.

What has now been said is deemed sufficient to show the fundamental importance of the preliminary inquiry before stated, viz., *whether there is any peculiarity, and especially any authorized peculiarity in the use of scriptural language respecting the mode of the divine subsistence and the person of Christ, as compared with the primary literal use of the same language?* The bare possibility of such a peculiarity is indeed sufficient to show how much may depend on ascertaining whether it be a matter of fact. It clearly appears, if I mistake not, from what has been said, that if the language is characterized by no peculiarity in its use, that is, if it is employed in the primary, literal meaning of the words, then it involves undeniable and manifold contradiction and absurdity; that if there is no peculiarity in the use of the language, except one which is *unauthorized*, then the language is incapable of any reliable interpretation or meaning—any which can exempt it from utter worthlessness in respect to the ends of writing and speaking; but that if there is an *authorized* peculiarity in the use of the language, then its actual meaning, whether contradictory or not, can be ascertained, according to the principles of interpretation applicable to the case, with as much precision and certainty as the meaning of any other language. If we make one further supposition—that the meaning thus ascertained should prove consistent—then on the decision of the preliminary inquiry before stated, depends nothing less than the question, whether we have in the Scriptures a revelation from God or not. From the supposition of *no peculiarity*, or of an *unauthorized peculiarity*, or of even an *authorized peculiarity in the use of the language with an absurd meaning*, it follows that we have not such a revelation. It is only on the supposition of an *authorized peculiarity in the use of language whose meaning is free from all absurdity*, that we can pretend that the Scriptures are a divine revelation.

Regarding the language of the Scriptures now under consideration as used in a peculiar and yet authorized manner, I do not propose to enter, to any extent, into what may be called the merely verbal exegesis of those texts which fall within the range of the Trinitarian and Unitarian controversy. The importance and the necessity of this mode of investigation in this controversy, whatever defect in one respect may have characterized it, I do not deny or doubt. It has been however, so often adopted, and conducted with so much particularity, and in my view, with so much success so far as the defense of the Trinitarian exposition requires it, that I regard it as superfluous to engage in it minutely in the present discussion. The subject in controversy labors more at other points than at those in respect to which relief is either needed or to be expected from a merely exegetical inquiry guided by text and context, and proceeding on the assumption of the inspiration of the writers as exempting them from contradiction and absurdity. To what purpose is it that the Trinitarian shows from the grammatical structure and the context, that one passage after another teaches the doctrine of the Trinity or the divinity of the Saviour, if this be all? All this, in the view of his opponents, both Unitarians and Infidels, only serves, in its legitimate bearing, to convict the scriptural writers of multiplied contradictions. On this ground the Infidel, admitting the justness of the interpretation, rejects the inspiration of the writers. On the same ground the Unitarian, admitting the inspiration of the writers, rejects the interpretation. Thus both deny the *truth* of the Trinitarian doctrines; and will deny it, until they are met with something more than what I call a merely verbal exegesis of the particular texts in controversy. Something more is plainly demanded; something which shall decisively exempt these texts from the charge of contradiction, whether the writers were inspired or not; something which shall show that their meaning, when ascertained by those laws and principles which are alone applicable to the peculiarities of the case, whether the meaning be *true* or false, is not self-contradictory or absurd.

The history of the progress of Unitarianism in this country, as well as some recent limited tendencies toward it, clearly indicate the necessity, not only of explaining the doctrine of the Trinity, of insisting on the possibility of its truth, and of removing all presumption against its truth, but of showing how the peculiar language of the Scriptures is fully accounted for and authorized in view of the nature of the subject and the circumstances of the case; on what principles such peculiar language ought to be interpreted; and what, when interpreted on these principles, is its actual meaning.

Having explained my own view of the doctrine of the Trinity, and having, as I claim, shown the possibility of its truth, and that there is no presumption against, but rather a strong hypothetical presumption in favor of its truth,

I now proceed, as I proposed, to show—

II. That the language under consideration is characterized in its use by *some* peculiarity.

By this I mean that the language is turned from its primary to a secondary meaning. On this point, the question is exclusively with those who deny or do not admit the inspiration of the scriptural writers, but maintain that the language is characterized by *no peculiarity* in its use, and therefore to be interpreted as literal language in the ordinary meaning of the words.

This opinion, I shall attempt to show, is not only unsupported by the slightest evidence, but is contrary to the most abundant and decisive *proof* of which the nature of the case admits.

It is unsupported by the slightest evidence. A large class of words are so often turned from their primary to a secondary meaning, that the *mere use* of one of them furnishes no evidence that it is used in its primary meaning, unless there is also an entire want of evidence of any change. Many of the words of common use are oftener employed in a secondary and peculiar, than in their primary meaning,—nor is any degree of evidence from the mere prior use of such a word in one uniform sense, decisive proof that the word, in a present instance, is not used in one that is new and different. This is at once set aside by evidence of a change in its import. Hence mere prior use is no evidence at all of the primary import of a word in a present instance, unless there is also an entire want of evidence of a change in its meaning. The prior use therefore, of the word *God*, and of the *personal pronouns*—and the same is true of other terms employed on the subject under consideration—cannot in itself be evidence of the lowest kind, that in the application of them in the case before us, they are not used in a secondary and peculiar meaning.

Again: that these words in the case under consideration are characterized by no *peculiarity* in their use, is contrary to the most abundant and decisive proof of which the nature of the case admits. The absurdity of a primary literal meaning of language, though not *a proof*, amounts to a *presumption* of a secondary and peculiar meaning. Words when turned from their primary meaning, if interpreted in that meaning, for the most part result in contradiction and absurdity. At any rate, in view of such changes, and with no opposing evidence of such a change in a given case, the absurdity resulting from a primary literal meaning always affords a strong presumption of a secondary and peculiar meaning. If now we add to these considerations the known good sense of the writer or speaker, including only ordinary qualifications for using language correctly, and if the contradictions of the ordinary and literal meaning are too palpable and gross to be attributed to such a writer or speaker, the presumption of a peculiar use of language is greatly increased. From this point, the proof, as the case may be, may be greatly increased. If it be one in which the writer evidently intends to be understood at the time,—and I speak only of such cases,—and if the language on the supposition of its peculiar use when justly interpreted, gives an obvious, consistent, true, and important meaning, the proof of a peculiar use becomes absolutely decisive. And further, if, in addition to these things, the language, on the supposition of peculiar use and meaning, is not only the necessary language for the purpose, but the most natural and the best which could be employed for the purpose, then the proof of peculiar use is yet further augmented. And further still, if there is abundant proof of the divine inspiration of the writer or speaker, uncounteracted by the slightest evidence from any absurdity or contradiction in the meaning of his language, *on the supposition of an authorized and peculiar use*, then the proof of it is the most abundant and decisive of which the nature of the case admits.

Now all this proof of the peculiar use of language, as we claim, exists in the case under consideration. In the first place we have the palpable and superabundant contradictions and absurdities involved in the common meaning and use of it, which are so strenuously urged by the Infidel and Unitarian, and in this fact we have a presumption against the common use and meaning, and in favor of one that is peculiar. In addition to this we have the familiar fact of the frequent peculiar use of language, with no opposing evidence in the case, and hence a *strong* presumption of a peculiar use and meaning. In connection with these things, we have in the third place, the undeniable good sense of the writers, including at least all ordinary qualifications for a correct and proper use of language. The Infidel must not here assume the contradictions of the writers as involved in the common use and meaning of their language, and allege these as proof of their want of good sense, and of their utter disqualification to use language correctly. This is begging a main question in debate. He is bound, in view of the common and familiar fact of a peculiar use of language, to admit the possibility of such a use in the present case, and further to admit the exemption of the writers, if on the ground of such a use they can be exempted, from all absurdity in their actual meaning. The question of their good sense and their ordinary qualifications to use language correctly, is not to be decided on the unauthorized assumption of a literal use of language and its consequent absurdities. And yet it is only on *this grossly unauthorized assumption*, that there is even a pretense for doubt on this point. Of the good sense of these men, and their ordinary qualifications as writers, we fall back for proof on what they have written and the manner of their writing in respect to other things than the subject under consideration. We appeal to the system of morals and religion which they inculcate, as the only one known to man which is not essentially defective, absurd, and preposterous in the view of unperverted reason; we appeal to their philosophy as unparalleled for its profundity and self-evident truthfulness—to their theology as alone in exhibiting God as worthy of the veneration and love of his creatures—a philosophy and theology which degrade and disgrace all that ever proceeded from the Porch and the Academy; we appeal to their integrity, their sober-mindedness, their singleness of aim and absorption of purpose; we appeal to the grace, the pathos, the sublimity of their style—to their simple and beautiful narration, their powerful argumentation, their weighty conclusions, the grandeur and beauty of their conceptions, the richness and splendor of their imagery; we appeal to their unswerving steadfastness, pressing the conscience of a guilty world with the most unwelcome truths, laboring amid the fires of martyrdom, standing alone with God for his cause and his truth;—in a word, we appeal to the unparalleled excellence of the matter and manner of their writings, their holy lives, their successful labors, their triumphant deaths, and affirm that the world has seen no other men, who in respect to character and capacity, were so well qualified to put a revelation of God on record, as the writers of the Scriptures. Or if this should seem extravagant, as it may to our Infidel opponents, from the want of reflection on the best means of attaining the ends of giving a revelation to this world, it is sufficient for our present purpose to say, that the writers of the Scriptures were in a high degree, or if this seems too much, were in an ordinary degree as writers qualified for their work. Taking even this low view of their qualifications, we affirm that the contradictions and absurdities involved in the assumption of their ordinary use of the language under consideration are too flagrant, too multiform, and too often repeated, to be attributed to such writers as these, especially in view of the possibility that the language should have a meaning *de usu loquendi*, exempt from these absurdities, and that therefore the proof from their character and qualifications as writers, in connection with the strong presumption before stated of *some* peculiarity in the use of language, is absolutely decisive. That such men as Aristotle, Locke, Reid, Edwards, when treating on subjects of unusual thought,—subjects difficult if not impossible to be comprehended in all their elements or relations,—subjects on which themselves can hardly be said to have familiarized their own knowledge by an oft-repeated reflective analysis of their complex conceptions, should fall into unsuspected contradictions, is not incredible. But there are some errors supposable in the use of language on ordinary subjects, so egregious that they are, so to speak, beyond the capacity of men of ordinary understanding. That such men as the writers of the Scriptures should ignorantly or inadvertently fall into such palpable self-contradictions as are charged upon them,—contradictions so entirely on the surface, so multiform, and so weakly ridiculous, that the writers must be sure to know and avoid them,—is as incredible as that they should have uttered with the same frequency and in literal language, the familiar absurdity that whatever is, is not, or that a part is equal to the whole. The incredibility of this is the exact measure of the proof, as thus far presented, of some peculiarity in the use of the language under consideration.

Here also we appeal to familiar cases of merely verbal contradiction, as obvious, if not as direct, as language can express. Such cases often occur in the Scriptures, and not less frequently in common life, but who hesitates to admit a peculiar use of language, and to interpret accordingly? Who, in interpreting such language as the following—"They twain shall be one flesh," "I and my Father are one," "God is love," "God is a rock"—does not assume as unquestionable, a peculiar use of the language? Who, in view of the known character of the writer or speaker, in connection with the palpable absurdity of a literal meaning, the frequency and established propriety of a peculiar use of language in other cases, and the possible consistency and truth of a meaning of the language in either of these cases when interpreted as used in a peculiar manner, does not decide at once that it is used in a peculiar manner and is to be interpreted accordingly? So we say that in the case under consideration, the good sense of the writers and their qualification to use language correctly,—in view of the absurdity of the ordinary use and meaning of their language, the frequency and propriety of a peculiar use, and the possible consistency and truth of a meaning of it when interpreted as used in a peculiar manner,—remove all doubt in respect to the fact of a peculiar use as the only basis of its just interpretation.

Here, so far as the present topic in debate is concerned, we might stop in the argument, but the proof, as we claim, is cumulative. If the language when interpreted as used in a peculiar manner, would give not only a consistent and obvious, but a pertinent and important meaning, as we have seen that it would, then the proof of a peculiar use is increased. If, in addition to these things, and on the supposition that the writers designed to teach the doctrine of the Trinity, there is no evidence that the language, being interpreted as used in a peculiar manner, is not the necessary or even the most natural and best language for the purpose of the writers—and we are authorized to say that there is no such evidence, there being no pretence that there is,—and if, still further, on the supposition of the above design of the writers, there is abundant evidence that the language, when interpreted as used in a peculiar manner, not only may be, but is the most natural, the best, and even necessary for the purpose of the writers—as I hope to show hereafter—then the proof of an authorized peculiarity in its use is greatly augmented, for these things are exactly what in all probability would be true on the supposition of the peculiarity of the language for the purpose specified, and what could not be true on any other supposition. And further still, if we add the most satisfactory proof of the divine inspiration of the writers—and this must be admitted in view of their possible exemption from all absurdity in their meaning—then the proof of a peculiar use of the language under consideration is the most abundant and decisive of which the nature of the case admits.

THE TRINITY.

V.—THE MANNER IN WHICH LANGUAGE IS USED IN THE SCRIPTURES RESPECTING THE MODE OF THE DIVINE SUBSISTENCE AND THE PERSON OF CHRIST, CONTINUED.

III.—Erroneous assumption of both parties.—Language so used cannot be interpreted.—Position not distinctly avowed.—Both parties improperly assume the inspiration of the writers.—Is not the Infidel right?—Language may be modified, but not without warrant.—The warrant not shown by the Trinitarian.—Trinitarians assume an unauthorized use of language—Three forms of the doctrine of the Trinity adduced.—Four laws of usage stated.—Applied to these forms of the doctrine.—Evil consequences of this mistaken assumption.—The Unitarian also modifies important terms without warrant, e. g., in insisting that God is applied to Christ in an inferior sense.—Principle of interpretation discussed and applied.

I PROCEED next to show—

III. That it is erroneously assumed both by Unitarians and by Trinitarians to some extent, that the language under consideration is characterized by an unauthorized peculiarity in its use.

Language used in an unauthorized and improper manner—in other words, in violation of the laws of usage—would, as we have seen, be utterly incapable of any reliable interpretation, and must of course fail to accomplish the purpose of language. Such a use of it is therefore one of the most incredible of all suppositions. Besides, all those which we have alleged to show that that under consideration is characterized by some peculiarity of use, decisively prove that it is not an unauthorized and improper peculiarity. Indeed, the supposition of such a use of language by the scriptural writers, in the view of any one who has the least knowledge of their writings and their character, is so preposterous, that no one can be found to assert the fact. This is not pretended even by the Infidel. To whatever other methods he has resorted for the purpose of impairing the divine authority of the scriptural writers, he has never assumed that they use language in a manner which renders it incapable of any meaning, either absurd or consistent, false or true. Nor will such a use of language on the part of these writers be claimed or even admitted by either Unitarians or Trinitarians.

I do not then, charge either the Unitarian or Trinitarian with formally maintaining that the language under consideration is used in an unauthorized and improper manner; but I claim that both, in no unimportant respects, do actually proceed in their interpretation, on the erroneous and groundless assumption of such a peculiarity in its use. Both, I have no doubt, would at once admit, that any meaning of the language which depends on such an assumption is wholly groundless and unwarranted, and would at once renounce it, could they be convinced that they actually proceed upon it in their mode of interpreting the language. My object then, is not to dwell on the error of making this the basis of interpreting the language, for there is no such necessity. The error is palpable and will be readily conceded by all. What my present purpose requires, is to show, that both Unitarians and Trinitarians in their interpretation of the language under consideration, do, to no inconsiderable extent, proceed on the confessedly erroneous assumption of an unauthorized and improper peculiarity in its use.

The unauthorized peculiarity, the assumption of which I ascribe to the Trinitarian, and that, the assumption of which I ascribe to the Unitarian, differ from each other, and yet both depend or rest on two others, which in the circumstances of the case, and as employed in the interpretation of the language, are entirely gratuitous. The one is the assumption of the inspiration of the scriptural writers; the other, the assumption of the modified use of terms, either by extending or restricting their ordinary meaning.

Both the Trinitarian and Unitarian then, assume an unauthorized and improper peculiarity in the use of the language, inasmuch as they both proceed in their respective interpretations of it, on the gratuitous assumption of the inspiration of the writers.

The Trinitarian proceeds on this: It will be admitted, that both the Unitarian and the Infidel strenuously insist that there is no authorized and proper peculiarity in the use of the language by which it is capable of a Trinitarian meaning, or by which any Trinitarian meaning can be freed from absurdity by the laws of a just interpretation. This then is the question, and on this point the only one, viz., is there such an authorized peculiarity in the use of the language, as by the laws of interpretation will exempt it from the charge of absurdity? If not, the charge of absurdity must be admitted. How then does the Trinitarian meet the charge? He appeals *merely* to the inspiration of the writers to disprove the alleged absurdity of their language. Or if he devises a meaning by his own ingenuity which he regards as free from absurdity, he propounds it as a possible and not as the actual meaning, obtained by the laws of interpretation applicable to a peculiar and proper use of language, duly ascertained and determined.* He does not show, nor pretend to show, any authorized and proper peculiarity in the use of the language, as a warrant for so modifying and determining its actual meaning, as to exempt it from absurdity. He therefore proceeds on the assumption of an authorized and improper peculiarity in the use of the language. Instead of showing, on the ground of an authorized and proper peculiarity in the use of the language, that it gives a consistent meaning according to the laws of interpretation applicable to the case, he abandons all pretense of its proper use, and for the purpose of exempting it from the charge of absurdity, relies solely on the gratuitous assumption of the inspiration of the writers. He thus virtually concedes that the language, if properly used, involves irretrievable absurdity. Denying of course its *proper* use, he proceeds on the assumption of its *improper* use; in other words, he assumes that it is characterterized by an unauthorized and improper peculiarity. This, of course, if admitted, would render the language incapable of any reliable interpretation or meaning. Such a de-

* In so doing there is a palpable error. There is an important difference between *a possible conception of the subject*, which is self-consistent, and *a possible meaning of language*, which is self-consistent. The mind, in the present case, may form a conception of some threefold distinction in the Godhead which shall be self-consistent; but it will by no means follow, that this conception *can* constitute the meaning of *the language* which the Scriptures employ to express a threefold distinction in the Godhead; in other words, that the language actually employed will admit of such a conception, and does not require a very different one of the subject, as its only possible meaning. It is quite supposable—not to say that it is commonly the fact—that what Trinitarians propound as *a possible self-consistent meaning* of the language, is not so; but at most, *a self-consistent conception of the subject* which the language will by no means admit of as its actual meaning; and which can therefore, in no respect exempt it from the charge of an absurd meaning. It is at this latter point that the Trinitarian errs.

fense of a Trinitarian meaning is utterly insufficient and groundless. So far as it proceeds on the assumption of the inspiration of the writers, it is a mere *ex concessis* argument with the Unitarian, which can have no weight with the Infidel who denies their inspiration ; while, so far as it proceeds on the assumption of an unauthorized and improper peculiarity in the use of language, it is wholly without foundation, and can give no satisfaction to a candid and enlightened inquirer after truth.

In a similar manner, at least in one respect, the Unitarian proceeds in maintaining his interpretation of the language. In defending his own, he is under the necessity of setting aside the Trinitarian meaning. This he does ultimately on the ground of the inspiration of the writers. He assumes the absurdity of the Trinitarian meaning, and denies it to be the actual one, because it is inconsistent with the inspiration of the writers. The Infidel also assumes the absurdity of the Trinitarian meaning, but maintains it to be the one intended by the writers, according to the laws of usage, and as such, decisive proof against their inspiration. Thus the Unitarian argument for the rejection of the Trinitarian meaning, is merely an *ex concessis* argument with the Trinitarian. It leaves the Infidel unassailed, and for aught that appears to the contrary, strong in his position, and can have no influence to establish the Unitarian doctrine. It is true that the latter claims to interpret the language as used in an authorized and proper, though peculiar manner, and on this ground to exempt it from all absurdity of meaning. But I am not speaking of the method which he adopts in defending his own doctrine, but of the ground on which he rejects the Trinitarian meaning of the language under consideration. This, I say, is simply the absurdity of this meaning, and its inconsistency with the inspiration of the writers. He avows the principle, that the absurdity of the meaning is a sufficient reason for rejecting it, though we cannot decide what the actual meaning is. It is plain then that he rejects, and regards himself as entitled to reject, the supposed absurd meaning of the language in view of the inspiration of the writers, though he could devise no authorized and proper use of it which would result in a consistent meaning. Here I might ask, does the Unitarian even pretend that what he claims to be an authorized and proper use of the language, and which results in a consistent meaning, would ever reveal itself to an unbiased interpreter of the language, who did not first assume the absurdity of a Trinitarian meaning? Would he resort to this ground except to avoid what he deems an absurd meaning, as that which is inconsistent with the inspiration of the scriptural writers? If he did not assume and believe their inspiration, would he not take common ground with the Infidel, and deny their inspiration on the ground of this absurdity? Be this as it may—and we may see how it is hereafter—when the Unitarian presses his Trinitarian opponents with giving an absurd meaning to the language of inspired men, and urges them to abandon it, though they cannot decide what its actual meaning is,—when he places his whole reliance on this argument as decisive against a Trinitarian meaning,—what is this but rejecting that meaning solely on the ground of the inspiration of the writers, and thus assuming an unauthorized and improper use of their language? This surely, is not meeting the argument of the Infidel. It is at most a mere *ex concessis* argument with the Trinitarian, resting on the assumption of the inspiration of the writers, one which can have no influence to lead the Infidel to abandon the charge of absurdity against the writers, nor his denial of their inspiration. He insists that if the language, being interpreted in the usual manner, gives an absurd meaning, then to reject this merely on the ground of the inspiration of the writers, is to assume that they use language in a grossly unauthorized and improper manner,—a manner palpably inconsistent with their inspiration. And what can be more just? If the language of the scriptural writers, according to the laws of usage, and irrespective of their inspiration, will give no other but an absurd meaning, then such is their actual meaning. To say otherwise is to assert that an absurd meaning, which is fully proved by the laws of interpretation to be the actual meaning of the writers, and which being thus proved to be so, is the most decisive proof that they are not inspired, is proof that it is not their actual meaning because they are inspired. It is to deny a fact which is fully and decisively proved,—viz., absurdity of actual meaning, because it is inconsistent with another assumed fact, of which, from the nature of the case, there can be no proof. Surely, if the scriptural writers use language in such a manner, that by the laws of just interpretation, and irrespective of their inspiration, it gives only an absurd meaning, and yet expect to be exempt from the charge of absurdity, only on the ground of their character, or of their inspiration, they use language in a grossly unauthorized and improper manner,—a manner not less inconsistent with their inspiration than is the absurdity of their actual meaning.

Thus both the Trinitarian and the Unitarian, the one in adopting and the other in rejecting a Trinitarian meaning of the language under consideration on the assumption of an unauthorized peculiarity in its use, proceed on ground utterly insufficient. This the Trinitarian does in denying the absurdity of his meaning solely on the ground of the inspiration of the writers; and this too, the Unitarian does by rejecting the Trinitarian meaning solely on the same ground. In both cases, the premises are insufficient to meet the objection of the Infidel, or rather, as involving the assumption of an unauthorized and improper use of language, are utterly insufficient to establish the truth of either meaning.

It is true indeed, that if either the Trinitarian or Unitarian be supposed to be in the right, the other must be supposed to be in the wrong. But there is another question,—whether either is in the right. The Infidel claims that both are in the wrong,—that they alike fail in their attempts to extricate the scriptural writers from the charge of absurdity, and to establish truth. Till this claim is fairly met, it is to no purpose that either the Trinitarian or Unitarian, in the controversy between themselves, should bring the other to adopt his meaning of the language by the mode of reasoning commonly adopted by these parties. This is not all which the exigencies of the case demand. There is yet a common enemy in the field to be vanquished, before either party can achieve a victory for truth, which ought not to be lost sight of in the controversy between them. This common enemy is the candid and successful inquirer after truth. To what purpose is it, that either the Trinitarian or Unitarian puts the other in the wrong, if neither is in the right?—that one defeats the other in their mutual conflict, only to secure a more signal triumph to a common adversary?

The truth is, that the meaning of the scriptural writers, whether absurd or not, false or true, must be determined, if at all, on other grounds than those adopted by the Trinitarian or Unitarian. To convince an unbiased inquirer after truth, by a valid process of reasoning, that the meaning of the language is not absurd, and that either a Trinitarian or Unitarian is its actual meaning, it is not enough to rely on the inspiration, and direct proofs of the inspiration of the writers. The proofs against their inspiration, claimed by the Infidel, must be overthrown. It must be shown that the language is not the ordinary language of men using terms in their primary literal meaning, and that it is characterized, not by an unauthorized and improper, but by an authorized and proper peculiarity in its use. It must then be interpreted according to the peculiar principles applicable to language when thus used in a peculiar manner. The meaning thus obtained, whether absurd or consistent, false or true, will be the actual meaning. This being thus ascertained, then if it be shown to be free from all absurdity, and if thus the direct proof of the inspiration of the writers be shown to be unimpaired by the alleged absurdity of the actual meaning, then and then only will the truth of that meaning be established.

Having thus considered the unauthorized peculiarities in the use of the language which are assumed by both Unitarian and Trinitarian, as they may be said to rest on the assumption of the inspiration of the writers, I now proceed to consider them as they rest on the assumption of a modified use of some of the important words.

On this point let me not be misunderstood. I do not say then, that the assumption of a modified use of the language is unauthorized. There is, in my view, the most decisive reason for maintaining that some of the important words are used in a modified meaning. What I maintain is, that the Trinitarian assumes some *particular* modified meaning of the language without showing or pretending to show, *de usu loquendi*, the warrant or reasons for so doing, and when in some cases no such warrant exists. Proceeding, as I claim, in his interpretation of the language, on such insufficient ground, he not only subjects himself to the successful assaults of his opponents, but leaves a Trinitarian meaning of the language unsupported and undefended. Strongly impressed with the proofs of the inspiration of the writers, having to contend for a Trinitarian meaning chiefly with those who also admit their inspiration, and regarding the mode of interpretation adopted by his opponents as entirely groundless, the Trinitarian has been satisfied to insist on the alternative either of adopting a Trinitarian meaning of the language, or of going openly into the ranks of Infidelity. Pressed in return however, by the Unitarian and Infidel, with the charge of those absurdities and contradictions which result from interpreting the language in its primary literal meaning, he resorts (without pretending to show the least sufficient warrant for so doing) to *a modified use* of some of the principal words, and of course to an interpretation of them, which for aught he shows to the contrary, is wholly gratuitous and arbitrary. In this way, as I now claim, he has failed effectually to vindicate, as he might have done, a Trinitarian meaning of the language.

This I shall now attempt to show from the manner in which Trinitarian writers have proceeded in interpreting the language under consideration.

Trinitarians then have interpreted the language of the Scriptures as teaching in some general import that there is *one God in three persons.* Individuals however, though agreeing in this general result, have differently modified the word *God*, and the word *person*, or the personal pronouns as applied to the Father, the Son, and the Holy Spirit,—some giving one, and some another more particular meaning to these terms. With this fact in view, two material questions arise, viz., *whether this class of interpreters, or any of them, have shown, or attempted to show, that de usu loquendi, there is any sufficient warrant for modifying the meaning of these terms as they have done;* and *whether the particular modified meanings which they have given to these terms are not made to rest on an unauthorized and improper use of the language?*

In respect to the first of these questions, I know of nothing which can give the least plausibility to an affirmative answer. It will be sufficient on this topic to refer to the distinguished Trinitarian writers, whose views we have already stated. Who then of them all, from Bishop Bull to Professor Stuart, however he may have modified the import of the terms, and however he may have supposed that by his ingenuity he has rescued the language from the charge of absurdity, has even attempted to show, *de usu loquendi*, any sufficient warrant for modifying its meaning as he has done? And here the question is not, whether by gratuitously assuming the inspiration of the writers, Trinitarians have inferred that there can be no contradiction in the actual meaning of the language; nor whether by modifying its meaning in a manner wholly arbitrary, they have been able to devise a possible conception of the subject which is exempt from contradiction; nor whether there is in fact a sufficient warrant for modifying the meaning of the language; nor whether, when duly modified, its meaning is free from all contradiction. But the question is—have Trinitarians even attempted to show that, according to the laws of usage, there is any sufficient warrant for modifying the meaning of the language as they have modified it? It is undeniable that words may be properly turned from their ordinary use to a new and before unheard-of meaning, and thus be used in either a more extended or limited sense. These changes are subject to certain fixed laws or rules, and when made according to these laws, there is in every case, not only good and decisive evidence of the fact of a change, but also of what the change is. On these principles, very different specific changes of this general class are fully authorized, and constitute as proper a use of language as any other. Now that the word *God*, or the phrase *one God*, and the *personal pronouns* as applied to the Father, the Son, and the Holy Ghost, have in the use of the scriptural writers been changed into their actual from their primary meaning, all Trinitarians will admit. But what advocate of the Trinity has ever attempted to show this fact,—to show what the changes are, on what principles of usage they are authorized, and having done this, to fix the precise import of the language in its changed and yet authorized and proper use? I can only say, that I know of no such attempt on the part of any Trinitarian author, and I do not believe that any has ever been made. On the contrary, so far as I know, Trinitarians confessing and obliged to confess, that the language, if used in its ordinary meaning, is replete with absurdity, instead of first showing an authorized and proper peculiarity in the use of it, and then by a just interpretation of its meaning exempting it from absurdity, whether the writers were inspired or not, have relied *solely* on the assumed inspiration of the writers for exempting their language from this charge. Thus to rest the vindication of the writers from this charge *solely* on the ground of their inspiration, is to proceed on the assumption of an unauthorized and improper use of the language.

I next inquire as proposed, whether the modified meanings which Trinitarians have given to the language under consideration, at least to some extent, *do not proceed on the ground of an unauthorized and improper use of the language.* I do not affirm that all the modified meanings given to the language by Trinitarians imply an unauthorized and improper use of it on the part of the scriptural writers: nor do I regard all the modified meanings adopted by Trinitarians which I consider as exegetically groundless, as necessarily false. What I maintain is, that some prominent Trinitarian meanings proceed upon and imply an unauthorized and improper use of the language by the scriptural writers.

The Trinitarian meanings of the language which are now under consideration, constitute what may be called certain particular forms of the doctrine of the Trinity, which are adopted by different classes of Trinitarians. I select the three following as examples for my present purpose,—viz., that which asserts the eternal generation of the Son, and the eternal procession of the Holy Spirit; that which asserts that the three persons of the Godhead are three distinct divine minds or agents, each being a complete subsistence; and that which asserts a threefold distinction in the Godhead denoted by the personal pronouns, without describing affirmatively at all what this threefold distinction or tri-personality is.

In respect to each of these forms of the doctrine of the Trinity, the question now is,—whether the meaning given to the word *God*, or the phrase *one God*, and that given to the word *person*, or to the *personal pronouns*, do not proceed upon and imply an unauthorized and improper use of the language by the scriptural writers?

In the first of these forms, the word *God*, or the phrase *one God*, is used to denote the Divine Being, or one Divine Being in three persons,—the Father, who from eternity begat the Son; the Son, who from eternity was begotten of the Father; and the Holy Ghost, who from eternity proceeded from the Father and the Son. Can then, the words *God* and *person*, or the *personal pronouns*, be turned by the scriptural writers from their primary literal meaning, to that which is here given them, according to those laws of usage which control such changes in the meaning of words?

What then are the laws of usage? Among them are the following, the specification of which will be sufficient for my present purpose,—viz.:

1. That there is good and sufficient reason for the change.

2. That when a word is turned from its primary to a secondary meaning, it must be used either in a more restricted or in a more extended sense than its primary meaning.

3. That when the word is thus changed, it must admit of an obvious, definite, and consistent meaning.

4. That in the case supposed, there must be good and sufficient evidence of the new and modified meaning of the word.

The foregoing laws of usage, in turning words from their primary to a secondary meaning, are so obviously indispensable to the purposes for which language is employed, that I deem it quite unnecessary to illustrate or to confirm their authority. The mere statement of them is sufficient to show, that if the violation of them, or of even the second and the third, is involved in the use of language in a secondary meaning, that use is unauthorized and improper, and the language incapable of any reliable interpretation.

I proceed then to say, that if the scriptural language under consideration is used to express the present form of the doctrine of the Trinity, it is used in violation of each of the foregoing rules or laws of usage. And first in respect to the word *God*. The word *God*, in its primary distinctive meaning, denotes a self-existent, eternal, independent, immutable Being. These ideas of God are essential elements in any and every authorized conception of him as a Being. But according to the present form of the doctrine of the Trinity, the one God is neither self-existent, nor eternal, nor independent, nor immutable. The second and third persons of the Godhead have a derived and dependent existence, or distinct subsistence, and yet the three persons are the one God, and this Being is self-existent, eternal, independent, and immutable. This conception is plainly impossible to the human mind, and for such a use of the word *God*, or for so turning it from its primary meaning, no good and sufficient reason can be given. Nor is the word, according to this form of the doctrine of the Trinity, used in any part of its primary distinctive meaning only, nor in the whole of that with some additional meaning. Nor does it admit of the supposed meaning as obvious, definite, and consistent; for the meaning is one of the most unobvious, palpably indefinite, and self-contradictory, conceivable. Nor is there the least evidence from the Scriptures, the only source of evidence in the case, that it is used in this meaning. We know indeed, that the advocates of this form of the doctrine of the Trinity have their proof-texts to allege. We shall only say, that in view of the circumstances of the case, and of the results of enlightened and unprejudiced interpretation, we do not think that an examination of this class of texts is required in the argument.

We now come to the supposed use of the word person, or of the personal pronouns, as these are applied to the Father, the Son, and the Holy Ghost, in this form of the Trinitarian doctrine, in which the distinct personality of each of the persons in the Godhead consists in or depends on a peculiar fact; in the case of the Father, that he from eternity begat the Son; in the case of the Son, that he was from eternity begotten of the Father; and in the case of the Holy Ghost, that he eternally proceeded from the Father and the Son; each of the persons being in essence and attributes identically one and the same. Now, by what law of usage can the personal pronouns be changed from their primary to such a secondary meaning as this? By what law can they be properly employed to express the facts of *eternally begetting*, of *being eternally begotten*, and of *eternally proceeding from*, rather than the words circle, triangle, or quadrangle, or than the letters x, y, and z? Plainly no possible reason can be given. Nor can it be pretended that this new meaning in either case is any part of the primary meaning of the word, and much less the whole of it with some additional meaning. Still less, if possible, can there be a pretense that the alleged new meaning is either obvious, definite, or consistent, or that there is the slightest evidence of its being the actual meaning. Thus every law which we have specified, as regulating the changes of words, is violated by the supposed use of the personal pronouns as they are applied to the Father, the Son, and the Holy Ghost, in the Scriptures. Having shown the same thing in respect to the use of *the God* as interpreted by this class of Trinitarians, it follows, that in their interpretation they proceed on the assumption that the scriptural writers, in changing this language from its primary to a secondary meaning, have violated the fundamental laws of usage which regulate such changes, and have of course used it in an unauthorized and improper manner, which renders it incapable of any reliable interpretation whatever.

I now recur to the second form of the doctrine of the Trinity above specified. This affirms that the three persons in the Godhead are three distinct divine minds or agents, each being a complete subsistence.* Understanding this language in its only possible meaning, it does not affirm but denies the existence of one God, or of one divine being; inasmuch as it does not affirm but denies the existence of one divine substance with even one divine phenomenal nature. If it implies, what it does not assert, viz., one common substratum or substance in which the whole is united as one thing, still this whole does not include one substance with even one phenomenal nature, and something more,—not one substance with three phenomenal natures—but one substance (which cannot be properly called a substance) with three distinct divine minds or agents, each of which being affirmed to be a complete subsistence, is necessarily conceived to be a distinct divine being in the ordinary import of the word. This is affirming three Gods in one God. Thus the meaning of the word *God*, or the phrase *one God*, or one divine being, instead of being an extension or restriction of the ordinary meaning of the language, and so including the essential primary conception of a being, and any part of the primary meaning of the language, is wholly a new one. It is true that in this case, the full, ordinary meaning of the word *person*, even that of a being, is retained. But then the word being in the phrase *one divine being*, entirely loses its primary, ordinary meaning; for what is now called *a being*, instead of including the essential idea or conception of a substance as that to which a phenomenal nature directly pertains, excludes this conception, and substitutes for substance in this necessary import, a mere vinculum or bond by which three distinct divine beings are united or combined, not into one being, but into one thing. Now for such a use of the terms *God*, *one God*, *one divine being*, there can be no good and sufficient reason. It does not imply a unity which need be or can be for any purpose characterized as oneness of being, nor is there any reason why the fact, supposed in this mode of the divine subsistence, would not be, but decisive reason why it should be expressed by other language. At the same time, as we have shown, the supposed use of the language excludes

* This form of the doctrine should be distinguished from that which affirms that three persons are *incomplete* subsistences.

every essential conception in the primary meaning of the word *being*, and involves in every possible authorized meaning of it, obvious self-contradiction. Nor will it be pretended that there is or can be any evidence that when the Scriptures speak of the existence of only one God, they mean three Gods so united by something, that the whole is not one being in any possible meaning of the word. According then to what has been said, it is plain that the advocates of the present form of the doctrine of the Trinity proceed on the assumption that the scriptural writers, in turning language from its primary to a secondary meaning, violate the fundamental laws which control such changes, and of course use language in that unauthorized and improper manner which renders it incapable of any reliable interpretation.

Let us now consider the third form of the doctrine of the Trinity before specified, which having obtained considerable prevalence, claims consideration. In respect to the unity of God it may be thus stated,—that God is one being—*numerically* one in essence and in attributes; that the Father, the Son, and the Holy Ghost, has *numerically* the same perfections; that the Son possesses not simply a similar or equal essence and perfections, but numerically the same as the Father and the Holy Ghost.*

This conception of God as *one being* is simply the ordinary conception of one being, as consisting of one substance or essence, and one nature, called his attributes. The error in respect to this language is not that its use is characterized by an unauthorized and improper peculiarity, but that it is characterized by no peculiarity at all. They who affirm this view of the divine unity also affirm that God,—not in respect to his relations, or modes of acting or revealing himself, but as *a being*, —is *tri-personal*. It is obvious then, that as there is no change in the use of the phrase *one God* or one divine being from its ordinary use, there must be such a change in the use of the word *person*, or the doctrine of one God in three persons is no other than the palpable self-contradiction of one God in three Gods. Nor is this all. No supposable change in the meaning of the word *person*, from its ordinary meaning, can exempt this form of the doctrine of the Trinity from self-contradiction, for

* Stuart's Letters to Channing.

still tri-personality is made a predicate of God as an element of his being, i. e., of the mode of his subsistence. While therefore it affirms that God is numerically one being in essence and in attributes,—in other words, that his whole being consists of one essence and one nature, called his attributes,—it asserts that something more pertains to his being, viz., *tri-personality;* that is, that the whole of the being is not the whole of the being. This definition of the unity of God therefore, precludes all possibility of tri-personality as a predicate of his being, and subverts the Trinitarian doctrine of one God in three persons. Vain therefore, is the attempt to maintain the existence of *one God in three persons*, without proceeding on the ground of some authorized and proper peculiarity in the scriptural use of the terms *one God.* Trinitarians must either take ground with the Infidel, and with him impute self-contradiction to the scriptural writers; or they must abandon the doctrine of the Trinity as taught in the Scriptures; or they must show some authorized and proper peculiarity in the scriptural use of Trinitarian language, that is, of the phrase *one God*, and of the personal pronouns as applied to the Father, the Son, and the Holy Ghost. The latter they are bound to do according to their own principles. For if the tri-personality of God was revealed to scriptural writers for the purpose of being communicated to others,—and that such was the fact every Trinitarian maintains,—then the scriptural writers could not use the phrase *one God* in such a meaning, as in the view of others would exclude and deny the tri-personality of his being, without using the language in an unauthorized and improper manner. They were bound by the laws of language to use the phrase *one God* in such a meaning as would accord with their knowledge of the subject, and of course in such a manner as not to exclude and deny the tri-personality of the Godhead. With the extension of their knowledge of God's mode of subsistence, their meaning of the word *God*, and of the terms *one God*, would extend. To suppose them then to use this language, —as this class of Trinitarians do,—in simply its primary meaning,—to denote a being consisting of one and only one substance or essence, and one nature called his attributes, so that the essence and attributes of the Father, and of the Son, and of the Holy Spirit, are *numerically* the same, as we conceive the essence and attributes of a man to be numerically the same, is to suppose them not only to utter contradiction in asserting the unity and tri-personality of God, but to use the word *God*, and the phrase *one God*, with their knowledge of the subject, in an unauthorized and improper manner. It is true, that on the present supposition, the writers would not use the language in an unauthorized and improper manner by turning it from its primary meaning; but by not turning it from that meaning when the exigency of the case required. The erroneous assumption then which I ascribe to this class of Trinitarians, is not that these writers *turn it from its primary* to an unauthorized and improper use, but that they employ it in an unauthorized and improper manner by using it in its primary meaning.

In respect to the *personal pronouns*, I claim that this class of Trinitarians assume an unauthorized and improper peculiarity in their use, as they are applied by the scriptural writers to the Father, the Son, and the Holy Ghost. I have already presented what I regard as a full account of the meaning which this class of Trinitarians give to the language now under consideration. Whatever may be thought of the consistency or inconsistency of the different forms in which this view of the tri-personality of the Godhead is presented, one thing seems quite undeniable,—that it proceeds on the assumption, that the personal pronouns are not used to express either the whole or a part of what must be considered their distinctive primary meaning, but only the very general idea or conception of a threefold distinction in the Godhead. It is true, that it is said that there is a distinction which lays a foundation for the application of the personal pronouns I, thou, he, which renders it proper to speak of sending and being sent, &c. At the same time however, "separate consciousness, will, power," &c., are denied. It would be impossible then, that this class of Trinitarians should consider the personal pronouns, in their present application, as used in any other manner than to express the very general conception of a threefold distinction in the Godhead. Now, if this be so, these words are not only turned from their primary meaning, but they are turned from it in violation of every law of usage which regulates such changes. In the first place, there can be no good and sufficient reason for the supposed use of these pronouns rather than of any other words, or than merely algebraic signs. Again, according to the supposed use and meaning of them, they retain no part of their primary distinctive meaning, by which a person is distinguished from that which is not a person, or one person from another. Nor do they admit of any obvious, definite, and consistent meaning in the supposed use. For as we have shown, in view of the definition of the unity of God adopted by this class of Trinitarians, these pronouns can express no meaning, no conception of any thing which can be called tri-personality, or a threefold distinction in the Godhead, the existence of which is possible in the nature of things. And further, instead of any evidence of the supposed meaning, which is wholly precluded by the impossibility of the thing to be proved, there is decisive evidence to the contrary. Nothing can be plainer, than that the scriptural writers use the personal pronouns, in their present application, in at least some of their distinctive primary meaning; that is, in some of that meaning by which a person is distinguished from that which is not a person. Even those whom we now oppose, admit that the threefold distinction which they affirm, renders it proper to speak of sending and of being sent, &c. They even claim that these distinctions, notwithstanding they disclaim any affirmative description of them, and deny all distinction in respect to essence and attributes, may exist in regard to attributes or essence.

It thus appears that many Trinitarians, in their interpretation of the Trinitarian language of the Scriptures, proceed on the assumption of an unauthorized and improper peculiarity in the use of that language. Such a use of language admitting of no reliable interpretation, it follows that the meaning given it, and of course the doctrine derived from it, is utterly groundless. The meaning given to the language in each instance is wholly arbitrary—given at the pleasure of the interpreters; given when the words interpreted furnish no possible reason for the meaning actually given rather than any other; given when any other words would have furnished as much evidence of the same meaning, on the part of the writers, as these; given when the words are so used, that according to the laws of usage they no more admit of or require one meaning than another; given when the words cease to be words, by being so used as to convey no possible meaning whatever; given when the same ideas and conceptions respecting God's mode of subsistence, might as well be imputed to the scriptural writers, had they used no words on the subject.

Again: the error which we are now considering has not been unconnected with consequences to the cause of truth which are much to be regretted. It is to this error, as it exists on the part of Trinitarians, that in the present connection I desire now to call attention, and this in relation to only one of its consequences. To say nothing then of the extravagance, the deficiency, the indefiniteness, the unintelligibleness, and even the absurdity which characterize different statements of the doctrine of the Trinity, and which in view of their authors seem to be required by the language and authority of inspiration itself, Trinitarians generally have placed such an *exclusive* reliance on this authority for successfully maintaining their doctrine, that they have done almost nothing adapted to the purpose of exempting it from absurdity in the mind of the Unitarian, and still less in the mind of the Infidel. They have scarcely attempted to unfold any authorized peculiar use of scriptural language on this subject or the peculiar principles of its interpretation, and in this way to ascertain its precise import and vindicate it from the charge of absurdity. This, though it does not justify or palliate the charge of absurdity against every Trinitarian meaning of the language, leaves the plausibility of the charge unremoved, and is, in my estimation, a serious deficiency in the mode of defending the truth. A more plausible mode of assailing the Trinitarian would be to show that he does not justify, *by the laws of interpretation*, even any consistent meaning which he contrives to give to scriptural language. Another general principle however, will show how inadequate is the mode of reasoning adopted by the Trinitarian. If, in a case in which the writer or speaker intends to be understood, no proper and peculiar use of language arising from the nature of the subject or other cause will authorize the rejection of a contradictory and absurd meaning, or the adoption of any other as the actual meaning, then we are not at liberty to reject the former or to adopt the latter. Whatever *presumption* against the absurd as the actual meaning may arise from the character of the writer, it cannot be *good proof* against its being the actual meaning where there is no other evidence against, but abundant other evidence for its being so, in the just interpretation of the language. It is on this principle only that respectable and even the ablest writers can be, as they often are, convicted of uttering absurdity. On the same principle the Trinitarian rejects the inferior or limited sense of the word *God*, given by Unitarians to the word when applied to Christ. For so doing he assigns two reasons: that there is in the instances of such an application of the word no evidence for, but decisive evidence against its being the actual meaning; and that the Unitarian adopts it as the actual instead of the Trinitarian meaning, for an insufficient reason, viz., because regarding the Trinitarian meaning as absurd, it is inconsistent with the inspiration of the writers, whereas he ought to receive the Trinitarian as the actual meaning, if the laws of interpretation give it as such, and this notwithstanding that in his view it is inconsistent with the inspiration of the writers. But if the Unitarian is forbidden thus to fall back on the inspiration of the writers, and *merely* for this reason to deny that an absurd meaning is their actual meaning, why is not the Trinitarian forbidden to deny, *merely* for the same reason, the absurdity of the meaning itself? He is; and is as unprotected from the assault of the Infidel as the Unitarian is in his position. Both the Trinitarian and Unitarian are bound by logical consistency, either to be Infidels by denying the inspiration of the scriptural writers, or to show,—after having ascertained by the laws of usage and just interpretation, irrespectively of the inspiration of these writers, the actual meaning of their language,—that this meaning is free from all absurdity. If these things are so, then in the unauthorized uses which the Trinitarian and Unitarian make of the inspiration of the scriptural writers in obtaining the meaning of their language, there is no substantial difference, though in another material respect there is between these parties an important one. The Unitarian, as it may appear, in defense of his meaning of the language under consideration, has no valid ground on which to stand, and therefore, little as he suspects it, takes the position of an unauthorized use of the language and of arbitrary interpretation, and at the same time absurdly maintains the inspiration of the writers. It may also appear that the Trinitarian, in maintaining his meaning of the language, has valid ground to take, viz., that of an authorized peculiarity in the use of the language, according to which its meaning can be ascertained and exempted from all absurdity by the just laws of interpretation, the inspiration of the writers be defended, and the doctrine of the Trinity in its true form established. If there is such ground for the Trinitarian, he is bound to take it. Not to do so, is at best to furnish an inadequate defense of what he regards as revealed truth, and even to abandon the Scriptures to the ruthless desecration of the Infidel.

I now proceed to show as I proposed, that the Unitarian resorts to *a modified* use of some of the important terms under consideration, without any sufficient warrant for so doing; in other words, that in changing the meaning of some of these terms from primary to secondary, he assumes an unauthorized and improper peculiarity in the use of them by the scriptural writers. It is true that in thus modifying this language, he claims to proceed on the ground of an authorized and proper peculiarity in its use; that in respect to some of the terms, they are properly and warrantably employed in *an inferior or restricted sense*, and in respect to others, that they are properly used *by personification.*

We say then, that *Unitarians*, in this mode of interpreting the language, proceed on the presumption of an unauthorized and improper use of it by the scriptural writers. This they do in maintaining that the word *God* is applied to Christ in the Scriptures, in an *inferior and limited sense.* Now if this be so, —if the scriptural writers use the word God in this application to denote that Christ, as a being, is any thing less than a divine being,—then we claim that the manner in which they use it for this purpose is unauthorized and improper. We admit that the word may be and is properly, in some cases, turned from its primary literal use, and employed in an inferior sense. But then this turning of words from their primary to a secondary meaning is, in all cases, subject to some fixed law or principle which cannot be violated without using it in an unauthorized and improper manner. What we claim then is, that if the scriptural writers use the word in its present application in an inferior sense, as maintained by Unitarians, they violate the principle or law of change which is applicable to the case, and so employ the word in an unauthorized and improper manner. This will appear by recurring to this principle, and to those which are adopted by Unitarians in the interpretation of the language.

The general principle or rule then, which is applicable to such cases, is, *that a word is to be considered as used in its com-*

mon literal meaning in every case, unless good and sufficient evidence to the contrary is furnished by the case itself. The justness of this principle is manifest at once, if we reflect that to suppose a word turned from its primary literal import, to another, without good evidence of the change and of the new meaning in which it is used, is to suppose the language not to convey the meaning of the writer or speaker, and therefore not to be properly used. Whatever may be the meaning of the writer or speaker in such a case, his language conveys none. If we are led by some accidental circumstance to conjecture or guess concerning it, still his language, furnishing no sufficient evidence of what it is, is plainly used in an unauthorized and improper manner. The question then arises, what is good and sufficient evidence that language is used, not in its primary but in a secondary meaning? I answer, negatively—

First—That the *mere* absurdity or falsehood of its primary literal meaning, is not such evidence. Unitarians maintain the principle,—and a very convenient one it is, with their gratuitous assumption of the absurdity of a Trinitarian meaning, for their purpose in this controversy,—that we may reject the primary literal meaning of language if it be absurd, when the mere words will bear it, though we cannot decide what is the actual meaning. This may be true in some rare cases, as in the utterance of a prophecy whose import is to be understood only in its fulfillment; or in certain other cases, when the design is present obscurity which is to be removed by future explanation; or when the antiquity of a book, or various readings, or errors in transcription, &c., deprive us of those means of deciding the actual meaning of language which were possessed by contemporaries of the writer. But what has this to do with the case in hand,—a case in which the writers are divinely commissioned to reveal truth for the instruction of all mankind, and in which they profess, and plainly design, to convey a meaning through the language which they employ? Here the principle can have no application. Mere absurdity or falsehood, whatever *presumption* it may do in other cases, can afford none in this, much less become *proof* of another meaning than that which is absurd. The writer not only may, but the proof is decisive that he does utter an absurdity. The language, justly interpreted, either expresses an absurd meaning or it does not. If it does, then an absurd meaning is its actual meaning, and cannot be rejected as such. If it does not, then the absurd meaning is not the actual meaning, and is to be rejected, not because it is absurd, but because it is not, by just interpretation, the actual meaning. Why then talk of rejecting a meaning which is given by the laws of interpretation, merely because it is absurd? Is it said, that nothing is more common in the correct mode of interpreting language, than to reject a supposed meaning merely because it is absurd? I answer, never. Aside from the character of the writer, the manner of writing, and other considerations, the absurdity of a meaning can never be reason for rejecting it as the actual one. Language is capable of being used in a definite meaning, and when properly employed, gives that which is intended. When therefore, a writer intends to convey a definite meaning, if his language justly interpreted does convey such an one, and can convey no other, and when the meaning thus conveyed is absurd, he is charged with uttering absurdity. In what other way can any one ever be convicted of uttering absurdity? How else can Unitarians, even with a show of honesty in their own view, charge Trinitarians with absurdity in affirming that there is one God in three persons? And if the sacred writers use language properly when using it in this manner, why does not the Trinitarian use it *properly* in conforming to their example? and why is not his language to be interpreted accordingly? Why is not the Unitarian, and every other interpreter of the Scriptures, to conform to the same inspired model of propriety? And then what a revelation from God would that be, the language of which, according to just laws of interpretation, expresses only an absurd meaning, and must therefore be supposed to have another actual meaning, though none can tell what! If this is not to suppose the language to be used in a peculiar manner, which is altogether unauthorized and improper, it is difficult to say what would be. It is to no purpose to say that the writers were divinely inspired. What warrant have inspired writers more than others, to use language for the instruction of mankind in such a manner, that according to the laws of just interpretation, it expresses only an absurd meaning? What vindication is it, when it is once conceded, that correctly interpreted, they actually utter absurdity, that they do not utter absurdity, because they were inspired? Would it not be more consequential to say, they were inspired to utter absurdity? Be this as it may, if they utter absurdity according to a correct interpretation of their language, they do the same whether inspired or not inspired. Absurdity is as good evidence against inspiration, as inspiration is against absurdity. Inspiration can have no influence as evidence against an absurd actual meaning in any case, unless the language according to correct interpretation, will express another meaning than the absurd one.

The principle of interpretation we are considering, is one of those vaunted principles of Unitarians—and the more entitled to examination on this account—by which divine revelation is to be rescued from the contempt of the Infidel. We cannot but think however, that to reject an absurd meaning as the actual, and when it is proved by the only evidence on the question to be the actual meaning *solely* because it is absurd, or *solely* because it is absurd and because the writers are supposed to be inspired, is the last expedient that a wise advocate of a divine revelation will adopt in its defense. By so doing, the Unitarian not only adopts a principle which is preposterously and flagrantly false, but he subjects himself to the charge of weakly begging a main question in debate with the Infidel, and the sacred writers, to the charge of utter incompetence for their work. He begs a main question in debate with the Infidel, by assuming the inspiration of the writers, while the Infidel alleges, as proof against their inspiration, the conceded absurdity of their writings according to the just principles of interpretation. Thus the Unitarian concedes the absurdity in the meaning of the language justly interpreted, and denies the absurd meaning to be the actual meaning, not on the ground of any law of interpretation, but only on the ground of the inspiration of the writers. The Infidel claims, that the language, correctly interpreted, and independently of the inspiration of the writers, abounds in absurdity. This being conceded by the Unitarian, he assumes the inspiration of the writers when conceding the fact which disproves it, and on this assumption denies the absurd meaning to be the actual meaning, when conceding the fact which proves it to be such. With how much respect for revelation will such advocacy inspire the Infidel? Further: the Unitarian subjects the scriptural writers themselves to the charge of incompetence for their work. He concedes that they use language which, according to the only just principles of interpretation applicable to the case, expresses only an absurd meaning. This he denies to be their actual meaning in direct defiance of decisive proof that it is their actual meaning, and solely on the ground of its absurdity, and of the inspiration of the writers, and affirms another to be the actual meaning, which lies far beyond the reach of human discovery. And thus the sacred writers use language for the purposes of revelation! They so use it that when correctly interpreted, it expresses nothing but absurdity, and this, thus clearly and decisively expressed as the only meaning of the language, is their complete vindication from the charge of absurdity—they mean nothing which can be understood by what they say, and yet what they say is to be received by the world as a revelation. Is this an authorized and proper use of language, or is it an unauthorized and improper use of it, which comports rather with idiocy than with competence to write a revelation from God?

II.

HUMAN SINFULNESS.

I.—ALL MEN ARE TOTALLY DEPRAVED.

I. The doctrine explained.—What the doctrine is not.—Distinguished from total depravity *by nature.*—Must be consistent with just views of the nature of holiness and sin.—II. The doctrine proved (1.) from Scripture.—Remark on man's enmity to God.

I SHALL, I., explain the doctrine of the *total depravity* of all men. By this doctrine, I mean that

All mankind (*without the interposition of divine grace*) *are, in respect to their first moral character, wholly and positively sinful.*

To prevent misapprehension, I remark still more particularly, that in this proposition I do not intend to assert that

Every thing which pertains to man, and to which a name may be given in the classification of mental phenomena, is sinful; nor that all men are as bad as they can be; nor that they are equally wicked; nor that they are simply destitute of holiness in distinction from any thing positively sinful; nor that there are no men in the world who through grace are good.

It is, if I mistake not, in respect to the particulars now specified, that errors in stating the doctrine of human depravity most frequently occur. I have designed to avoid these in the statement which I have given. Thus it cannot be said, that the representation is that every thing that pertains to man is sinful, for the predicate of sinfulness is confined to his moral character. This, it is true, involves all those *complex* acts to which the words moral or sinful can be properly applied, but it does not include what in more analytical language may be properly called acts or states of mind. The acts of the intellect and of the will—the excitement of constitutional susceptibilities—may be properly spoken of as distinct acts, but of no one of them analytically considered is moral quality predicable. In all cases, as we have before shown, when we predicate moral quality of an act, we denote one which is complex, or made up of what may be properly spoken of as distinct mental acts. Nor can it be objected to the statement now given, that it represents all men to be as wicked as they can be, or to be equally wicked, since it is too plain to be denied, that all men may be wholly sinful, and some be far worse than others. It is indeed true that the practical governing principle of men, if our doctrine be true, must be the same in kind, and to a certain extent the same in degree in all men. Beyond this however, there is room for indefinite diversity in the degrees of this principle. Nor does the statement now given countenance the error, that the depravity of men consists in the destitution of holiness, for it asserts positive sinfulness. Nor is it consistent with another opinion, that the moral character of man is partially good and partially bad, for it predicates entire sinfulness of his moral character. Nor does it deny that there are good men in the world, for there may be many through the interposition of divine grace, and yet without such interposition the moral character of all may be wholly sinful.

In further explanation of the present statement I remark, that it distinguishes the doctrine of *the total depravity of men* from the doctrine of the total depravity of men *by nature.* The importance of this remark results from the fact, that some divines have made substantially the statement now given of the former doctrine as the true statement of the latter. They suppose that to say that man is depraved without the interposition of grace, is the same thing as to say he is depraved *by nature.* This however, is not only shunning a main point in the controversy, but it is obviously incorrect. For although it be conceded that all men are depraved without the interposition of divine grace, and although it may follow as an inference that this depravity is *by nature*, yet the fact is not specified in the language of the statement, since the depravity may be, for aught that is asserted to the contrary,—as our opponents have maintained it is,—owing to *the circumstances* of men, and not to their *nature;** i. e., unless it be assumed that the interposition of grace is *not* included in their circumstances, since if

* Adam became depraved without the interposition of grace, or it may at least have been so. But he did not become depraved by nature, but by circumstances.

it should be assumed as included, it would be properly ranked with the influence of bad example, bad education, &c. Whether therefore, the depravity of men is to be ascribed to their *circumstances* or to their *nature* is not settled, but is designedly left undetermined by the present statement. It also leaves the question concerning the sinfulness of infants untouched, since it confines the predicate of sinfulness to moral character without deciding *when* that commences.

Further: to a right apprehension of the doctrine now stated, it is necessary that we form just notions of what constitutes moral character, or rather what constitutes it wholly and positively sinful. Generally speaking, moral character consists in a man's governing purpose, evinced to us by that course of specific action or conduct to which it leads. When therefore, we speak of it as wholly and positively sinful, we intend that the man is the subject of that supreme love of the world—that preference of worldly good to all other, which leads to that course of specific action or conduct which is the appropriate result of such a governing principle. It is however to be remarked, that strictly and properly speaking, the governing principle itself constitutes moral character, since we never hesitate to decide on character where the governing principle of a man is clearly evinced, whether it be by a course of conduct or by a single action, or even in some cases *by words* merely. When therefore I say, that the moral character of mankind is wholly and positively sinful, I mean that they are the subjects of that supreme love of the world,—that preference of earthly good, or that selfishness, or that selfish principle, or that corrupt and wicked heart, or that sinful disposition, call it by what name you will,—which governs its subject in all his specific actions or conduct.

II. I proceed now to prove the doctrine.

The proofs are derived from the Scriptures, also from observation and experience.*

From the Scriptures.—Gen. vi. 5: "And God saw the wickedness," &c. This, though generally given, is not of itself perfectly decisive, for from the connection it admits of being viewed as spoken only of the men of that particular age—the

---

* The remainder of this lecture was taken from the notes of one of Dr. T.'s pupils.

antediluvian—though it admits also of being considered a universal declaration. But in connection with the text we find (Gen. viii. 21), "The imagination of man's heart," &c. This is a conclusive proof-text, for it gives the fact as *universal*. Ps. xiv. 5, x. 36, cxl. 53, and Is. lix. are on this point as Paul explains them and applies them in Rom. iii. 9–19, to all men, where also the argument for *universal Justification* is founded on the fact of *universal sinfulness*. These are very decisive. Jew and Gentile are alike here. The only attempt at evasion of the strong description in these texts, is on the ground that the Psalmist in some cases includes good men of whom he could not mean to predicate total depravity, while Paul says there are none. "All men are not *so* wicked—all do not curse and steal." But if the Psalmist included them, it is no proof of contradiction, for some are renewed. The exceptions to his declarations are so few as not to need a formal notice, or to constitute a warrant against his making a general declaration. Writers seldom make exceptions when they are few or trivial. But how is Paul to be justified? I answer, the principle of moral action in men is *one*; it is adequate to any degree of wickedness. Paul does not mean to say that all are guilty of murder in overt deed, and the texts should not be so interpreted. In them *positive sinfulness* as well as *negation of holiness* is asserted of all, for "none do good," but all are active in sinning. Jer. xvii. 9: "The heart is deceitful," &c. This is a strong passage. Heart means the heart of man. It is a universal proposition without qualification, and needs none. Eccles. ix. 3: "The heart of the sons of men is full of evil." A universal proposition.

The universal call of the Gospel upon all men to *repent* is proof of total, universal depravity. What is the repentance required? Not a change from one degree of goodness to another, but a change of *moral* character. This implies a previous deficiency in moral character. God commands all men everywhere to repent;—why, if not sinners? "The whole need not a physician" (Matt. ix. 12). But the Bible calls none sinful but those who are wholly so. It characterizes them as those that believe not the Gospel—"loving the world"—"not loving the Father"—"not for him but against him." These qualities it predicates of all renewed persons, and hence calls on *all* to change this nature. The Scripture doctrine of Regeneration proves this doctrine. This involves the same change—an entire new moral character in kind—and implies previous entire sinfulness. Thus, "if any man is in Christ, he is a new creature: old things are passed away," &c. (2 Cor. v. 17; Col. iii. 9; Eph. iv. 22.) "Old man corrupt," an entire change from old to new man; now holy—before sinful. The doctrine of Justification also. This is represented as the Justification of the ungodly—of sinners, of enemies. (Rom. iv.; Gal. iii.; Rom. v. 6–10; Heb. ii. 9.) "Christ tasted death for every man." What then are all men but sinners, enemies, &c.? For Christ came to call not the righteous, but sinners to repentance (εἰς μετάνοιαν). The Scriptures divide men into two, and only two classes, viz., the righteous or imperfectly holy, the wicked or the positively and wholly sinful. They represent the renewed as sanctified in various degrees—some possessing the very *least* degree of holy principle that can be called so, and yet views these as among the righteous and as possessing a positive, decisive, and essential distinction from the wicked. If then the *least* degree of holy principle ranks its possessor among the righteous, how much can any other possess? Evidently something less than the *least* possible. If the wicked have not the least possible good principle, are they not totally depraved? Eph. ii. 1–5: "And you hath he quickened," &c. This is a strong passage, the language of which is figurative but not the less obvious and precise—"originally children of disobedience"—"fulfilling the desires of the flesh" —"wherein ye walked," a walking, *living death*, "by nature children of wrath, even as others." There is only one attempt at evasion here. Unitarians say that Paul reckoned himself among the wicked that his language might not sound harsh. John vii. 7: "The whole world *hateth* me," &c. The *world* in the Bible is used to represent the wicked, *all* in their natural state, as in 1 John v. 19. So other passages. The Scriptures do not say men hate God *per se;* the devils said, "We know thee that thou art the Son of God," but they hate me "*because* I testify."

Remarks.—In representing the depravity of man, preachers should use much caution. There has been much erroneous and injudicious preaching on the enmity of the heart towards God. It is too generally considered to be *overt hatred* of God, and when presented to many minds where that state of feeling does not exist because they may never have had such distinct views of God as to call it out, they know from their own consciousness that they have not that state of heart, and you cannot convince them of the contrary. The Bible never so represents the matter. You must adopt the Bible sense of the words hate, enmity. See Deut. xxi. 15; Matt. vi. 24; Luke xiv. 26; Prov. xiii. 24; Matt. i. 3; Rom. ix. 13; John xii. 25, where hate is used in the sense of a *less degree of love.* This less degree of love, leading the person exercising it to treat the less esteemed object in some respects as an enemy, is properly termed "enmity," "hatred." Luke xiv. 26: "Hateth not his father," &c. Whenever their interests come into competition with God, they are to be sacrificed, thus in a sense treating these persons as enemies. So loving God subordinately is properly called hatred, and the nature of such subordinate love to God, love leading us to disregard all his great and benevolent designs, is equivalent in its effect to positive hatred. James iv. 4 explains this so. Sinners do not hate God for his own sake. Even Satan would not. Unitarians and Universalists love God amazingly—that is, *their* God.

But in some minds it is true that there is overt enmity towards God, and this enmity, secret and lurking as it may be, can be presented so that the subject of it shall *see*, *feel*, and *admit* it. And thus to present it, tasks the skill of the preacher. Exhibit to sinners a pure and just God who testifies that their works are evil—the God of the Bible as ever present with them, and determined eternally to punish them for their sins, —suppose him ever at their side, witnessing every act, reproving every sin, and they will feel troubled at his presence—they will wish to be rid of such a being—they will be conscious of the overt enmity of their hearts rising against God, a feeling of hatred which is more than a less degree of love. They will then acknowledge that the carnal mind *τὸ φρόνημα τῆς σαρκός*, "friendship of the world is enmity against God"—that the principle tending to sacrifice God and his interests to self is hatred. But without such exhibition, sinners will complain of false, slandering accusations, and hence go away enraged rather than softened by the truth.

HUMAN SINFULNESS.

II.—ALL MEN ARE TOTALLY DEPRAVED.—(*Continued.*)

(2.) The argument from experience and observation.—Certain traits of character are adduced against its truth.—Considered under three particulars.—Traits specified, are innocence of childhood, honor, gratitude.—They are shown to be not morally good.—Argument on the application of the words good, lovely, &c.

THAT this argument is relied on by both the contending parties, is quite decisive of its insufficiency on one side of the question or the other.

On one side, it is maintained that there are certain traits of CHARACTER belonging in greater or less degree to all men, even the worst, at some period of life, which are *morally good*, and that these are decisive proofs that the first moral character of men is not wholly depraved. I propose—

1. To ascertain what these things are;
2. To show that they are not morally good; and,
3. That so far as moral quality can be supposed to pertain to them, they are sinful.

1. What are these things?

And here my object will be to show, that *they are either involuntary constitutional propensities simply; or they are subordinate volitions—acts of will—choices to gratify constitutional propensities.* Here we have to encounter the ambiguities of language in one of its most perplexing forms. The difficulty is, to ascertain with precision what is meant by the language in a case in which the words employed in different applications have different meanings. The following catalogue of names may be sufficiently extensive for our purpose: "The innocence and purity of early childhood, natural affection, compassion, kindness, honesty, veracity, fidelity, gratitude, honor, patriotism, humanity."

The first, "the innocence and purity of early childhood," is phraseology having a generic import. What then is meant by it? So far as I can conceive, it must mean at least some one of the following things: an entire exemption from sin and moral defilement previous to moral agency, and of course, to moral character; or perfect obedience to the divine law after moral agency commences; or some specific virtues which are not included in the specific enumeration; or these specific virtues themselves; or exemption from all sin without positive obedience to the divine law; or exemption from some particular sins. These are the only senses in which I can imagine the writers who speak of "the innocence and purity of childhood," to use the language.

I now inquire, what are the things meant in the more specific part of the catalogue? Some of these terms are ambiguous, that is, are used by good authority in different senses. Thus the phrase *natural affection* often denotes the feeling or emotion which a man has toward his offspring or other kindred, and which is merely a *constitutional* feeling or emotion. Thus viewed, it is an involuntary state of mind which, like our propensity for food or drink, may or may not precede a given act of choice, but which, in its own nature, is not an act of choice. In like manner we use the words compassion and humanity, to denote the same thing as we express by the terms *compassionate and humane feelings*, meaning states of mind which are not voluntary—not acts of choice, but which may or may not be the basis of particular acts of choice. In each of these uses we designate simply *constitutional* propensities, excited in view of their objects, as distinguished from any act of the will, and this without deciding whether there is a subsequent act of choice to gratify or to deny the propensity, or whether the man gives dominion to the propensity, or subordinates its gratification to other and more worthy objects of affection.

But we use the same terms to denote different things. Thus a man may love his reputation, or his wealth, or his Maker, more than he loves his child, and yet truly love the latter; and this love we call *natural affection*. So he may love his child more than he loves his reputation, or his wealth, or his Maker, and still we call this love *natural affection*. The same thing is true respecting the use of the words *compassion* and *humanity*. The specific object of these emotions is *suffering*, that is, each is a propensity or desire to relieve suffering in the primary import of the term. But a man may love the public good more than the relief of the culprit condemned to punishment, and still feel *compassion* for the sufferer; or his compassion may lead him to relieve the sufferer at the sacrifice of public good.

The same things may be said of the word patriotism or love of country. A man who loves his Maker or a universe more than his country, may still love his country and be the best of patriots; or he may love his country more than God and a universe besides, and still be applauded for his patriotism.

The word *honor* may be used in a similar manner. A man may love God more than the honor which cometh from men, and still love his reputation or character; or he may love honor more than God, and though a duelist and a murderer, be extolled as a man of honor. The same things are true of the use of the words *kindness* and *benevolence*. There is, as we have seen, a constitutional propensity in every man which can find its gratification in the happiness of others; and a man may choose to impart happiness to others for the pleasure of seeing them happy, when to do so interferes with no other and higher selfish interest of his own, although he has not fixed his heart in supreme affection on the highest happiness of the universe, or on the glory of God; and although the act itself only furnishes the means of vice. This is that species of kindness which gives money to the mendicant drunkard. Or a man may show kindness because his chief object is to secure the greatest amount of happiness to others; or to glorify God. Or he may perform the same act from a regard to reputation, or to any other private personal end; and the name of kindness may, according to an authorized use of the word, be applied to describe the act in each instance specified.

Gratitude is another word which may be properly used in very different meanings. Sometimes it denotes merely the love of the gifts of a benefactor, or of him for his kindness, without any love of his character; or it may denote the love of his gifts as this love blends with the love of his character.

It is then quite obvious, that some of the principal terms in the above catalogue may, on the authority of usage, be employed to denote widely different things.

The other words, though used in various senses, are never used to denote merely constitutional propensities, since their objects are external acts; but always a voluntary purpose or principle, or at least to include such a state of mind. Thus honesty denotes either a purpose to render to every one his due, or the external act itself, or both. Veracity, a principle or purpose to speak truth, or the speaking of truth, or both; but when these terms are used to denote the principle of honesty or of veracity, they often denote things in some respects *essentially* different. Thus, a man may purpose to be honest, and true, and faithful, to promote his reputation or his pecuniary interest, or to avoid the evils of disgrace, or poverty, or civil punishments; or he may form this purpose from a supreme regard to the will and the glory of God. Nor can any one fail to see, that while honesty and veracity may, with propriety of language, as usage decides this propriety, be applied to such purposes, be the object or end of the purpose what it may, the purposes themselves essentially differ as their object or end differs.

Should it here be said, that a man may purpose to be honest and truthful for the pleasure of being so, and in this sense be governed by the purest and best principle, I readily admit, that in popular language a man may be said to be honest for the pleasure he takes in being so. But the question is, what is the meaning of this language? And to settle this, we must decide on the object which affords the pleasure. This must be the acts of honesty. But what is there in acts of honesty to afford pleasure to the mind? I answer, that they give pleasure as acts which, in their true nature and tendency, subserve the highest good or the glory of God. And if this be the pleasure proposed, his ultimate end is the glory of God, i. e., his principle is the same which I before described. Besides this import of the phrase, *for the pleasure of being honest*, there is one other,—the avoidance of self-reproach in being dishonest, or securing self-complacency in acts of honesty. If this be the motive in an enlightened mind—a mind which has just views of the ground of self-complacency in right moral action—then it implies the same thing, for no mind can find true self-complacency in such acts, except as they are the dictate of a supreme regard to the will and glory of God. If the motive be simply to avoid the fears of punishment or the pains of remorse, which a guilty conscience often inflicts, this is as truly a selfish consideration, as when the motive is worldly advantage or any other good short of the glory of God. So that in whatever language we may describe the motive, the principle of honesty must be, as it may, either a purpose to promote reputation or profit, that is, some worldly inferior interest, or a purpose to glorify God.

Thus it appears that the terms in the foregoing catalogue which have a specific import, denoting particular acts or states of the mind, may, according to usage, be employed to denote either,

Involuntary states of the constitutional propensities simply; or,

Specific volitions—acts of will—choices in which the mind chooses the gratification of some of its constitutional propensities.

Besides these, I know no other meanings of these terms.

I now proceed to show—

2. That these things are not *morally good.*

Before however, I enter into the direct examination of this topic, it is requisite that we decide on the true standard of moral goodness. After our previous discussion it is not necessary that we dwell long on this point. I would remark then, that reason and the Scriptures alike decide, that the lowest degree of moral excellence in man consists *in supreme love to God.* Reason so decides; for nothing is more obvious than that any other practical principle will sacrifice the greatest good to that which is less. The Scriptures so decide; for saith our Lord, "He that loveth father or mother more than me, is not worthy of me." And again, "He that is not for me is against me."

Again: it must not be forgotten that man is bound to be actuated and governed by this great principle of supreme love to God, in every particular voluntary action. "Whether ye eat or drink, or whatsoever ye do, do all to the glory of God."

Once more: the man who does not habitually act under this principle of supreme love to God, does uniformly and without exception act under the principle of the supreme love of the world, or of the selfish principle. No man can have two objects of supreme affection; and since there is no third object, God or the world must be supreme. "No man can serve two masters, for he will either hate the one and love the other, else he will hold to the one and despise the other. Ye cannot serve God and mammon."

The arguments of our opponents to show that the things in question are morally good, are derived from three sources,—*from an ambiguous and undefined use of the words good, lovely,*

&c., as applied to these things; from the nature of the things themselves, and from their practical results.

(1.) Let us then examine the argument from the use of the words *good*, *lovely*, &c. It is then readily admitted that these epithets are often applied, and in real and proper import, to the things in question. But it is a vital question, what is this meaning? There is a beauty in sights and sounds which may be called *lovely;* there is a natural grace in personal accomplishments of body and mind which may be called *lovely;* but no one supposes that there is the least moral loveliness or excellence. A particular medicine may be pronounced *good* in respect to its salutary efficacy in particular diseases, and yet were it used as a universal nutriment of the human body, it might be universal death. "Fire is a good servant, but a bad master." So kindness and fidelity among a company of highwaymen may be pronounced *good* by them in reference to their intercourse, and yet be enforced for purposes of plunder and assassination. When these terms are thus used, it is plain that they do not denote moral excellence or moral beauty. I ask then, what they mean when applied by our opponents to the things under consideration, and I insist on an answer. I am not to abandon the argument in deference to mere words. I concede that these things may, according to the authorized usage of terms, be called *good*, and *lovely*, and useful, and so on. But what then? Is the beauty of a landscape *moral loveliness?* Is the goodness of an article in the materia medica *moral goodness?* Is the utility of kindness and truth practiced by a band of assassins *moral excellence?*

So it is not denied that these things, contemplated as objects of natural beauty, and fitness, and utility, may be very justly pronounced *lovely* and *good.*

If they are considered, as some of them may be, as merely constitutional propensities, there is in them an obvious fitness to the present condition and well-being of man; for example, without a constitutional affection or regard for his offspring, what a wretched world would this be! So too, considered as subordinated propensities, i. e., subordinated in their indulgence and gratification to the will and glory of God, they are objects of beauty and of great utility. In this form they are not only duly regulated and directed by the supreme love of God, and therefore harmless, but in fact blend with it, and constitute together a state of mind or practical principle of greater power than could otherwise exist. For example, such love for children thus united with love to God in the parental bosom, is an object which we justly contemplate with an almost unparalleled delight, and without this associate, the love of God would itself be a less efficacious principle than it is in practical life.

Further: the things now under consideration, received as *voluntary states of mind*, or principles of action which respect simply the insulated gratification of constitutional propensities, without any reference to the will and glory of God, may in a comparative respect be pronounced good, although when considered as practical principles in their true nature and tendency, and especially as compared with the purer, higher principle of supreme love to God, they are deformed and base, yet compared with other practical principles which might be substituted for them, they are in a high degree useful, and in this respect may be spoken of as *good*. They prompt to many external acts which are right, so far as external acts can be right without rectitude of principle—acts which in external form are the same which the purest, best principles would dictate. They contribute largely to the peace and happiness of the community in which they prevail, compared with the amount which would result from baser principles. Man without them, unless the love of God were to take their place, would be far more depraved than he is with them. They operate also as mutual checks on each other in respect to the outbreakings of crime and the desolations of human happiness. For example, how much sensuality and profligacy are prevented by avarice? how much fraud and violence and murder by a supreme regard to reputation? In short, were they to give place to any practical principle, the love of God excepted, the world would be worse than it now is; and while men refuse to act from the only principle which is pure and holy, the wisdom and the goodness of God are conspicuous in rendering by these principles our existence on earth so comfortable and happy. All this we readily concede; we feel bound to gratitude toward our Maker in view of it, and we welcome our opponents to the concession in its full length and breadth.

It is here however to be remarked, that the concession that

we have just made concerning the things in question does not amount to an admission of moral excellence. Admit that they may with entire propriety be called *good*, and *lovely*, and *amiable*, and *charming*—is there nothing which these epithets may be used to describe but *moral excellence?* Is every thing which is properly termed good—either as the means of good, or as compared with something worse, or as it prevents evils which something else would produce—*morally good?* If so, then I ask what is there in the universe that may not, in some one or all of these senses, be pronounced morally good? For what is there—what sin is there which is not *morally good* in some one of these respects? Not only are the sins of men in this world *good* in some one of these respects—for any sin might be worse—but the sins and the woes of the damned, as subservient to the ends of divine justice, may in this sense be pronounced *good.* What then is there in the fact that these things may be pronounced good, which shows that the word is not applied in a sense as remote as possible from that of *moral goodness?* And what appears in respect to our opponents who resort to this use of the word good as the basis of their argument? Nothing to show why we are not to adopt Mr. Hume's standard of moral excellence, and plead in extenuation of the charge of total depravity, the utility of athletic limbs and broad shoulders, or of the beauty of taper legs, or of an aquiline nose; nothing to show that they do not either through ignorance or perverseness confound all moral distinctions, and like this prince of Infidels substitute a moral standard for that of God's revelation, according to which, moral excellence as truly pertains to the features of the face as to the love of God in the heart.

HUMAN SINFULNESS.

III.—ALL MEN ARE TOTALLY DEPRAVED.—(*Continued.*)

Argument from experience and observation continued.—Traits in question are not morally good.—Argument on the nature of the features adduced.—Considered as simply constitutional affections.—Reply to objection, that not to have them is sinful.—The same considered as voluntary practical principles.—Third source of argument—from external action.—Habitual obedience to God the only legitimate evidence.—Habitual violation of one command decisive against goodness.—The good adduced may result from selfishness.

In the preceding lecture, I entered upon the argument to show that certain things in the character of unrenewed men are not *morally good.* I examined the argument of our opponents derived from the application of the words *good*, *lovely*, &c., to the things in question. Two remaining sources of argument before specified, now claim consideration. I proceed then—

(2.) To examine the argument of our opponents, derived from *the nature of the things* in question.

The first on the catalogue is "the innocence and purity of early childhood." Here I shall examine the various meanings of this phrase. If then by innocence and purity our opponents mean *perfect obedience to the divine law*, then in ascribing this to any human being, they contradict their own repeated declarations that all men sin—declarations which imply that none are innocent. Besides, they assert what they cannot prove, for not a human being can be found to testify that in early childhood he perfectly understood and perfectly obeyed the law of God. If by innocence and purity they mean certain *specific virtues* which are not included in the specific enumeration, we have no means of ascertaining what these virtues are, nor whether they exist, and the assertion of something undefined and unknown is unworthy of notice; or if any or all of the virtues included in the specific enumeration be meant, then the terms "innocence and purity" ascribe nothing additional to the character, and leave us to decide simply whether these supposed specific virtues are real. Or if by "innocence and purity" be meant an entire exemption from sin in a moral agent without positive obedience to law, this is absurd and impossible, since in such a being innocence and purity can consist in nothing short of perfect obedience to law. Or if by "innocence and purity" be meant exemption from some particular sins, this may be admitted, and yet sin may reign in the heart. Or if we are to understand by "innocence and purity" an entire exemption from sin or moral defilement,—previous to moral agency, and of course to moral action and moral character,—then they are not proof that the first moral action, when it is done, and the moral character when it is formed, is not wholly sinful. I now ask, whether the terms "innocence and purity" can denote any thing but some one or more of the things which have been supposed? If not, then they can describe nothing which can be alleged in mitigation of the charge of total depravity in the first moral character.

I now come to the *specific* things in the enumeration; and as we have shown, *some* of the terms of this part of the catalogue, as natural affection, compassion, kindness, honor, &c., may according to usage denote either *simply constitutional propensities, whether subordinated to the glory of God or to some other chief end;* or *voluntary acts,—choices to gratify these propensities without any regard to any higher end.*

Considered then as constitutional propensities, we say there is nothing *morally* good in them. Common sense decides that no moral quality pertains to a mere constitutional desire for the welfare of a child, or for reputation, or for the relief of suffering, for the promotion of others' happiness—more than to such a desire for food or drink, or than to the circulation of the blood, or the operation of the digestive organs. Again: substantially the same propensities belong to the irrational animals—to the lion and the tiger, the sheep and the dove, as well as to man. Further: if moral goodness pertain to these constitutional propensities, then the greater their strength and the more they are excited, and the greater their practical influence, the greater the degree of their moral goodness. A parent who sacrifices his country from the strength of his affection for his child, has more of this virtue than if he loved his child less; and the hero or conqueror who devastates kingdoms from the love of glory, is more virtuous than if he loved his reputation less. If it be said that this is excess in these propensities, I admit it; still it shows either that moral goodness is in its own nature liable to excess, even to that which is sinful,—in other words, that either moral goodness may exist in so great a degree as to become itself sin, or that in these constitutional propensities there is no moral goodness. Once more: that considered simply as constitutional propensities they have no moral quality, is evident from the consideration that they do not decide whether the subject will duly regulate them in reference to the supreme good, or seek their insulated gratification. The fact that a man has a constitutional appetite for food does not make it certain that he will be a glutton, so neither does his constitutional love of his offspring determine whether he will love them excessively or not. He may do the one or he may do the other with the same constitutional propensity. Let him do which he will, the constitutional propensity remains with all its inherent moral excellence, if it possess any such excellence; and however much of a glutton or sot he may become, the constitutional propensity that prompts to his vicious indulgence is morally excellent. The same remark applies to every other constitutional propensity. If the constitutional propensities as such are morally good, they are so whether they be indulged to excess or restrained within due limits. Of course, as man cannot commit wickedness without proposing the gratification of some constitutional propensity,—nor of course without being the subject of such propensity,—he cannot therefore commit a crime without being the subject of some degree of moral excellence in the very act. Yea, according to a previous principle, the stronger the constitutional propensity which leads to the wicked choice and deed, the greater in this respect is his moral excellence. Thus there is a physical impossibility that a man should be wholly sinful in the perpetration of any crime; and not only so, but the more violent the constitutional propensity that prompts to it, the greater is the moral excellence which in this respect adorns his character. And then how good and lovely such propensities appear when they exist in the highest degree, and acquire such strength (for of such they are susceptible) as shall prompt both the purpose and the deed, which shall sacrifice God and the universe to their own insulated gratification!

But it will be said that Paul (Rom. i. 31, and 2 Tim. iii. 3) has decided that the destitution of these things is sinful, and that it follows therefore that they are morally good. I answer that the apostle has not affirmed that the absence of these things is sinful; mere destitution is nothing, and to speak of it as mere destitution, and as implying no positive state of mind, and yet as sinful, would be to talk nonsense. So does not the apostle talk, nor any other sound moralist. He asserts nothing more, than that to be without natural affection is *proof* of great wickedness. But does it follow from this, that if they had not been without it, they would have possessed moral goodness? Suppose a man has destroyed his constitutional appetite for food by intemperate drinking—does this prove that if he had not destroyed it, that it would have graced his character with some degree of moral excellence? Plainly not; he may still consult its gratification in gluttonous excess. Doubtless to extinguish or to smother into absolute inactivity any of our constitutional tendencies is sinful. It implies some voluntary act, the object or tendency of which is to destroy that which ought to be consecrated to useful purposes. To destroy any of my bodily members voluntarily evinces a sinful purpose, but shall we therefore concede to the casuistry that pronounces our features or our limbs, if well-formed, actual virtues? Man may doubtless so smother, perhaps extinguish, his natural affection for his offspring by debauchery and excess, that it shall have no practical influence, and thus be guilty of great wickedness; but he may also cherish that propensity of his nature, and consult supremely its gratification, and blaspheme God for crossing it, and be as wicked as had he destroyed it. If the want of natural affection then proves a high degree of wickedness, its existence is consistent with an equal degree of it. How then is it shown to be morally good?

It remains now to examine the things under consideration as *voluntary practical principles*, in which the mind fixes its preference on the gratification of some constitutional propensity without the least regard to the supreme good. We have already shown that the terms used to describe these "good things," as they are called, may denote simply such acts of preference. The question is, are these *morally good?* This cannot be pretended, in view of the true standard of moral excellence. According to this, no act or state of mind can be morally good, unless it be the supreme love of God, or in its complex meaning involve and be dictated by such love. But the acts now spoken of, it will not be pretended, are either the love of God itself, or that they involve it, and are dictated by it.

They do not in their own nature essentially imply or include the love of God, or even a thought of him. May not a man love his parents, or his children, or his neighbors,—may he not prefer to be honest, temperate, true, &c., without the least regard to God? Every one's own consciousness answers this question. Of course these affections, purposes, or principles, designated by the terms natural affection, temperance, veracity, kindness, &c., do not in their own nature necessarily imply the least moral goodness. I go further, and ask whether these principles and affections, as their nature is evinced to every one by his own consciousness, are not consistent with overt or direct enmity toward God? May not a man, for example, love his child so much as to hate any being who should take away from him the object of his affection, though that being be God himself? Now, without insisting on the positive sinfulness of such an affection for a child, I ask, has it, in its own nature, any moral goodness? Has an affection in its nature any thing morally good which is consistent with enmity to God? Plainly not. Here then our opponents have no alternative but either to deny the law of God to be the standard of moral excellence, or the universal decisions of human consciousness. If they deny the former, we shall leave them to a willful denial of the plainest of all truth, which exempts us from the obligation of further argument. If they deny the latter—the decision of human consciousness—we ask them to produce their witness, the man who will testify that he never could love his child at all, without also loving God supremely; or rather that, in his experience, the former affection necessarily involves the latter.

(3.) I proceed to examine the third source of argument, *the practical results;* in other words, the argument from external action. This is considered by our opponents as quite decisive of the goodness of the principles. Thus Dr. Ware asserts with confidence, that he has *seen* in children much to approve; and with the same positiveness, that even in the worst of men good feelings and principles predominate. It is hardly supposable that Dr. Ware should pretend to any knowledge of the nature of these principles as they exist in children and the worst of men, by direct inspection of their hearts. The question then is confined to *external action*, as the expression of *internal principle*, and is simply this, whether the external acts of kindness to kindred, friends, neighbors, and fellow-beings—acts of honesty, veracity, &c., in the common intercourse of life, are legitimate evidence of the least moral goodness.

1. Obedience habitually universal to God's commandments being *known to us*, is the only legitimate evidence of holy principle (John xv. 14, and xiv. 15–23; 1 John v. 18). Such is the nature of the human mind, that right moral principle will maintain an *habitual* influence on the external deportment. At the same time, incidental or occasional aberrations from the path of duty are not inconsistent with the existence of right moral principle. This is the only criterion by which we are authorized to pronounce any man good, or as having *any* correct moral principle. That we may apply the principle of judging in any case, so much of the deportment of an individual must fall under our observation, as to satisfy us that he habitually renders a universal obedience to God's commandments. Our mere ignorance that he does any thing inconsistent with such habitual obedience, through a partial and limited knowledge of his deportment, will not authorize us to pronounce him influenced by correct moral principle. We must have positive evidence, and this must be furnished by such an acquaintance with the general course of action or conduct, that there shall be no room for rational doubt that good moral principle governs the man.

There is a certain course of external deportment which, in itself, as it falls under our observation, is no evidence for or against correct moral principle, and forbids us to form a decisive judgment. So far as it falls under our observation, it may, on the one hand, be quite unexceptionable, and yet we may see and know so little of the man, as to be utterly unable to pronounce concerning his principles of action; i. e., according to the first rule now given, we may *not* know that he does or that he does not render an habitual, unreserved obedience to all God's commandments. On the other hand, some single act may fall under our observation, which in itself is decidedly sinful, and yet a more extended acquaintance with the deportment of the individual might require us to believe him habitually governed by rectitude of principle. In such cases we are bound not to judge at all.

2. Any allowed or habitual violation of one of God's com-

mandments, is decisive proof of the total want of correct moral principle (James ii. 10). The equity of this test rests on the fact, that allegiance to God is but one and a universal principle; one allowed act of disobedience shows therefore an utter destitution of such a principle, and that when the will of the creature and the will of the Creator come into competition, the right of superiority is awarded to the former, and God dethroned from the supremacy which belongs to him.

It ought here to be remarked, that in many cases in which we are authorized to decide nothing positively, we may so far presume that a man is or is not governed by right principles, as to regulate our own conduct in reference to him according to such a presumption. But such a presumption is widely different from a pretended infallible judgment, founded on legitimate evidence.

In the admission of members into the Christian church, we proceed not on the principle that we can pronounce or even form a confident judgment of the personal piety of the individuals, but on the ground that they propose to perform an act appropriate to real Christians, and that we have no evidence that such is *not* their character.

I now proceed to the inquiry, whether according to these only legitimate rules of judging of the moral principles of others from their external conduct, we are authorized to pronounce the particular external conduct under consideration, evidence of such principles in the heart.

1. In applying the first rule, the question is, whether allowing all that can be claimed, it will furnish the requisite evidence of an habitual universal obedience to God's commandments. And I answer, that the acts themselves obviously do not amount to that which the rule requires.

2. In applying the second rule, the question is, whether it does not, in the case supposed, absolutely *forbid* us to pronounce the principle of the conduct to be good or bad, i. e., forbid us to form an opinion. It certainly must be admitted on the one hand that the external conduct now alleged in proof of correct moral principle may exist, and as it falls under our observation be no proof of a bad moral principle. All that we see may be quite unexceptionable. We go further (since the case now supposes that we know the moral history of the individual but imperfectly), and readily admit that all that we do know of

him is quite consistent with correct moral principle,—that it is that which does mark the deportment of every good man, and therefore forbids us to pronounce that the subject of it has *not* such a character. But does it at the same time authorize us to pronounce that *he is a good man?* This is the question, and the one on which the main inquiry chiefly depends. I answer then, that the simple facts now alleged, being all that is known, we are not authorized, but forbidden to pronounce that the subject possesses the least moral goodness.

This position rests on the principle, that all that we know of the individual may be the dictate of mere selfishness. This I prove—

First, from the Scriptures (Matt. x. 37, and Luke xiv. 26). Now these and similar declarations undeniably prove that natural affection may be supreme in the heart, and thus preclude the least regard to the authority of God.

The story of the young ruler seems to have been put on record for the express purpose of correcting the error of our opponents on this subject. Never did all that is attractive and imposing in the natural character of man blend in higher perfection than in that of this lovely youth. Yet when the Saviour applied to his heart the true test of allegiance to God, how was the emptiness of all his boasted virtues detected! Did he yield a ready compliance—a cheerful submission to an acknowledged command of the Most High? Was he ready to sell all and give to the poor, and take up his cross and follow Christ? He was sad at the utterance of such a requisition, and went away grieved, for he had great possessions. The comment of our Lord was, "How hardly shall they that have riches enter into the kingdom of God!" Here then is brought out the most determined ungodliness of heart—a selfish, sordid attachment to riches—which rejected a known command of God, and showed that his authority was excluded from the whole inner man. The same *amiable qualities* then, with the same *fatal deficiency*, MAY exist in other men.

The apostle has carried this principle still further. Thus he says, "though I bestow," &c. (1 Cor. xiii. 3).

HUMAN SINFULNESS.

IV.—ALL MEN ARE TOTALLY DEPRAVED.—(*Continued.*)

Argument continued from experience and observation.—The good characteristics alleged are considered in childhood and in adults.—Shown to be positively sinful, so far as they have any moral quality, by the nature of moral action and the true principles of judging of it.

The object of the present Lecture is to show, that the argument from experience and observation fully and unanswerably supports the doctrine *of the total depravity of man.*

This I shall attempt to show from the nature of those things which are alleged to the contrary, and from the true rule of judging of moral character.

It is here proper to remark, that that class of men who profess to be, or may be supposed to be, the subjects of a change of moral character by grace, are not to be included in the argument. They are exceptions according to the statement of our doctrine.

I shall pursue the argument in reference to children and those of more advanced age.

I. In reference to children.

We are told that "innocence and purity" are characteristics of early childhood ; and the meaning is, that they are innocent and pure before they form a moral character. This allegation then, has nothing to do with the question, since we can form no estimate of moral character before moral character exists.

Again : it is said that infants early show affection, and gratitude, and attachment to those from whom they receive kindness. And who does not? It is the striking characteristic of sinners, that they love those that love them ; and though these terms may denote other than mere selfish affections, yet we have shown that we are not authorized from such ambiguous manifestations, to assert that the things thus described proceed from a right moral principle. We must know something more then of children before we can, with a proper warrant, decide the question at issue. What then is the fact, when there is a full development of the governing principle to our observation? They show affection and attachment, it is said, to those who show them kindness, which they would do on the supposition of their total depravity. But how is it with respect to those who do not show them kindness—when even those who give them the highest proofs of affection cross their inclinations? We see a decided spirit of selfishness, manifested in acts of dissatisfaction, resistance, and violence; and not only no manifestations of right principle, but such manifestations of the selfish principle as *oblige* us to pronounce them wholly under its influence.

It is said that infants are not cruel, but that a child takes pleasure in torturing insects from gratification afforded by witnessing violent motion, &c., and that by an appeal to his compassion he is easily made to desist. The fact implied, that a child never tortures an insect with a knowledge of its sufferings, is palpably false. That peculiarly forcible appeals to their compassion and sympathy will often overcome the power of the temptation, at least for the moment, is admitted. If the assertion, that a child never tortures an insect from mere cruelty, mean that he never does it from the pleasure felt in mere suffering, this is also admitted; and it is also admitted and maintained, that no such principle exists in any human bosom. There is no such thing as cruelty or malignity consisting in delight in mere suffering. Every human being has a constitutional susceptibility to the happiness of all sentient beings. To suppose a corresponding susceptibility to the misery of other beings *per se*, is to suppose a contradiction; that is, we should be capable of loving and hating the same thing in the same respect. But cruelty, if it exist at all, must proceed from the purpose to gratify, as it is supposed to do in the present case, some innocent propensity. What then shall we say of such a purpose to inflict torture on insects? What is the difference, in point of principle, between this and the purpose to take the life of a fellow-being, to gratify our innocent propensity for wealth or honor? In both cases it is barefaced selfishness. I need not say that it is a selfishness always witnessed in children, and the objection admits it. Nor need I add, that thus witnessed, it obliges us to affirm that they are completely selfish.

Again: the proneness of children to falsehood, it is said, is the result of example, education, and circumstances. The reply to this is, that example and education are a part of the circumstances; and if children in their *circumstances*, as soon as they discover the connection between falsehood and their own selfish interests, lie and deceive, then it is proof which obliges us to decide that they are supremely selfish.

Without considering other particulars in the conduct of children, these are enough for our purpose. Taking then the very account given of these things by our opponents themselves, they are selfishness in as palpable forms as it can exist. That these characteristics are to be found in all children, at least so early as we are warranted from observation to form any judgment at all of their moral character, will not be denied. But they are acts which bespeak the entire selfishness of the heart, and require us so to judge according to the rule which the Scriptures give and reason sanctions.

In confirmation of the supreme selfishness of children, I might refer to the constant and indispensable necessity of an appeal to their selfishness, in some form, to prevent its outbreak in others. "He that spareth the rod, hateth his son," &c. (vide Prov. xiii. 24). An analysis of all that influence which restrains children and youth from vice, would show that it consists wholly in those considerations which address the selfish principle, and that the love of God is not in them.

We might also rest an argument equally conclusive on the decisive manifestations by children of an indifference and aversion to God.

We say then, that the very characteristics of children which are alleged as virtuous, are mere operations of the selfish principle, and that, according to the rule of judgment which we have stated, the proof is absolute and decisive of the supreme selfishness of the human heart in early childhood.

I proceed to consider—

II. The moral character of man in more advanced age.

Here it is to be remarked, that some of the characteristics alleged in extenuation of the charge of depravity, are themselves mere operations of the selfish principle. But while some of these characteristics are mere operations of selfishness, and as such decisive of the selfish principle, there are others, as honesty, truth, and kindness to neighbors, which cannot be pronounced, from the nature of them simply, to be the effects of selfish principle. They may be selfish or they may not be, so far as the nature of them determines. To prove that they are so, we must resort to collateral evidence and the application of the true rule of judgment.

This is true of the so-called natural affections. These are merely selfish so far as they have any moral quality. For it is to be remarked, that natural affection, contemplated as a physical property, or as subordinated to the love of God as it is in good men, has no more moral quality than the propensity for food. The want of it is not sin, but only an evidence of a sinful heart, as refusing to take food would be.

Here the precise question is (with the exception already made), whether, in every case in which we are authorized to judge of moral character, we are not obliged to pronounce on the existence of the selfish principle to the exclusion of all love to God. Now to authorize a positive judgment, our knowledge of the individual must be either perfect, extending minutely to his whole moral history, or if imperfect, it must extend to something which in its own nature is decisive of moral principle.

That we have that perfect knowledge of any individual which will enable us to judge of his moral principle on the ground of such knowledge, cannot be easily believed. Imperfect however as it is, have we not known in the most faultless of those of our acquaintance, in whom there is no reason to believe that renewing grace has produced any change of moral character, something which amounts to unequivocal proof that the love of God is not in them? Viewing their moral character as it is by nature, as it has been independently of any transformation from the commencement of moral agency, has not a moderate familiarity furnished us the knowledge of some known habitual sin, either of omission or of commission? With all that is fair and unexceptionable, with the exactest honesty and truth, with great liberality to the poor, with compassion for the suffering, and great assiduity in promoting the temporal well-being of a family or neighborhood, have we not found a neglected closet or Bible, or some habitual sensuality, or an utter worldliness of spirit, or insensibility to the spiritual and eternal interests of fellow-beings, or constant violation of the duties of the Sabbath, or at the least, a decisive indifference or aversion to all communion with God in the ways of his appointment? If our knowledge has extended to these things (and if not, we are not competent to make a decision), have we not actually found some one or more of them palpably marking the deportment of the individual, and proving beyond a doubt that his heart is not right with God? There can, I think, be but one answer to this question. What then is the legitimate conclusion from our experience and observation, with respect to the moral character of man? When so moderate a familiarity with others as we have now supposed, detects in those of the most blameless external deportment such decisive marks of ungodliness of heart, when all our acquaintance whom we know equally well are below these in the scale of morality, when there are other hundreds or thousands of whom we know still less, furnishing still more unequivocal proofs of the same fact, what is the legitimate conclusion respecting the moral character of man from experience and observation? Does not the mind at once rest in this result, that similar knowledge OF ALL would detect similar proof of ungodliness, which this degree of knowledge discovers in the most faultless of those who are known? Shall we be told that the fairest specimens have not fallen under our observation, and that others have witnessed what we have not? But this is denying the evidence of *our* experience, and making the experience of others, or rather their testimony concerning their experience, the test of truth. But we will admit the testimony, and challenge our opponent to produce the individual whose moral character by nature is unstained by any allowed or habitual sin. If he is to testify concerning his experience, this must be his testimony. He must not say that there are those whom he *does not know* to be thus guilty, unless he testifies that he does know their entire moral history, for this would be testimony of mere ignorance, when it must be the result of a perfect knowledge of the whole man, and positive to the point of his entire exemption from any known habitual sin. But such testimony cannot be adduced. The proof then from our own experience remains unimpaired. It is all to one single point, *the entire selfishness of the heart*, and that in cases, so far as there is any evidence to the fact, of the most faultless human characters, and there is not a particle of evidence to the contrary. All that can be said with any pretense of weakening our conclusion is, that there are cases to which our knowledge does not extend, and concerning which, from actual knowledge, we come to no conclusion. But what does such ignorance amount to? What if *all* that I know of one individual is, that he is externally blameless in regard to honesty, and truth, and charity; and that knowing more of another who in these respects is equally blameless, I know that he is without the love of God, does this prove that the former possesses it? And if, in every similar case in which my knowledge is more extended than in regard to the first individual, I find all with the moral character of the second, have I not good reason to conclude that the first is in the same predicament?

Here an important principle which the human mind unperverted, unavoidably adopts, and which the Scriptures teach, may be introduced as giving absolute conclusiveness to the argument: "As in water face answereth to face, so the heart of man to man" (Prov. xxvii. 19).

On the foregoing principle rests the conclusiveness of the argument from the history of man, as made known to us by written records or oral testimony. In these ways we come to the knowledge of facts which prove depravity, and we find none which impair the evidence from those which are known.—(Edwards on Original Sin, chap. i. secs. 6, 7, 8; Dwight's Theology, Serms. 29, 30.)

Having thus shown the proper application of the true rule or principle of judging of moral character, I shall now attempt to show, that all men adopt this principle and make this application of it in reference to the very characteristics under consideration, in all cases in which they can be supposed to form an impartial judgment of human character.

On this subject it is believed that there is no want of evidence, but rather a want of candor—not so much error in what men in fact believe, as there is difficulty in bringing them to confess it. We are not willing to criminate others when our sentence condemns ourselves. Still we believe the truth and the evidence may be obtained, and that it may be made to appear, that notwithstanding the common denial of our doctrine in words, the actions of men, which speak louder than words, decisively show the belief of it. Now there is such a thing as what we term a knowledge of human nature—a knowledge of *man* as man. It supposes certain laws of voluntary action, certain principles which are common to all; and the science of human nature is especially conversant with these laws and principles, and presupposes that here is a field capable of being explored, and that in it actual and certain discoveries may be made. The field is actually explored by every man, and to a certain extent with entire success, so that there is in fact no subject better understood by mankind generally, than the commanding practical principle of human nature. The key to the discoveries is, that "as face answereth to face in water, so the heart of man to man." And while each possesses such a knowledge of his own heart, and traces the actions of others in their true bearings, he discovers in these unequivocal manifestations a perfect accordance between one heart and every other. The knowledge is of great practical utility, and is in fact the basis and the directory of all the intercourse between man and man.

Nor in making this estimate of human nature, that is, of *man*, is the uniform conclusion respecting his governing principle at all weakened by any exceptions in the case of the sanctified. These are so few in number, and the manifestations of another and a better spirit are so feeble, fluctuating, and doubtful, that to keep on the safe side of the question, in all practical judgments, these exceptions are not taken into the account. Here then let the inquiry be made, what is the estimate which men form for all the practical purposes of human intercourse, of the commanding practical principle of human nature? Let the inquiry be made in reference to the manifestation of that principle in those acts of honesty, truth, and kindness, which are regarded by many as such lovely features in human nature. If it appear that they do in fact decide, and that they decide according to the true rule of judgment, that these are the dictates of pure selfishness, and in as palpable forms as in acts of rapine and murder, then the question must be settled.

HUMAN SINFULNESS.

V.—ORIGINAL SIN.—VIEWS.

Imputation as a general term.—Not held by the Jews.—Nor by the Greek Church.—Originated in a mistake of Augustine.—Imputation as now used has five significations.—General form in which original sin is received by the Orthodox.—Five different forms in which it is taught.—Importance attached to some of them by some parties among the Orthodox.

The doctrine of Original Sin has been held by theologians in a variety of forms. So different have been these particular forms of the doctrine, that it is difficult to present one which is general and shall be common to them all. The most general form in which it has been held is, that as a consequence of the sin of Adam, a corrupt or depraved nature is propagated to all his posterity. Some who advocate the truth of this general statement, maintain that this corrupt nature is sinful and ill-deserving, while others deny its sinfulness and ill-desert, and regard it as corrupt or depraved only as leading to sin with its ill-desert. Those who maintain this propagated nature to be sinful and ill-deserving, have adopted different views of the mode in which it becomes thus sinful. These, or the more prominent and important of them, may be comprised under the general doctrine of *Imputation;* at least as some have chosen to use this word, though as I think, improperly.

It has been claimed that the doctrine of the Imputation of Adam's sin to his posterity was held by the Jews. The Old Testament however, gives not the least support to such an opinion; while the Chaldaic Paraphrases go no further in the language which they use on the subject, than the idea that temporal death comes on his posterity, on the principle that had they been in the same circumstances as Adam, they would have done as he did,—a principle, as some may suppose, like that of Paul in Heb. vii. 9, 10: "And as I may so say, Levi also, who receiveth tithes, paid tithes in Abraham; for he was yet in the loins of his father," &c. How far this *quasi* assertion of the apostle can have any thing to do with any doctrine of imputed sin, it may be difficult to see.

In the ancient Greek Church the doctrine of Imputation cannot be found. Origen, Chrysostom, and Cyril considered temporal death in this world, not as the *punishment* but as a *consequence* of the sin of Adam. "The Latin Church, on the other hand," says Knapp, "was the proper seat of the strict doctrine of Imputation." This writer, after ascribing the origin of the doctrine to the false mode of interpreting the words of Paul in Rom. v. 12, 13, and particularly to the rendering of ἐφ' ᾧ, *in quo* by the Vulgate, says, "This opinion was then associated with some peculiar philosophical ideas then prevalent in the West, and from the whole, a doctrine *de Imputatione* was formed in a sense wholly unknown to the Hebrews, to the New Testament, and to the Grecian Church." He adds—"We may hence see the reason of the fact, that the Grecian teachers, e. g., those in Palestine, took sides with Pelagius against the teachers of the African Church."

As the word *Imputation* has been and is still used, there are several different forms of it. The more prominent of these are the following:—(1.) The proper doctrine of Imputation as taught by Augustine, and maintained by the western churches, and in their symbols. (2.) The doctrine of Imputation by representation or federal headship, as taught by some Lutheran theologians, and by Witsius in his Economy of the Covenants. (Vide Knapp, vol. 2, p. 49.) (3.) The doctrine of Imputation as founded on the *scientia media* of God, or his foresight of the consent of posterity in Adam's sin. (4.) The doctrine of Imputation by the sovereign transfer of Adam's sin to his posterity, as taught in a work highly recommended by some divines in this country, published under the title of "Gethsemane." (5.) The doctrine called by Dr. Owen, *Putation*—that God considers and treats the posterity of Adam *as if they were guilty*, or had committed his sin; meaning, that they are guilty of that sin only. as being liable to punishment on account of it. How these different forms of the doctrine called *the Imputation* of Adam's sin to his posterity may, as they have been explained by their different advocates, run into each other, it may be difficult if not useless to determine. I propose such notice of each, by fuller explanation, and also by some particular examination of them, as shall at least enable you to judge of their truth by comparing them with the teachings of the Word of God. I shall begin with what I consider the more proper form of the doctrine. This I deem an important preliminary inquiry to our investigation of the doctrine of *the total depravity of man by nature.*

The object of our inquiry then, is to ascertain the general form of this doctrine as taught by the Reformers and those who, after them, have adopted their views, and also the changes and modifications it has undergone by a class of Orthodox theologians within the last forty or fifty years, especially in New England. The general form of this doctrine as taught by the Reformers, and as it has extensively prevailed among the Orthodox since their time, may be thus stated, viz., that all men have a corrupt and sinful nature by birth, which nature is corrupted in Adam.

Rightly to understand the import of this statement of the doctrine, it is necessary to consider it in two parts: one, the corrupt nature of men, which, though considered in itself, or abstractly from our connection with Adam, is not sinful and deserving of punishment, is yet considered as evil and pernicious, as it tends infallibly to that sin or moral evil which does deserve punishment. The other part of the doctrine respects the manner in which this nature is truly and properly esteemed sinful by our connection with Adam. This connection with Adam, according to this doctrine, amounted to a constituted *oneness* between Adam and all his posterity, so that when Adam sinned by knowingly and freely transgressing the divine law, and thus corrupting his nature, all his descendants did in God's estimation also sin in the same manner, thus corrupting their nature. Hence they, being *one* with Adam, *quoad hoc*, though very diverse from him in other respects, are born with a nature which is sinful and corrupt, and which has become so, exactly in that manner in which Adam's nature became corrupt.

While this form of the doctrine of Original Sin, or depravity by nature, has been most prevalent among the Orthodox since the time of Augustine, yet it has been held and taught under some diversity of modification by different individuals of the same school at different periods. So far as I know, it had however not received any important modification as adopted by any considerable portion of the Orthodox community, until since the time of Dr. Hopkins and Dr. Edwards. For the last forty or fifty years, the doctrine has undergone considerable modifications in this country, especially in New England, till the Orthodox clergy in New England almost universally, and to a considerable extent in other parts of this country, have rejected at least one important part of the doctrine, viz., that which represents Adam's posterity as *one* in him and sinning in him. While these have agreed in the rejection of this part of the doctrine, and would also agree in some very general forms of stating the doctrine of *total depravity by nature*, they would differ widely in respect to their more specific forms of statement.

The more prominent and different specific forms of the doctrine of Original Sin, so far as, in my view, they demand particular notice, are the following:

1. The doctrine of Imputation as taught by Augustine.*

2. The doctrine of Putation as taught by the Princeton school, by Storr, and others.

3. The doctrine of a created or propagated *sinful* nature, sometimes called Physical Depravity.

4. The doctrine of a corrupt nature not sinful, but resulting in sin in all cases.

5. The doctrine of voluntary sin, traced by some to divine efficiency, and by others to the innocent constitutional propensities of man in his circumstances. Whether however, this fifth form, in either of its more specific forms, can be properly called original sin, may be supposed by some to admit of a question. Dr. Emmons maintained the first sin of Adam to be the only original sin. As the sin with which the subsequent sin of the race is *in some manner connected* as a consequence, the New Haven divines would probably consent to call it *the original sin*. But in respect to any *original sin* as a predicate of Adam's descendants, they would perhaps agree to call the first sinful volition, or act of each individual, original sin. Hitherto they have designated nothing by the phrase. They maintain still the general doctrine, that *all men are totally depraved* by nature, and this in its true Orthodox meaning; and on this ground claim, on this subject, an Orthodox standing.

In respect to these different specific views, it cannot be pretended, in my own opinion, that, strictly speaking, any one of

* The doctrine of "Spermatic Animalculæ," as maintained by some, or that the race were seminally in Adam, as taught by Dr. Gill and others, I shall pass without further notice.—(Vide "Knapp's Theology," vol. ii. p. 49.)

them is essential to Orthodoxy, since they are each of them adopted to the exclusion of every other by those who are ranked among the Orthodox, and since they all agree in that general form of the doctrine which is opposed by the anti-orthodox. When the question is, what is Orthodoxy on this point? the answer should be such as all who are properly esteemed Orthodox would subscribe to; since, on any other principle, the Orthodox are distinguished from the Orthodox, and not from the opposers of Orthodoxy.

The general forms of stating the doctrine to which the Orthodox as a class or party would subscribe, are such as these, viz., *that all men are depraved by nature;* that all mankind come into the world in such a state, that without the interposition of Divine grace, they will sin in every instance of moral action. All who should subscribe to these would be Orthodox *quoad hoc*, all who should deny would not be.

With respect to *two* of the above-named *specific* statements, viz., physical depravity and constitutional propensities, I know not that any have pretended that either is essential to Orthodoxy, whatever they may have supposed to be essential to truth. With respect to the *first* and *third*, viz., that of our oneness in Adam, and that of physical depravity, etc., each is strenuously maintained by the opposers of Orthodoxy, and by some among the Orthodox themselves, to be essential to Orthodoxy. Whether it be so or not, seems to be the only point which it is necessary to decide that we may answer the question before us, viz., what is the Orthodox doctrine of Original Sin? The inquiries are two, viz.: First, is the doctrine of our oneness in Adam and sinning in him essential to Orthodoxy? This inquiry is answered by the fact already stated, that this doctrine has not only been denied for a long time by the Orthodox of New England, but is also denied extensively, probably by a majority of the Orthodox clergy of the United States.

The other inquiry, viz., whether physical depravity be essential to Orthodoxy, is the topic of principal interest. Decided by the undeniable fact, though very many of the Orthodox ministry and Churches have believed and strenuously inculcated this doctrine, there is no pretense that it has obtained the sanction of any Orthodox Confession of Faith, or is to any extent worthy of the notice of standard Orthodox writers. To the representation that some of this class of theologians held this doctrine, some plausibility may perhaps be given by garbled quotations from their writings, or by unguarded passages which are plainly inconsistent with fuller statements of their views. The doctrine never became a test of Orthodoxy even in New England. It was indeed taught by Dr. Burton, of Vermont, who published a volume in its defense. It was however, strenuously opposed by Dr. Hopkins and Dr. Emmons, and their disciples, among whom were many of the more prominent divines of the country, who, though maintaining that all sin consists in the volitions or voluntary exercises of the mind, never suffered in their reputation for Orthodoxy. Indeed, they themselves strenuously insisted that they were the only consistent Calvinists. Hopkinsionism was indeed strongly disapproved by many of the Presbyterian Church, but chiefly on the ground of other peculiarities of doctrine, *resignation* and *Divine efficiency*, rather than for holding the exercise scheme.

These different forms of the doctrine of Original Sin, I propose to examine hereafter. I deem it however highly important, in the mean time, to ascertain with precision the form of this doctrine, as taught by Augustine, and maintained by the Reformers and the Reformed Churches, with unimportant exceptions, till the present time, and as uncontradicted by any considerable portion of this Church, except in New England, in the time of Hopkins, Emmons, the younger Edwards, and others who followed them.

HUMAN SINFULNESS.

VI.—ORIGINAL SIN.

Views of Augustine, Calvin, and Edwards.

WHAT I now call the proper doctrine of original sin is, generally speaking, the doctrine of the Imputation of Adam's first sin to all his posterity, on the ground of *a constituted personal identity* of Adam and his posterity. I have already given a general explanation of this doctrine. The more full and particular form of this doctrine may be unfolded as follows: God, in creating man, created not merely Adam, but mankind, human nature, Adam and his posterity, as one moral whole, one moral person, determining this oneness or identity by his sovereign constitution. The human race, man as thus created and constituted one moral person, was *created morally upright*, so that, as God's work, what Adam was as *created*, his posterity were also as *created*. The first sin of Adam was thus the sin of all his posterity—their *voluntary act* as truly as it was his. They committed the same sin which Adam committed, both in number and in kind, and on the only equitable principle of imputing sin to any being, it was imputed to Adam and to his posterity,—to Adam because he committed it, and to them because they committed it. Thus the only original sin of Adam's posterity is the sin which each of them, as one moral person with Adam, being like him created upright, committed, and as truly as did Adam commit his original sin, and being then committed by each just as it was by Adam, it was imputed to each just as it was imputed to him. It was the act of each, the sin of each, the fall of each, the apostasy of each, and of all his posterity, just as it was of Adam himself. It is this sin, with all its *corruption and guilt*, and with this *only*, that each of the posterity *is born, not created;* for, as a creature, he, like Adam, was made *morally upright;* so that man, each individual of the race, not God, is the author of his own sin.

Such is the ancient and proper doctrine of Original Sin, which first received its definite and permanent form in the statements of Augustine, in his controversy with Pelagius, early in the fifth century, which by Pope Zosimus, after having pronounced Pelagius sound in the faith, was decreed to be Orthodoxy, was afterward generally adopted by the scholastic theologians, then by the Reformers—by such men as Gomarrhus, Stapfer, Turretin, and others—was introduced into the confession of the Westminster divines, and has been thus perpetuated in the Orthodox church, to a greater or less extent to the present time, having been more ably defended by Jonathan Edwards than by any other advocate.

The first error on this subject began earlier in the Christian church, in the unauthorized assumption, that the apostle in Romans v. 12, &c., asserts, that infants are sinners, or that all men *are born* sinners. Thus Origen and others of the earlier fathers, to account for this sin and depravity of all, before actual sin was supposable, resorted to the theory of pre-existence in another world, when each individual sinned in his own proper person. Augustine however,found as he supposed, the true origin of this depravity or sin in all men at birth, in their prior existence in Adam,as created in him in the manner explained.

Augustine's Language and Views.—He says (on Eph. x. 6), "Quicunque ex illo uno multi in se ipsis futuri erunt, in illo uno unus homo erant"—"They who from that one shall be *many* in themselves, in that one were one man." Again: "We were all in that one man, since we were all that one man who fell into sin, through that woman who was made from him previous to transgression. The form in which we were to live as individuals had not been created and assigned to us, man by man, but that seminal nature was in existence from which we were to be propagated" (De Civ. Dei., xiii. 14). "In Adam all have sinned, as all were that one man" (De Pec. Mer., i. 20). "Infants belong to human nature and are guilty of original sin because human nature sinned in our first parents." Again: "All sinned in Adam; the human race were in the loins of Adam." And also, "Infants derive from him the guilt of sin and the punishment of death." These passages from Augustine are deemed sufficient to unfold his view of original sin. In confirmation of the view ascribed to Augustine, I refer to

Tholuck and Neander. Tholuck says: "Augustine proceeded on the realist view that God did only ONCE CREATE, placing the whole of each species in the first individual, so that all subsequent existence is nothing more than the manifestation and development of what has a previous being. Inasmuch then as at the first the man Adam was, when he fell, both individual and species, the species also fell in him. Acute expositions of this view, and a philosophical application of the Aristotelian principles *de universalibus in re* to the doctrine of Imputation, are to be found among the schoolmen, e. g., Anselm and Odoardus, in 'De peccato originali.'"—(Tholuck on Rom. v. 12—'Εφ' ᾧ, pp. 158–9.) Neander in his Church Hist., vol. ii. p. 609, says: "Augustine supposed, not only that this bondage under the principle of sin, by which sin is its own punishment, was transmitted by the progenitor of the race to his posterity, but also that the first transgression, as an act, was to be imputed to the whole human race; that the guilt and penalty were propagated from one to all. This participation of all in Adam's transgression, Augustine made clear to his own mind in this way: Adam was the representative of the whole race, and bore in himself *the entire human nature* and kind in the germ, since it was from him it unfolded itself. And this theory would easily blend with Augustine's speculative form of thought, as he had appropriated to himself the Platonico-Aristotelian Realism in the doctrine of general conceptions, and conceived of general conceptions as the original types of the kind realized in individual things. Furthermore, his slight acquaintance with the Greek language, and his habit of reading the Holy Scriptures in the Latin translation, led him to find a confirmation of his theory in a falsely translated passage of the Epistle to the Romans, viz., v. 12."

Thus it appears that the ancient and the prevalent doctrine of the Imputation of Adam's sin, until a recent period received its form, as well as derived its origin from the false speculative philosophy of a converted heathen philosopher, who from his ignorance of Greek, and of the use of universal forms of expression, misinterpreted the apostle in Rom. v. 12; supposing him to speak of infants, he applied his ingenuity and philosophy to show that Adam and all his posterity were, *ex ordine Dei*, *one man*, *one moral person*, infants included. and so committed the same sin which Adam committed.

Calvin's Views.—I speak of his views as given in his Institutes, which were written in early life; for, in his Commentary on Rom. v. 12, written in his maturer age, he expressly affirms that the apostle had no thought of infants.* The proposed exhibition of his views will be given, by reading selected passages from his Institutes.

Calvin says, Inst., B. ii. ch. i. secs. 5, 6, p. 299, "We are fallen from our original dignity," i. e., we were all created in Adam "upright," for this was the decisive proof-text; "but we all sinned before we were born, and when born we have the corruption which each contracted in the sin in Eden." There was a vast difference, in the view of the Reformers, between the character in which we were created, and that in which we were born, for we all, on the realistic theory, were created in Adam, and were as pure and holy as he. They use such phrases as "the honors bestowed on us at our creation;" "God at the beginning formed us;" "we cannot think on the primeval dignity," &c.; "in the person of the first man we are fallen," &c. But we are born depraved on account of the transgression which intervened. When Calvin in this chapter, uses the term "*man*," he means the *race* as existent in Adam. "He suffered not alone, but involved all his posterity." "This is that corruption which the fathers call *original sin*, meaning by sin the depravity of a nature originally pure." Again: "Even before we see the light of day, we are in God's sight impure and sinful." "Adam was the root, and we were necessarily vitiated in him." Speaking of our corrupt nature, he distinguished it thus: "Our *nature*, not as created but as vitiated in Adam." "Now let us dismiss those who dare to charge God with their corruptions, because we say that men are naturally corrupt." He says our sin proceeds not from God, and speaks of "our sin in Adam." He speaks of a "natural depravity which did not originate from nature, but is an adventitious quality not innate, but natural in the sense of belonging to all;" "and therefore infants themselves, as they bring their condemnation into the world with them, are rendered obnoxious to punishment by their own sinfulness, not by the sinfulness of another."

* I admire Calvin's intellectual greatness and candor; and especially in changing his opinions on this subject, and on that of limited Atonement, after he had acquired a high theological reputation by his Institutes.

It is plain that Calvin held to no transfer of Adam's sin and guilt to his posterity, they being innocent, but only an imputation, charging, reckoning, as in Rom. v. 13, of each one's own sin to him, the sinning agent. The other, viz., the reckoning of one person's sin to another, as though he committed it, and holding him liable for an act he never perpetrated, is not *Imputation* but *putation*, as Van Mastricht, who knew well the doctrine of Calvin, says (Lib. iv. ch. ii. sec. 10): "Imputatio autem, non consistit in mera *putatione*, quâ Deus putet fœdifragium protoplastorum, non ab ipsis tantum perpetratum fuisse, sed *actualiter* et personaliter, etiam ab omnibus eorum *posteris:* esset enim in hoc error manifestus," &c.

So that the doctrine of the Princeton professors, who give up oneness with Adam, yet retain the sin and liability of his transgression in each of his descendants, is not the Imputation of the Reformers, nor Imputation at all.

President Edwards stated the objection to the doctrine of our oneness or identity in Adam, thus: "That it implies *falsehood*, and contradiction to the true nature of things, as hereby they are viewed and treated *as one* who are *not one*, but wholly distinct" (p. 445).

Now if the doctrine of Edwards is, that Adam and his posterity are viewed by God as one, or what is the same thing in effect, that Adam and his posterity *are one*, when *in truth* they are *not* one, but *wholly distinct*, then his doctrine does imply falsehood, and a contradiction to *the true* nature of things.

"But," says Edwards, "this objection is founded in a false hypothesis and wrong notion of what we call sameness or oneness among created things; and the seeming force of the objection arises from ignorance or inconsideration of *the degree* in which created identity or oneness with past existence, in general, depends on the sovereign constitution and law of the supreme Author and disposer of the universe."

The question then is, what is this *wrong notion* of what we call sameness or oneness among created things, which Edwards ascribes to his opponents? It is plainly, what may be called the common idea or notion of oneness, when applied to any thing or being. What then is the true meaning of the language, what the idea or notion which the mind forms and expresses, when we say of a thing, it is the same now that it was before? Plainly this, that what it was and was not, as a thing, it is now that thing and not another, so that nothing can truly be predicated of it at one time which cannot be at another, except difference of time. If therefore, Adam and his posterity are one thing or being, and if identity or sameness can be *truly* predicated of them at different times, then of that one being nothing can be truly predicated at one time of its existence, considered as a being or thing, which cannot be truly predicated of it at another time of its existence, except difference of time. Now we know that Adam existed before his posterity, and that what he was and all he was as Adam, as a being or thing, he was while his posterity had no existence; and that of course as a being or thing, and in all that he was as a being or thing, he was wholly a distinct and another being from each and all his descendants.

We also know that each one of the posterity of Adam existed after Adam derived existence from Adam as a progenitor or father, and what each was, and all he was as a being, he was distinct from Adam, and not the same being but another. Now with this notion of identity and distinctness, Adam could not be his posterity nor could his posterity be Adam. Of course to say that Adam and his posterity are *one moral being*, is a contradiction to the true nature of things.

But says Edwards, "Created identity or oneness with past existence, in general, depends *in degree* on the sovereign constitution of the Supreme Author and Disposer of the universe." But how is this? He says:

"Some things being most simply considered are *entirely distinct* and *very diverse*, which are yet so united by the established law of the Creator in some respects, and with regard to some purposes and effects, that by virtue of that *establishment* it is with them as if they were one." This is very guarded and very equivocal language, when the question is about the truth and reality of things. Why does not he say absolutely, as the case required, that they are in truth one and the same thing? Instead of this he says, "*it is with them as if they were one.*" What is with them *as if they were one?* Does he mean that we conceive of them and speak of them as if they were one when they are not so in truth? Then while he predicates *diversity* and *distinctness* of them, he also affirms that while we falsely conceive them to be one they are in truth not one.

But in the next sentence he comes to the point in an example of a tree a hundred years old, and which has not perhaps one atom of matter the same. He says directly, that "this tree is *one* plant with the little sprout that first came out of the ground." Here then, with what he calls *entire distinctness and diversity* in things,—viz., of the present component atoms of the tree from the atoms which composed the *sprout* that first came out of the ground,—we have the oneness of two, viz., the tree and the sprout, unequivocally asserted. But then, as if afraid to risk his own assertion in this unqualified form, he retreats, in the conclusion of his sentence, from an absolute assertion of oneness to the conditional proposition, *as if it were one!*

But he comes back in the next sentence to this form of statement, viz., that it has been the pleasure of God *to constitute a union* in these respects and for these purposes, *naturally leading us to look* upon all as *one.*

He gives another example of the same kind in the body of man at forty years of age, as being one with the infant body which first came into the world, from whence it grew, though now constituted of different substance, and the greater part of the substance probably changed scores if not hundreds of times, and though it be now in so many respects *exceeding diverse,* &c., &c., yet God deals with it *as one body.* He gives other examples to show that a thing which when *most simply considered* is entirely distinct and very diverse from another thing, and yet is by divine establishment or constitution, as he says, as if it were one and the same thing, or, as he says, is one and the same thing, or as he says, is treated by God as if it were one and the same thing. Now here four very different predicates are made of the thing which is entirely distinct and very diverse from another thing, viz.: first, that it is with them, that is, with the thing which is entirely distinct from another, and that other from which it is so entirely distinct, "*as if they were one;*" the second, that they are naturally looked upon by us "*as one;*" and third, that they are dealt with by God *as one;* and fourth, that they are one.

Let us look at these different predicates. One is, that in respect to two things which are *entirely distinct* and *very diverse,* "*it is with them as if they were one thing.*" This is certainly true in many cases. We conceive of the supposed sprout and the tree a hundred years old, and speak of them, and in many respects act in regard to them, as if they were one and the same thing, and in these respects *it is with them* as if they were one and the same thing, though in *the truth and reality of things*, *most simply considered*, they are *not* one and the same thing. This is a case in which our conception is that involved in an acquired perception, as when we conceive of the rising and setting of the sun, and involves a rash and false judgment concerning the truth of things, which is corrected by our reason, or a true knowledge of things as they are in truth and reality. The language we use in the case is the language of mere appearance, and our conduct proceeds on a false conception and judgment, as it does in a thousand cases, in which the rash and false judgment, as the basis of our conduct, answer all the purposes of practical life as well as the true conception and judgment. Now what does this amount to? Why simply to this: that the things which are conceived of and spoken of, &c., as one and the same thing at different times, are *not in truth one and the same* thing at different times, but very different things, and that we in so regarding them, regard that to be true and real which is false, and involves a contradiction to the true nature of things. I ask then, is this the oneness and identity of Adam and his posterity intended by Edwards? If so, it is not real,—it is a oneness and identity only in appearance, and to assert a oneness and identity as real and true is to assert a known falsehood; as if one were to say, in view of the known facts in the case, that the sprout and the tree a hundred years old are one and the same thing, or that the sun rises and sets. Though in such cases the mind assents to the truth of the false proposition without reflection, yet the moment we reflect on our actual knowledge we necessarily pronounce the proposition in these cases *false*.

The second predicate of things entirely distinct and very diverse is, "*that they are naturally looked upon by us as one.*" If it can be properly said that it is natural to us to judge rashly and falsely in respect to certain objects of perception, as we in fact do to a great extent, as when we predicate sweetness of sugar, cold of ice, &c., then in the present case it may be truly said, "*that the things so entirely distinct are naturally looked upon by us as one.*" But then, natural or not natural, in so looking upon them, i. e., in so conceiving them, we conceive falsely. They are not, and we know that they are not one.

The third predicate of things entirely distinct, &c., is, that they are treated as if they were one by God. This we admit. But then to say that they are treated by him as if they were *one*, is to concede that they are not one. And the question is, how is it proper or fit that God should treat a human body, which we know is not the same that existed at a previous time, as if it were the same? I answer,—the present distinct and different body is connected with the same soul; the object of inflicting evil on the body is to inflict *evil on the same soul* which committed the sin for which it is inflicted, and this is accomplished by producing certain effects on the present though different body, as truly as were it the same as that which existed in connection with the soul when the sin was committed.

The fourth predicate is, that things which are entirely distinct and very diverse *are one.* This we deny without qualification, maintaining that there is no sense or meaning of the language in which it can be true. The tree a hundred years old is not one with the sprout from the acorn; the body of a man is not one with the body of the infant; and so of every example which Edwards gives of distinctness and diversity, and also of oneness. It is true, and this is all that is true in this case, we, in common modes of conceiving and speaking of these things which we know on due reflection to be entirely distinct and diverse, conceive falsely and speak falsely; just as when we say the water runs, the kite flies, the sun rises and sets, sugar is sweet, and ice is cold. The error in the mind of Edwards, in predicating oneness of things entirely distinct and diverse, consists in assuming that the language which men adopt to describe appearances merely is the language of truth, or rather, that the conceptions of things which we form in our rash and hasty judgments of reality, and which rest on mere appearances, are true conceptions of reality—in other words, that what on due reflection we know to be false, is also true, and known to be true.

Edwards, Calvin, and others, have yet another mode of presenting the subject of the identity of Adam and his posterity; as when they speak of God as having formed or created *us*, or *the species*, or *human nature*, when he created Adam and Eve. Calvin, B. ii. secs. 1–3, and other places. Edwards when he speaks of the sin by which the species rebelled (p. 437), and of man *as made upright*, meaning, as he says, *the species* which

God at first made upright. Now this must mean one of these two things: either that God, when he created Adam and Eve, created them upright, and in so doing created that kind or sort of a being whom we call *man*, upright; or it must mean that when he created Adam and Eve, he created the individuals who constitute the human species, and so created the species, all men, upright. In the first meaning all that is said is, that the two individuals of a species were created upright, without intending to predicate the same fact in any sense or in any respect of *the posterity* of the two individuals. Was this then their meaning? Plainly not. The mere assertion of such a fact *simply* respecting Adam and Eve, was not at all to the purpose of these writers. The object of asserting that the species (that man, &c.) was created upright, was to assert a fact which should clear God from the charge of creating the descendants of the first pair *sinners*, and so being *the author of sin;* a fact which would bear them out in saying that "God formed *us* in his own image" (Calv., pp. 258, 260, 265, *et. al.*); that the sin of one was common to all (p. 263); that our nature, when spoken of as corrupt, is not characterized *as created* by God (p. 265); that this corruption is not the work of God, but the consequence of OUR degenerating from OUR primitive condition; that *man* was favored with rectitude by the divine goodness (p. 269); that it is a depravity which did not originate from nature, but an adventitious quality or accident, and not a substantial property originally innate (p. 270); that it was the same sin in number and in kind as committed by Adam and his posterity; that it is not a guilt additional to that of the first apostasy, but identical with it—the sin by which *the species* rebelled; that moral dispositions must be *concreated* with human nature, though God did not create a sinful disposition, &c., &c. (vide Edwards). Now to what purpose does Edwards say these things, "the sin by which the species rebelled, if the act of rebellion was only that of Adam and Eve, as human beings, and in no respect that of their posterity?" To what purpose that the sin of the first apostasy became the sin of the posterity, *their* sin, *in reality* and propriety, by virtue of *a union*, &c.; that this sin is not *theirs* merely because God *imputes* it to them, but is *truly* and *properly* theirs, and on *that ground* God imputes it to them?

HUMAN SINFULNESS.

VII.—TOTAL DEPRAVITY BY NATURE.

Plan of discussion.—Different theories explained.—(1.) Imputed sin.—(2.) Putative sin.—(3.) Want of original righteousness.—(4.) Divine efficiency.—(5.) Physical depravity: arguments against this.—(*a.*) Does not explain the fact.—(*b.*) Is self-contradictory.—(*c.*) Disproved by the proof alleged in its support.—(*d.*) Makes God the author of sin.—(*e.*) Inconsistent with acknowledged truths.—(*f.*) Not taught in the Scriptures. Gen. v. 3; Job xiv.; xv. 14; Ps. li. 5; lviii. 3; John iii. 6.

The present inquiry assumes the fact of the total depravity of all men, and respects simply the ground or reason of the fact.

Those who have maintained the general doctrine of depravity *by nature*, have understood the phrase by *nature* in different senses, and thus have ascribed the fact to different specific causes, or have adopted different specific theories to account for the fact.

My design is—

I. To refute some of these theories; and,

II. To state and defend what I regard as the true account of the universal sinfulness of mankind.

I. To refute some of these theories.

1. The theory or doctrine of imputed sin. This doctrine I have already described. I propose to consider it in another place, viz., when I come to inquire into the connection between Adam's sin and that of his posterity.

2. The theory of putative sin. This theory maintains that men are born depraved, without ill-desert, and are nevertheless justly liable to punishment on account of Adam's sin. A theory which maintains an *innocent depravity*, *sinless sin*, *guiltless guilt;* a just liability to punishment without ill-desert deserves no further consideration. (Vide Storr's Biblical Repertory.)

3. The theory which represents the depravity of man as consisting in the want of righteousness, and this to be sinful or ill-deserving. We have already exposed the unsoundness of this theory, by showing that the want of righteousness is nothing,

and that sin can be predicated only of positive mental exercise or action.

4. The theory of direct divine efficiency. This theory concerning the origin of human volitions, considered as *a philosophical* theory, I have already examined, and have attempted to show that it is both unphilosophical and contrary to the decisions of common sense. If this be so, and if the language of the Scriptures which is supposed to teach this theory or doctrine will bear any other meaning, then this is not its true one; since we must not do violence to both common sense and sound philosophy, by giving to the language of the Scriptures a meaning which both forbid.

According to this principle I remark, that the language of the Scriptures which is supposed to support this theory, does not support it; for it will bear another meaning, and therefore requires it. The language of the Scriptures is the language of common use, and is to be interpreted as such. But nothing is more common in all languages, especially that of the Bible, than to ascribe to one that which he does, not by his own direct efficiency, but by the direct agency of another. *Quod facit per alium, facit per se.* Solomon built the temple, but not by his own direct agency. God is said to have given the law on Mount Sinai, but Stephen says (Acts vii.) that it was given by the ministry of angels. In 2 Samuel xxiv. 1, we are told that God moved David to number Israel; but in 1 Chron. xxi. 1, the same thing is ascribed to Satan.* Similar instances might be cited. These are enough to show that the mere form of expression decides nothing on the point before us, and that we are left to the decisions of common sense and sound reason. If these decide against the doctrine of the production of sin by direct divine efficiency, and we have shown that they do, the point is settled. The language of the Bible does not teach this doctrine.

That God, as providential Governor, purposes all sin, and that this is consistent with his moral perfection and the free agency of man, we have already shown. Such being the providential purposes of God, it is in perfect accordance with the usage of language, in similar cases, to ascribe the event of

---

* In respect to the point at issue, vide Eph. ii. 2. The spirit that now *worketh* in the children of disobedience (ἐν ἔργῳ).

sin to God; and this, while the form of the phraseology is not designed to ascribe, and the nature of the subject forbids us to ascribe it to him in any respect which is dishonorable, and still less the least direct efficiency in the production of sin; nay, even while in other instances, and for other purposes, it also perfectly accords with usage to deny in terms equally absolute, that God purposes sin rather than holiness in its stead. (Ezek. xviii.) As the foundation for submission, confidence, and joy under the government of God, it were immeasurably desirable that the providential purposes of God should be known to extend, in some respect, to all actual events. To exhibit for these useful practical purposes this truth, is the obvious design of those scriptural declarations which we are now considering. At the same time when this truth is perverted, or rather to prevent its perversion, it is in other instances, so far as the mere phraseology is concerned, though not really, absolutely denied. Nor is such a use of language either unusual among men in like cases, nor in any respect unjustifiable or to be wondered at. The known nature of the whole subject, what God is and what he is not, as a providential and moral Governor, what holiness and sin are, what men are as free moral agents, together with common sense and common honesty, are sufficient to prevent a false interpretation of the language in either case; to prevent, on the one hand, the denial of God's providential government as the basis of confidence and joy under all the evils of life; and on the other, such views of the *mode* of its execution as are palpably inconsistent with the perfection of his Moral Government over free and accountable agents. *Language*, *words*, are nothing; they may be, according even to the best usage, contradictory in the most palpable form, provided the meaning be plain and consistent.

It may be said, that according to some of the principles now adopted, the doctrine of divine influence in the production of holiness must be rejected. This I readily concede, provided there are no peculiar reasons for receiving it, which do not exist for receiving the theory under consideration. That there may be such reasons is apparent, since in the first place the nature of holiness and sin are so essentially different, that God may do that consistently with his moral perfection, to render holiness certain, which he cannot do to render sin certain. If we suppose God to have established that general form of Moral

Government over men, which, as applicable to the whole race, is best fitted to the ends of infinite wisdom and goodness, we may still suppose such occasional changes in it, even by miraculous interposition, as shall render holiness certain when sin had otherwise existed, without any impeachment of the divine character. But to suppose God thus to interpose to render sin certain when holiness had otherwise existed, is to impute to him the character of a tempter to sin, or of the author of sin, in a manner highly dishonorable, and even criminal. In the second place, *the mode* of divine influence in the production of holiness may be very diverse from *that* which the present theory asserts respecting the production of sin. *This* renders sin necessary by a physical necessity, and destroys therefore its nature. *That* may secure the existence of holiness in men in perfect consistency with the nature of holiness. If it be said that God can also produce sin in the *same mode* of agency now supposed, I answer, that this is to abandon the theory of efficiency now under consideration. Besides, to suppose a divine interposition to produce sin, like that which is now supposed in the production of holiness, implies that otherwise there had been holiness, and holiness in the circumstances in which God required it,—a supposition which is liable to the objection that it makes God a tempter to sin, or a blameworthy author of it.

If it be asked here, whether there is *no conceivable mode* in which divine influence may render the existence of sin certain, consistently with the moral perfection of God and the accountable agency of man, I answer, that I know not but there may be. To suppose such an influence, which in the mode of it should be a part of the established system of things, and which man as a moral agent under the motives to holiness has power to resist, may, for aught I know, be as consistent with God's perfection and man's free agency, as an influence which, though resulting from motives or constitutional propensities merely, renders sin certain. But to suppose such an influence is not only wholly gratuitous in regard to evidence, but is useless for every purpose of doctrinal consistency, and so perplexing, so difficult of explanation, and so remote from the ordinary notions of the human mind, that we may safely say that it cannot be found in the Bible; that it ought never to be introduced into popular instruction, or to become in any instance an article of faith. But, in the third place, there may be a peculiar phraseology adopted by the sacred writers respecting the agency of God in the production of holiness, which shall oblige us to ascribe holiness, though we do not ascribe sin, to such agency. What is true in this respect we shall have occasion to inquire hereafter.

5. The theory of physical depravity.

This theory, according to our preceding remarks, has not been adopted to any such extent by standard Orthodox writers as to entitle it to special consideration. So many however among the Orthodox have adopted it, and even strenuously contended that it is the only rational and scriptural account of human sinfulness, that it deserves some attention.

The theory is, that God creates man with a physical or constitutional property or attribute of the soul, which consists in a propensity, taste, relish, or disposition to sin, and which is in itself sinful, and the cause of all sin. (Vide Woods' Essay.)

We have already had occasion so far to consider this theory as to show that sin is not predicable of any physical or constitutional property of the soul. It may be well however to examine it still further, as a theory designed to account for human sinfulness. Considered as a theory, it is in my own view liable to the following objections:

First—It gives no account of what it professes to account for. The object of the theory is to account for sin. But how is this done by tracing all sin to a previous sin? If this constitutional propensity, taste, relish, or disposition is itself sin, how is it the cause of all sin? This plainly cannot be, unless this sin be the cause of itself, which is absurd. Nor is this all. According to strict truth all sin consists in a *sinful disposition*. Neither external specific acts, nor the specific volitions to perform them, have any moral quality, viewed abstractly from the *disposition* which prompts them. The inquiry therefore, *whence is sin*, can have no real and proper meaning unless it include the sinful disposition itself. The present theory then, teaches that *all sin* is the cause of *all sin*, and therefore gives no rational account of any sin. Besides, every theory which professes to account for sin must either involve the palpable absurdity of making sin the cause of all sin, or give no account of the cause of all sin, or trace it to some cause which is not sin. The present theory therefore, view it in what light you will, leaves the inquiry, *whence comes sin* or depravity in man, just where it finds it. The only import which the language used can have is, that all sin *except the sinful disposition* is to be traced to the sinful disposition. But all sin consists in the sinful disposition itself. But how can this be, except all sin be traced to all sin? But to the main question, or rather to the only real and proper question, viz., *whence comes this sinful disposition?* it does not even in pretense give an answer.

Secondly—This theory asserts what is self-contradictory and absurd, and therefore impossible in the nature of things, and this in two respects. It asserts that a created property of the soul is sinful; and also that this created property is a propensity to sin, meaning by the latter, that sin as such is the object of the propensity; the absurdity and impossibility of both we have already sufficiently shown.

Thirdly—The only argument alleged in support of this theory proves it to be false. This argument is relied on with so much confidence that it claims a careful consideration. It consists in appeal to the decisions of the common sense of mankind in all nations and ages, and of the Scriptures also, by which it is claimed that all actions, whether virtuous or vicious, are to be traced to an antecedent disposition, temper, or affection of the mind, which is before action as a tree is before the fruit, and as a fountain is before the stream.* To the truth of this proposition I most unhesitatingly and unequivocally subscribe. Reason, common sense, and the word of God fully support it. But then the question is, what is the import of the proposition, as one sanctioned by common sense and the Scriptures? Particularly, what is meant by *all actions?* This term is in common use applied to what we have had occasion to denominate subordinate actions, whether mental or external, and if we ask for facts which evince the truth of the proposition before us, we are and must be exclusively referred to those instances in which the actions that proceed from the disposition are subordinate. For example, we are told that acts of fraud and lying, of theft and murder, which are perpetrated for the attainment of money are to be traced to an *avaricious disposition;* the acts of the hero and conqueror to an *ambitious disposition*, and the acts of men, the object of which is to obtain worldly good, to *a worldly disposition.* Now these are the facts, and in kind

---

* Vide Edwards on Original Sin, p. 259, *sqq.*; compare p. 166.

the only facts that can be appealed to in support of the proposition before us. They show beyond all question that the actions which proceed from the *disposition* are of that class which we call specific acts; and also, that the disposition, temper, or affection of mind is itself an act of preference. For what is an *avaricious disposition* but a preference of money; and what is an ambitious disposition but a preference of fame or honor; and what a worldly disposition but a preference of worldly good? I ask for an instance, in which, according to popular use, the word *disposition*, *temper*, *affection of mind*, or any synonymous term, is used to denote that which is moral, and as the cause or source of moral actions, and in which it does not denote a mental preference? No such instance can be adduced. Of course the very argument, or rather the facts appealed to in the argument for the theory under consideration, overthrow this theory. They show that the *disposition*, *temper*, *affection of mind*, call it what you will, which is universally acknowledged to be antecedent to actions, and which is itself moral, and determines also the moral quality of actions, is itself a *mental preference*. It is then a mental act,—as really an act of the agent as are the acts which it dictates. It is therefore *not* a constitutional property of the soul. The theory which maintains that it is such is therefore false, and is decisively shown to be so by the very argument and the only argument which is alleged in its support.

The argument derived from the Scriptures on this point is substantially the same as that now considered. It is founded in those texts which trace specific actions to the heart; such as these: "Out of the heart proceed evil thoughts, murders, adulteries, fornications, thefts, false-witness, blasphemies" (Matt. xv. 19). "A good man out of the good treasure," &c. I ask then, what do the Scriptures mean when they speak of the heart in such a connection? What does such language mean in common usage? What but the governing purpose or affection of the man; that supreme regard for some object or end as his chief good which controls and dictates the whole course of specific moral action. What is a proud heart, or an avaricious heart, or a worldly heart, but a heart whose supreme affection is fixed on the objects specified by the epithet connected with it, i. e., on reputation, on wealth, on the world? But the supreme love of an object is a preference for that object to all others. It is of course an act of a voluntary agent; and therefore is not and cannot be a constitutional property of that agent. While therefore the Scriptures and common sense concur, the world over, in tracing all subordinate actions to the heart, to the *disposition*, &c., there is nothing like evidence to the point, that this thing called heart, disposition, &c., is a constitutional property of the soul. On the contrary, the meaning of the language in every such case, and therefore *the fact* is, that there is a mental preference, a real choice, an act of the voluntary agent, in which some one object or end is preferred to every other. The Scriptures and common sense then concur in the decision, that the theory of physical depravity is false.

Fourthly—This theory exhibits God as the author of sin in a manner most dishonorable to himself and revolting to the human mind. The mode in which it represents him as producing sin in his creatures is not that of temptation (which, whatever may be the guilt of the tempter, does not of course exonerate the sinner from blame), but it is by a creative act. Of course it excludes wholly and absolutely all agency and action on the part of the sinner—every thing of the nature of co-operation and concurrence; and he becomes a subject of sin, as the mere passive recipient of it, by the act of his Maker. Such a mode of production implies also, on the part of him that produces the sin, an unqualified preference of the sin produced to holiness in its stead. And what a view of God is this! Allowing that sin, guilt, really pertains to the created property of the soul, to what agent does the guilt of it belong? That the question may be truly answered, I ask, who designed it,—who produced it? Not man, but his Maker. Why? From a direct and unqualified preference of sin. How? Not in a manner that involves the least particle of responsibility on the part of the creature, since he has no more power to avoid sin than to avoid existence. No demon can be conceived to be so exclusively and so criminally the author of sin in others as God is represented to be by this theory. The force of this argument is derived from the alleged MODE of God's producing sin, viz., that it is A MODE which necessarily involves on his part a preference of *sin to holiness*, all things considered. We have already seen that he may decree sin without this dishonorable preference of sin to holiness. Not so, if he creates or propagates it.

Fifthly—This theory is inconsistent with many acknowledged truths.

1. It is inconsistent with natural ability, and of course with human responsibility—no natural ability to act right.

2. It is inconsistent with moral inability, for this implies natural ability.

3. It is inconsistent with total depravity. There cannot be total depravity without accountability.

4. It is inconsistent with the principle, that the will is as the greatest apparent good. No good in sin *per se*, or as distinguished from *natural* good, and of course no apparent good.

5. It makes sin good in itself, and the only real good to man as a moral being.

6. It is inconsistent with facts—e. g., the first sin of Adam.

7. It is inconsistent with law. God should prohibit the propensity.

8. Motives, the terms of salvation, &c., are a mockery.

9. It is inconsistent with the necessity of Regeneration by the Holy Spirit, the only change necessary being not a moral, but a constitutional change.

10. It involves the Arminian dogma of grace to make man a moral agent.

11. It supports the Arminian doctrine of the self-determining power of the will; the object of the propensity being a sinful volition or choice, we cannot choose to gratify this propensity but by choosing a sinful choice.

12. To sin must be the chief end of man. (Vide "Christian Spectator," 1832, p. 456.)

Lastly—The passages of Scripture which are supposed to teach this doctrine do not teach it. Before I proceed to examine them, I would state a principle of interpretation which is applicable to all, and which I shall have occasion to apply in the argument, viz., *that the language will bear another meaning than that which asserts the doctrine of physical depravity, and that this fact, in connection with the absurdity of the doctrine and the law of usage, is decisive that they require another meaning.* By applying this principle to this class of texts, I would not intimate, that if we allow the doctrine of physical depravity not to be an absurdity, that the texts alleged would support it. On the contrary, I shall attempt to show that if it be admitted that the doctrine is free from all absurdity, they furnish it no support.

I now proceed to examine these texts.

Gen. v. 3: "And Adam begat a son in his own likeness, after his image." It is wholly gratuitous to assert, that "likeness" or "image" in this text denotes a resemblance or sameness in moral character, for it may be that of constitutional properties as distinguished from moral character. Nor would it be a mark of weakness in the historian, as some pretend, to tell us that man who was at first created in this respect, like his Creator, begat a son like himself. It has been often said, that we cannot suppose Moses to utter so trivial a fact as that Adam begat a son, who was, *in kind*, the same being, &c. But this is contrary to fact in other cases. (Vide Gen. i. 24, &c.) The writer did think it important to tell us, that like produced like in other things. Nor is the statement of this universal law trivial. Let the objector read Gen. ix. 6, 1 Cor. xi. 7, James iii. 9, and Acts xvii. 28, and then say whether it be a mark of weakness to utter the truth, that man has a nature that likens him to God. Vide Doederlein: "Gen. v. 1–3, teaches that man who bore the likeness of the Divinity, begat a son like himself, exalted by the same endowments and privileges" (vol. i. p. 578). According to the principle stated then, this text requires another meaning than that now opposed. For the third verse asserts that Adam begat a son "in his own likeness," i. e. (ver. 1) in the likeness of God. Again, if we admit likeness in moral character to be intended, the text teaches nothing like the doctrine of physical depravity. It does not decide in what the moral character consisted, what was the proximate cause of it, nor *when* it commenced. Nor, if it be conceded that it decides that it commenced *at birth*, does it affirm that it consisted in physical depravity, rather than in voluntary action. If we are obliged to suppose one or the other, the latter is by far the most rational. But to say that a father begat a son who, in moral character, was like himself, is not saying that which obliges us to discard both reason and common sense in order that we may understand what is said. Accordingly, such men as Calvin, Edwards, &c., who held that we are *born* sinners, believed that we become sinners by sinning in Adam, being one with him; nothing being more remote from their thoughts than created sin.

Job xiv. 4 and xv. 14: "Who can bring a clean thing out of an unclean? Not one." "What is man that he should be clean, or he which is born of a woman, that he should be righteous?" The interpretation given by Morus of the former of these texts is, "Who can make that holy, which is so plainly unholy?" But conceding that these texts assert, as we will admit the last clause of the latter does, the moral impossibility that sinful parents should have any but sinful offspring, that is, that they certainly will be sinners, still this amounts merely to the fact that all who are born into the world become sinners; and neither fixes the *time* nor the *manner* in which they become so. The import of these passages is therefore fully exhausted, without supposing them to teach the doctrine of physical depravity.

Ps. li. 5: "Behold, I was shapen in iniquity, and in sin did my mother conceive me." David here uses figurative phraseology. If the language be literally interpreted, it is rather an imputation of sin to his mother than a confession of his own, and contradicts all those texts which teach that sin begins at birth. Besides, if sin consist in acting or doing, then the language cannot be literally interpreted without contradicting the apostle, who decides that children, before they are born, do neither good nor evil (Rom. ix. 11). Or rather, interpreting this declaration of the apostle correctly, it is an unqualified denial that children before birth are the subjects of sin at all, since otherwise his reasoning in this instance amounts to nothing. We are then obliged to consider the language of the Psalmist as figurative, and either to exclude wholly the notion of sin prior to birth, or else deny the principle laid down by the apostle. For, if there is another kind of sin than *doing evil*, then he reasons inconclusively, and contradicts himself, according to the common interpretation of Rom. v. 12. Obviously then, the Psalmist here uses figurative phraseology, in which he confesses that he had sinned from a very early period of life, as it were from the very beginning. (Vide Morus, vol. i. p. 448.)

Conceding however that the passage does, in violation of every dictate of sound reason and common sense, assert the existence of sin before birth, still it does not decide in what the sin consisted, but leaves us with what of reason and common sense may remain, to decide whether it consisted in physical depravity, or in voluntary action; and this, if indeed it must consist in one or the other, with a strong balance of probability in favor of the latter, since the former involves a contradiction in the nature of things.

Ps. lviii. 3: "The wicked are estranged from the womb, they go astray as soon as they be born, speaking lies." If this passage is to be literally interpreted, still it does not teach the doctrine of physical depravity, for the sin ascribed to the wicked is that which consists in action, viz., in going astray by speaking lies. But the language is obviously figurative, since children neither go nor speak at their birth. Common sense therefore, which must determine the true meaning of the passage, limits it to this general and indefinite import, that the wicked are estranged from God at a very early period, even as early as the commencement of moral agency and moral action. On the true import of the Hebrew phrase, "from the womb," see Morus, vol. i. p. 447. He supposes that this language denoted that the thing spoken of showed itself early, had become inveterate, that it had not lately begun, or in one instance, but was of very frequent occurrence. He cites (Ps. xxii. 9–11, and Job xxxi. 18) some objections to this application of the first of these texts; particularly, the marginal rendering is, "thou keptest me in safety." John ix. 34, he considers as a strong description of a man very wicked; and as a form of speaking which shows the design and import of such phraseology among the Jews. Kuinoel thinks differently of this passage. (Vide his Comment. on John ix. 2.)

John iii. 6: "That which is born of the flesh, is flesh." (Vide Kuinoel *in loc.*) "In supposing yourselves the partakers of the blessings of Messiah's kingdom, because you are the children of Abraham, you greatly err. He that is born of men, is a man; you therefore, as Jews, have no superior excellence, nor are better fitted for the happiness of Messiah's kingdom than others. You therefore must be born again, since the qualifications for this kingdom are very diverse from any thing that comes by natural descent." That the passage will bear even this import I see no reason to deny. At the same time a further meaning, viz., your natural birth secures a sinful character, and therefore you must be born again, will, I think, better accord with the analogy of faith. The word σάρξ, in the last instance, has probably the same signification as σαρκικόν, and the meaning of the passage is, that every man who is born into the world falls under the dominion of his constitutional appetites; in other words, becomes a sinner. I need not say how remote such a doctrine is from that of physical depravity.

If the language of the Bible was even more direct, if it asserted that men sin *as soon as* they are born, it would not admit of the doctrine of physical depravity, nor even properly understood, assert the very *instant* in which sin begins.

HUMAN SINFULNESS.

VIII.—TOTAL DEPRAVITY BY NATURE.—(*Continued.*)

True account.—II. Theory explained.—1. No property of the soul sinful.—2. Nature not corrupted by oneness with Adam.—3. Constitutional propensities not sinful.—4. Excitement of propensities not sinful.—5. Disposition, which is the cause of sin, not sinful.

I PROCEED to consider as I proposed—

II. The true account of the universal sinfulness of mankind.

Remarking then, that the Orthodox universally will subscribe to the general proposition, that mankind are depraved by nature, while all others would deny the truth of it, and while the Orthodox would differ among themselves in regard to the specific import of the phrase *by nature*, I now propose, first, to explain what I understand to be the true import of the phrase in the proposition, that mankind are depraved by nature; and, secondly, to vindicate the explanation.

First—To explain the phrase *by nature.*

When then I affirm, that all mankind are totally depraved *by nature*, I mean, *that such is their constitution or nature that in all the appropriate or natural circumstances of their existence, they will uniformly sin from the commencement of moral agency.*

It is here to be remarked, that according to this explanation of the doctrine of depravity *by nature*, the depravity or sinfulness of mankind does not *consist in* any thing which can be called *nature*, in the primary sense of the word. Nor can this be said without the most palpable impropriety in the use of language, nor without the most palpable absurdity in things.

When it is said that mankind are depraved by nature, or are sinners by nature, &c., the obvious design is to describe the cause, ground, or reason of their depravity, and the language specifies this cause, ground, or reason to be *nature.* The depravity is therefore said to be *by* nature, not to consist in nature; to result from nature as its cause or reason. To say then that *nature* is depraved, or that depravity consists *in nature*, is to confound the effect with its cause. If the proposition that mankind are depraved by nature is true, in the only possible meaning of the language, then the proposition that *nature* or *their nature* is depraved or sinful, if the word nature be used in the same import, is most palpably false; since this is to say, that the cause of depravity or sin, i. e., of all sin in man, is itself sin. More particularly I would say, that the proposition that mankind are depraved by nature cannot mean either of the following things:

(1.) It cannot mean that any attribute or property of the soul—any thing which is either *created* or *propagated* as a property of the human mind, is sinful. Aside from the monstrous and revolting absurdity of supposing God to create a sinful nature in men, and to damn them for the very nature he creates, the Scriptures unequivocally teach that all men are now created *in the image of God* (James iii. 9).

(2.) The doctrine cannot mean that mankind have a sinful nature which they have corrupted by being one in Adam, and by acting in his act, or sinning in his sin. To believe that Adam and his posterity are *one moral person*, or *one moral being*, and that by virtue of this personal identity, all Adam's descendants acted in his act or sinned in his sin—as truly in God's estimation committed the first sin of Adam as he did—are as truly guilty of that sin, as *justly* exposed to punishment on account of it, as Adam himself, and did as really by acting in that act, corrupt their nature as Adam corrupted his,—I say to believe this, I must first renounce the reason my Maker has given me, and then disbelieve the oath of God to the contrary, entered upon the record, (Ezek. xviii. 3, 4.)

(3.) Nor can the doctrine imply that any of *the constitutional propensities* of the mind are sinful. Sin is not predicable of constitutional propensities, but only of the choice to gratify them in contravention of the divine will. All these propensities were in Adam when perfectly holy,—they would belong to every human being if perfectly holy. The *man* Christ Jesus possessed every one of them, for "he was tempted *in all points* like as we are, yet without sin."

(4.) Nor does the doctrine teach *that any degree of excitement* in these propensities, or *any desires* for their gratification, prior to the choice or preference of it, is sinful. The man who always triumphs over *the excitement* of them—who duly subordinates all his desires of inferior good to the will of God, is a perfect man. This form of self-government is the substance of all duty ; and the greater the propensity, the stronger the desire for the forbidden good; if governed, controlled, denied by the will, the nobler the act of obedience. "He that ruleth his spirit is better than he that taketh a city." "The trial of your faith is precious." "Blessed is the man that endureth temptation."

(5.) Nor does the doctrine teach that there is any *disposition*, propensity, or tendency to sin, which is the cause of *all* sin, and which is itself sinful. There is an obvious difference between *a disposition, propensity, or tendency to sin* which is prior to *all* sin, and *a sinful disposition.* There are in fact both. There is what may be truly and properly called a disposition, or tendency, or propensity to sin, which is prior to and the cause of *all* sin in man. And there is also, as *a consequence* of this disposition or propensity to sin, what with equal propriety may be called *a sinful disposition*, which is the true cause of all *other* sins, *itself* excepted, i. e., all that can be called wrong-doing in executive action. Now of the former disposition or propensity to sin which is the cause of the latter, i. e., of the *sinful* disposition, I say it is not sinful ; all the sin pertains to the latter. All sin must have a cause. The first sin must have a cause ; which cause can neither be morally right nor wrong—cannot itself be sin. The cause of all sin, even of the first sin, itself sin ! Whence then came the first sin ? Do you say from a previous sin, as its cause ? Then you say, there is a sin before the first sin. The fallen angels and our first parents were once holy. Whence came their first sin ? Do you still say from a previous sin ? And what sort of philosophy, reason, or common sense is this ? A sin before the first sin—sin before all sin ! Do you say there must be *difficulties* in theology ? I ask, must there be *self-evident absurdity*, even the most palpable *nonsense ?**

* The whole embarrassment on this part of the subject results from the different *senses* of the words *disposition* and *propensity*, in their various applications and connections. Thus if we speak of a *disposition* or *propensity to sin* as the *cause* of *all* sin, or as Edwards says, "as a prevailing liableness to sin," the *disposition* and *sin* are so distinguished as cause and effect, the former being spoken of as the cause of *all* sin, that it is perfectly plain that we cannot mean that *the disposition to* sin is itself sin. But if we speak of a disposition to sin as the cause of overt acts of sin, as acts of fraud, falsehood, &c., &c., then we mean a *sinful* disposition, a disposition involving the preference or choice of its object ; this latter disposition being the sum and substance of all sin, and the consequence or effect of a disposition to sin in the former import of the word. This is the true *usus loquendi*, a due attention to which only can save theologians from the most palnable absurdities.

HUMAN SINFULNESS.

IX.—TOTAL DEPRAVITY BY NATURE.—(*Continued.*)

True theory further explained.—Theory thus explained, defended.—(1.) Exempt from absurdity.—(2.) Explains the facts.—(3.) Consistent with the universality of human sinfulness.—(4.) Is Orthodox.—Quotations from Edwards.—(5.) Supported by the Scriptures.—Objections considered.—(1.) Universality of sin does not prove depravity by nature.—Objection considered under several particulars.—(*a.*) Occurrence of sin in Adam.—(*b.*) Freedom of will.—(*c.*) Bad example.—(*d.*) Circumstances.—(*e.*) Necessity of trials.—2d Objection: Inconsistent with free agency.—3d Objection: Inconsistent with the moral perfection of God.

Having examined and attempted to refute some of those theories respecting the fact of human depravity which I deem false, I now proceed to consider, as I proposed, the true account of the universal sinfulness of mankind.

Remarking then, that the Orthodox universally will subscribe to the general proposition that mankind are depraved *by nature*, while all others would deny the truth of it, and while the Orthodox themselves would differ in regard to the true import of the phrase, *by nature*, I propose to state and explain what I understand by this phrase, and to vindicate the statement.

When I say that mankind are depraved *by nature*, I mean that the depravity which I have already described and proved to pertain to mankind, *is truly and properly traced to the physical or constitutional propensities of man for natural good which belong to man, as a man, in the circumstances of his existence as the cause or occasion of it;* or thus: *that certain properties of man for natural good, which constitute a part of his nature whether he be sinful or holy, with the appropriate circumstances of his existence, are the ground, reason, cause, or occasion of his depravity.*

By this however, I do not intend that these propensities become the cause or occasion of sin, viewed abstractly from their objects, or from the circumstances of temptation in which man is placed; since it is obvious, that propensities without objects to excite them, can neither evince their existence nor become the occasion of sin. Nor do we ever in common speech, when we ascribe an event to the nature of any thing, exclude the circumstances in which that thing is placed, or in which its nature acts and shows itself. Nor, on the other hand, when in common speech, we ascribe an event to the *circumstances* of a thing in distinction from its *nature*, do we exclude its nature from all connection with the event; since neither the nature of the thing without its circumstances, nor the circumstances of the thing without its nature, would be followed by the event. So that, in strict metaphysical or philosophical language, both *nature* and *circumstances* are the canse or occasion of the event spoken of. In proper phraseology however, we are accustomed to speak of *nature* and *of circumstances* as if one *excluded* the other; and to affirm that the nature of a thing and *not* its circumstances, or its circumstances and *not* its nature, is the ground or reason of a given phenomena. Thus it may be said of one tree, that it is owing to its circumstances that it bears bad fruit; and of another tree, that it is owing to its nature.

Now this popular mode of speaking not only conveys a very precise and definite meaning, but is of great utility; and the question is important, what is its meaning, and to what cases or facts is the one form of phraseology truly and properly applied, and to what the other? I answer, that it is truly and properly ascribed *to the nature* of a thing when it is its invariable consequence in the appropriate circumstances of its existence; and that it is truly and properly ascribed to *the circumstances* of a thing when merely, by any change of these circumstances, there is a change in the event. To illustrate by example. A tree, which in all possible circumstance or under every variety of circumstances within its proper place of existence, bears bad fruit, is by nature bad; or the badness of the fruit is properly ascribed to the nature of the tree. Another, which in one set of circumstances bears bad fruit, and in another set of circumstances good fruit, is not properly said to be a bad tree by nature; but its bearing bad fruit is properly ascribed to its circumstances. Now here arises a very important question in respect to a tree. And who does not see the practical utility of the distinction denoted by the phraseology under consideration, or of deciding whether a tree's bearing bad fruit is owing to nature or to circumstances? In the one case, the natural course would be to cut down the tree and burn it; in the other, to preserve it with care, and to bestow on it a more perfect culture.

Now these forms of phraseology, modified indeed so far as the different nature of physical and moral phenomena demands, are applied to the latter. Thus we ascribe the sin of our first parents to temptation; i. e., to certain external circumstances and *not* to nature, because it resulted obviously from a change of circumstances. But we ascribe the depravity of their descendants to nature and *not* to circumstances, on the supposition that under all circumstances essential to their proper state of existence they become depraved.

Again: when I ascribe the depravity of man *to nature*, I do not mean that nature is *an efficient* natural cause, nor an occasional natural cause of human sinfulness. This, the nature of the predicate forbids, whether the sin be ascribed to nature or to circumstances. We are speaking of sin, i. e., of moral action, which of course implies moral agency; a fact which obliges every one to understand the language under consideration, with the requisite limitation. Besides, to say that one thing is *by* another, does not designate the latter as the efficient natural nor an occasional natural cause of the former. Indeed, this form of expression is probably used more frequently to denote an *occasion* or *causa sine qua non*, than to denote an *efficient cause*, while nothing is more common than to use it to denote an occasional moral cause. When therefore I say that depravity is *by nature*, I mean simply that *nature* is the occasional moral cause of the universal sinfulness of mankind. I mean that *nature* is a cause therefore, which, though certainly followed with depravity, is yet as truly subject to man's powers of moral agency, as it would be were all his acts perfectly holy.

These remarks may sufficiently explain what I intend by the general phrase *by nature*. In regard to the specific statement which ascribes the depravity to our constitutional propensities for natural good, I remark that I do not intend to exclude the weakness or imperfection of our intellectual powers from all connection with human sinfulness. It may be true that greater perfection in these powers at the commencement of accountable existence would, even with our present propensities for natural good, prevent this depravity; and that in this respect the imperfection of our intellectual powers is in some sense connected with it. Nevertheless, this connection is indirect and remote, since the degree of excitement in the propensities for natural good, and not voluntary action, is the direct result of this intellectual imperfection, and voluntary action the proximate result of excitement in these propensities. These propensities therefore are the immediate springs of voluntary action; they are its *proximate cause*, rather than any state or acts of the intellect. It is therefore, in respect to this more *direct* and *proximate* relation of our constitutional propensities for natural good to voluntary acts, that I speak of them as its cause. It is for the *proximate* cause or occasion of human depravity that we are inquiring.

To vindicate the theory now stated and explained, I remark:

1. It is exempt from all philosophical absurdity and embarrassment. It is possible, that God should create free moral agents with such propensities for natural good, that in the circumstances essential to their proper place of existence, they should uniformly sin. The truth of this remark will appear in answering objections.

2. This theory accounts for all sin; i. e., for the first sin of all the descendants of Adam, and for their continuance in sin. This may be fairly assumed until the contrary is proved. I would observe however, that the theory before us does not profess to account for all sin, and of course for the *first sin* in men, by ascribing it to a *previous* sin, or rather, as we have before shown, by ascribing all sin to itself as its cause. It traces sin to a *cause* which is not itself sin. To say that voluntary agents may be led uniformly into sin by the strength of propensities and appetites which are not in themselves sinful, is certainly, when considered in itself, not an unphilosophical account of the fact. If so in one case, it may be so in all. What becomes of the assertion that it cannot? Angels—Adam sinned.

3. The theory is proved to be correct by the universality of human sinfulness. The fact of the universal sinfulness of mankind we have already proved, be their circumstances what they may. The question in view of this fact is, whether this depravity is to be ascribed to the nature of men, or to their circumstances? I answer, if this inquiry is to be understood and answered in a manner strictly metaphysical, we must say that the depravity of man is to be ascribed to both his subjective nature and his circumstances. Indeed, I will not say that it is wholly contrary to a correct popular mode of speaking to say

this. (Vide James i. 14, 15.) At the same time I maintain that it is also a correct popular mode of speaking, to ascribe this depravity *to nature*, and that when the object of the inquiry is to decide to *which* of the *two causes* it is to be ascribed, implying what is undoubtedly true, that it may with perfect truth and propriety be applied to one or the other exclusively, according to the usage of terms, the only correct answer is, that it is be ascribed *to nature*. This, as we have seen, is always done in those cases in which no change of circumstances changes the result; and the present is such a case. We have therefore precisely the same reason, and all the reason, to ascribe the depravity of men to their *nature*, which we have or can have in any case, to ascribe any phenomenon or consequence to this cause. Why, for example, is it proper to say that a stone is *by nature* heavy, or that *by nature* when unsupported it tends toward the earth? Simply because in all circumstances of its existence we know that such is the fact. It is therefore to no purpose to say, if mankind were to be placed in some supposable circumstances, the result might be holiness and not sin. Be it so. In like manner, if a stone were placed in some other circumstances than those which pertain to its proper place in the system,—for example, within the attraction of the sun,—it would not fall, but rise, and it could no longer properly be said that it was *by nature* heavy. So it might be true of mankind, that in some other circumstances than those which pertain to their proper place of existence, they might be holy. This however, affects not the truth nor propriety of ascribing their sinfulness to their *nature*, since in all the circumstances which belong to their proper place in the system, they all become sinful. If therefore it be proper and true, as the language is used, in any case whatever, to ascribe any phenomena or effects *to nature*, then it is both proper and true to ascribe the sinfulness of man *to the nature* of man.

The force of this argument depends on the incontrovertible principle, that uniformity of event proves the cause to be uniform. The event in the present case therefore, cannot be properly ascribed to any particular circumstance or combination of circumstances in the case of any of the human race, because it is the same in all circumstances which essentially belong to their proper state of existence. To suppose what would be or would not be, were man's state of existence essentially changed, is wholly nugatory and vain, amounting only to conjecture, where nothing can be known or determined. The only proper method of reasoning is, to take man as we find him, and to adopt in reference to his actual state and to the known phenomena, the true principles of reasoning. If these conduct to the conclusion that man is *by nature* depraved, this conclusion we are bound to adopt.

To the preceding argument many objections are made which demand examination. I ought however to remark, that some at least of these objections are made not against the theory now stated and explained, but against that which asserts that the nature of man is itself sinful, and that against such a theory the validity of these objections must be admitted.

4. This is the true doctrine of Orthodoxy.

In support of this position I give the following extracts from Edwards on Original Sin:

"If any creature be of such a nature that it proves evil in its proper place, or in the situation which God has assigned it in the universe, it is of an evil nature. That part of the system is not good which is not good in its place in the system; and those inherent qualities of that part of the system which are not good, but corrupt in that place, are justly looked upon as evil inherent qualities. That propensity is truly esteemed to belong to the *nature* of any being, or to be inherent in it, that is the necessary consequence of its nature, considered together with its proper situation in the universal system of existence, whether that propensity be good or bad. It is the *nature* of a stone to be heavy, but yet if it were placed, as it might be, at a distance from this world, it would have no such quality. But seeing a stone is of such a nature that it will have this quality or tendency in its proper place here in this world where God has made it, it is properly looked upon as a propensity belonging to its nature; and if it be a good propensity here in its proper place, then it is a good quality of its nature; but if it be contrariwise, it is an evil natural quality. So, if mankind are of such a nature that they have a universal, effectual tendency to sin and ruin in this world where God has made and placed them, this is to be looked upon as a pernicious tendency belonging to their nature."—(Part I. ch. i. sec. 2.)

"A propensity to that sin which brings God's eternal wrath

and curse (which has been proved to belong to the nature of man) is evil, not only as it is *calamitous* and *sorrowful*, ending in great *natural evil*, but as it is *odious* and *detestable*, for by the supposition, it tends to *moral evil*, by which the subject becomes odious in the sight of God, and liable as such to be condemned and utterly rejected, and cursed by him. This also makes it evident that the state in which it has been proved mankind are, is a corrupt state in a *moral sense*, that is, that it is inconsistent with the fulfillment of the law of God, which is the rule of moral rectitude and goodness. That tendency which is opposite to that which the moral law requires and insists upon, and prone to that which the moral law utterly forbids, and eternally condemns the subject for, is doubtless a corrupt tendency, in a moral sense."—(Part I. ch. i. sec. 3.)

"In order to account for a sinful corruption of nature, yea, a total native depravity of the heart of man, there is not the least need of supposing any evil quality *infused*, *implanted*, or *wrought* into the nature of man by any *positive* cause or influence whatsoever, either from God or the creature; or of supposing that man is conceived and born with a *fountain of evil* in his heart, such as is any thing properly *positive*. I think a little attention to the nature of things will be sufficient to satisfy any impartial, considerate inquirer, that the absence of positive good principles, and so the withholding of a special divine influence to impart and maintain those good principles, leaving the common natural principles of self-love, natural appetite, &c. (which were in man in innocence), leaving these, I say, to themselves, without the government of superior divine principles, will certainly be followed with the corruption, yea, the total corruption of the heart, without occasion for any positive influence at all. And that it was thus indeed that corruption of nature came on Adam, immediately on his fall, and comes on all his posterity, as sinning in him, and falling with him."—(Part IV. ch. ii.)*

The Bible accords with this theory. Eph. ii. 3: "And were by nature, φύσει, children of wrath," &c. This is popular phra-

---

* *Quere?* Does the Bible authorize such assertions as those of Edwards, concerning "*propensity to sin*," "*proclivity to sin*," "*tendency to sin*,"—or does it, at the utmost, only assert the uniformity of the fact, and that it is *by nature*, or that the antecedent is in the ἐπιθυμίας, &c?—(Ephes. ii. 3; Jas. i. 14, 15.)

seology, and the only place where sin is said to be by nature. It was common among the Greeks to say φυσικῶς, as we say naturally in a loose, popular acceptation of the term. But in the same verse Paul shows that he did not mean a nature sinful *per se*, for he states the sin to have been actual, voluntary. It was "having conversation among sinners," "*fulfilling* the desires of the flesh and of the mind," ποιοῦντες τὰ θελήματα (and this though *dead*, "dead in sins," and yet walking), *doing*, acting out the promptings of the carnal propensity, but not in feeling or having them. Paul was an advocate for voluntary sin, if any. Rom. ii. 14: "For when the Gentiles do by nature,φύσει," &c., has been employed by Pelagians as a proof that all are not depraved by nature, but that some do right by nature. Some Orthodox attempt a defense by saying that the apostle speaks hypothetically, i. e., *when* they do it—i. e., should they do it. But this is hardly fair, and cannot be believed. He speaks of actual cases. I answer: If it did show that some few by nature were not depraved, it would not disprove the general doctrine of depravity. We say "all men are mortal"—"all have died," and yet Enoch and Elijah did not. So in this case, had there been a few exceptions, Paul would not feel a need of stopping to specify them in stating the general doctrine of human depravity. Universal propositions are rarely true to the letter. But the apostle here is only showing what men did without a revelation by the light of nature, which shows that he could use the term nature out of its strict philosophical sense, i. e., not to denote the *subjective* nature. He was contrasting the Gentiles with the Jews under a revelation. But in Eph. ii., "among whom we all"—Jews and Gentiles—"had our conversation." Texts which trace sin to propensities which are plainly involuntary. James i. 13, 15: This is a metaphysical account of the process of sinning. "But every man is tempted *when*;" tempted in the sense of *tried*. Then when lust (ἐπιθυμία), which means simply desire, good or bad, fixing the mind upon any thing. See Luke xxii. 15: ἐπιθυμίᾳ ἐπεθύμησα φαγεῖν, κ. τ. λ., i. e., I have greatly desired to eat, &c. Phil. i. 23: ἐπιθυμίαν ἔχων εἰς τὸ ἀναλῦσαι, κ. τ. λ., I am in a strait, &c. It is then a generic name for desire, and not necessarily lust in a bad sense. In this passage then, the apostle enters into the cause, ground, or reason of sin. He supposes a nature with propensities, and objects appealing to them and dictating the preference of themselves to God. Here is a nature in its appropriate circumstances. From these results the *ἐπιθυμία*, the desire of the good preferred by the objects of the propensities. But this state is not sin, for not till lust or desire hath conceived doth it bring forth sin. This *συλλαβοῦσα τίκτει*, conceiving and bringing forth sin, is only a figurative expression for yielding to or gratifying that desire: philosophically expressed, it would be the volition or elective act of the mind by which the forbidden object was taken instead of God. So accurately has the inspired apostle given the common-sense, metaphysical account of the mode and reason of sin. See also 1 John ii. 15, 17: *ἡ ἐπιθυμία τῆς σαρκὸς καὶ ἡ ἐπιθυμία τῶν ὀφθαλμῶν, κ. τ. λ.* The passages that speak of the flesh and the spirit, *σὰρξ καὶ πνεῦμα*, as opposed to each other. Gal. v. 16–20: This say I then, walk in the Spirit, and ye shall not fulfill, *ἐπιθυμίαν σαρκὸς οὐ μὴ τελέσητε*, and these are contrary the one to the other, so that which ye would, ye do not: *ἵνα μὴ ἃ ἂν θέλητε ταῦτα ποιῆτε.* There is no *cannot* in the Greek. He then enumerates the works of the flesh, and we shall find that they are all in view of objects which appeal to some constitutional propensity in itself not wrong. The perverse indulgence of some natural propensity, leads to each of these sins without supposing an hereditary propensity, having for its object an independent *sui generis* gratification in sin itself, for its own sake. Rom. viii. 5, 6: *τὸ φρόνημα τῆς σαρκὸς.* If there is a propensity to sin *per se*, how is it that the apostle never mentions it? Those texts represent Regeneration as a moral change mostly, not a change of physical constitution. The nature of sin is everywhere represented in the Bible to be the preference, choice, in some form of mammon, to God. The Bible is unintelligible if this is not the meaning. The objections to this theory prove it true.

Remarks.—The terms "nature," "innate," &c., applied to depravity in our common acceptation of them, are apt to mislead our minds as referring to something constitutional. But not so with the word natural. Hence in speaking of depravity, we have used the word physical instead of natural. In abstract propositions, where it is difficult to judge by the nature of the subject, &c., the primary meaning of words should be given them. It is on these terms that controversy has its beginning, middle, and end.

THE OBJECTIONS DO NOT DISPROVE THE DOCTRINE.

Obj.—It is said that universality of sin in man is no proof of depravity by nature.

This objection is supported by the opposers of the natural depravity of man by several arguments.

1. It is alleged, that the occurrence of sin in Adam utterly invalidates the proof of the depravity of man by nature, derived from the universality of sin. The force of this objection depends wholly on what is meant by *the depravity of man by nature.* If this means that man is the subject by nature of a *sinful disposition* previous to all sinful acts or volitions, the objection is unquestionably valid; for, as Dr. Woods admits (and thus abandons the entire argument from the universality of sin, to prove depravity by nature in his sense of the language), the case of Adam proves that a holy being may change from holiness to sin. It is to no purpose to say, that there must be even in a holy being *a sinful* disposition previous to any sinful acts or volitions. For still there is in fact a change implied from holiness to sin, and therefore a state of holiness previous to a state of sin, and of course, previous to a sinful disposition. But if one man, and that the parent of our race, may change from holiness to sin, without a previous *sinful* disposition, then the whole race may sin without a previous sinful disposition. Of course the supposition of depravity by nature, meaning a *sinful disposition* by nature as a created attribute, is not necessary to account for the universal sinfulness of man.

But by the doctrine of total depravity of all men by nature, we do not understand a sinful disposition as the foundation of all sinful volitions. We mean by depravity, a sinful volition itself, or rather, a sinful elective preference which becomes predominant in the soul, and comes into existence through that in the physical constitution and in the circumstances of men, which is the ground or reason of the fact, and in reference to which reason, such depravity may be properly said to be *by nature*, or to be *natural.* The question then is, whether the sin of Adam shows that it is unnecessary to suppose that the above *cause* or *reason* of the universal sinfulness of men actually exists.

To decide this question, it is necessary to settle two others,—whether Adam sinned without any reason existing for the fact in his constitution and circumstances; and whether we can suppose that his posterity become universally sinful, and only sinful, without any such ground or reason of the fact.

As to the first of these questions, it is no other than whether man can act voluntarily, without some reason for the existence of the particular act rather than for the existence of its opposite, which we have already discussed and decided. Whatever this reason may be, we have also seen, that it must be resolved into the constitution and circumstances of man.

As to the second question, this is easily determined when we have decided the first. For if we cannot suppose *a single* event like that now under consideration, without some ground or reason for it, we certainly cannot suppose a constant uniformity of the same event without some ground or reason for such uniformity. The only question that can remain is, whether this necessary ground or reason of the uniformity of the event is such, that the event itself may be said to be by nature, or to be natural. By the event, we mean a predominant sinful volition in all men, and the reason of this fact we have already shown to lie in the constitution and circumstances of man; and we have also shown, that to say that an event which uniformly results from such a cause may, according to the strictest propriety, be termed *natural*, or be said to be *by nature*. It follows therefore, that the universal depravity of man proves that he is depraved by nature.

If it be asked, why may not the sin of Adam, resulting as it did from the same cause as that from which the sinfulness of his descendants results, be said to be *by nature*, I answer, because there is an important difference in the two cases. Adam did not sin in all the appropriate circumstances of existence; but his descendants do sin in all the appropriate circumstances of their being. Had those in which Adam was placed remained unaltered, there is no evidence that he would have sinned at all. But let those of his posterity change as they may, within any limit in which they can be said to be the appropriate circumstances of their being, and they uniformly sin. But we have before shown that the phrase *by nature*, in this and in all cases, assumes that the being of whom we speak is in the appropriate circumstances of his being. While therefore, there would be no propriety in saying that Adam was a sinner, or became depraved *by nature*, there is the most perfect propriety in saying that his posterity, on the present supposition of universal sinfulness, are depraved *by nature*.

2. It is said that the universality of sin may be accounted for by man's free will, without supposing depravity to be by nature. Free agency or the free agent is the efficient cause of sin, but the question is, why does he choose wrong instead of choosing right in all cases?

3. It is said, that the universality of sin may be accounted for by bad example. In addition to the arguments of Edwards it ought to be remarked, that bad example and bad education are only *circumstances of our being*, and whatever may be supposed to be their influence, it only amounts to our doctrine; for, as we have seen, if man is depraved in the appropriate circumstances of his being, then his depravity is owing both to his constitution and his circumstances, and in our meaning of the terms he is depraved *by nature*.

4. It is said that the universality of sin may be accounted for by the circumstances in which men come into existence; these being such that the passions get the start of reason. So undoubtedly it may be, but what is this but saying that men become depraved or are depraved by nature, in the proper sense of the term? Thus Edwards answers this objection by saying that the strength of appetite and passion which this hypothesis assigns as the cause of prevailing wickedness, amounts to a prevailing propensity to sin, and is altogether equivalent to a *natural* tendency (p. 236).

5. The necessity of trials in order to virtue are said to be a sufficient account of the sinfulness of man. This objection differs not substantially from the former, and is refuted in the same manner.

Obj. 2.—It is said that the total depravity of man by nature is inconsistent with the free moral agency of man.

The force of this objection, if it have any, must lie either in the fact that man's depravity is certain, or in the nature of that which is the ground or reason of such certainty.

1. The former topic we have largely investigated, and if I mistake not, have fully shown that certainty of action is consistent with the most perfect freedom of action. I shall not here formally resume the consideration of this part of the sub-

ject, but supposing the principles of the argument to be well understood, shall rather inquire whether our opponents, especially Dr. Ware,* has not decisively admitted the truth of our main principle—that certainty of action is consistent with freedom of action, and thus in this respect abandoned his objection to our doctrine.

In his "Answer," &c., p. 51, Dr. Ware expressly asserts, that it is possible that a being constituted as man is, may depart from the path of duty and become a sinner at any moment; that by such an act he becomes a sinner in the sense in which it is said in the sacred writings, that there is no man that doeth good and sinneth not.

Here then two things are conceded; the one is, that man may in perfect consistency with his moral agency become a sinner, and that every man will in perfect consistency with his moral agency *certainly* sin *once*. But if it be consistent with his moral agency that every man should *certainly* sin once, then it is consistent with his moral agency that he should *certainly* sin twice, thrice, indeed, in every instance of accountable action.

Nor is this a solitary concession of Dr. Woods. On p. 53 he says, "There may be what we term *a moral certainty* respecting any child that is born into the world, that if it live to become a moral and accountable being it *will become* a sinner."

On pages 95, 96, Dr. Ware has still more explicitly and fully asserted that the certainty of action is consistent with moral freedom. Thus he says: "Upon the supposition of that moral freedom, which I maintain to be the true ground upon which man is justly accountable for his actions, deserving of praise or blame, and a proper subject of reward and punishment, every action of every human being *is as certain before it is performed as afterward.* Suppose men to have that liberty which the scheme I advocate attributes to them, it is *as certain* beforehand how they will act as upon the scheme of necessity; that is, it is *absolutely certain* how they will in fact use that freedom. And speaking of it merely as an abstract truth, we may say it is *impossible* that they should not use their freedom as they actually will use it."

Now what more than this have the Orthodox contended for

---

* In his reply to Dr. Woods.

in respect to the certainty of human action as consistent with praise and blame? Has Dr. Ware ever read the writings of the Orthodox? Does he know what their views of this subject are? If not, he is inexcusably ignorant. If he has, then he has read in the famous works of the two Edwardses that "metaphysical or philosophical necessity is nothing different from certainty." "In this sense I use the word necessity, when I attempt to prove that necessity is not inconsistent with liberty." (President Edwards' Works, vol. v. p. 26.) "Certainty," says Dr. Edwards, "is the necessity in question." (Diss., p. 39.) *Necessity* then as used by the Orthodox, is the self-same thing which Dr. Ware calls *moral certainty.* Why then does he pretend that there is a difference between them? But not to reproach him with ignorance or falsehood, he has abundantly conceded that *certainty* is perfectly consistent with accountability and freedom, and on this point fully agrees with the Orthodox.

But we may carry this point a little further, and ask, have the Orthodox used any stronger language on the subject than Dr. Ware uses and professedly vindicates? "It is *impossible,*" says he, "that they should not use their freedom as they actually will use it;" and yet he also maintains the accountability of man as deserving praise or blame, and as a proper subject of reward and punishment. Let Dr. Ware now assume the task so triumphantly assigned by him to Dr. Woods, that of showing how "a being may be justly required to do what in all the circumstances in which it is placed, it is *impossible* for it to do" (p. 63).

Thus on one page Dr. Ware has declared one thing, and on another declares the contrary. Are the Orthodox chargeable with any grosser contradiction? But is Dr. Ware fairly chargeable with real contradiction? Certainly with contradiction in terms, but we think not with contradiction in ideas. The solution of the matter is, that in the one instance he has used the word *impossible* in a sense totally unauthorized, and which totally misrepresents the opinion of the Orthodox which he professes to state; in the other instance, he is driven to use the word *impossible* in the same sense in which the Orthodox use it on this subject, to denote *moral certainty.* Thus he has explained our terms as he ought, and as we explain them, and thus he uses them; and by this very simple and equitable process has perfectly unfolded our consistency. We say then, *if* Dr. Ware understands the sense in which he uses terms, *if* he will interpret the same terms when used by the Orthodox in the same sense as that in which he uses them himself, and *if* he will keep the fear of God before his eyes, he will never again (vide Dr. W.'s Ans., p. 63) charge the Orthodox doctrine of depravity with being inconsistent with moral freedom, on the ground of *moral necessity.*

From the abundant concessions of this principle by a late controvertist of our doctrine, we may safely affirm, that the *certainty* of sinful action in man is not inconsistent with his free moral agency, and from the illustrations formerly given of the principle, *that certainty of action is consistent with freedom of action.*

2. The next inquiry is, whether the nature of that which is the ground or reason of the certainty of sinful action is not inconsistent with moral freedom?

The answer depends wholly on what that is supposed to be, which is the ground of the certainty of sinful action. If it be that which has the nature and influence of a physical cause, the objection is valid. But we have abundantly shown that such is not the nature and influence of that which is the reason of the certainty of man's sinfulness.

According to our statement of the doctrine of depravity by nature, the ground or reason of man's depravity lies in his innocent physical propensities, and his circumstances. The question therefore is, whether such a *ground* of certainty of action is inconsistent with moral agency?

This question in its abstract form, it is supposed, has been already sufficiently discussed. Indeed, if we admit the certainty of human action, and who does not admit it, then we ask what can be the original ground or reason of such certainty but that which we have now supposed? Without pursuing this subject in the manner in which we have already considered it, it may be more useful to inquire on this point into the actual state of the controversy as it exists at the present time in this country, taking Dr. Ware's views of the subject as the medium of representation.

In his Letters (pp. 23, 24), Dr. Ware says, that all the wickedness which the Orthodox ascribe to men, supposing it to be real, may be satisfactorily accounted for on the ground of the innocent physical propensities of our nature and the circumstances in which we are placed. Here then the ground or reason of human sinfulness supposed, is precisely that which we say is the real ground or reason; and this Dr. Ware tells us is a satisfactory account of the matter.

Nor is this a solitary instance in which Dr. Ware has attempted to show that this specific ground of sin in man is perfectly consistent with man's moral agency. (Vide Letters, p. 21, *et al.;* Ans., pp. 51, 53, and 89.) In doing this, the fact is, that Dr. Ware has adopted an hypothesis which, so far from being one which he can claim, is of Orthodox invention, and was adopted in this self-same controversy by some of the ablest defenders of Orthodoxy long before Dr. Ware was born. It would not be difficult, it is believed, to show that Augustine and Calvin maintained substantially the same view of the subject which Dr. Ware adopts, and would have believed to be purely Unitarian. It is sufficient however for our purpose, that President Edwards maintained it in its full extent.—(Works, vol. vi. pp. 427, 431.)

It is true that in one respect between this hypothesis of Edwards and that of Dr. Ware there is one circumstantial difference. President Edwards supposes the withdrawing of a divine influence, the presence of which would prevent the sin of men. But he does not suppose such influence to be essential to moral agency, nor that the withdrawing of it does not leave man as perfectly a free moral agent as Dr. Ware can imagine. This divine influence withdrawn, Edwards supposes the ground of the certainty of man's sinfulness to consist in his innocent natural appetites and passions, and so does Dr. Ware.

Now how it looks for a man in the attitude of a controversialist on this subject to set himself forth, I do not say as the author of an hypothesis of this kind, but to claim it as exclusively Unitarian, or rather as anti-Orthodox, when the same subject has been so long in controversy, and when the most distinguished Orthodox writer on the subject had propounded the same hypothesis in an essay of universal celebrity, long before Dr. Ware knew his right hand from his left. Whatever explanation Dr. Ware might give of this fact, one thing is certain,—if this hypothesis be just and satisfactory when adopted by Dr. Ware, it is equally so when adopted by the Orthodox.

Obj. 3.—It is said that the doctrine of total depravity by nature is inconsistent with the moral perfection of God. The force of this objection, if it have any, must like the former lie either in the certainty of man's sinfulness, or in the nature of that which is the ground of this certainty.

How the certainty of sin in man is consistent with the moral perfection of God, we have already attempted to show.

This being admitted, it only remains to show that that which constitutes the ground or reason of this certainty is consistent with the moral perfection of God, and this is done by showing as we now have, that this ground or reason of the certainty of sin is consistent with the free moral agency of man. If God for some end worthy of his infinite benevolence, has seen fit to give man existence in such circumstances that sin is the certain consequence, and if at the same time the certainty of the event results from a cause which is perfectly consistent with the moral agency of man, then the justice of God in the punishment of man is undeniable. For if such a being thus rebelling against the holy laws of his Maker ought not to be punished, it is impossible to conceive that the punishment of a creature by his Creator can be just.

The two objections against the doctrine of the total depravity of man by nature, which we have now been considering, have ever been the chief reliance of the opposers of this doctrine. Such is strikingly the fact in the late controversy in this country. Dr. Ware, whether he adduces an argument from reason or from Scripture in opposition to the Orthodox doctrine, scarcely fails to present in some form the supposed inconsistency of the doctrine with the free agency of man and the moral perfection of God, as the basis and strength of his argument. Now it is very unfortunate for these grand objections of Dr. Ware, as it was for the same objections when made by Dr. John Taylor, that the doctrine against which they are brought is not the doctrine of the Orthodox. By this I do not mean, that none of the Orthodox have maintained those views of man's depravity against which these objections are brought. But I mean, that many of the Orthodox have not maintained such views—I mean more—that the Orthodox *as a class* or party have not. Those who have, I cheerfully abandon to Dr. Ware's animadversions, with the hope, and I may say with the expectation, that to some extent he and his associates in this cause will correct their error. But why should the Orthodox party be held responsible for opinions which only *some* of that party have embraced? Why should this be, when some of the ablest defenders of Orthodoxy have explicitly disclaimed the views thus charged upon them? If the question respect the sentiments of individuals, let the individuals who embrace it be called to answer for themselves. If it respect the doctrine of the Orthodox as a class or party, let it be stated in a form to which they as a class or party either have assented or will assent. The fact is, that the controversy on this subject respects not the inquiry, whether the doctrine opposed by Unitarians is not liable to the objections which they allege against it, but whether this be the real doctrine of the Orthodox. This previous question must be settled, or the controversy will have no very satisfactory or successful termination. The contending parties will continue to fire *by* and not *at* each other, and either keep the field, waxing bolder in fight, or retire alike confident of victory.

HUMAN SINFULNESS.

X.—TOTAL DEPRAVITY BY NATURE.—(*Continued.*)

Objections to the theory.—(4.) Infants are sinners.—The position of the author defined.—That infants are sinners inconsistent with this on one supposition.—I. Opinions of Orthodox writers.—II. The doctrine of the Scriptures.—1. Supposed proofs for the doctrine.—2. It is claimed that the Scriptures teach that infants are sinners at the moment of birth.—Remarks on classification of proof-texts.—(1.) This cannot be true.—(2.) It contravenes common sense.—(3.) Violates the laws of usage.

I HAVE examined the three principal objections to the doctrine of TOTAL DEPRAVITY BY NATURE alleged by the opposers of this doctrine, viz.: that universal depravity can be accounted for without tracing it to nature; that it is inconsistent with the free moral agency of man; and also with the moral perfection of God. These are the objections of Pelagians and Arminians,—objections which, we have seen, lie in full force against certain forms of stating the doctrine of depravity by nature, but which, as I trust, have no force, nor even plausibility, when alleged against that form of this doctrine which is maintained in these lectures. The importance of this view of the doctrine as the only one which can be defended against Pelagian or Arminian objections is obvious.

There is however, another class of objections which are alleged, not by the opposers of the doctrine of depravity by nature in every form of it, but by some Orthodox writers, against that maintained in these lectures. Most of these objections we have already had occasion to examine in the defense of our doctrine. There is but one more which requires further notice, viz.:

Objection 4.—That infants are sinners.

It has been then extensively maintained, that the Scriptures clearly teach that infants are sinners, and that this fact is inconsistent with the doctrine of *depravity by nature* advanced in a former lecture.

Those who have advocated this doctrine have held it under very diverse forms. From the time of Augustine (for before there is no pretense that there was any settled Orthodoxy on this point) to the time of Dr. Edwards and Dr. Hopkins, it was held by the Orthodox generally under that form of Imputation which exhibits Adam and his posterity as *one moral person*, and his posterity as sinning in him, i. e., in his first transgression, by acting in that act as truly as Adam himself, and so corrupting their nature just as Adam did his, and thus, though *created* holy, as born with this sinful or corrupt nature.

Since the time of the younger Edwards and Dr. Hopkins, this doctrine has been very materially modified and changed by many Orthodox divines. These writers led the way in these changes, maintaining that all sin consists in the voluntary mental exercises of the sinner, the latter tracing all such exercises to divine efficiency producing or creating them. Others of this class of divines, none indeed however who are entitled to consideration, have held this doctrine under the form of physical depravity; others, under that of mere liability to punishment, including a corrupt nature without ill-desert, and calling this the doctrine of Original Sin by Imputation. All these maintain that sin begins in all men at least as soon as they are born. There is yet another class who hold the doctrine of depravity by nature, as stated in a former lecture, viz., *that such is the nature or constitution of the human mind, that all mankind in all the appropriate or natural circumstances of their existence will uniformly sin from the commencement of moral agency.*

Of the several theories or forms of this doctrine which I deem groundless, except that of imputed sin (which I propose to examine hereafter), I have already said sufficient.

My present object is to inquire whether the Scriptures teach the doctrine of infant depravity, *in that particular form of it* which affirms in exact literal language *that infants either at or before birth are sinners.* I say, *in that particular form of it;* for I wish not to be misunderstood on this point. I would then distinctly affirm, that in my view the Scriptures do teach that all mankind do and will in fact sin from the commencement of their moral agency; that they sin so early, that in *popular language* it may be properly said that they sin from the first, from the beginning, sin as soon as they can; that there is no such interval between birth and sin as rendered it necessary, that in the popular language of the Bible that interval should be specified. The doctrine which I oppose is that form of it which is derived from pressing the language, the mere words of the Scriptures, to their utmost possible meaning as mere words; and maintains that the object of the sacred writers was to assert, in exact literal language, that sin in all men begins at the very moment of or before birth.

The question then now before us, is not so much what depravity consists in as when it begins. It is not whether mankind may be properly said to be sinners from the first, &c., in the loose and indefinite language of common life, but whether the language of the Bible is to be interpreted on this subject to the letter; and whether therefore the popular language of the Bible, as thus interpreted, is the precise and exact form of statement which is to be adopted in scientific theology.

Before I proceed to discuss this question, I will answer the objection to our doctrine of depravity, which is derived from infant depravity, on the admission of the fact. Conceding then that infants are sinners either before they are born, or at the very moment of birth, how is this inconsistent with the doctrine which I have advanced? Plainly in no respect, unless it be assumed that they are not moral agents at or before birth. The objection which maintains that it is impossible that they should be moral agents so early, and that therefore they are sinners in some other way than by committing sin, we have answered already. As to that form of the objection which maintains that they *commit* sin either at or before birth, and thus asserts *their moral agency* when they sin, there is plainly no inconsistency between this fact and the doctrine that they sin as soon as moral agency begins, for it neither affirms nor denies the period when moral agency commences.

I state this answer as sufficient, provided we take no more definite position in respect to the character of infants than what is implied in our statement of the doctrine of depravity. I cannot however but think, that the cause of truth—of scriptural doctrine—requires that we go further on this subject. What I propose then in the present lecture, after a brief view of the opinions of some Orthodox writers, is to inquire what God in his word requires us to believe on this controverted subject.

I. I will briefly as may be, ascertain the opinions of some

Orthodox writers. The views of Dr. Dwight, as given in his Theology, I have attempted to exhibit in a tract already published.* Amid some *apparent* and only verbal incongruity, sufficiently guarded however by explanations to prevent misapprehension, he, I think, very clearly maintains, that infants are sinners by voluntary exercises or acts. Dr. Edwards obviously held also, that all moral quality pertains exclusively to voluntary exercises or acts, and probably that these are produced by divine efficiency, although I find nothing very definite in his writings respecting the time when they begin. The old Calvinists, properly so called, from Augustine to Dr. Green, agree with President Edwards in affirming that "infants are not capable of moral action at all;" incapable of what they called *actual sin*. This is true of the Westminster Catechism and other Orthodox formulas.

Dr. Hopkins says, "that as soon as they begin to act, they (infants) sin, and that it cannot be *precisely* determined *how soon* this is." (Syst., vol. i. p. 327.)

Dr. Emmons says, "It is certainly supposable that children may exist in this world *some space* of time before they become moral agents; but how long that space may be, whether an hour, a day, a month, a year, or several years, as many suppose, we do not presume to determine. But during that space, whether longer or shorter, they are not moral agents, nor consequently accountable creatures in the sight of God or man." (Sermons, 1825, p. 257.)

Dr. Woods says, after affirming again and again that all sin "is the action of a rational and accountable being," "I make it no part of my object in the present discussion to determine *precisely* the *time* when moral agency begins. There are difficulties in the way which I feel myself wholly unable to surmount. My position is, that as soon as they are moral agents they are sinners." (Reply to Ware, pp. 83–88.)

Prof. Stuart goes still further, as do many others, affirming that infants are not sinful.

I now proceed—

II. To the doctrine of the Scriptures.

Here I propose—

---

* An Inquiry into the Nature of Sin as exhibited in Dwight's Theology, by Clericus. New Haven, 1829.

1. To examine the supposed proofs of infant depravity from the Scriptures; and,

2. To offer proof to the contrary.

1. Under the supposed scriptural proofs of infant depravity, the first thing that claims our attention is—

(1.) The proof-texts alleged in support of the doctrine.

These however, I have already had occasion to examine, and have shown that they do not admit of the interpretation which supports the doctrine of infant depravity, but require an interpretation which is opposed to this doctrine. The passage in Rom. v. 12, I shall examine hereafter. Instead of a minute examination of these supposed proof-texts, I propose to specify some of the more prominent, and to show that, according to *the true method and principles* of interpreting them, they do not teach the doctrine of infant depravity. These principles I am more disposed to examine at some length, on account of their bearing on other controverted doctrines.

The question then is one on which diversity of opinion is obviously the result of adopting different principles of interpretation. It would seem indeed, that the true principles of interpreting the sacred volume, at least in respect to those more common modes of expression which occur in all languages, and in regard to which, mankind, except in cases of controversy, are universally agreed, ought to have been settled among professed theologians long before this. To what purpose is it that we read the same Bible, and make it the supreme and ultimate standard of faith, if we interpret its language by no fixed, but by entirely different principles? Plainly, correct principles of interpretation alone can give correct results, and nothing but the established authority and controlling influence of such principles can produce harmony of sentiment among the professed believers in divine revelation. I have long believed that the grand source of error and of diversity of religious belief lies in this,—that the interpreters of the sacred volume have no settled and controlling laws of interpretation. Were these laws fixed and applied as they might be, we should see an end to most of the theological controversies.

The passages relied on by the advocates of infant depravity may be reduced to two classes, viz.—first, that class which teach *the universality* of sin in men; secondly, that class which speak of *the time* of its commencement. They are such as the following: *The whole world is guilty before God; that all are under sin; that all have sinned; that the wicked are estranged from the womb; that they go astray as soon as they be born; that the imagination of man's heart is evil from his youth; that which is born of the flesh is flesh.*

2. It is claimed that these and similar passages of Scripture teach that *infants are sinners at the indivisible moment of birth.*

To this interpretation I proceed to state the following objections:

(1.) This interpretation *cannot be true.*

It will be admitted, that a meaning *which cannot be true*—which involves known absurdity or self-contradiction—cannot be the real meaning of an inspired declaration. This is as obvious as it is that the Word of God cannot teach falsehood. In deciding then the real meaning of any scriptural passage, it must first be ascertained that the one proposed expresses *what may be true*, or does not express a known falsehood. On this preliminary decision all interpretation of the sacred oracles must proceed, since otherwise we are authorized to give a meaning to the Word of God which we know cannot be true, i. e., to ascribe to it known falsehood. On this preliminary decision the interpretation given by the advocates of infant depravity to their proof-texts depends. They assume that their doctrine may be true, or that it is not a known falsehood, and rest this assumption of course solely on the authority of their own reason—their philosophy. With what propriety then do they reproach their opponents with deciding the same question on the same authority? Why accuse them, as if it were a crime, "of sitting in the chair of philosophy and prejudging the case?" They do the same thing—decide it on the authority of their philosophy. While we, on the authority of reason or of philosophy, believe that infants are not capable of sinning at the precise instant of their creation,* they decide on the same authority *that they are.* I say then, in their own language, "this is a very compendious way of settling the question. The man who makes this decision, sits in the chair of philosophy and prejudges the case." But says Dr. Spring,

---

* This argument applies only to that form of the doctrine maintained by Dr. Spring, viz., that infants sin *as soon as* (literally) they are created.

(whose doctrine I have now especially in view, and whose language I quote), "who knows best whether infants are capable of sinning—God, only wise, or the presumptuous objector?" Here Dr. Spring infers that infants *are capable* of sinning, on the assumption that God has decided that they *are* sinners. But this he could not do without first assuming that it *may be true*, and having done so, determines that the Scriptures teach that they are sinners, and thence infers that they *are capable* of sinning. He therefore not only begs a main premise in his argument, but he sits in the chair of philosophy, and falls under the same rebuke which he administers to the presumptuous objector, "Wherein thou judgest another, thou condemnest thyself."

But the question is not, whether an interpreter of the Word of God must first decide on *the possible truth* of the meaning which he adopts. This he must do. This Dr. Spring does; and if he may and must do this, so may his opponents. The question therefore is this—whether this prior decision, made on philosophical grounds, is rightly made,—it is, whether that is *a possible truth* which is decided to be such? This is the question on which the correctness of the interpretation depends. If it is not *a possible truth* that infants are sinners, in the sense maintained by Dr. Spring, then his interpretation must be rejected. The principle is law, that no meaning can be the real meaning of the Word of God unless it *can be true.*

We say then, that the meaning given to the passages of Scripture under consideration is not *a possible truth.* It *cannot be true* that the *exercises* or *acts* of the soul are its essential properties. The position is absurd and self-contradictory, and therefore must be false. It supposes a soul with all its essential properties, and thus qualified to act, while it is yet without one essential property, viz., action; i. e., a soul with all its essential properties, without its essential properties—a soul which is not a soul—a thing that is, and yet is not. The Bible surely does not teach such an absurdity.

The same thing is true of the doctrine that infants are born guilty of Adam's sin, by virtue of being one with Adam. That Adam and his posterity are *one moral person*, or one moral being, and that the latter committed the self-same sin which Adam committed while as yet they were not in existence, is not a possible truth. It involves the palpable contradiction that beings who are *not* the same being, are the same being; that those who did not exist and act, did exist and act.

The doctrine of a created or constitutional propensity to sin, which is itself sinful, is also fraught with self-contradiction. We know what sin is, and what it is not. We know that sin can no more pertain to the created properties or constitutional propensities of the mind, than to the features of the face, or the form and structure of the human body. To say therefore that a constitutional propensity of the soul is sinful, is as absurd and self-contradictory as to say that the soul is solid and extended, or that matter thinks and wills: it is saying that that is sinful which is not and cannot be sinful. But we need not dwell on this topic. Our opponents all disclaim this form of the doctrine of infant depravity.

Nor is there any form in which the doctrine that infants sin at the precise instant of their creation or of birth, *can be true.* Sin is predicable only of that state of mind which we call *preference* or *choice.* Every act of preference or choice involves *the perception* of the objects which it respects, a knowledge of their nature and relations, a comparison of them as sources of good or happiness to the mind. These mental acts must precede the act of will, analytically considered. To suppose that there can be an act of choice or preference without them, is to suppose that man can choose without perceiving the object chosen, and prefer it to another object without perceiving that also which is absurd and impossible. But if these mental acts are necessary to an act of choice or preference, then it is plain that such an act cannot in every sense be simultaneous with the soul's existence. In other words, the existence of an agent, and of the acts of perceiving, &c., must in some sense precede the analytic act of the will; i. e., precede the act of sinning. The doctrine then, that infants are sinners at the precise instant of existence, in every conceivable form of it, is self-contradictory—*cannot be true*, and therefore is not taught in the Word of God.

(2.) The interpretation which we oppose contravenes common sense. It will be admitted that every unbiased mind, supposing the Scriptures to be silent on the subject, would decide that infants do not and cannot transgress a known rule of duty at the very instant they are born. Do the Scriptures then contradict this decision, and oblige us to abandon this judgment of common sense? We answer, that there is a strong presumption against this. It is setting the Bible against those decisions and judgments of the human mind, in which we do and must repose, as the basis of human action in all the affairs of life. Is the Bible then such a book? Does it do the same violence to common sense, which it would do had it declared that all infants are born accomplished mathematicians or orators? Does the Word of God thus task human faith? Is this the book which its divine Author consents shall be tried at the bar of human reason, and which demands only a rational faith of rational beings? Can it be supposed for a moment that any passage of the divine Word, which will even admit of another meaning, actually teaches that infants knowingly transgress a rule of moral action at the precise instant of birth?

But not to rest the matter here. What is common sense? It is the competent, unperverted reason of the human mind, whose decisions, in the interpretation of the Scriptures, are to be relied upon as infallible. Man must know *some things* beyond the possibility of mistake, or there is an end to all knowledge and all faith. Otherwise, all his deductions and all his faith have no sufficient basis. He cannot prove the being of God, his perfections, nor the inspiration of his Word, nor decide on the import of a single sentence it contains. An infallible conclusion must depend on infallible premises. If there are no judgments or decisions of the human mind which are entitled to unhesitating confidence, then is universal skepticism authorized. But if there are such judgments, the question is, what are they? Plainly those in which the human mind is competent to decide correctly, and does decide without perversion. Thus the common decision of the unbiased mind, that the bread and wine of the Eucharist are not the literal body and blood of Christ,—that infants are not born with the muscular strength and intellectual acquirements of manhood, are decisions of the competent, unperverted reason of man. They are to be relied on as infallible judgments. So in the present case. The human mind is competent to decide whether infants at the moment of birth are capable of transgressing a known rule of duty. If not, all attempts of our opponents to support their decision must pass for nothing. If not, no confidence is due to other like judgments, and the very foundations of faith are subverted. But if the mind is competent to decide in one or the other of these opposite decisions, it is perverted; and the question is, in which? We say, in the decision that infants are sinners at the precise moment of birth. This doctrine is a theological peculiarity. Its origin can be traced to theological controversy. It was unknown in the early Christian Church; was derived probably from the philosophic doctrine of Realism in the fourth century; was devised to carry a point in polemic theology, and has therefore no other or higher authority than a speculation of heathen philosophy. We might specify other adequate causes of mental perversion in this case. We might show also, that in forming the opposite decision, no possible cause of mental perversion is even supposable, and that the mind is as prone to judge correctly in this matter,as in deciding that an infant at the moment of birth has not the qualifications of a general or a statesman. Indeed our opponents themselves, if they would not constantly assume that the Bible contradicts this decision, i. e., if they would not always beg the question, must admit, that the judgment of the unbiased mind in all ages and in all countries, would be, that infants are not and cannot be sinners at the moment of birth. This then is the decision of common sense,—the judgment of that competent, unperverted reason which God has constituted the ultimate umpire on every vital question of truth,—those which relate to his own being—his perfections—his character —the divine authority of his Word, and the import of every sentence it contains.

Is it said that we make an undue use of reason and exalt reason above revelation? But is it an undue use of reason to employ it honestly and without perversion in deciding questions for which it is fully competent? Then reason has no place. Man is not to use it. None of its decisions are entitled to confidence. We know indeed, that reason may be perverted where it is competent; that it may judge even confidently where it is utterly incompetent to decide, and that from *the abuse* of reason great evils result. But does it therefore follow that it has no *legitimate* use, or that such an one is exalting reason above revelation? Can the decisions of competent, unperverted reason contradict God's revelation? Then are the foundations of all rational faith swept away. Then let the frank avowal be made, and the Infidel exult in the concession, that the pretended revelation of God cannot stand when tried by human reason. Not so its divine Author. His triumphant challenge to an unbelieving world is, "*bring forth your strong reasons;*" "*come now, and let us reason together.*" Here we take our position and affirm, that common sense—the competent, unperverted reason of man—is an umpire whose decisions the Word of God neither does nor can contradict. The question then is this: Is not the doctrine that infants are sinners at the precise instant of their creation, contrary to common sense? Is it not absolutely incredible to the unsophisticated mind, that infants at the precise instant of birth have that knowledge of right and wrong, and of those moral relations which are requisite to moral responsibility and accountable action? We answer yes; and are therefore confident that the Bible does not teach that infants transgress known law at the precise moment in which they are born.

(3.) The interpretation which we oppose violates the great principles and laws of usage. Laying aside the impossibility of the truth of this interpretation, and the infallibility of the decisions of common sense, we now appeal to those principles which regulate the use and interpretation of the language of common life. We say then,

In the first place, the language of the Scriptures is to be interpreted, *not on the basis of an unusual philosophy, but in accordance with those ideas or conceptions of things which are common to the minds of men.* That the Bible is designed for the instruction of mankind generally, is a fact which must have a most important and decisive influence on the subject-matter of the book. This must lie entirely within the limits of the apprehension of the minds whose instruction is designed. All those elementary ideas, notions, or conceptions of the nature of things which constitute its comprehensive statements of truth, must therefore be those which are common to mankind. The Scriptures do indeed reveal complex truths, which are beyond all possible as well as beyond all actual discovery by the unaided mind of man. This they do however, not by conveying any new elementary ideas or notions of the nature of things, but by compounding and abstracting, and otherwise modifying those which have been already acquired by the mind. Limitations do indeed necessarily pertain to every revelation made to our finite minds; while some of these result from the limitation of our faculties, others arise from the perfect adaptation of the revelation itself to the end for which it is given. General and popular forms of truth, compared with scientific abstractions and analyses, are not only the most useful, but the only intelligible forms of truth to the common mind. Since then it is but a self-evident proposition, that whatever is revealed to the common mind is intelligible to that mind, it follows that the Scriptures have nothing to do with any unusual, unobvious, far-fetched, and unnatural notions of the nature of things. So far as the revelation goes, that elementary philosophy which the people possess—those ideas or conceptions of the nature of things which are common to the minds of men—absolutely restrict the use, and therefore control the interpretation of scriptural language.

The same thing may be shown in another way. Words are the signs of the ideas or conceptions of things. Of course they can be used and understood no further than the ideas or conceptions of which they are the signs have been already acquired by the mind. Hence also, that language may be the vehicle of thought or meaning from one mind to another, the words used must be signs of the same ideas or conceptions in both minds. For example, we cannot understand the import of the law, "Thou shalt love the Lord thy God with all thy heart," without having first acquired just and adequate ideas or conceptions of the things signified by the words, *God*, *heart*, *love*, &c., according to the intention of the Lawgiver. Here then a very important question arises, what are the ideas or conceptions which the Lawgiver intends to excite in our minds by this language? In other words, *what* and *how much* meaning belongs to these words in the intention of Him who uses them? In respect to the word *God*, the design is not to convey to our minds that vast and comprehensive conception in all its fullness, which the infinite Being forms of himself. Here is necessarily some limitation. So in respect to the words *heart* and *love;* and the design is not to send the mass of mankind to the schools of philosophy,—to the subtle metaphysician, the profound analyst of mental properties and mental phenomena,—to learn what things are meant by these words of the divine law. If this law is intelligible to the common mind, then that mind possesses all that knowledge of the nature of things which is requisite to the correct understanding of the language of the law. The same remark, with some unimportant exceptions, applies to the entire revelation of God. This revelation being designed for the instruction of mankind generally, is not concerned with those scientific abstract notions or conceptions which are peculiar to philosophers, nor with any notions of things that lie without the track and range of ordinary minds. It deals in truths more extensively known—in things less minute, more palpable, and more familiar. It employs those more general ideas and notions of things which are common, which lie within the limits of ordinary research, and whose truth or accordance with the reality of things is tested by the practical business of human life, and settled as a matter of certainty by the common mind. These are the ideas or conceptions of the nature of things with which the Bible is conversant. They constitute the common stock and property of the common mind in all ages and all countries; the only medium through which the Bible can, according to its design, become intelligible to all people; the grand materials of extending and improving our knowledge on the most important of all subjects. These high ends the Word of God proposes, not by imparting new elementary ideas to the human mind, but by combining, abstracting, and variously modifying those which already exist, in forms level to common apprehension. The peculiar notions, the far-fetched and out-of-the-way conceptions of philosophic inventors, have no place in the sacred volume. It deals exclusively in those obvious, natural, and easy ideas and notions of the nature of things which are common to mankind generally. These, and these alone, are the ideas or conceptions which human language, from its very nature, can possibly render intelligible or useful to the mass of mankind. These therefore alone constitute the *meaning* of that book which is designed for their instruction. We are brought then to this important and irrefutable principle in deciding the meaning of the sacred Scriptures —*that the meaning must not include any unusual philosophy, but must exclude it, and be confined most rigidly to those elementary ideas or conceptions of the nature of things which are formed by the common mind.*

In view of this principle, we now ask whether the doctrine of infant depravity, at the precise moment of birth, in any of its forms, ever entered the common mind as one of its obvious and natural conceptions? Laying aside all the speculations of philosophic minds, and all the theories devised for controversial purposes, is it a natural, obvious, common conception of the human mind, that infants are sinners at the precise instant of birth, by voluntarily transgressing known law, and this as an essential property of the soul; or by having sin either created or propagated in them as a constitutional propensity of the mind, like our constitutional propensity for food or drink; or by committing, as one and the same moral being with Adam, the self-same sin which he committed? Would either of these notions or conceptions ever have entered the head of any plain man of ordinary understanding? Would such a man ever think or conceive that mental acts are mental properties, any more than that all causes and effects are identical; or that constitutional propensities are sinful any more than bodily members; or that we committed Adam's first sin by being one with him, any more than that he, by virtue of the same connection, committed all our sins? Does that Book which is designed to instruct, reform, and save mankind, thus depart from the track and range of human thought, and confound and perplex all sober sense and sound reason?

With these views of the subject-matter of the Scriptures, the language of the book is, as we should expect it would be, in perfect accordance. We proceed then to say,

In the second place, *that the language of the Bible is to be interpreted, not to the letter in defiance of the plain dictates of sound reason and common sense; not with the minute accuracy of philosophic statement or verbal exactness; but only with that degree of precision which pertains to all popular speech and writing, and which the nature of the subject, the connection, and other circumstances determine.* The book which we call the Scriptures was written chiefly by plain men, and was addressed to plain men. While therefore it deals in the generalities of popular truth, it also of necessity adopts popular language. It adopts it, with all its remoteness, so far as mere words are concerned, from technical and philosophic precision. For the most part the sacred writers are even careless of every thing, except so to exhibit truth as to secure its influence on the popular mind. Provided their general meaning, or more correctly, some general comprehensive truth, be clearly and impressively presented, it betrays no concern to guard against captious objections, subtle misconstructions, nor even verbal incongruities. Words, so to speak, with them are nothing. Meaning is every thing. If this be obvious, true, consistent, important, their object is attained. Accordingly they present the weightiest truths in popular forms of speech, and commit them, though at the risk of being perverted and explained away, to the sound discretion and honest simplicity of the reader. Nor is the popular language of the Bible the least of those circumstantial proofs which confirm its divine origin. Instruction in this form is obviously best fitted to the great end for which a revelation is given; and while an honest mind, aided by its previous knowledge of things, and guided by that incidental evidence which always attends the use of such language, will be sure to discover its actual import, the very structure of popular language precludes all other safeguards against misconstruction. The law which governs its interpretation is emphatically common law—law which results from no statute enactments or arbitrary dictation of any man or any body of men. It is the law of custom, the law of usage—law which is generally understood and successfully applied in the language of common life—law which conducts the honest mind to infallible results, and which is therefore clothed with infallible authority. To interpret the Scriptures then with the minuteness of special pleading, or with the precision of philosophic or technical phraseology,—to press the language to the letter, or to the utmost precision of meaning which the mere words will bear, and thus to violate the law of common usage—is an outrage on the dignified simplicity of the Word of God from which every well-informed and candid mind must revolt.

In confirmation of these views of the subject we might appeal to the highest authorities. The great principle of Ernesti, *ne resecemus ad vivum—do not cut to the quick*—a principle, the violation of which has brought more dishonor upon the Word of God than every other false mode of interpretation, applies here. Mr. Burke, than whom there is not a more competent judge, says, "I do not conceive you to be of that sophistical, captious spirit, or of that uncandid dullness, as to require for every general observation or sentiment, an explicit detail of the correctives and exceptions which reason will presume to be included in *all* the general propositions which come from a reasonable man." We have still higher authority. Paul himself once found occasion, in the character of an interpreter, to recognize and apply the very principle for which we are contending.

"But when he saith, 'all things are put under him,' it is manifest that *he* is excepted who did put all things under him." As if he had said, the language is not to be interpreted to the letter. Reason and common sense decide that the exception, though not specified in words, is to be made.

But let us appeal to the language of the Scriptures itself. "Let the dead bury their dead" (Matt. viii. 22). "God did tempt Abraham" (Gen. xxii. 1). "Neither tempteth he any man" (Jas. i. 13). "By the works of the law shall no flesh be justified" (Gal. ii. 16). "Was not Abraham our father justified by works?" &c. "Was not Rahab the harlot justified by works?" (Jas. ii. 21, 25). "As having nothing, yet possessing all things" (2 Cor. vi. 10). "Whosoever shall keep the whole law and yet offend in one point, is guilty of all" (Jas. ii. 10). "And she was a widow who departed not from the temple, but served God with fastings and prayers night and day. And she, coming in at that instant, gave thanks," &c. (Luke ii. 37, 38). These passages are cited as specimens of scriptural usage which show beyond all question, that the language of the Bible is not to be interpreted to the letter. Indeed no other book probably would suffer so much as this from this mode of interpretation. The reason is, that it is written pre-eminently in the language of common life—in language of great looseness so far as mere words are concerned, and in the interpretation of which the reliance, instead of being on words merely, must be chiefly on the connection, the nature of the subject, and on those diversified circumstances which decide the meaning. Is then the meaning of this language obscure or doubtful? Not at all. Are these *real* contradictions, i. e., contradictions in the meaning? By no means. Let the real meaning of any two passages, or of any single passage containing a *verbal* incongruity, be ascertained, as it easily may be, and we always find a perfect harmony of import. But how shall such consistency be made out if we interpret to the letter? How is this, if with a "sophistical, captious spirit," or with "uncandid dullness," *we cut to the quick*, giving to every word the utmost meaning it will possibly bear? In the passages just cited, we should have literally dead men required to bury literally dead men; God tempting no man, and yet tempting Abraham; absolute poverty, and yet the possession of all things; a man keeping *the whole* law, and yet in one respect not keeping it, and thus not keeping it in any respect; a woman who never departed from the temple, coming into it, and engaged in fasting and prayer without sleeping night or day during her life. If all this is ridiculous, it only shows what the principle of interpretation is from which it results.

When however we speak of the want of philosophic precision in the language of the Scriptures, we are sure to excite alarm and call forth contradiction. The very men who never fail to appeal to the same fact when they have occasion to expose the errors of others, deny and execrate it when turned against their own favorite opinions. We are at once told, "if the language of the Scriptures is to be interpreted with such indefiniteness and want of precision, then its import becomes altogether uncertain, nothing can be decided respecting it with confidence, and every one is left to give what meaning he will to the sacred oracles." We might answer to this, that if these formidable consequences follow from the want of rigid and exact verbal precision in the language of the Bible, still *the fact* itself is undeniable and notorious—so notorious, that the refutation of the present charge is called for only because perverseness can make it, and because ignorance and credulity can be imposed on when it is made.

But the charge is groundless. For what is this so-called *indefiniteness* of popular language, which is deemed so portentous to the cause of truth? It is *not* indefiniteness in respect to any thing—not in respect to one idea which is of the least importance to be expressed or determined by the use of such language. The only possible pretense is, either that the language does not express something of which we know nothing,—or something which is absolutely of no moment in regard to the object or end of speaking or writing, and therefore not worth expressing,—or which no one can be rationally supposed to think of, and the very expression of which would be so entirely useless or unnecessary, as to disgrace the writer and to insult the reader by supposing that he had not the requisite discernment and integrity to make the proper exceptions and limitations. And what if such indefiniteness does belong to the language of common use, and to that of the Bible? Is there therefore nothing definitely said, when all is said which is worth saying, and said too with all the precision of meaning which is requisite to the ends of popular speech or writing?

Indeed what higher degree of precision is either desirable or practicable? How could the great purposes of language be answered, if every conceivable exception or qualification pertaining to the common forms of expression were to be formally specified? What if, in speaking of some general characteristic of man, or of a nation, we should always encumber our statements with the exceptions and qualifications which the case of some individual man, woman, child, or new-born infant might require, if truth *to the letter* were requisite? What if we may never name the date of any great event in this world, nor even that of its creation, unless we specify the precise instant, even the indivisible moment, in which the event occurred? What if we could never give the hour of the day with sufficient precision and truth, without specifying minutes, seconds, and half-seconds? And will any one gravely say, that in these common forms of expression there is an objectionable indefiniteness,—a want of precision which renders the import uncertain, and defeats the very end for which language is used? But is it so? Is there even the least indefiniteness or uncertainty in regard to the meaning, and all the meaning which the writer designs to express? Is not what he intends to say, and what he does not intend to say, as obvious to the candid and discerning, as had he stated, explained, qualified, and expounded after the manner of a plea in chancery? Would this expedient of cumbrous additions have rendered the meaning more precise, definite, or obvious? Is it not as accurately conveyed, both negatively and positively, as it can be by any other use of words? We think even more so; especially to the popular mind. If we appeal to facts, we find that no other use of language is exempt from misapprehension to such an extent among mankind generally. The moment a writer departs from ordinary usage by his definitions, qualifications, and exceptions, the common reader, if he is not lost in the labyrinth, is led to interpret by dismissing the judgments of common sense—those conceptions of things which are common to the human mind, and which constitute the surest possible criteria of the import of language, together with all the ordinary circumstantial means of ascertaining the meaning of language; and to place his dependence on mere words. He thus substitutes one of the most uncertain and doubtful kinds of evidence for the highest and best which the nature of the case admits.

We now appeal to the usual forms of expression in common life and in the Scriptures. Take the following: *Men* reason, brutes do not. *All* men value their reputation. *Everybody* was there. *All* Europe was agitated by the conquests of Bonaparte. The French nation are distinguished for affability and politeness. "Preach the Gospel to every creature." "Behold, *the whole city* went out to meet Jesus, and besought him" (Matt. viii. 34, xxi. 10; Mark i. 33). "And set *all the city* in an uproar" (Acts xvii. 5, xxi. 30). "Live peaceably with all men." We entered on the business *as soon as* we met. "*As soon as* the days of his ministration were accomplished, he departed to his own house" (Luke i. 23). "Him therefore I hope to send presently, *so soon as* I shall see how it will go with me" (Phil. ii. 23). He has *always* sustained a bad character. He was a liar from *the beginning.* "Showed him all the kingdoms of the world *in a moment* of time" (Luke iv. 5). "Our light afflictions which are but for *a moment.*" "I have guided her (the widow) *from my mother's womb*" (Job xxxi. 18). "*From a child* thou hast known the holy Scriptures (2 Tim. iii. 15).

The reader will perceive that these examples comprise two forms of phraseology—that the one affirms *universality* and the other describes *time;* and that to ascertain the true mode of interpreting these forms of expression, is to determine the true interpretation of those scriptural texts which are now under discussion.

How then are the above forms of expression to be interpreted? We answer, not to the letter—not with metaphysical or verbal precision. Let them be reviewed individually, and let such an interpretation be given, and how obvious, and how flagrant the perversion of the language! One form of expression thus interpreted, will assert that every new-born infant reasons,—that every new-born infant values his reputation,—that every infant in France is affable and polite,—that every infant in Jerusalem came out of the city to meet Jesus,—that Paul forbade all contention with infants at the very instant of birth,—and that all of this description were actually engaged in the uproar at Thessalonica! The other class thus interpreted, will assert, that in a meeting of gentlemen for business the common salutations of civility were omitted,—that Zacharias, when his ministration ended, without one intervening act, mental or bodily, departed to his house,—that Job became the benefactor of the widow the instant in which he was born, and that Timothy at the same moment actually possessed important knowledge of the written Word of God! More need not be said to show how remote from all correct usage of language, and how repulsive to common sense and sound reason, is this *ad literam* interpretation of the sacred oracles. We even feel that we owe an apology to our readers, to be derived from the "uncandid dullness" of some men, for thus extending our refutation of such a principle.

The question then returns, how are such forms of expression to be interpreted? We answer, according to the known or acknowledged nature of the subject, and the predicate—the connection, and other circumstantial evidence which may attend the case. By these, in all instances of the proper use of language, the meaning may be determined with great facility and entire success. In most instances, the nature of the subject and predicate will be sufficient for the purpose. Thus when we are told that certain men "set all the city in an uproar," the known incapacity of the new-born infant to partake in the tumult forbids the interpretation which includes them as engaged in it. When Paul speaks of his light afflictions *for a moment*, the known duration of his sufferings shows that he meant the whole of life. And when Job represents himself a benefactor from his mother's womb, the nature of the case shows that he means from that early period in which the performance of acts of kindness are supposable.

To apply these principles then to the case before us. When it is said that all have sinned, or Jews and Gentiles are all under sin, the language can no more be supposed to include infants at the precise instant of birth, than when it is said, that all men value their reputation, or all men reason, &c. When it is said that "the whole world is guilty before God," the language can no more be understood to include infants, than when it is said "the whole city went out to meet Jesus, and besought him," &c. When it is said that "the wicked are estranged from the womb—they go astray as soon they be born," the language no more predicates sin of infants at the moment of birth, than Job, in the same form of expression, predicates of himself active beneficence toward the widow at that instant.

But we shall be asked, how soon do the Scriptures on these

principles decide that mankind sin? Our answer is, as soon as the known or acknowledged nature and circumstances of the case will allow any reasonable man to suppose that they can sin. In our view, very early—so early, that their first moral character is sinful—so early, that God in his Word has not thought proper to make any account of the interval between birth and sin, nor to give us any more definite knowledge on the subject.

The true principle of interpreting the popular language of the Scriptures in those passages in question is, that all sin who can sin, and as soon as they can. The importance of this principle in its bearing on the denial of human depravity by Unitarians and others, compared with the *ad literam* interpretation, is obvious.

But we need not say more on this part of the subject. All we ask is, that the question may be fairly met on the grounds where we have placed it.

HUMAN SINFULNESS.

XI.—TOTAL DEPRAVITY BY NATURE.—(*Continued*).

Fourth objection to theory (continued), viz., that infants are sinners.—Other supposed Scripture proofs examined.—(II.) Argument from Justification.—(III.) From Regeneration.—(IV.) Sanctification from the womb.—(V.) Destiny at death.—(VI.) Argument from their sufferings and death.—(VII.) Argument from infant baptism.—Proofs against infant depravity.

In the preceding lecture I began an examination of the supposed proofs of infant depravity, and considered the principles of interpretation which apply to the proof-texts alleged in support of this doctrine. I now propose to examine other supposed scriptural arguments for the depravity of infants.

II. The argument from Justification may be thus stated: The Scriptures teach that all who are justified, are justified through the blood of Christ. As none but sinners can be justified through the blood of Christ, it follows that infants must be sinners, or that they cannot be justified at all. Here the objection might be left, it being as obvious that infants are no more included under this universal necessity, or even thought of in such scriptural declarations, than they are when we are required to preach the Gospel to *every creature*, or to live *peaceably with all men*. But this is not all. Infants, unless they can *believe*, cannot be justified through Christ, even if they are sinners. The doctrine is as broadly laid down in the Scriptures, that *faith* is as truly necessary to Justification, as the blood of Christ. "He that hath not the Son hath not life." "He that cometh to God *must* believe," &c. If it be said that infants are capable of believing this concerning God, I have only to say, that if any can receive this, and choose to receive it without any proof either from reason or the word of God, they are welcome to their faith.

III. The argument from Regeneration is substantially the same as the preceding, deriving all its plausibility from the *universal forms* of scriptural language, which any novice in interpretation knows are not to be construed as extending to infants. Besides, what is Regeneration? It is a moral change produced by the Spirit of God. It is, through this divine influence, "putting off the old man and putting on the new man;" it is ceasing to do evil and learning to do well; it is making ourselves a new heart and a new spirit—an intelligent, free, voluntary mental act, and none the less so because it is produced by a divine influence. It is therefore an act which is as impossible in the case of infants, as that of faith or repentance, or of calculating an eclipse. Besides, if we suppose it to be some other change—one which may be wrought in the infant mind—still, if actually wrought, the subject cannot be saved without faith; nor can a change in the structure of the mind be a moral change,—a change from holiness to sin. This necessarily implies a degree of intelligence of which infants are not capable, involving the knowledge of God, of the nature of sin and of holiness. I ask then, if any infant as such—an infant born at one moment and dying the next—is capable of such knowledge, and therefore capable of the change which necessarily involves such knowledge?

IV. It is claimed that some infants have been sanctified *from the womb*, and this is proof at least of *their capacity for holiness*. This argument rests on two false assumptions,—the one that the phrase *from the womb* denotes the *very moment* of birth; the other, that *sanctified* denotes, made the subject of *holiness or moral excellence*. The first assumption has been shown to be groundless. The second needs only a brief examination. The first text I notice is in Jer. i. 5. This is obviously a mere declaration of God, that he had appointed or separated Jeremiah, in his divine purpose, to the office of a prophet before he was born. (Compare Gal. i. 15; vide Rosenmüller, *in loc.*; Lev. xx. 26, and xxvii. 21; vide Schleusner, Αφοριςμ.) Besides, if the passage teaches that he was made holy, it teaches that he was so before birth, and of course he was not born a sinner, and could not be regenerated. There is then one exception to the universality of the facts contended for.

Another passage relied on is Luke i. 15 (vide verse 41), in which John the Baptist is said "to be filled with the Holy Ghost even from his mother's womb." Here it may be granted that "filled with the Holy Ghost" means regenerated or made holy; still the phrase "from his mother's womb," as we have shown, is indefinite, and leaves the precise moment of time undecided, and at most only shows that he was regenerated in very early life. (See Kuinoel, *in loc.*)

V. It is asked what becomes of infants, if they die without sin. I answer first, that they are as well off,—that their state is as desirable if they die without sin as if they die with sin. If they sin at the very moment of birth we have no evidence of their conversion, it being impossible to hold any communication with their minds; and the Bible being silent as to any assertion that they are saved. Nor is this all. On the scheme of our opponents they are infallibly lost, for they are sinners. But we have seen that they cannot repent, believe, or become holy; and the Scriptures decide that all sinners who do not repent, believe, &c., must be damned. If that large portion of the human race who die in early infancy are born sinners; if none of them can be saved except they repent and believe—except *they* put off the old man and put on the new—then how many of these are born, sin, die, and perish forever under the curse of God, before it is possible, that with any adequate knowledge of sin, of duty, of God, or the Saviour, they should renounce their iniquity by turning to God, or believe in him as a rewarder of those who seek him?

But a presumptuous curiosity still asks what becomes of those who die in infancy? I answer, a wise and benevolent God disposes of them without telling us *how*. Why should he tell us? *Cui bono?* We have no access to their minds, and can do nothing to instruct them, or in any way to contribute to their salvation, except in prayer and confidence to commend them to God. This we can do whether we know or not the precise moment when sin commences in the human mind. To give us knowledge merely to gratify our curiosity, and especially when by so doing, the occasion for the high and useful duties of submission to his will, and confidence in his government, would be either impaired or taken away, is not the manner of God. That we may, with unhesitating confidence, and with prayer for his blessing, commit such children to his hands, should be the great, the only object of solicitude to the Christian parent. It is certainly possible that children who die in infancy, should, in another state of being, wake up in angel purity, and their song forever speak of the grace that *saved* them alike from the character and the doom of a sinful world.

VI. The argument from the sufferings and death of infants is briefly this,—that suffering and death are the consequences of sin in the subject, and therefore infants are sinners. In support of the principle that all earthly calamities, and especially death, are the consequence of sin in the subject, the following texts are cited. The words of Eliphaz in Job iv. 7, "Who ever perished, being innocent?" and Rom. v. 12. The latter passage I shall consider hereafter. The former is not a divine declaration, though I hesitate not to admit the truth of it in real import. I only say respecting it, that it is one of those *universal forms* of expression, in which the speaker had no thought of an infant. Again, the principle which constitutes the premise of the present argument is contradicted by our Saviour in John ix. 2, 3. Here it is plainly asserted that this great calamity was not on account of the sin of the unhappy subject of it.

That the death of children in infancy is no evidence of their becoming sinners at birth, is decisively shown by the fact that they die *before* birth. If it be said that they sin before birth, then the doctrine that they first sin at birth is given up. And not only so, but that they sin before birth is denied by Paul, Rom. ix. 11. If now it be said that they are not human beings before birth, I answer, that in the language of the Scriptures and of all other usage, they are. The Mosaic law regarded the killing of an infant before birth as shedding man's blood, and so do the laws of every civilized people. Paul calls them children before they are born.

But it is claimed in this argument, that the object of Paul in Rom. v. 12, is to teach that sin is as universal as death among human beings, and that we have no warrant for denying the absolute universality of sin, in view of the absolute universality of death. I might say that even death is not absolutely universal in this world, for Enoch and Elijah did not die. But not to insist on this, I readily admit that if we have *no warrant* for denying the *absolute* universality of sin, viz., in the case of infants, then the above reasoning would be valid. But we have such a warrant, as we have sufficiently shown,—one which obliges us to make the exception in the case of infants. But I shall show hereafter, that the apostle in this passage, neither spoke of the death nor of the sin of infants; that he had not a thought respecting them.

VII. The argument from infant baptism claims that baptism

is proof of the sin of the subject. On this assumption the argument entirely depends. I answer then, that baptism, as a divine ordinance, affords no such proof.

First. Christ was baptized, though not a sinner. This is decisive that the ordinance, as such, does not prove sin in the subject. If it be said that this was a peculiar baptism, a ceremony of consecration to his priestly office, I answer, this is gratuitous. But whatever it was, the rite was administered to him as fulfilling all righteousness. Baptism then, in some cases and for some purposes, may be administered without previous sin in its subject. I therefore remark—

Secondly, that whether baptism is a proof of sin in its subject, depends wholly on what it is, or on the reason or end of its administration in the particular instance or instances in which it is administered. If administered in one case with a specific design or reference in that case, and not with the same design in others, then it is in each instance just what it is in that, and it is no more. Now we know that it was not administered in the case of the Saviour with any reference to sin in the subject. Again: we know that in the case of adult believers it was administered with another design, viz., as a sign of the remission of sins, and of course that in these instances it is proof of sin in the subject. Now where is the proof that it is administered to infants with the same design, or that it is the same thing in their case as when administered to adult believers? I say there is no evidence on this point. There is decisive proof to the contrary, as our opponents themselves must admit on their principles; for they concede that it is not the sign of Regeneration or of remission of sin in the case of infants. Of course it is *not* in one instance what it is in the other. (Vide Morus, vol. ii. p. 517.) And this utterly destroys the argument. Nor is this all. What is baptism in infants, when it is once conceded that it is not a sign of remission of sin or of Regeneration? Why, say our opponents, it is a sign that they need remission and Regeneration as sinners, i. e., it is a sign of their sinfulness. And is it so? Have we such an ordinance from God? Has he appointed the very emblem of purity as the sign of impurity and corruption? This is incredible. Or if it be said that it is not a sign of moral impurity, but of the necessity of moral purity, then I ask for the proof. What right has any man without warrant to unfold the import of such an ordinance in a manner so entirely arbitrary? Besides, it involves the subject in gross incongruity. In the case of adults it is a sign or seal of what is; in that of infants it is not, nor yet even a sign of what *will be*, but only a sign of what *need be;* and yet no more a sign of what need be in that class of children than in all others. In adults it distinguishes one class from another in view of a difference. In infants it distinguishes, if at all, one class from another without denoting a difference. Surely all this is arbitrary, and said for a purpose of defending a favorite opinion.

But what is infant baptism, and what does it denote or signify? I answer, and this on the principle of my opponents, as exhibited in all their formulas of doctrine—baptism has one general, common character, viz., it is a sign and seal of a covenant. This I suppose it was in all cases. In that of adult believers, it is admitted to come in the place of circumcision, and the apostle virtually declares it to be such a seal when he says Abraham received the *sign* of circumcision—a seal of the righteousness of the faith, &c. (Rom. iv. 11). Thus it is a rite which certifies the validity of the covenant, and in all its particular promises. As applied to believers, it signifies the fulfillment of those promises in them which respect them as adult believers. As applied to the infant children of believers, it signifies the validity of the promises which respect *them*. Comprehensively, the promise which respects them is, that of this class of children God will perpetuate a spiritual seed in the world, and each baptized child is thus exhibited as one of this class; his baptism is the sign of this fact, and the seal of this promise, and this is all that it is.

I come now to the scriptural argument against Infant Depravity.*

The only importance of this, is to show that sin consists in free moral action, by the removal of an objection drawn from this source. The doctrine of infant depravity exposes the Bible to the sneers of Infidels, and to its rejection by men of intelligence and reason. I allege the case of the child Immanuel (Is. vii. 15, 16; viii. 4). "Before the child shall know to refuse the evil," &c.; "have knowledge to cry, my father." Here is *one* child at least who, till about three years old, was not

* From the MS. notes of a pupil.

to know good from evil. If it refers to Jesus, then a portion of the race, other children, cannot know and cannot have sinned. There are passages in which children are spoken of as "not knowing good from evil." "Your children which in that day had no knowledge between good and evil" (Deut. i. 39). To this some object that it may mean that particular sin for which others were excluded from Canaan. There is no indication that this was meant; but we will allow them to adhere to their literal interpretation, 'no knowledge of good and evil.' Again, Jonah iv. 11: "And should not I spare Nineveh, that great city, wherein are more than six-score thousand persons that cannot distinguish between their right hand and their left, besides much cattle?" It is objected, 'there could not be so many infants in one city.' There could be in those times and regions, for the population exceeded all that we see in modern times. In this passage then, God is giving Jonah a reason why he spared Nineveh. What logic is it to say, that he spared it because there were one hundred and twenty thousand persons in it who *deserved* punishment? The weight of the reason consisted in their innocence. There are passages in which infants are called *innocent*. Jer. ii. 34: "In thy skirts is found the blood of the souls of the poor innocents." Ps. cvi. 38: "Innocent blood," &c., of souls, &c., sacrificed. Jer. xix. 4. 2 Kings xxi. 16. But the last does not certainly mean infants. It may mean pure, free from blame, or clear, free, quit from an obligation. On what ground will they pronounce these infants, whom inspiration characterizes as innocents, deserving of eternal death? Do they say it means comparatively innocent? Let them adhere to a *literal interpretation*. Passages which speak literally of the time when sin begins, seem to me to be very indefinite. Such as speak of going "astray from the womb" are evidently figurative. But Gen. viii. 21: "The imagination of man's heart is evil from his youth," &c. *Youth* is a period of very indefinite length. All we can say is, they sin very early.

HUMAN SINFULNESS.

XII.—CONSEQUENCES OF ADAM'S SIN TO HIS POSTERITY, AND THE CONNECTION BETWEEN THAT SIN AND THESE CONSEQUENCES.

Subject divided into two parts.—I. The fact of a connection.—General statement variously modified.—Proved (1,) by narrative in Genesis.—Also by the assertions in Romans v. 12, 18, 19.—II. Mode of connection.—It is not true (1,) that Adam's posterity are created with a sinful nature, nor (2,) that they are guilty of his sin.—The doctrine involves absurdity, injustice, and is unsupported by the Scriptures.—The principle is denied in the Scriptures.—Not guilty of his sin by being counted as one with him, through a sovereign act of God.—Nor by putative act of God.—Biblical Repertory and Christian Spectator.

That sin and death, with that class of evils to which in this world our race were doomed after the apostasy, come, in consequence of Adam's sin, on his posterity, is an opinion almost universally received by believers in Divine revelation. The more particular consequence, viz., the sinfulness of his posterity, is that respecting which there has been great diversity of opinion, and which now claims our particular attention.

The subject naturally divides itself into two parts, viz.:

I. The fact that the sinfulness of mankind is in consequence of the sin of Adam; and—

II. The mode of connection between his sin and this consequence.

I propose—

I. To prove the fact, that the sinfulness of mankind is in consequence of the sin of Adam.

Those who have maintained this general form of the fact have frequently connected with it specific statements, which in my view the Scriptures do not authorize. Thus it has been confidently asserted, that had our first parents not sinned, sin and death would never have entered the world,—that the death of mankind is to be considered as exclusively the consequence of Adam's sin, and in no respect the consequence of their own, so that all men would die though they were sinless or holy,—that had the penalty of the law which Adam transgressed been executed according to the strict principle of Moral Government and exact letter of the law, Adam would have had no posterity.

I advert to these opinions chiefly for the purpose of remarking, that caution is requisite in this case, as in most others, lest we give to the general forms of scriptural language a more particular meaning than they are designed to convey. It is, if I mistake not, from the want of this that most of the theological controversy in the Church arises, and especially on the subject now under consideration.

It will be admitted by those from whom I may differ on the topics just stated, that the language of the Scriptures, at least so far as words or forms of statement are concerned, gives us only the general fact, *that the sinfulness of mankind is in consequence of the sin of Adam.* But it is maintained that this general form implies the other more particular facts. This I deny. It may be true, that God determined that if Adam sinned, his posterity should be sinners, and also, that had Adam *not* sinned, some, or even all of his posterity should sin. God may determine that the small-pox should be introduced into a community by one man; and still it may be true, that were it not to be thus brought, it would be introduced in some other way. So also it may be true, that the death of mankind is a consequence *indirectly* of Adam's sin, and *directly* a consequence of their own sin. Again, it may be consistent with the strictest principles of law or Moral Government, that when Adam had sinned, God should delay for a time, as men do in civil governments, the execution of the penalty, and that our first parents, even without the system of redemption, should have lived long enough under a merely legal dispensation, to people the earth with their descendants. If these things are so, then plainly there can be nothing to justify the above specific statements which are so often made. Instead then of adopting these conjectural and unauthorized implications, I take only this general position, as that and that only which the Scriptures authorize,—*that the sinfulness of mankind is in consequence of Adam's sin.*

I proceed to support the truth of this position by the following proofs. I allege—

1. The account given by Moses of the fall of our first parents, and its consequences.

From this narrative we learn that God designed that Adam

and Eve should be the progenitors of a race. Gen. i. 28: "God blessed them and said, 'Be fruitful, and multiply, and replenish the earth, and subdue it.'" The form in which marriage is instituted plainly shows the same thing. "Therefore shall a man leave his father and his mother, and shall cleave unto his wife, and they shall be one flesh" (Gen. ii. 24). The fifteenth and sixteenth verses of the third chapter very clearly show, that not only the serpent but the woman were acquainted with the design of God to people the earth with human beings as the descendants of the first pair.

Again: we shall now see that this narrative of Moses gives yet other facts, which clearly show that sin and death, with other evils, were the consequence of the sin of Adam.

Particularly, an economy of grace was immediately introduced as consequent on the sin of Adam; it respected his descendants as truly as himself, and essentially changed their condition from what it would have been under a merely legal economy. In Gen. iii. 15, an economy of grace is revealed: "It shall bruise thy head, and thou shalt bruise his heel." The work of the Redeemer is described by an apostle as consisting in destroying him that hath the power of death. (Vide Heb. ii. 14; 1 John iii. 8.)

Who then can doubt that certain consequences of Adam's sin to his posterity were the grounds in respect to which this economy of grace was adopted? Who can doubt as to the specific consequence that *they were to be sinners*, and in this character to need a Saviour? And yet who can on this point decide any thing more specific? Whether they would or would not have sinned if Adam had not, who can tell? It might be true that if he sinned, they would sin, and it might also have been true, that had he not sinned, they would not have sinned. While then the simple fact, that in consequence of his sin, they would sin, is all that can be inferred from the narrative, this fact itself is most clearly taught.

Another fact consequential on the sin of Adam is, that Paradise is changed into a world of thorns and briers, of toil and pain and death. By this change, it was obviously designed as the residence of a sinful race, and clearly indicates its character. Again we see not only that the sinful character of Adam's posterity, but also that these ills of life, and death itself were consequential on his sin. But who can say any thing more than this?

Who can decide from this narrative whether death is or is not the consequence of Adam's sin, exclusively of the sin of his descendants; or whether it is or is not directly the consequence of their sin, and indirectly of his, as the latter is the ground of the certainty of the former?

Another fact is conspicuous from this narrative, that death and other evils consequent on Adam's sin, both to him and his posterity, are not the result of a strictly legal process. If so the economy of grace was vain, since it accomplished nothing. Death, with other earthly calamities, does not imply any violation on the part of the Lawgiver of the principles of law; nor yet are they what these principles demand as the full execution of the legal penalty. These evils are inflicted under an economy of grace, and are blended with manifold mercies. They were denounced subsequently to the establishment and disclosure of such an economy. Even death, the greatest of them, may be, and often is a blessing, being an entrance into bliss eternal. Death was as truly destroyed when the promise of redemption was made, as when Christ died; i. e., though an evil, it was not a penal evil—it was an evil as included in a system of moral discipline for sinners under grace; it was an evil, and as such, a *consequence and proof* of sin and condemnation, but not a legal penalty. These evils therefore, are not inflicted on men, nor was this implied in this sentence, in the way of legal process. They are indeed inflicted on sinners and on those who deserve them, and even still greater evils.

Now from all these facts in the Mosaic narrative, we unavoidably conclude that sin and death, with other evils, were in a most palpable and striking manner the consequence of Adam's sin. For why this change from the original dispensation of law—why this economy of grace? Why this world of thorns and briers, the appointed residence of a race yet to exist? Why this destiny to toil and pain, and sorrow and death, in respect to all who should live on the face of it? Is there or is there not some single event, whence in some way of connection all this originated? No one can read the Mosaic history and doubt that there was such an event, and that it was the sin of Adam in Paradise. He must see that the grand object of the historian was to convince us that this is such a sinful, dying world as it is, under the government of God, as the consequence of Adam's sin.

Here however, we must guard against certain particular inferences, which though the narrative of Moses does not expressly deny, it does not authorize. Who dare say it authorizes us to assert that the sin of Adam is *the direct proximate cause* of the sin of his posterity? The narrative does not imply this, while the nature of sin in man and the known proximate cause, as previously explained, forbid such an inference. Neither may we infer as a revealed doctrine, that death comes on men in no sense for their own sin. For had not their sin been certain, God might not have doomed them to certain death. If it be said that infants have no sin of their own, and therefore do not die for their own sin in any sense, I answer, this may be true, and yet the Scriptures may have used that general phraseology which decides nothing respecting infants. Their case may have been unnoticed, and the Scriptures have expressly decided in general terms that men die in the character of sinners.* On this supposition, death, though it comes in one respect as the consequence of the personal sin of each, comes as a mark of God's displeasure with each—comes as *a proof* of sin in each; still as it does not come in the way of a strictly legal process, it may also be connected with Adam's sin as well as with their own.

In further proof of our position I allege—

Rom. v. 12, 18, 19: "Wherefore as by one man sin entered into the world," &c. "Therefore as by the offense of one (or better, as by one offense), judgment came upon all men to condemnation." "By one man's disobedience many were made (or became) sinners." These passages cannot be understood to teach less than that all mankind become sinners in consequence of Adam's sin.

I now proceed to consider—

II. *The mode* of connection between Adam's sin and that of his posterity.

It is obvious that one thing may be supposed to be the consequence of another in many ways or *modes* of consequence, and that simply to affirm that one thing is *by another* or *by means* of it, or is *a consequence* of it, decides nothing in respect to the *particular mode* of the connection. It is, if I mis-

---

* The very passage in Gen. iii. 16–19, itself shows that the evils threatened respected *not* infants but adults.

take not, in this general and indefinite manner that the Scriptures exhibit the connection between Adam's sin, and the sin and death of his posterity. This has given rise to much gratuitous and unauthorized speculation; and there are few subjects in theology in respect to which the language of Scripture has been more unreasonably pressed, or on which opinions so groundless and absurd have been held with so much tenacity. Whether revelation enables us to answer every minute inquiry respecting the mode of this connection or not, it is believed that from the known nature of the subject, and from what the Scriptures teach, we can decide in the most important respects what this *mode* is *not*, and also what *it is*.

This I shall now attempt, remarking—

1. That the posterity of Adam do not become sinners as a consequence of his sin, by being created with a *sinful nature*, or by having such a nature conveyed to them by the laws of propagation. This point has been already discussed.

2. Adam's posterity do not become sinners as a consequence of his sin, *by being guilty of his sin*. This theory or doctrine has been advocated under some diversity of specific form. Some have maintained that we are guilty of his sin by *transfer;* i. e., that God in the exercise of absolute sovereignty *transfers* the guilt of Adam's sin to his posterity, without respect to any personal acts or personal ill-desert on their part; thus making them guilty when otherwise they had been innocent.

The absurdity and injustice involved in this doctrine are its sufficient refutation, since they are so palpable and gross that we are fully authorized to say *a priori*, that the doctrine itself is not to be found in a revelation from God. It is replete with absurdity, for what greater can there be, than that the guilt of one being should become the guilt of another—yea of the millions of his descendants to the end of time? We might ask, was the whole or a part of the guilt of Adam transferred? If the whole, why did he not become innocent by the transfer? If a part, how was it divided between him and them? Was it equally or unequally divided? Was he as guilty as had no division been made, and each of them as guilty as he? or was the portion of each lessened at all by the division? I may further ask, whether it could be thus divided into parts, and each part be equal to the whole; whether guilt like matter be infinitely divisible, and even whether when divided into parts as indefinitely as the supposition demands, there could be enough for all, and each the object of a just condemnation?

More gravely now I ask, what is guilt? What is guilt if it be not a personal thing, pertaining to the action, and solely to the action of an agent who acts? Plainly, if this be not true of all that can be called guilt, the human mind has no conception of it. If it be true of all that can be called guilt, then the doctrine is chargeable with the contradiction of affirming that a thing which is not guilt is guilt. There is no escape from this, but by denying that guilt pertains exclusively to the action of an agent; and this is folly too great to be reasoned with.

The injustice which the doctrine imputes to God is still more revolting. "Shall not the Judge of all the earth do right?" And is there no appeal to the reason of man in respect to what right is? If not, then why does God himself so often appeal to human reason on this very question? Every such appeal is an admission that men do know what right or equity is; what it demands and what it forbids. If not, then there is an end, not only to all reasonings and conclusions in theology, but to all confidence in God. If there be no standard of right or equity on which human reason is competent to decide, where is our proof of his justice or goodness? How can we reason or judge at all in respect to either his character or his government? But if there is such a standard, if there is an eternal rule of right which human reason does and must understand, and by which it must judge, or be of no use to man, then the appeal is fairly made to human reason. I ask then, what violation of the eternal rule of right more palpable, than *to transfer* the guilt of one being to another; than to count another guilty, and to punish him for another's act? Admit that such a principle obtains in the moral administration of God, and what are the consequences? He who is not guilty becomes truly guilty; yea, he who is holy may be really and at the same time as guilty as the guiltiest, and be treated accordingly. Such a principle subverts every thing; law, equity, moral government, moral character, in respect to both God and man are overthrown, and the righteous as well as the wicked have cause for consternation and dismay.

Again: this doctrine derives no support from the Scriptures. Allowing the possibility that it should be found in the Bible, still no passage can be properly understood to teach it which will admit of any other meaning. Before a doctrine so revolting to reason and common sense can be palmed upon the Word of God, it must be shown that the language cannot be interpreted in any other but the absurd meaning, and this I affirm to be impossible in respect to any passage cited to support it.

Further: the passages depended on for the support of this doctrine require another import. They are those which speak of God's *imputing* sin and righteousness. We read that "Abraham believed God, and it was imputed to him for righteousness," that is, his faith was reckoned as the ground of favor instead of perfect obedience or of righteousness; of course he had none by *transfer*. Shimei, who deserved death for cursing David, prayed thus: "Let not my lord *impute* iniquity unto me." Whose iniquity? Not another's, but plainly his own; as if he had said, let me not be punished as my crime deserves. God, it is said, imputed sin to the children of Korah, Dathan, and Abiram, on account of their father's sin. But I answer, that there is no more evidence that these children were punished *for being guilty of their father's sin*, than there is in every other case in which children die. Indeed their death, for aught that appears to the contrary, may have been *to them* on the whole a real blessing, and not a punishment, while it was evil to the parents, and might subserve the useful purpose to others to awe them from similar crimes.

Other examples are referred to, viz., Job xxi. 19: "God layeth up his iniquity for his children." Jer. xxxii. 18; 1 Sam. xv. 1–7, and 19. These are examples in which certain evils come on those who deserve them for their own sins, or they are not. If they are, they have no relevance to the question. If they are not, they are cases in which the evils brought on the children may be, on the whole, blessings to them. Another passage is appealed to. Ex. xx. 5: "Visiting the iniquity of the fathers upon the children unto the third and fourth generation of them that hate me." (Vide Emmons' Ser., vol. i. p. 305.) This passage must be interpreted so that "them that hate me" shall be *the children that hate me*, in which case the evil is deserved by the children; or it must mean the children of *parents who hate me*, in which case the evils are not *penal*, but may be disciplinary, as in the case of a drunkard's children, to whom certain evils consequential on *his* crimes may be real blessings.

But the view of this passage now opposed is plainly contradicted by the following passages: Deut. xxiv. 16; 2 Kings xiv. 6; 2 Chron. xxv. 4; Jer. xvi. 11, 12, 13.

Once more: this doctrine of transfer is explicitly denied in the Scriptures. Ezek. xviii. 20: "The soul that sinneth, it shall die." "The son shall not bear the iniquity of the father." Vide also Jer. xxxi. 29, 30. A more explicit recognition of injustice in any procedure, than in that of punishing children for the sins of their fathers, cannot be well conceived; nor a more formal vindication from the charge of injustice on the part of God be named. The charge is, that an innocent posterity are punished for the iniquity of the fathers; in a proverbial form of expression, "The fathers have eaten sour grapes, and the children's teeth are set on edge." The vindication by God himself is a point-blank denial of the fact, accompanied with the severe and terrible rebuke, "What mean ye, that ye use this proverb concerning the land of Israel, saying, The fathers have eaten sour grapes?" &c. (Ezek. xviii. 2). Who that reads this chapter will dare to repeat such a charge against God?

Another form of the doctrine, *that Adam's posterity are guilty of his sin*, and that in which it is taught by its ablest advocates, is, that Adam's posterity, by the sovereign constitution of God, are *one* with Adam, and thus are truly and properly considered as acting in his act; and so committing one and the same sin which Adam committed. This theory is encumbered with absurdities, and involves imputations on the Divine character not less revolting than those which pertain to the theory of transfer. If we are one in Adam, and so guilty of his sin, then also was Adam one with us and guilty of our sins; and without saying what a monster of iniquity this representative of the human race must be, having committed each and every sin that has been and shall be perpetrated from the beginning to the end of time, the question naturally arises, whether *we* have in fact any sin at all to answer for, since all sins were committed by our common father. Or if it be said, and this is said, that Adam and his descendants are one *complex* person, one *moral whole*, then how much sin pertains to each according to an equitable distribution among the parts? And further, it would seem that in the dispensation of punishment or pardon, this same *moral whole* must share alike in the calamity and the blessing; i. e., so much sin as is punished must be so punished in the several parts of this *moral whole*, and so much as is forgiven must be remitted to the several parts of this *moral whole*. On which principle of equity can one be wholly subject to punishment, and another wholly pardoned? If any given number of sins for example, be pardoned, they must be pardoned in respect to the being to whom they belong; i. e., in the present case in respect to the complex whole, and as there cannot be punishment so far as there is pardon, each individual has a fair claim to his portion of the benefit.

But not to dwell on such absurdities, what shall be said of a Moral Government in which such a principle is acted upon, and what of its author? The mind unperverted by theological system-making cannot fail to see what appalling consequences must follow from the adoption of the principle, that one being is to be considered and treated as having acted in another's act; nor indeed that God himself cannot make it true that one being is another, or the act of the one is the act of the other. No constitution or covenant of God can make it true, that a being can sin before he exists. All that can be said in extenuation of these "fooleries" is, that great and good men may believe the most palpable absurdities without seeing them to be such, when they suppose themselves obliged to adopt them in defense of revealed truth.

There are two sources of argument on the part of those who maintain the doctrine that *we are guilty* of Adam's sin, which in their view at least ought not to be passed without notice: one is the fact that children suffer extensively in consequence of the sins of parents, according to the very laws of nature which God has established; the other is the scriptural text, Rom. v. 12: "Therefore as by one man sin entered into the world, and death by sin; and so death passed upon all men, for that all have sinned."

The fact that children suffer in consequence of the sins of their parents is undeniable. But in what *way* or *manner* of connection? Is it on the ground that the sins of the parents are the sins of the children? That all the calamities of children are not inflicted on this principle, we are taught by the Saviour himself (John ix. 2, 3). The question is, what proof is there that any are inflicted on this principle? To say that they are inexplicable on any other, is saying nothing to the purpose, since many, like that now adverted to, are inexplicable on this. Indeed, if they are accounted for in this way, the inexplicableness of the procedure is still increased. The truth is, that both reason and Scripture oblige us to class the sufferings of infants, be the proximate causes of them what they may, under the category of evils, which may be, whether we can or cannot tell *how they are*, consistent with God's moral perfection. At any rate, who shall say, that to account for the sufferings of infants we are bound to believe nonsense?

But it is not difficult to account for the sufferings of children which are consequential on parental crime. The child of a drunkard becomes decrepit, deformed, and feeble. This to him may be a great blessing, in supplying useful discipline, as restraint on vice, and in other ways.

4. There is another form of the doctrine of Imputation, which may be called Putation,—that the posterity of Adam are guilty of his sin, or that they are liable to suffer the consequences of Adam's sin, without being the subjects of ill-desert in any mode.

This is only another, and so far as the Orthodox are concerned, a modern form of the doctrine of *Imputation.* It is that maintained in the "Biblical Repertory," published at Princeton, and by Professor Hodge in his "Commentary on Romans." It may be thus stated,—*that God regards and treats all men as sinners on account of Adam's sin, without their being the subjects of ill-desert, either by transfer or by Imputation, or in any other way.*

In a controversy between the "Biblical Repertory" and the "Christian Spectator" in 1831, Professor Hodge undertook to defend this form of the doctrine of Imputation. He appealed first to the authority of such writers as Augustine, Calvin, Turretin, Owen, and Edwards. The "Spectator," in reply, maintained that no one of these writers held this form of the doctrine of Imputation. The rejoinder of Professor Hodge consists substantially in abandoning this ground of authority which he had taken with so much confidence at the outset, by saying, "that it was no concern of his whether these standard writers, to whom he had appealed, held the doctrine or not!" (Vide "Christian Spectator," 1831, p. 497.)

The difference between the professed doctrine of Professor Hodge and the writers referred to is, that they held that the posterity of Adam are truly ill-deserving, and regarded as so on account of Adam's sin, and that he maintains, except when he contradicts himself, that no ill-desert whatever belongs to the posterity of Adam on account of his sin, though God regards and treats them as sinners; thus virtually maintaining that God regards that to be true which is not.

Thus Professor Hodge says, "that Adam's first act of transgression was *not*, strictly and properly, that of his descendants;" that community in action, transfer of moral character, are no part of the doctrine of Imputation; that their doctrine (that of the Old School) includes neither the idea of any mysterious union of the human race with Adam, so that his sin is strictly and properly theirs, nor a transfer of moral character; he denies that the moral turpitude of that sin was transferred to us, and even the possibility of such a transfer. They say, that Imputation does not involve a transfer of moral acts or moral character, that the ill-desert of one man cannot be transferred to another. They maintain that the word *guilt*, as applied in the present controversy, denotes simply *liability* to punishment, and that no ill-desert belongs to Adam's descendants, as the previous ground or reason that the evil consequences of his sin come upon them.

Such, in many different forms, are their statements of *their* doctrine of Imputation.

Let us now hear all this contradicted by the same writer. He says: "In Imputation there is, *first*, an ascription of something to those concerned; and, *secondly*, a determination to deal with them accordingly." Again: "When Paul begged Philemon to *impute* to him the debt or offense of Onesimus, he begged him *to regard him as the debtor or offender*, and *to exact of him whatever compensation he required*." He describes this as "laying the conduct of one *to the charge* of another, and *dealing* with him accordingly." Here plainly are two things—a *first* and a *second*—an ascription of conduct and a determination to deal, &c. Paul not only begged Philemon to look to him for remuneration, if wronged by Onesimus, but to regard him as *the offender*. If language can express the idea, Paul requested Philemon to accuse *him* of the misconduct of his run-away slave, and also to exact compensation for any wrong done. In accordance with this, Professor Hodge says, "When Adam's sin is said to be imputed to his posterity, *it is intended* that his sin is *laid to their charge*, AND they are punished for it, or are treated as sinners on this account." Who makes this charge? God. Is it true or false? If true, then Imputation involves more than liability to evil consequences. If false, then God does not make it. Thus while we are told in formal statements, professed explanations, that *Imputation* involves *mere liability*, on the part of Adam's posterity, to certain consequences of Adam's sin, we are also told that it involves laying Adam's *sin to their charge.*

The reason for this exhibition of contradiction is to show the fact of an entire agreement *in things* between New England divines and the conductors of the Biblical Repertory, according to some of their statements. It is time to cease all disputation except about words.

In maintaining the form of Imputation now under consideration, its advocates attempt to give it plausibility by appealing to certain transactions among men. The cases to which they refer are those in which one is *said* to do what another does, and is also held responsible for his act; or in which what one has done is said to be put to the account of another; e. g., the monarch is said to do the act of his representative or minister, and to be bound by it. So the relation of one who employs an agent—the parent for a child, and particularly the case of Paul and Onesimus are referred to. Between all such cases and the one under consideration, there is one essential difference which is fatal to the cause in support of which the appeal is made, viz., in all these cases the language used, and the responsibility which exists, is founded on *a prior consent or stipulation, either expressed or implied*, to be held responsible. The only question is, whether the evil consequences of Adam's sin come upon his posterity on this ground, viz., of their previous voluntary consent, expressed or implied, to be held responsible for Adam's act? This is out of the question. How then can the fact that certain consequences of Adam's sin come on his posterity, be accounted for on the principle of the voluntary assumption of another's responsibility?

To expose more fully the groundless nature of this appeal in the case of Paul and Onesimus, let us suppose Paul to have used the language of those who claim that he meant what they mean. Suppose he had said to Philemon, 'If Onesimus has wronged thee, or oweth thee aught, lay it to my charge; not merely regard me as becoming liable by my consent to be responsible for the consequences, but charge and accuse me of all the misconduct of your run-away slave; if he has robbed you, or defamed you, or burned your house, or killed your children, accuse me of these things openly and before the world.' Had the apostle said these things, would it not have amounted to proof of insanity? And yet, according to our brethren, he might have said them with perfect truth and propriety. They represent God as doing the very thing which Paul in such language would have requested Philemon to do, and which of course Philemon, had he complied with Paul's request, would have done. He would have laid to the charge of Paul all the crimes of this run-away slave; and the great apostle, even after his conversion, would stand before the world, in the proper use and true meaning of language, charged with and guilty of these crimes, as truly, in the belief of Professor Hodge, as Adam's descendants are charged in the Bible with Adam's sin. This indeed would be done with the consent of the apostle, while in respect to Adam's descendants, his sin is charged upon them, and they are made liable to its consequences without their consent, *ex ordine Dei.*

Some hold the doctrine we have been considering under another form. They say that Adam was *our federal head or representative.* This language is sometimes used to describe the same thing as that of *transfer;* sometimes that of *Imputation;* sometimes that of *Putation;* and sometimes to denote simply the doctrine, that in Adam there was such a trial of human nature, as to show us that there is no reason to suppose that it would have been better for his posterity to have been tried as he was, than it now is. This I do not deny. It certainly *may be* so. Indeed there is a high probability that it is better for us to be what we are in nature and circumstances, than to have been what Adam was in this respect. On this principle some proceed to make an inference wholly unwarranted, viz., that it is just in God, as Professor Hodge maintains, to regard and treat us as sinners on account of Adam's sin; i. e., to bring upon us the penal evils of his sin. This is an outrage on justice. What if I, had I been created with the same constitution in kind and degree, and placed in the same circumstances with Borgia, or any other cut-throat of the hierarchy, should have committed the same crimes, can I therefore be justly considered and treated as if I had committed them?

HUMAN SINFULNESS.

XIII.—CONSEQUENCES OF ADAM'S SIN TO HIS POSTERITY, AND THE CONNECTION BETWEEN THAT SIN AND THESE CONSEQUENCES.

Rom. v. 12–19, considered.—Falsely interpreted.—I. Reasons for this untenable.—1. Rendering of ἐφ' ᾧ.—2. No rendering of ἥμαρτον supports this doctrine.—3. The drift of the argument does not support it.—The apostle does not teach that infants are sinners, nor that death is the legal penalty of sin.—"*All have sinned.*"—"*Death by sin.*"—Argument from fourteenth verse.—The death spoken of is not penal.—Signification of κατάκριμα —Nature of the case.—The death common to all men.—It takes place in this world.—Denied by the apostle to be legal penalty.—Arguments from the prevalence of death from "Adam to Moses."—II. Proofs against this interpretation are decisive.

I PROPOSED, in the preceding lecture, to show—

I. The fact, that the sinfulness of mankind is the consequence of the sin of Adam; and,

II. To consider *the mode* of connection between that sin and this consequence.

After attempting to prove the fact as now stated, I entered on the consideration of *the mode* of connection between Adam's sin and the sin of his posterity; and attempted to show particularly the absurdity of the doctrine, that his posterity are guilty of his sin by Imputation, in the different forms of this doctrine; also that the Scriptures give no support to, but rather explicitly deny it. This led to an examination of the scriptural argument with the exception of the passage in Rom. v. 12. I now propose to examine this much-controverted passage.

If what has been said be true, there is at least a strong presumption, not to say decisive proof, that this text gives no support to the doctrine, that the descendants of Adam are guilty of his sin in any sense in which this language can be used. To suppose that it can be derived from this text, is to suppose the apostle to lay down a principle which has no countenance from other parts of the sacred volume, which is contrary to all reason and common sense, and which is also in the most explicit terms denied, and denied in terms of severe rebuke by God himself.

In considering this passage of Scripture, I propose—

First—To examine the reasons given for the interpretation which I oppose; and,

Secondly—To offer proofs against this interpretation.

First—To examine the reasons for the interpretation which I oppose.

1. The rendering of the last clause of the twelfth verse thus, "*in whom* all have sinned." The Vulgate, and many of the older commentators, translate the words ἐφ' ᾧ, *in whom.* Against this rendering there are the following reasons: (1.) The antecedent is too remote. (2.) 'Εν ᾧ would be used if this were the meaning. (3.) 'Αμαρτάνειν ἐπί τινι (*to sin in another*), is a conception unknown. (4.) The assertion ἐφ' ᾧ παντες ἥμαρτον, is explained, or rather the idea or meaning is developed in the following verses, 13th and 14th, and indeed in the whole passage to the end of the chapter. This we shall see hereafter. Professor Hodge rejects the rendering *in whom.* The rendering *unto which*, is, I think, supported by the most evidence. (Vide Doddridge *in loc.* Vide also examples from Greek writers in Stuart's Com., *in loc.*)

2. It is claimed that ἥμαρτον may be understood, *have sinned by Imputation.* As we have seen, there are two forms of the doctrine of Imputation. One is, that the posterity sin by being one and the same person with Adam, and by committing the same sin, in number and kind, which he committed. It is worthy of remark, that the word ἁμαρτάνω always denotes to sin *by acting*, in the view of those who adopt this theory. Thus Turretin says, "the word ἥμαρτον properly denotes some actual sin" (pecatum aliquod actuale). He states expressly that they who sinned in Adam, before they exist, are considered as sinning in him and themselves to have sinned.—(Instit. Theol., vol. i. p. 481.)

According to another form of the doctrine of Imputation, it is claimed that ἥμαρτον may be rendered, *treated as sinners*, or *regarded and treated as sinners, without personal ill-desert.* That God should *regard* a being as a sinner who is not, is intuitively absurd and impossible. Or if it be said that the meaning is, that all are *truly regarded* as sinners, then they are sinners and ill-deserving. In support of this rendering of the word ἥμαρτον, we are referred by some commentators to other passages. Two of these only we shall notice, and merely because Professor Hodge has referred to them. One is in Gen. xliv. 32, or xliii. 9. The literal rendering is, *I shall have sinned.* Nor is there any thing decisive that this does not give the exact meaning; i. e., there is nothing to show that Judah did not intend to say, I shall have sinned in violating my promise to protect and restore the child. It may be however, I will *consent* to be regarded as a sinner, so far as this is possible, without being in fault, i. e., *to be treated as a sinner.* Supposing then, that one man says to another in a case like this, *I shall have sinned*, meaning only, *I consent to be treated as a sinner*, does it follow that a God of equity and truth can use the same language in the same meaning in respect to all mankind, and this when not one of them has sinned, nor even consented to be treated as a sinner? Supposing it to be proper to say, *I have sinned*, meaning simply that *I have consented to be treated as a sinner*, can God say *that all have sinned*, in the same sense, when not one has *consented to be treated as a sinner?* This would be a palpable falsehood.

The other passage is in 1 Kings i. 21. Here the literal rendering is, "I and my son Solomon *shall be sinners;*" i. e., in the view of Adonijah, and other political demagogues. Supplying the ellipsis, the phrase *shall be sinners* has its literal meaning. Bathsheba affirming that herself and son would be in fact, though erroneously in her view, *esteemed sinners* or offenders by Adonijah. Suppose however that she had another meaning, viz., that Adonijah would, without believing her and Solomon to be actual offenders, treat them as such; does it follow that because usage would justify her in saying, we shall be sinners, meaning we shall be treated as sinners when we are not, by a wicked king and his coadjutors, that God uses the same language in the same meaning in respect to the whole human race? What if, in such a case of flagrant injustice, usage sanctions the use of the phrase *we shall be sinners*, to denote we shall be treated as sinners when we are not; does it follow that it is possible that God should actually use similar phraseology to mean that he treats the whole human race as sinners when they are not? And yet it is solely on the authority of such usage that Prof. Hodge claims that God declares that the whole human race *have sinned*, meaning that under his government they are regarded and treated as sinners without any personal ill-desert. Surely these examples do not furnish the shadow of a pretense that such is or can be the meaning of the apostle when he says, "*all have sinned.*"

3. It is claimed that the interpretation now opposed is required by the scope of the passage, the drift of the apostle's argument, and undeniable facts. This argument, which consists of several particulars, may, it is believed, be presented in its full force, thus: "The apostle, it is said in the 12th verse, clearly asserts a connection between the sin of Adam and the sin and death of all mankind; and he does this, as is manifest from the subsequent context, for the purpose of tracing a connection between the sin of Adam and the condemnation of mankind, which resembles the connection between the work of Christ and the Justification of believers. Thus it is said, that when the apostle asserts that "by one man sin entered into the world, and death by sin, and so death passed on all men;" that "through the offense of one many be dead;" that "by the one offense *judgment* came on all men unto condemnation;" and that "by one man's disobedience many were made sinners," we are forced to understand the apostle as teaching, not the acknowledged truth, that all men are sinners in consequence of Adam's sin, but *the more particular* truth, that they are sinners in Adam, or are guilty of his sin, or are regarded and treated as sinners on account of his sin. In support of this position, it is said that there is no other way of accounting for the universality of the penal evils summarily comprised in the word *death*, especially as these evils come upon infants. For as the infliction of penal evils implies the violation of law, the universal infliction of these evils cannot be accounted for by the violation of the law of Moses, since men died before it was given; nor by the violation of the law of nature, since even those die who have never broken that law. To strengthen this argument, we are told that the apostle *by death* does not mean merely natural death, to which all men and even infants are subject, for this might be accounted for by the violation of the law of Moses, or of the law of nature, or by their inherent depravity; but death stands for any and every evil judicially inflicted for the support of law, and especially for the great fact that men begin *to exist out of communion with God;* i. e., God instead of entering into communion with them the moment they begin to exist, as he did with Adam, and forming them by his Spirit in his own moral image, regards them as out of

his favor, and withholds the influences of his Spirit. It is asked why is this? And the answer is, that Paul tells us that it is for the one offense of one man that all thus die. The covenant being formed with Adam, not only for himself but for all his posterity, or Adam being placed on trial, not only for himself but for the whole human race, his act in virtue of this relation is regarded as ours. God withdrew from us as he did from him; in consequence of this withdrawal we begin to exist in moral darkness, destitute of a disposition to seek our happiness in God, and prone to delight in ourselves and the world. Thus the sin of Adam ruined his posterity.

Such is an outline of the argument, as given by a late advocate* of the doctrine, that the posterity of Adam are guilty of his sin.

To some of the positions contained in this reasoning I assent, and from others I entirely dissent. I assent unequivocally to the positions that the apostle asserts a connection between the sin of Adam and the sin and natural death of all mankind; and of course a connection between the sin of Adam and the sin of his posterity, with the condemnation of all mankind according to law; that the sin of Adam and the sin and condemnation of mankind resemble in one respect the work of Christ and the Justification of believers; i. e., the sin and condemnation of mankind are connected with the sin of Adam, and the Justification of believers is connected with the work of Christ. I also admit that the covenant with Adam was made not only for himself, but also in an important respect for his posterity; that Adam was placed on trial for the whole human race, and that in virtue of this relation, and in consequence of his sin, his descendants begin to exist without a prevailing disposition to delight in God, and are prone to delight in themselves and the world; and that all, as soon as they become moral agents, sin and fall under God's condemnation, *directly* for their own sin, and indirectly in consequence of Adam's sin.

There are other positions in the foregoing reasoning which I unequivocally deny. Particularly, first, that the apostle teaches that the posterity of Adam are in any sense guilty of his sin, or that they are regarded as sinners and treated as such on account of Adam's sin; secondly, that he teaches that the evils

---

* Prof. Hodge; vide Com. on Rom. v. 12, &c.

which come on mankind in this world are *penal* evils, or the punishment properly so called of Adam's sin, or of their own sin; and thirdly, that he teaches any thing whatever concerning infants.

It is manifest from the foregoing reasoning that the question is, whether Paul in this passage teaches the doctrine of Imputation, or that we are guilty of Adam's sin, in either of the forms in which it has been maintained. And it is equally manifest, that so far as this reasoning can possess the least plausibility, it depends on two questions, viz., whether Paul teaches that the evils brought on mankind in consequence of Adam's sin are *penal evils*, and whether he teaches that infants are sinners.

Before I proceed to consider either of these alleged facts, I have one remark to make,—that if we admit that the apostle asserts them, neither of them nor both together prove that he teaches the doctrine of Imputation in either form of it. Supposing then, that the apostle teaches that infants are sinners and suffer the penalty of sin; which is the most rational to conclude, that they are sinners by actually sinning, or by Imputation; sinners by that which alone can be sin, viz., the transgression of law (vide Rom. iv. 15; 1 John iii. 4), or sinners by that which cannot be sin? I know that it is affirmed by those whom I oppose, that infants cannot be sinners by transgressing law, or by actual sin. This they decide, as well they may, on the authority of reason or common sense. But I ask, how can they consistently do this when they have also decided that infants are sinners, and when in their full conviction Paul has not only said, that "where there is no law there is no transgression" (Rom. iv. 15), but also that "sin is not imputed when there is no law;" and when another apostle has said, that "sin is the transgression of the law?" Is it not exalting reason above revelation, to say that there is some other kind of sin than that of transgressing law? If the apostle teaches that infants are sinners and bear the penalty of sin, then plainly it remains for the word of God and human reason to decide in what their sin consists. Shall we say that sin consists in that and that only, in which the word of God, and reason, and common sense decide that it can alone consist; or in imputed sin, in which it cannot consist? There is far less philosophical absurdity in supposing infants to be sinners *by actual sin* from birth and before birth, than in supposing them to be sinners by *imputed sin.* Augustine, Calvin, Turretin, the Westminster divines, Edwards, never boldly ventured to contradict the apostle's plain assertion, "that sin is the transgression of the law, and where there is no law there is no transgression;" but said "all sin being a transgression," &c.

I now proceed to show that the apostle does not teach that infants are sinners, nor that the death of which he treats is the legal penalty of sin.

(1.) He does not teach that infants are sinners. We assert that no proof of the doctrine can be found in the passage before us, unless the word of inspiration is self-contradictory. At least we may say, in view of the very peculiar and incredible nature of the supposed fact, that if this passage or any other asserts it, it must be asserted in a form which shall be so unequivocal as to admit of no other construction. The mere assertion has the same aspect of incredibility beforehand, as that infants at the moment of birth, are accomplished orators, mathematicians, or generals.

But let us examine the arguments supposed to be furnished by the passage itself.

The first we notice is taken from the universal form of the apostle's phraseology, "all have sinned." This mode of interpreting universal forms of expression we have already sufficiently considered, to show that it not only does not authorize, but absolutely *forbids* the extension of it to infants. In addition to what has been said on this point, it is to be remarked that the apostle uses the same form of phraseology in predicating universal sinfulness of mankind, without including infants. (Compare chap. iii. 9 with verse 23; and also chap. ii. 32; and Gal. iii. 22, especially the last.) But what is still more decisive, he makes the necessity of faith to Justification to be coextensive with sin; i. e., he teaches that every sinner must be justified by faith. This shows decisively that he speaks only of those who are capable of believing, and not of infants. Can infants believe in God or in Christ? If not, are they damned for imputed sin, without the least benefit from the Atonement of Christ?

But let us test the question by the law of usage and the dictate of common sense. Look at such sentences as the following: "All men value their reputation." "All men reason."

"All Europe was agitated by the conquests of Napoleon." "Preach the Gospel to every creature." "Behold the whole city went out to meet Jesus and besought him." "And set *all* the city in an uproar." "Live peaceably with all men," &c., &c. Precisely like these is the case under consideration. The topic discussed was, whether both Jews and Gentiles (all men capable of sinning and capable of faith) were sinners; and the reason for saying that Paul never thought of infants in the phrase *all have sinned*, is as decisive, as for saying that they are not thought of in such forms of expression in other cases. Reason and common sense decide that it is as impossible that infants should sin in Adam's sin, or in any other way, as that infants should walk or engage in the mob at Thessalonica. All usage of universal forms of expression proceeds on the principle, that their meaning is to be limited by the universally known and acknowledged nature of things.

The second reason alleged for including infants is, that infants die, and that we must understand the apostle to teach in the phrase *death by sin*, that sin, at least among human beings, is as universal as death. I answer, this argument depends entirely on the correctness of the principle already stated. In other words, the question is this,—whether the apostle means to say that death is the consequence of sin, and thus proves sin in those cases in which they are, according to reason and common sense and the word of God, without sin and incapable of sin? Suppose it were to be said in the language of common usage, that all men take food because they know that it is necessary to sustain life. Could this language be justly interpreted to include infants? It will not be pretended. But why not? Infants take food as well as other human beings. Why then are they not to be included in the above proposition? Plainly because reason and common sense say that they are incapable of the knowledge predicated. But reason and common sense decide with the same infallibility that they are incapable of actual sin. This our opponents all admit. I have already shown that there can be no other sin than actual sin. That death is a predicate common to both infants and those who have passed the period of infancy, is no more evidence that it is a consequence and proof of the sin of the former, because it is of the sin of the latter, than the fact that the taking of food is a predicate common to infants, and also to the rest of the world, is a proof that infants take food with the conviction of its necessity to sustain life, because adults take it with such conviction. I admit that if the common predicate in the latter case could be supposed to result from a common cause, the conviction of the necessity of food to sustain life, if this were the dictate of common sense, and if usage did not sanction the supposed universal form of speech without extending it to infants, this form of expression must be interpreted to include them. But as the facts are, we are compelled by the laws of usage to exclude infants, and to say with the most assured confidence that they are not even thought of. These decisive reasons exist in the case before us for saying that the apostle, when he said all men die because they are sinners, had no thought of an infant.

A third reason for the opinion that infants are included by the apostle, is taken from the 14th verse: "Nevertheless death reigned from Adam to Moses, *even* over them that had not sinned after the similitude of Adam's transgression." The last phrase it is said must refer to infants, or to infants and idiots, since these are the only individuals during the interval between Adam and Moses of whom it could be true* that they "had not sinned after the similitude of Adam's transgression." I answer, (1.) that according to the theory of Imputation, infants are one in Adam, and therefore sinned exactly after the similitude of Adam's transgression. Being one and the same moral person, committing, as Edwards, Stapfer, and others say, the same sin in number and in kind, and corrupting their nature in this act just as Adam did in his, how could it be otherwise than that they sinned in precisely the same manner in which Adam sinned? (2.) It is not true that infants and idiots are the only individuals of that period who could not sin after the similitude of Adam's transgression, for the adults having no revealed law like that which Adam violated, could not sin like him.

But it is said that the apostle refers to all who lived in this interval, as dying on account of imputed sin, and to make the case more decisive to his purpose, he uses the distinctive particle καὶ, *even*, to distinguish a particular class from others, viz., *infants*, in respect to whom no possible doubt could exist whether they had sinned after the similitude of Adam's transgression.

---

* Here, by the way, an assertion is rejected because it is impossible.

It is obvious indeed, that unless the apostle has shown that he had reference to some others than adults, it would be difficult to prove from their case that he meant to say that only the imputed sin of Adam was the cause of their death. On this supposition a *possible doubt* might arise whether he thought of imputed sin. But there is no evidence that he referred to infants, but rather proof to the contrary. For (1.) the distinction claimed is a distinction without a difference; for the adults of that period could no more have sinned after the similitude of Adam's transgression than the infants, nor yet as much so, according to the theory of Imputation; for as adults guilty of actual sin without a revealed law, it is impossible that they should sin as much like Adam, as Adam did like himself, while infants as *one* with Adam must have sinned exactly as Adam did. (2.) If the apostle distinguishes infants from adults, it is by this peculiarity—that they had not sinned after the similitude of Adam's transgression—clearly implying that the adults had sinned after the similitude of Adam. But this is not only not true in respect to a revealed law, but if true would spoil the reasoning ascribed to the apostle; for how could the case of those who had sinned after the similitude of Adam's transgression be brought to prove that they died for *the imputed* sin of Adam. If our opponents affirm that the adults of this period sinned after the similitude of Adam's transgression, then they must give up the doctrine of death for imputed sin. If they say that they did not, then the difference claimed between them and the infants of that period did not exist; and to suppose the apostle to refer to infants in the clause in question, is to suppose him to make a distinction without a difference; i. e., to resort to downright falsehood in argument. Our opponents may hang on either horn of this dilemma which they prefer. I answer, (3.) that the word *καὶ*, *even*, has not necessarily, as it occurs in this passage, the force of a distinctive particle in the manner asserted. It may be used merely to give greater point and force to the instance to which he appeals. Suppose that the apostle had said that (actual) sin was in the world until the giving of the law of Moses, and that some denied or doubted it on the ground that during that interval there was no revealed law of which sin could be the transgression. Suppose now the apostle to set aside all doubt on the point, and appeal to an undeniable matter of fact, viz., that death reigned over all men during that period, even over them who had not sinned under a revealed law or after the similitude of Adam's transgression. I ask, could any form of expression be more natural, more exactly what we should expect him to adopt? There is then not a particle of evidence in this clause, that the apostle thought of infants. (4.) I ask why he referred to this interval at all? Plainly there was some peculiarity in respect to it, decisive of the point he wished to establish. But what was the point, and what the peculiarity? His point, it is claimed, was to prove that imputed sin was in the world until the law of Moses. But what peculiarity would enable him to prove this? Was it in the case of those who were adults or not infants? And what was it? There was none which could show that they were sinners by Imputation, for their case no more proves this than that of those who lived after the law of Moses. For if it had been asserted that those who lived after the law of Moses, died as transgressors of that law, or for not receiving it, as the Jews supposed the fact to be with respect to the Gentiles, still it might be said that the former died for transgressing the law of nature. How then would the death of this part of mankind prove the doctrine of imputed sin? Plainly not at all; and this is admitted virtually by our opponents, who bring forward no proof on this point till they find the apostle, as they say, referring to the infants of that period. The whole strength of the apostle's reasoning is therefore derived from the case of infants who lived and died before the law was given by Moses. But surely there was *no peculiarity* respecting the infants of that period at all to the purpose of the apostle, more than in the death of all others of this class. Infants, after the law, could no more die as *actual* sinners, than infants before the law; and if this proves that they die for *imputed* sin, it proves it in all instances as much as in that of infants before the law. No possible reason then can be given why the apostle referred to death prior to the Mosaic law as a proof of imputed sin. The death of the adults would not furnish an argument, nor would the death of the infants of that period more than the death of all other infants. It is plain then, that the apostle did not attempt to prove imputed sin, nor refer for this purpose to the death of infants before the law.

If now we suppose the object of the apostle in referring to those who lived and died between Adam and Moses, was to prove that they died as the consequence of actual sin, though they had not sinned against a revealed law, then the case is fully and decisive to his purpose. Nor is it possible to assign any other object or design for his referring to that period in this manner. He has obviously done so as a peculiarly clear case in which there was sin, and also in which sin is not imputed; i. e., was not punished with death as the penalty of any revealed law having such a penalty. Neither the case of Adam, nor of those who lived after the Mosaic law, would so well answer his purpose; for it might be said with some plausibility, that these died under law with the penalty of death, or that death in these cases was the legal penalty of sin. Again, it is manifest that in his reference to this period he included the adults, and whatever peculiarity there was which availed to his purpose in argument, it respected the adults of this period compared with those of any other. But these adults no more die for imputed sin, as we have seen, than others. The only conceivable peculiarity in their case, is that which the apostle unequivocally specifies, that they sinned and died when there was no law revealed. They being under the law of nature only, were *ἄνομοί*, or "without law;" death could not be to them a legal penalty, or when sin was not imputed, i. e., not punished with death as a legal penalty. This being the only conceivable peculiarity on account of which the apostle referred to the adults of this period, so it is the only conceivable peculiarity on account of which he could have referred, if he would have referred at all, to the infants; for the peculiarity in the case of the adults and of the infants must be the same. Unless therefore we suppose that the infants sinned and died as the adults died,—i. e., sinned and died without a revealed law; i. e., actually sinned under the law of nature,—then the apostle could not have referred to the infants of that period at all.

5. To say that the apostle referred to infants as sinning by Imputation, is to beg the main question in debate, that infants can sin by Imputation. The thing is impossible in the nature of things, in every sense of the language. It is contrary to reason, common sense, and the Scriptures, and it might as well be said that *not to sin after the similitude of Adam's transgression*, means that they sinned by conception or respiration, as that they sinned by Imputation. Who devised this mode of sinning? Philosophical theologians, and on the authority of

the realistic philosophy; devised it in order to support a palpably false interpretation of universal forms of language; devised it for lack of ingenuity to see how all men could be said to be sinners, and without supposing all men to include infants; devised it to support error and to carry a point in false theology. If such nonsense is to be ascribed to an inspired apostle, to what respect is inspiration itself entitled?

I give here the following extract from Tholuck's Commentary on Rom. v. 12:

"'Ἐφ' ᾧ. Augustine proceeded on the realistic theory, that God having *performed but one act of creation* had placed *the race in the first individual*, so that all further existence was nothing else than the appearance and development of what was already *in being*. Since now in the beginning *the first individual* and *the race existed together*, it followed that the race fell *in him*. Subtle explanations of this view, and philosophical applications of the theory of the *universalibus in re* to this dogma of Imputation, are given by the schoolmen; e. g., Anselm, and Odoart, in his essay De Peccato Originali."

Having thus attempted to prove that the apostle in the passage before us did not refer at all to infants, I now proceed to show as proposed—

(2.) That the death of which he treats is not *penal*, or is not the legal penalty of sin.

It is the assumption that the death here spoken of is the legal penalty of sin, which I consider as the first and grand error of nearly all the interpretations of the passage. It deserves particular inquiry, why it is that interpreters have so commonly been led to adopt this view. I know of but one reason which has the least plausibility,—a plausibility existing only in words, if even so much can be said of it. This reason is derived solely from particular forms, or rather one particular form of expression used by the apostle. Three or four are commonly cited, in proof that he teaches that the death of which he speaks is a penal evil.

Let us examine these so far as the force of the language, *de usu loquendi*, can be supposed to decide any thing on the question, and then appeal to other considerations.

The first passage which occurs is, "By one man sin entered into the world, and death by sin, and so death passed upon all men, for that all have sinned." What is there in this text to show that temporal death, as a common event to all men, comes on them as a penal evil, either as the penalty of Adam's or of any other man's sin? Plainly, nothing thus specific is asserted. That the sin which has entered the world was introduced into it by one man, and that the death which has entered the world comes by sin, and comes to all men because all have sinned, is all that is affirmed. But this is not saying that death or sin comes on men as a penal evil, for it is quite possible that these evils should come in some other mode of consequence or connection than that peculiar to sin and its legal penalty; and to assert that they cannot, is gratuitous, and to beg the main question in debate.

Another passage relied on is, "Through the offense of one many be dead, or have died."

There is another, which in words has more plausibility. 'For the judgment was of one offense unto or in condemnation.' Here much is supposed to depend on the words *κρίμα*, rendered *judgment* or *sentence;* and *κατάκριμα*, rendered condemnation. It is assumed that *κρίμα* is the sentence of a judge, and that *κρίμα εἰς κατάκριμα* is a sentence of condemnation to bear the penalty of the law transgressed by him on whom it is pronounced. I reply, that the word *κρίμα* is obviously a generic term, like our English word judgment, at least when applied to the character and conduct of others. (Vide Matt. vii. 2; John ix. 39; Rom. xi. 33; 1 Cor. xi. 34, compare 32d verse.) Κρίμα, then, may denote any judgment or sentence in respect to the character or conduct, and especially determining or ordaining consequences. This word is used to denote *condemnation* in the sense of pronouncing one exposed to or liable to punishment, as worthy of punishment, as well as the act of dooming one to punishment.

As decisive on this point I appeal to John iii. 18: "He that believeth not is condemned (*κεκριταί*) already, because he hath not believed," &c. None will pretend that every unbeliever is absolutely and hopelessly condemned to bear the legal penalty of sin, or that he is doomed absolutely to this punishment. The meaning of the text is, that because of his unbelief he is in respect to character guilty, or deserving of the penalty, and as such justly exposed to it. Is there any other sense in which all men can be said to be condemned or under condemnation in this world of mercy?

Look at a similar case among men. Suppose one arraigned for the crime of murder before a judge having the prerogative of pardon, as God had by virtue of the promised redemption; he comes to pronounce sentence; and suppose too the sentence to involve the decision that the accused is guilty of the crime charged, by dooming him to that to which he could not be condemned were he not guilty, even as plainly as a sentence bringing him to the scaffold; would not usage justify us in saying—would not all the world say, that the accused was condemned? and when the main question, and from the nature of the case the only possible question was, whether he was guilty or not, and as such exposed to the penalty, would not this be called a sentence to condemnation as certainly and as properly as a sentence dooming absolutely to bear the penalty?

Whether therefore the phrase, *sentence unto or in condemnation*, denotes a sentence dooming to legal penalty, and thus involving its actual execution, must be decided, not by the mere words, but by the instances to which they are applied, or something in the connection. So far as the nature of the case is concerned, I only remark here—intending to examine this more fully hereafter—that the sentence spoken of by the apostle was pronounced under an economy of mercy for all men, even for all who are delivered from the penalty of the law, and therefore could not be a sentence dooming all men actually to bear the legal penalty.

Let us now look at the connection. Here however, we must keep in mind the precise point at issue. It is not whether the sentence pronounced on Adam, and also on his posterity, implied their sinfulness, and of course *their just exposure* to the legal penalty as sinners, nor whether it actually and absolutely doomed them to temporal death on account of their sinfulness, but whether it absolutely condemned them to bear *the legal penalty* so that there was no escape; i. e., was it a sentence of hopeless condemnation to the legal penalty? It is to no purpose to say that the death to which they were hopelessly doomed, was a part of the evil of the legal penalty. Be it so. This it must be in the nature of the case, if they were to suffer any evil even in the form of discipline or chastisement, for the penalty included the highest degree of evil of which they were capable. But if it was only a part of the evil of the penalty, then it was not the penalty itself; nor was it even penal, because though it be an expression of some degree of displeasure for sin, it could not make a full or adequate expression of displeasure, and no evil can be *penal* which fails to do this.

What I maintain then is, that the sentence to condemnation pronounced on the human race was on account of sin and guilt, expressing God's displeasure, though not in that full degree which the infliction of the legal penalty requires, and deciding their guilt and just exposure or liability to the full legal penalty. The point in question then may be thus presented, whether this sentence was such as involved the just exposure of all men to the infliction of the legal penalty, or such as involved its actual infliction? On this point, leaving the nature of the case for future inquiry, I now appeal to the context. The apostle then, in the 16th verse, says that the sentence was of (for) one offense, *εἰς κατάκριμα*, but the free gift (*χάρισμα*) is of (for) many offenses (*εἰς δικαίωμα*) unto a provision for righteousness. Now if the *εἰς κατάκριμα* denotes an act of absolute condemnation to the penalty, the *εἰς δικαίωμα* denotes an act of absolute Justification. If the sentence unto condemnation involves absolute condemnation, or condemnation in the sense of dooming to bear the penalty, then the free gift unto an ordinance of righteousness or Justification involves absolute Justification. Thus the Universalist argues from the premises furnished by most commentators, and argues most unanswerably if the premises are true. But it is conceded by those with whom I now reason, that the *χάρισμα εἰς δικαίωμα* is a provision or gift not involving the absolute Justification of all men, but one which may be followed with the act of absolute Justification of all men, or is in one respect at least a sufficient ground for this act. It follows then, the *κρίμα εἰς κατάκριμα* is a judgment not involving an absolute condemnation of all men.

The very form of the expression shows this. Why *εἰς κάτακριμα* instead of *κρῖμα του κατακρίματος*, and *εἰς δικαίωμα* instead of *του δικαίωματος*? Again, in the next verse, the apostle expressly specifies a condition—*the receiving* abundance of grace and the gift of righteousness—of actual salvation; thus clearly implying that without this condition, i. e., on condition of impenitence and unbelief, men would perish under the penalty of sin; in other words, that the exposure to the actual infliction of the penalty was not absolute but conditional. But the sentence to *some death*—the death of which the apostle speaks—

was an absolute sentence. This then was not the legal penalty. Once more, that the gift of grace, or the grace of God in this provision for Justification and life, did not involve the actual salvation of any, is clearly asserted in verse 20th, "that grace *might* reign through righteousness," &c. Of course the sentence unto condemnation pronounced after the promise of a Redeemer, did not involve an absolute or hopeless condemnation to the penalty of sin.

The judgment then, the sentence *unto* condemnation, was not a sentence of condemnation; not a sentence absolutely dooming the race to eternal death—no such was ever pronounced on mankind—but a sentence pronounced under an economy of mercy dooming all men to return to dust, and clearly implying the sinfulness of all, and their just exposure to eternal death as the penalty of sin. Thus rightly to interpret the phrase *κρίμα εἰς κατάκριμα* is the key to the whole context, since on this, the interpretation I oppose entirely depends. The only question is, whether God ever sentenced the human race in consequence of Adam's sin, to bear the penalty of his law; i. e., absolutely and hopelessly doomed them to everlasting death. But he did sentence them absolutely and hopelessly to some death. What was it but temporal death, and temporal death because all have sinned, and yet temporal death under an economy of mercy? True, this sentence unto condemnation was pronounced by a Judge, but a Judge who had laid aside the terrors of legal majesty; and though frowning at sin, put on the smile of mercy to win back a rebellious world to his favor. This brings us to contemplate more particularly the nature of the case.

The death then of which the apostle treats in this passage, is the death to which all mankind were doomed after the apostasy of our first parents, in the sentence, "dust thou art, and unto dust shall thou return" (Gen. iii. 19). This will be admitted. I ask then, whether the apostle could have understood, or expected his readers to understand an event described by Moses in this language, to be what Prof. Hodge represents, viz., that men begin to exist out of communion with God? This, according to the Professor, is "the essence and sum of all evils"—"it is inflicted antecedent to them all," and was described in the language, "dust thou art, and unto dust shall thou return!" This is too much I think for sober exegesis.

Again: the death spoken of is not that which was threatened

in the law, and therefore is not the legal penalty. So far from it, that instead of pronouncing the sentence of the law, the first annunciation from the offended Lawgiver is the gracious promise, "the seed of the woman shall bruise the serpent's head." Here then we have not a legal process, arraigning, trying, and dooming to legal penalty, but THE PROMISE OF A REDEEMER;—not a sentence to bear the legal penalty, but redemption from that penalty. And are we to be told, that this proclamation of grace was instantly followed with the sentence of penal justice? Was man thus redeemed—thus placed under an economy of grace, and at the same moment doomed to bear the very penalty of the law from which he was reprieved by mercy? This is incredible,—impossible. The language of the sentence compared with that of the law, shows the same thing. The law says, "thou shalt surely die;" language which, as used in such a connection, as Jewish phraseology, perpetuated and explained in the New Testament (as we have already shown), denotes death in sin,—eternal death. What now was the sentence actually passed on Adam under an economy of redemption? Not, thou shalt *die*,—die under the curse of the law,—die in sin,—die hopelessly as an immortal being;—not, thou shalt depart from this world to the complete and endless misery threatened in the law. No; but, "dust thou art, and *unto dust* shalt thou return." By the law, man must have been doomed to the extreme of misery as an immortal being, by the sentence under grace, to temporal death with other evils. The death then which is here denounced and of which the apostle is speaking, is not the legal penalty of sin.

Secondly—The death of which the apostle speaks is common to all men. It actually came on Adam—it comes on all men under an economy of mercy; and what is more, it comes on those who are delivered from the curse of the law. It is a death which, in their case, as an evil, is destroyed. 2 Tim. i. 10: "To die is gain." Is this death, the penalty—the very curse of God's law?

Thirdly—It is death which takes place in this world. The apostle tells us, that it entered the *world* by sin,—that it passed upon all men,—that it reigned from Adam to Moses. And is this the legal penalty due to sin? Have the whole human race,—all men, Adam, Noah, Abraham, and all the patriarchs, actually died in their sins? Are all that ever lived in this world, now suffering the penalty of God's violated law? But it is said, and this is all that can be said with the least plausibility in support of the interpretation now opposed, that the same apostle often uses the word *death*, and particularly in chap. vi. 23, to denote the legal penalty. To this I reply, that the mere *word* decides nothing on the point, because it is wholly ambiguous in itself—one of the most so in the Scriptures—being used in different senses in the same sentence. The only mode of deciding its meaning is from the connection, from evidence furnished by the case itself. When then, in chap. vi. 23, we are told that "*the wages* of sin is death, but the gift of God is eternal life," the meaning is clear and decisive. *Death* as the wages, the penalty of sin, and as contrasted with eternal life, is undeniably eternal death. But with the same unerring certainty we say, that *death* which takes place in this world, which passes on all men, and which reigned from Adam to Moses, is temporal death. The apostle refers to a fact of history *in this world*, and reasons from it as one placed beyond all doubt and denial, the fact of universal temporal death. How is it possible that the love of system can blind the mind to truth so palpable! The reason why so many commentators suppose *death*, in this passage, to include the entire evil comprised in the legal penalty is, that the apostle most obviously aimed to prove that all men were sinners, and as such were under condemnation. Thus Professor Stuart admits that the death spoken of is *universal*, that this is *temporal* death, and that the apostle had this *particularly in view;* and yet that "this does not oblige us to infer that other parts of the penalty are designedly excluded" (p. 227). The error lies in supposing that the entire evil of penalty is included in the word *death*, whereas the apostle, by *the death* of which he speaks (temporal death, a universal palpable fact), simply proves that all men are *sinners*, and as such are *condemned to bear the full penalty of sin*, so far as sin and law condemn, while yet they are under an economy of pardoning mercy.

Fourthly—That the death spoken of in this passage is the legal penalty, is most explicitly denied by the apostle, in the immediate context. Having affirmed in the 12th verse that all have sinned, he proceeds to prove it. As if he said, contrary to what some may suppose, sin was in the world before the Mosaic law existed; but sin is not imputed, i. e., is not charged and punished in this world, when there is no positive revealed law, or when there is no such law with a penalty. As temporal death, the death of which the apostle speaks, was the actual penalty of the Mosaic law as a civil institution, it was very natural that those to whom the apostle wrote, should suppose, either that it was the *penalty* of some positive law, or that otherwise it was in no sense the consequence, and therefore that it was no proof of sin. While therefore the apostle asserts that sin was in the world before the Mosaic law, he is very careful to show that he did not rest this assertion on the fact that sin was imputed, i. e., charged and punished by the infliction of any legal penalty. Had he reasoned on this principle, he was perfectly aware that he would in fact, and in the view of his readers, have reasoned inconclusively. He was careful therefore to guard against this view of his argument, by saying that sin is not imputed when there is no law. But if the prevalence of sin in the world before the Mosaic law cannot be proved in this way, i. e., on the ground that it was charged and punished with a legal penalty, how can it be proved? Why, very obviously and conclusively; for although sin was not *imputed*, i. e., was not charged and punished with temporal death as a legal penalty, when there was no revealed law having such a penalty; nevertheless death *the consequence*, and therefore *the proof* of sin, reigned during the whole interval. Here then we have the explicit assertion of the apostle, that death did not come on mankind as a legal penalty.

The correctness of this interpretation depends entirely on the import of two phrases—"sin is not *imputed*," and "when there is no law." In my own view, when the former is applied to God, or when God is said *not* to impute sin, it means that *he does not both charge and punish the sinner, or inflict the legal penalty of sin.* When applied to God without the negative particle *not*, or when God is said *to impute sin*, the meaning is, that he considers, or knows the subject to be a sinner, and treats or determines to treat him as such by inflicting the legal penalty of sin. God never does the latter without also doing the former; i. e., he never inflicts or determines to inflict the penalty of sin on any except those whom he considers or knows to be sinners. But he does *remit* the legal penalty in the case of those whom he considers and knows to be sinners. To do this is not the direct and full converse of imputing sin, for he still *considers* them as sinners. It is however *not imputing sin*, because an essential part of the act of imputed sin is not done; the legal penalty is not executed. The proof of this is of course to be derived, not from the various uses of the word λογίζομαι, but from the phrase *not to impute sin*. A clear case, and one sufficient for my present purpose, is the prayer of Shimei, 2 Sam. xix. 19: "Let not my Lord impute iniquity unto me." Shimei does not ask his Lord not to *esteem* him a sinner, for he confesses his sin; but not to inflict the penalty, or to reckon and pronounce him a sinner to be punished. So in Ps. xxxii. 1, 2; Rom. iv. 8; 2 Cor. v. 19.

Another question is, what is the import of the phrase "*when there is no law*." Some understand it in the broadest sense; i. e., to denote neither a revealed law, nor the law written on the heart, or no law whatever. To suppose the apostle to use the phrase in this meaning, would be to suppose him to say in the entire sentence what is true, but what is entirely irrelevant to his purpose. What possible occasion had he to affirm that God never imputed sin when there is no law whatever, and of course no transgression? Who could suppose that God *imputed* sin when there was none? How could the fact enable him either by itself or in connection with any other fact, to prove that sin was in the world until the Mosaic law? His argument on this supposition must be this—and this has been the opinion of many commentators—that as God does not impute sin when there is no law whatever, therefore as God *did impute sin* to men before the Mosaic law, there must have been a law during that period. But this argument is built on a false premise. God did not *impute sin* to men; i. e., he did not bring temporal death on men as a penalty, nor execute any legal penalty on men universally in this world during the period specified. Besides, to suppose the apostle to assert this, is to suppose him to say, that *the death* which reigned from Adam to Moses was the full penalty of the law of that period, which none will admit who adopt this view of the passage. To say that this death was not the legal penalty, and that it was *only a proof* that God *considered men* as sinners, is to concede that it is no proof that God, in the true meaning of the language, *imputed* sin; for the phrase will not bear this meaning, viz., that of simply *considering* or *regarding* men as sinners.

But we can be at no loss concerning the meaning of the phrase, μὴ ὄντος νόμου, "*when there is no law.*" It obviously describes the condition of those that lived before the giving of the Mosaic law, when indeed there was a law written on the heart, but *no revealed* law. He thus by stating the principle that sin is *not imputed* when there is no (revealed) law, affirms *the fact* that it was *not imputed* during the period of which he speaks; i. e., it was not punished with temporal death as a legal penalty. Notwithstanding this fact, or as he says, "nevertheless," he maintains his position that "sin was then in the world until the law," and proved to be so, not indeed on the ground that it *was imputed*, but on that of another fact, the universal prevalence of death the consequence of sin. But the language of the apostle is decisive of this point. Compare Rom. ii. 12, 13, where to be *without law—not to have law—not having law*, is not having a *revealed* law. The plain meaning of the apostle in these verses is, that sin was not punished in this world by the infliction of *the legal penalty* when there was no revealed law, and that nevertheless death reigned from Adam to Moses. The following paraphrase will present the apostle's thoughts in this part of the passage: "I have said that all men, in all ages and nations, have sinned. Nor let any suppose that there can be no sin except in transgressing or rejecting the law of Moses, or that there was no sin in the world till this law was given; for sin was in the world before the law of Moses existed. True indeed it is, that sin was not then visited *in this world* with the infliction of a legal penalty, as it was under the Mosaic law. Nevertheless death, *which is by sin*, the consequence and proof of sin, reigned through that whole interval."

Fifthly—In confirmation of this view of the passage I ask, why did the apostle appeal in his argument to the prevalence of death from Adam to Moses? This period was evidently *distinguished* by some *peculiarity* decisive in its bearing on his argument. By what *peculiarity?* This is a vital question. I answer then, not that during this period there was absolutely no law by which was the knowledge of sin, and by which sin could be charged, for it is beyond all denial, that the law of nature was written on the heart during this period. Nor was it a peculiarity of this period that death was any more a consequence of Adam's sin, or that it could be *any more clearly shown* to be a consequence of Adam's sin, than during any other. For although it could be shown that death during this period was not the legal penalty of any *revealed* law, it could not be shown that it was not the consequence—I do not say the penalty—of the law written on the heart. As to the supposition that the apostle refers to infants, if we admit so strange a supposition, there is plainly nothing *peculiar* in respect to that class of infants. It is just as true that other infants had not violated the law of nature as that these had not. Besides, it is undeniable that he refers to the death of adults, and that there was some *peculiarity* in *their* case, as truly as in that of infants, which he deemed necessary to his argument. The question then is, what was *this peculiarity?* Not that they died on account of Adam's sin in any sense in which the adults of any other period did not die for Adam's sin. And furthermore, and let this be particularly noticed, that there was not according to the history of this period, any thing in the condition, in the character, or in the circumstances—not a solitary fact in any respect *peculiar* to that portion of the human race, by which the apostle could show in his argument that they died on account of Adam's sin. The fact then, and the only fact, on account of which he could have referred to the period from Adam to Moses was this: that during that period there was no law whatever of which the death that prevailed could be the legal penalty. If then the apostle attempted to prove the existence of sin during that period, by inferring it from the prevalence of death as the legal penalty of sin, he did so though there was no law, and when he himself asserted that there was no law of which death could be the legal penalty.

In opposition to this view of the subject, it is claimed that the apostle clearly teaches that the death of the period under consideration, was the penalty of Adam's sin. The argument for this doctrine may be stated in its entire force in this form: Death, as it takes place in the world, is and must be the penalty of sin; and as death from Adam to Moses could not be the penalty of either the Mosaic law nor of the law written on the heart, it must be the penalty of the law given to Adam, or the legal penalty of his sin. (Vide Hodge on Rom. p. 176.)

Such is the argument, and let it be noticed, that on this the whole question depends. If it is fallacious, all pretense that the apostle teaches that temporal death is *the legal penalty* of Adam's sin or of any other sin, must be abandoned. Let us then examine the argument. My first remark concerning it is—

That the main premise is wholly unauthorized. Where is the *proof* that death, as it comes on all men in this world, is and must be the legal penalty of sin? We say there is none on this point, and none is adduced even in pretense. The position is a mere assumption—a mere begging of the question in respect to the main thing in debate.

Again: this assumption is contradicted by plain matter of fact. Temporal death as common to mankind, as we have seen, is not and cannot be the legal penalty of sin, inasmuch as it takes place under an economy of mercy, and is actually endured by multitudes who are delivered from the legal penalty of sin.

Further: the assumption that death during the period spoken of is the penalty of any law whatever, is, as we have seen, expressly denied by the apostle. Thus he says, sin is not *imputed*, is not visited with a legal penalty when there is no law having a penalty; and this principle is brought forward as applicable to the period between Adam and Moses. He thus unequivocally teaches that there was no law of which the death of that period was the penalty of sin. On what authority then is it assumed, that all the death that takes place in this world is the legal penalty of sin; or that the death which prevailed from Adam to Moses, was the penalty of the law given to Adam? But this is not all.

If we concede that the death referred to was the penalty of sin, there is no proof that it was the penalty of Adam's sin, but rather proof to the contrary. There is no more reason for supposing the law of Adam to be in force as an existing law, than for supposing the law of Moses to be in force during that period. Why not then say that the death of that period was the penalty of the one law as well as of the other? Why might it not as well be the penalty of a law which had not begun to exist, as the penalty of a law which had ceased to exist? Or rather, if it must be regarded as the penalty of some law, why not regard it as the penalty of the only existing law, viz., the law written on the heart? It is to no purpose to say that many, especially infants, did not violate this law; for neither did they violate the law given to Adam. Besides, the question now to be answered is this—of what law was the death of *the adults* referred to, the penalty? Surely, to say it was the penalty of the law given to Adam, or the legal penalty of his sin, is not only gratuitous, but against the much stronger probability (if it was the penalty of any law) that it was the penalty of the only law which was then in existence, and which they had actually transgressed. To believe this,—indeed to believe that the death of infants was by anticipation the penalty of the law of nature, as one which they certainly would violate, is less irrational than to believe it to be the penalty of a law which they never had and never could violate.

Again: in all the history of the period under consideration, there is not a solitary fact which shows that death was the legal penalty of Adam's sin; while some of the most striking facts are decisive that in many instances it was not. None that can support this scheme has ever been specified, and for this reason, none can be found. The destruction of the world by a deluge, and of Sodom and Gomorrah by fire and brimstone, were well-known instances of death for personal sin, for actual transgressions. What an utter failure then in argument, to have referred to this period to prove that mankind died as the legal penalty of Adam's sin! There is not a fact to support such a conclusion, but many which most decisively prove the contrary.

But it is said, "that death must be the legal penalty of sin." But I ask, why it *must* be? Is there no other way in which death can be a *consequence* of sin, than as its legal penalty? Was the death of Abraham and of all the patriarchs, and of all the prophets and apostles, the legal penalty of sin? Plainly the position, the main premise of the argument under consideration, is a false one. "Death," it is said, "must be the legal penalty of sin." Where is the proof—where is the attempt at proof? It is the merest assumption, or rather a most palpable begging of the main question in the debate—How do these men know the truth of what they affirm? How dare they assert that death in this world is the legal penalty of sin, in face of the plain and undeniable fact, that it comes on all men under an economy of mercy,—comes on the individuals who are delivered from the legal penalty of sin,—comes on men who had no law with death as its penalty, when the apostle expressly declares that in such a case, sin is not visited with a legal penalty.

I now proceed as I proposed—

Secondly—To offer proofs against the interpretation of the passage which I oppose.*

It will be sufficient for the present purpose to show—

First—That the apostle teaches that death, considered as an event common to all men, is *not a legal penalty;* and secondly, that the sin, the universality of which he infers from the universality of death, is *actual* sin, and not the imputed sin of Adam.

First—The apostle teaches, that death considered as an event common to all men, is not a legal penalty. We suppose it will be admitted, that the apostle here refers to the sentence denounced after the fall, upon Adam and his race, as disclosing the facts respecting his sin and its consequences. Here then we might rest our present position. For, as we have shown that sentence was not the sentence of the *law*, nor was its execution the *penalty of the law.* Many die the death denounced in that sentence, who are delivered from the legal penalty. This we regard as absolutely decisive on the point now at issue.

But we are not obliged to leave the question here. The apostle in the very passage under consideration, has directly and formally disproved the doctrine that death comes on men as the *penalty* of any law whatever. He first asserts, that the sin which is in the world, came into it by one man. He next affirms, that death is by sin, and that death, as the consequence of sin, passed on all men because all had sinned. In confirmation of this statement, he appeals to a known and acknowledged matter of fact, viz., that before the Mosaic law, sin was in the world. "But," he adds, "sin is not imputed when there is no law;" i. e., sin is not charged and punished when there is no law. Nevertheless, death the *consequence* (not the penalty) of sin prevailed from Adam to Moses,—a period in which there was no law of which death could be the penalty. Sin therefore was in the world (as death, its consequence, decisively proves), even when there was no law with death as its penalty.

* The remainder of this chapter is taken from the Quarterly Christian Spectator, Vol. III. No. 2, pp. 316–328.

Thus, while the apostle decisively teaches that death is the consequence of sin, he proves that it is not the *legal penalty* of sin, according to any law whatever.

In confirmation of this view of the passage we ask, why did the apostle appeal to the prevalence of death from *Adam to Moses?* This period was obviously distinguished by some *peculiarity* decisive in its bearing on the apostle's argument. By what peculiarity? This is a vital question. We answer then, not by the fact, that death during this period was at all more a consequence of Adam's sin, or was more clearly *shown* to be a consequence of Adam's sin, than at any other period. Not that during the period there was no law, by which was the knowledge of sin, and by which sin could be charged; for it is beyond all denial, that there was such a law. What then was the fact peculiar to this period? Plainly this, and only this, that there was no law *threatening death* as its penalty. To suppose the apostle then to speak of death in this case as a legal penalty, is to suppose him to argue from a fact which directly contradicts his own doctrine,—to argue from the prevalence of death during a period in which there was no law that had death as its penalty. The object of the apostle then in referring to this period, is obvious. It was to show that death, *as an event common to all men*, did not come upon them as the penalty of any law whatever; but as an immediate consequence of personal sin, and remotely (in the manner before described) as the consequence of Adam's sin. Thus he proved from the universality of death, according to the original sentence under an *economy of grace*, that all men were under sin and condemnation.

But our brethren think, that the apostle appealed to the prevalence of death from Adam to Moses, for the very purpose of showing that death during this period came on men as the LEGAL PENALTY of *Adam's* sin. If this opinion can be shown to be wholly groundless, the main point at issue will be decided. We ask then, how does the prevalence of death from Adam to Moses, prove that it was the legal penalty of Adam's sin? The vast multitude destroyed by the deluge and in Sodom and Gomorrah, are well known to have *deserved* death themselves; to have died, in some respect at least, for their own personal sins. How then would such a case prove that men died solely for the sin of another? Surely, the apostle was unfortunate in referring to this fact to prove that death reigned as the legal penalty of *Adam's* sin exclusively, or in any respect whatever.

Again: how does this scheme exhibit the apostle in other respects as a reasoner? If we suppose that there was a law at that period, viz., that given to Adam, of which death was the legal penalty, then the apostle gravely asserts, according to our brethren, that *although* sin is never punished with death as a legal penalty when there is no law threatening death,—*nevertheless*, i. e., notwithstanding this incontrovertible principle,—sin was punished with death, when there was a law threatening death! In other words, the apostle *contrasts* the period antecedent to the law by Moses, with that which was subsequent, by placing them in direct opposition, the one to the other, and then proves that *there is no difference between them!*

But we shall be told (and here lies the strength of our brethren's cause), that the apostle *proves* that death from Adam to Moses was the legal penalty of *Adam's sin.* We ask then, how does he prove this? Not by his assertion of the notorious fact, that *actual* sin was in the world during that period, REIGNING *unto death*,—pervading the whole race, and bringing this consequence with it. Nor will it be claimed that the apostle asserts in direct terms, that death at this period was the legal penalty of Adam's sin. How then does he prove it? Our brethren reply, *by inference*,—by premises which unavoidably support the inference. Let us then examine the premises, and the conclusion derived from them. The apostle asserts, that sin is not punished with death as a legal penalty, when there is no law threatening death; and that death reigned before the Mosaic law, or from the introduction of sin to the giving of this law. Does it follow from this that death was the legal penalty of Adam's sin? It is as palpable a *non sequitur* as can easily be imagined. For how does the fact, that death reigned before the Mosaic law whose penalty was death, prove that death at this period was the legal penalty of the law given solely to Adam? If death could be a consequence of sin *in no other way* than as its legal penalty, then indeed the inference might claim some plausibility. But, as we have seen, it can be, and is in fact a consequence in some *other way.* And this exposes at once what we have always considered the error of our brethren, in deriving *this* inference from the apostle's premises. They assume that death *is and must be* the legal penalty of some law. Hence *their* reasoning (not the apostle's) is this. The apostle asserts that sin is not punished with death as a legal penalty, when there is no law threatening death; and that death reigned before the law, i. e., from Adam to Moses. Therefore, *as death is and must be the legal penalty of some law*, it follows that death at this period was the legal penalty for Adam's sin. This we say, is the argument of our brethren in its entire strength, so far as we can understand it. And whether it be conclusive or not, even thus stated, who does not see that it *adds* to the premises of the apostle the very position on which the whole inference depends, and takes for granted the very point in debate? "*Death is and must be the legal penalty of some law.*" Let this be proved. Let it be proved in opposition to plain matter of fact; otherwise the argument of our brethren clearly depends on that sort of paralogism, called begging the question. Do we state this too strongly? Let then the argument be formed which shall justify their conclusion, without *assuming* the position that death is and must be the penalty of some law. Surely an assumption so entirely gratuitous, can need no other refutation than to say that it is *merely* an assumption, and one which contradicts plain matter of fact. The doctrine that the millions of the human race who died from Adam to Moses, died under the legal penalty of *Adam's sin*, has plainly no other basis, than that the apostle expected his readers to draw such an *inference* from *his* premises; and to draw it in face of the plain matter of fact, that death comes on men under an *economy of grace*, and on many, who, we know, were *delivered* from the curse of the divine law. Surely such a doctrine has but a feeble claim to be ranked among the *articuli stantis vel cadentis ecclesiæ*,—the very foundation of the superstructure of redemption.

Secondly—We proceed to show that the sin, of which the apostle speaks in this passage, is not *imputed* sin, but *actual, personal* sin.

It is not *imputed* sin; i. e., it is neither sin which we have committed in Adam as *one* with him, nor is it the mere *liability* to the punishment of his sin. The former we need not discuss. The question therefore is reduced to this,—whether the phrase *all have sinned* means, that *all are liable to the legal penalty of Adam's sin, without ill-desert of their own?* Now we say, that the language in question never has this meaning, neither as used by this apostle, nor any other inspired writer, nor according to the ordinary use of language. To say then that it has this meaning in *this instance*, is to say it without evidence and against evidence. Let us then advert to the evidence alleged. It is said, that the phrase *all have sinned*, must include human beings who cannot be said to have committed actual sin. But if so, then we may suppose that they are said to have *sinned* in some other mode of sinning, as well as in that which is contended for. Other modes of sinning might be supposed quite as rational as that of being made liable to be punished for another's sin. And when we have once resorted to mere conjecture, we may as well suppose one thing as another, especially if the absurdity in the one case be no greater than in the other. But why must human beings be intended who have not yet actually sinned? Suppose it were said that *all men reason;* should we suppose the language to include human beings before they *can* reason? Shall we be told that they *die* before actual sin? But how does this prove that they are liable to death as the *legal penalty* of Adam's sin? Does the death of *all* sinless beings prove the same thing in respect to them? But we shall be told that the words of the apostle are, that "ALL have sinned." But who are the all? Plainly the *all men*, the πάντας ἀνθρώπους, Jews and Gentiles, whom the apostle is proving to be under sin and under law; and who therefore must be justified by faith, and not by the deeds of the law. And does his argument and his conclusion relate to human beings who *cannot* commit sin on the one hand, nor be justified by *faith* on the other? Is the apostle discussing such subjects in respect to beings who are not moral agents, and who can neither commit sin nor exercise faith? Is he applying his statements to beings to whom they can have no possible application? Can it be supposed that a writer like Paul, in arguing and illustrating the necessity of Justification by faith to both Jews and Gentiles, and founding his doctrine on the sinfulness of both, as subjects of a law which is to *stop every mouth*, intended that his declarations should be extended to human beings before moral agency? One thing is certain. Those whom the apostle proves to be sinners must, according to his argument, be justified *by faith.* Is this true of any human being before moral agency? We might as well suppose the laws of the land against theft and murder to respect such beings. But it will be said, that *all* means *all*, in the most extensive sense which the *word* will bear; i. e., we must interpret *to the letter;* we must disregard that great principle applicable to the interpretation of all popular language, *ne resecemus ad vivum.* But who does not know that this is pre-eminently a false and dangerous mode of interpretation? To see that it is false, apply it to the following passages: Rom. xii. 18; John i. 7, v. 23; Mark xvi. 15. According to this principle, the first of these passages gravely teaches, that we are not to quarrel with infants as soon as they are born! Such trifling is unworthy of any one who interprets the word of God. The mere use of the word *all* then furnishes not a particle of evidence. On the contrary, to interpret such general phraseology to the *letter*, is doing palpable violence to language, as the above examples and universal usage in like cases decisively show. But it will be said that, in the passages just cited, we have in the *known nature* of the things spoken of, a decisive warrant for some limitation of the language. True, and this establishes the principle, that the known nature of things *must* limit such language. And where have we this warrant for limitation, if not in the case now at issue? Look to the subject treated of, the scope and object of the writer, and especially to the known nature of the predicate, *sin*, without begging the question about *imputed sin;* and what more decisive reasons can be supposed for concluding, that the phrase *all have sinned*, does not denote beings who confessedly *cannot sin.* Plainly, we have as good reason for saying that a being cannot *sin* before moral agency, as for saying he cannot *believe* before moral agency.

But we shall be further told, that the phrase, "even over them that had not sinned after the similitude of Adam's transgression," describes those who sinned before moral action. We ask, how does this appear? Not from the assertion that they did not sin as Adam did. The difference between them and Adam, we have before shown, consists in this, that they did not sin under a *law with the penalty of death.* This is the distinctive peculiarity. But it may be said that the beings here spoken of, are only a particular *class* of those who lived between Adam and Moses, viz., infants and idiots. We answer, that if this be so, then the other class *did* sin after the similitude of Adam's transgression; for otherwise, one class could not be thus distinguished from the other. But if all except infants and idiots, during this period, sinned like Adam, then the sin of this period, by which death reigned, was chiefly *actual* and not *imputed* sin. Why then did the apostle refer to this period to prove that death came on all, *exclusively* of actual sin, and *solely* for the imputed sin of Adam? Surely, he intended to prove no such doctrine as this. But it will be claimed that the force of the word *even* is, to distinguish a part from the rest. The true force of this word as here used by the apostle (keeping in mind the precise shape of the question he was discussing), may be illustrated by an example. Suppose then the question in discussion to be, whether any ever had the small-pox except those who had not been vaccinated; as it was in the present case whether any died as sinners without being under a law whose penalty was death. Suppose that it was a known fact, that between the years 1800 and 1810 the entire population of a city or country, all of whom had been vaccinated, had been visited with this disease. How natural in discussing the question now supposed, to appeal to the *fact* and say, "the small-pox prevailed in that city from 1800 to 1810, even over them that had been vaccinated." So the apostle; death reigned from Adam to Moses, even over such as it may be supposed it never reigned over, viz., those who were under no law *whose penalty was death.* He thus states the fact that death prevailed during this period, and then distinguishes the manner in which they who lived during this period sinned, from that in which Adam sinned. Why then *must* this phrase denote human beings who sinned *before* moral action?

But the doctrine of imputed sin is contrary to the decision of the competent unperverted reason of mankind; i. e., contrary to common sense, and as such to be rejected. This expression of our opinion is not intended *ad invidiam;* and the reason is, that we intend *to prove* what we say. We claim then, that the reason of man is *competent* to decide in respect to the justice or injustice of the principle, that one being should be held liable to be punished without his consent, for the sins of another. This we have shown already. Again: aside from certain theological purposes, the decision or judgment of the human mind is uniform in condemning this principle. No one will hesitate to admit, that aside from some supposed theological exigency, such a principle had never been thought of, except as one of palpable injustice and oppression; that it had never been ranked among even the possible truths or principles of God's government; and that even now, aside from the supposed exigency, the united wisdom of man, were it to be consulted, would reject it with abhorrence. The very men who maintain it, are obliged to admit that God adopts directly the opposite as a *general* principle; while they themselves to a man reject it with detestation, in all the relations of human life. It has indeed been applied to the government of God by wicked men, to impeach the equity of his administration, and God has disclaimed it with the severity of indignant rebuke. It has been ascribed to earthly tyrants, to illustrate their oppressions and cruelties. But aside from these instances and the one now under consideration, it is unknown and unheard of in the annals of moral legislation. One thing then is plain and undeniable, as a matter of fact, viz., that this principle *was devised for a purpose.* Certain providential events, and the *supposed* import of an apostle's declarations, were regarded as incapable of defense, without it. For this purpose therefore it was devised—for this purpose, on grounds of equity, it has been exclusively applied. It has been applied *solely* to this purpose, with no evidence to justify its application, but the supposed necessity of the case; and in defiance of an otherwise universal, and confessedly correct judgment of the human mind. It has been applied solely to this purpose, though it confessedly involves the supreme Lawgiver in the palpable inconsistency of acting on opposite principles, as though both could be alike the principles of equity. It has been applied solely to this purpose, when otherwise it would have incurred universal execration. It was therefore *devised for a purpose*, and applied to carry a point in controversial theology; and more decisive proof of a perverted judgment cannot easily be imagined.

Nothing is more remote from our belief, than that they who have adopted this principle, have done so with a clear perception of its nature. On the contrary, we believe, that at first, the supposed necessity of the principle for controversial purposes, secured its admission and gave it currency; and that soon the sanction given to it by great and good men, with other causes, effectually served to conceal its otherwise palpable deformity. This however is no reason why its true nature should not be exposed; nor why, if it is contrary to the infallible judgment of the competent, unperverted reason of man, the fact should not be understood. If the Bible is to be interpreted at the sacrifice of all such decisions and judgments of the human mind, then let this principle of interpretation be avowed. Let it be defended, if it can be. But if not, then let the doctrine which involves such a sacrifice be rejected, although in a given instance, which is not the case here, we should be entirely unable to discover "the mind of the spirit."

We only add, that in our view, the doctrine of imputed sin, instead of relieving the passage from difficulty, only creates insuperable difficulties where otherwise none would exist. No one acquainted with the controversies respecting this text will pretend, that aside from this doctrine of Imputation, and the character and state of infants before moral agency, the passage presents any peculiar difficulties to the interpreter. Assumptions on this subject so unnatural, so strange, so foreign to the design of the writer, are the stumbling-stones at the outset. Let them be dismissed from the mind of the interpreter, as things which the apostle never thought of in writing the passage, nor expected his readers to think of in interpreting it, and we venture to say, that this passage, so long abandoned to controversy and obscurity, will be regarded as one of the most lucid in argument and striking in illustration, to be found in the writings of the apostle. We shall see, that God in his wisdom and goodness, determined to make such a trial of human nature in one man, that if he sinned, the merely legal system under which he was tried, should be modified by the introduction of an economy of grace; that under this economy, his descendants should be born with the certainty of commencing their moral existence in sin, and as sinners be doomed to temporal death; and that thus, universal sin and death by sin, were introduced into the world by one man. We shall further see, that these facts were appealed to, and this manner of death's coming on all men, was distinguished from the manner of its coming according to a legal process, for the purpose of showing the universality of sin in respect to men,—not as the descendants of Abraham, but *as the descendants of Adam;* not as Jews, but as men; and this for the further purpose of showing the universal necessity of that gracious Justification, not from *imputed sin*, but from "*many offenses*," which the gospel reveals. In accordance with this design, the apostle asserts and traces the similitude between Adam and Christ, in respect to the evils which come by the one, and the blessings which come by the other. Then, that he may vindicate and magnify the goodness of God toward us in the plan of grace, he shows also the striking dissimilitude between them. As if he had said, If in consequence of the sin of one man, sin and death and condemnation come on many, great as the calamity is, the grace of God by one man Jesus Christ, far surpasses, as a blessing, the calamity as an evil. More, far more is gained by one, than is lost by the other. For what if the sin of one results in these evils to all; the gift by grace, which is by one, is a provision for Justification from many offenses. What if sin hath abounded, grace doth *much more* abound. What if sin hath reigned unto death, even so shall grace to those who reject not its provisions, reign through righteousness unto eternal life by Jesus Christ our Lord. Behold the contrast! By the first Adam, we are indeed subjected to sin and death. By the second Adam, we may not only retrieve the loss, but reign in holiness and bliss which shall never change and never end. If paradise is lost, heaven may be gained. Is it credible that when the apostle's mind was engrossed with such a theme, and aiming to conduct his readers to such a conclusion, he should introduce and discuss the perplexing topic of the Imputation of Adam's sin to his posterity? Did he teach that the whole race, at the very moment of birth or before birth, were justly subject to the full penalty of God's law for the sin of Adam; and on the *justice* of such a doom, found the rich and abundant grace of God in man's redemption?

The sin which the apostle ascribes to all men in this passage, is *actual sin*. The word ἥμαρτον (have sinned) is used to denote *actual*, *personal* sin, and that only. Thus it is used by the apostle in this discussion. (Vide Rom. ii. 12, iii. 23.) If therefore any thing can be decided by language, this point is decided in the present case. For by what warrant are we told that the word ἥμαρτον (*have sinned*), means in this case what it never meant in any other? By what evidence are we called to believe that a word always used to denote what all the world, this particular instance excepted, understand to be sin, and regard as the only thing which can be sin, or properly called sin, denotes merely *a liability* to be punished, and this too, solely for the sin of another?

Further: the sin of which the apostle speaks in the 12th verse, is the same *kind* of sin of which he treats in the preceding discussion. This is undeniable, not only because the 12th verse is inferential from what precedes it, but because the apostle had been speaking of sin universally. But of what kind of sin, if indeed we are to suppose more kinds than one, had he been speaking? The sin of being "enemies to God," verse 10; the sin for which Christ was delivered, "*our offenses*," iv. 25; sin in respect to which "*all have sinned and come short of the glory of God*;" sin in respect to which both Jews and Gentiles *are all under sin;* sin by which all *have gone out of the way*, &c., &c., iii. 9–18; sin *under the law* which *stops every mouth*, and by which is *the knowledge of sin*, 19, 20; sin which is *without excuse*, because when they KNEW *God, they glorified him not as God;* sin committed under a revealed law, or the law written on the heart; sin consisting in all vile affections and abominable doings; sin consisting in *doing* things which they *knew* to be *worthy of death;* sin under the government of that God whose judgment is *according to truth* against them which *commit* such things, and who will render to every man according to *his deeds*. And now we ask, is this only *Adam's sin imputed?* Does this kind of sin, thus described as personal acts and doings, consist after all, not in personal acts, but only in being liable to be punished for another's act? Is not the principle of our brethren most explicitly contradicted in the clause—"who will render to every one according to *his* deeds?" Plainly, if language can distinguish one thing from another; if the apostle could describe what we mean by *actual, personal sin*, he charged this and this only on men. But this is the very sin of which he speaks, when he says in the passage under consideration, "WHEREFORE as by one man sin entered into the world." What sin, except that of which he had been speaking as common to Jews and Gentiles? As if he had said, Since the sin which I have proved to be common to all men, entered the world by one man, &c. And when he adds, repeating only what he had said before, that "*all have sinned*," does he mean that all are liable, though as yet *sinless*, to be punished for another's sin? Did the apostle prove all men to be the perpetrators of actual sin; did he describe the fact by the phrase *all have sinned*, and in that explicit manner too which we have seen; and does he now in the 12th verse, pursuing still his course of thought, turn aside to beings as yet personally *sinless*, and bring the same charge in the same language against them? We can as well believe that he is predicating sin of the primordial atoms that compose a human body.

The same thing is evident from the immediate context. "*By one man sin entered into the world.*" What sin, except that which is in the world? And is this nothing but the liability of personally *sinless beings* to be punished for the sin of another? Was this the sin and the only sin which entered the world, and by which death came? Is this the meaning of the apostle, that by one man liability to death on the part of beings as yet sinless, entered the world; and death by this liability to death, and so death passed on all men because all were justly liable to die for another's sin? Such reasoning we cannot charge upon the apostle. Again, "For until the law, sin was in the world." Does not the apostle here refer to the well-known historical fact of abounding actual sin? Had a world been destroyed by a deluge of waters; and Sodom and Gomorrah by a storm of fire and brimstone, and this for actual sin; and was there no sin in the world resulting in death but *imputed* sin; no sin but the sin of personally sinless beings? But this sin which was in the world, was *the* sin by which *death* reigned. The sin therefore by which death reigned from Adam to Moses, was *actual* sin.

Further: it will be admitted that the sin spoken of by the apostle, is that by which death prevails. And here the question is not, whether "in Adam all die," i. e., whether death is not to all, in some *mode*, a certain consequence of Adam's sin; but whether the apostle teaches that they die irrespectively of personal sin? We say, that he teaches that men die indeed as the consequence of Adam's sin, but not without *actual* sin of their own. Adam introduced death by introducing sin. By one man *sin* entered into the world. But how does death come? "Death *by sin*;" and *so*, by this connection, "death hath passed on all men, because *all* have sinned." We do not see how the language of the apostle could be more explicit, in asserting personal *sin* to be the proximate cause of death.

He traces the same connection between the *actual* sin from Adam to Moses, and the prevalence of death. For to what other sin could he refer when he said, "until the law sin was in the world?" But we have his own explanation of the fact. He describes the *very sin* with which he connects death, as *the offense* which *abounded* by the entrance of the *law*. But what had the entrance of the law to do with *imputed* sin? Nor is this all. He describes the connection in terms the most unequivocal. "That as *sin hath reigned unto death*." What is this but sin, pervading the world and bringing with it death as its consequence? And will it be said or thought, that the apostle ascribed such a dominion to any sin but *actual* sin? Or to put the question in its true form, is mere *liability* to death without personal sin, the *offense* which abounded by the law; the *sin* which reigned unto death?

Again: it will be admitted by all, that the sin of which the apostle treats, is that from which Christ died to procure our deliverance. In the preceding chapter then, we are told he was delivered for "*our offenses*." In this chapter we have not a word about deliverance from imputed sin, nor yet from the death which is the consequence of sin, but a Justification from "many offenses;" resulting not in exemption from that death which is common to all, but in *life*, *eternal life*. Is this a deliverance from imputed sin, and from death as its legal penalty? Surely the apostle has here taught no such redemption.

We only add, that the apostle has placed the point in debate beyond all question, by clearly and unambiguously showing that the *very sin* which is the consequence of one man's disobedience, is *actual sin*. After asserting in the 19th verse, that "by one man's disobedience many were made sinners," he adds in the next verse, "moreover the law entered that *the offense might abound*." We ask, what *offense?* Plainly the offense by which men became sinners in consequence of one man's disobedience. Was this then *imputed* sin—mere liability to punishment for Adam's sin? or was it *actual* sin? How could the law by Moses cause *imputed* sin or any other sin to abound, except *actual* sin? And what law could do this, except a law by which is the knowledge of sin? But this is the sin by which all are made sinners by one man's disobedience. *Actual, personal sin* then, is the sin which entered the world by one man. If any mode of describing this sin, either in its nature or its relation, in its effects or its consequences, can decide this point, it would seem that this question must be settled. Can the evidence now adduced be set aside by the groundless assumption of *imputed* sin? Could this assumption be shown to be a *possible truth*, would it even then avail against the evidence now adduced, to the fact, that *actual sin* was here intended? What then is the state of the argument, when even the possibility of the truth of such an assumption cannot be shown? Shall we do open violence to the dictates of common sense, by giving to the apostle's language such a meaning, when it not only admits of, but in view of the evidence in the case, absolutely demands another?

HUMAN SINFULNESS.

XIV.—CONSEQUENCES OF ADAM'S SIN TO HIS POSTERITY.

Exposition of Romans v. 12–21.

WHAT I now propose is, to exhibit the *mode* of connection between Adam's sin, and its consequences to his posterity, in that positive form in which, in my view, it is presented by the apostle in Rom. v. 12, &c. I proceed then to say in general terms, that contrary to what has been commonly supposed, the apostle represents

The mode of connection between Adam's sin and its consequences to his posterity, to be BY GOD'S SOVEREIGN CONSTITUTION, in distinction from *the mode* of strict legal procedure. Or thus, *the mode of this connection* was by God's sovereign constitution, ordaining an economy of grace immediately after the sin of Adam, so that his posterity commence their moral probation under a system of both law and grace; i. e., under a system in which law is so modified by grace, that while in its authority to command, and in its power to condemn, it is neither abrogated nor weakened, it is not in all its principles strictly adhered to, or carried out in man's probation on earth, but is in this respect partially, and may be wholly, through grace, dispensed with in determining man's relations to its sanctions, and to the rewards and punishments of a future state.*

With this general view of the apostle's representation before us, I now proceed to his more particular views of the subject.

His object in the 12th, 13th, and 14th verses, is to show that all the posterity of Adam became sinners, and subject to temporal death in consequence of his sin, and yet in such a way or mode of connection as not to exclude their individual responsibility for their own sin, nor to imply that temporal death was

* What the cause or reason in each individual's mind is, that he sins in his first moral act, is an inquiry untouched by the apostle in this chapter. We shall treat of it hereafter.

the legal penalty of sin; but in such a way BY GOD'S SOVEREIGN CONSTITUTION, that *the sin* and just (not actual) condemnation of all men to bear its penalty, must be inferred from their connection with Adam as his descendants. (Vide his conclusion in the 19th verse.) For this purpose, he obviously in the 12th verse refers to the historical narrative in the 3d chapter of Genesis. The facts, as the record shows, respected the progenitor of the human race, and all his descendants, as moral beings, and were such as no human ingenuity would ever have surmised. Adam, the father of us all, sinned; and instead of being at once visited with the infliction of the legal penalty for sin, was placed with the race who were to descend from him, under an economy of grace (Gen. iii. 15). Under this economy, and in entire consistency with its nature, a sentence, *on account of sin*, was pronounced upon him—not however in the language of the legal threatening, "THOU SHALT DIE"—but a sentence of very different import, a prominent part of which is, "dust thou art, and unto dust shalt thou return." This, though dooming him to temporal death only, being a sentence *on account of sin*, implied of course his just exposure to the full penalty of the law, or eternal death. At the same time, this narrative is so conducted as decisively to show, that not only the revealed economy of grace, but the sentence to temporal death under this economy, respected not Adam only but his whole posterity. God had in our first parents made a trial of human nature, of the kind of beings called men, placing them as it would seem, in circumstances the most auspicious to a happy issue. Nor is it for human reason to say, that exactly that system of things in respect to Adam and his descendants which God in his sovereign counsels had determined on, was not the dictate of infinite wisdom and goodness. This system or constitution under which he determined to give existence to a race of moral beings, as disclosed in the narrative by Moses, was however so aside from the ordinary notions of the human mind concerning the government of such beings, as scarcely to be credible were it not revealed. Obedience with reward, or disobedience with penalty, had been the natural expectation. But God had determined that if the first progenitors of all sinned, not to deal with them in exact retribution, but at once to introduce an economy of mercy, and what perhaps is no less strange under this economy, to bring into existence their posterity with such a nature and in such a condition of being, that from the first—or very early in their first moral character—they would become sinners, and that all with this common character should be subjected to the common doom of returning to dust, i. e., to temporal death. Accordingly when Adam sinned, the first great announcement respecting him and his posterity, is AN ECONOMY OF GRACE in the promise, "The seed of the woman shall bruise the serpent's head." Then under this economy follows, not the sentence dooming all to bear the penalty of the law, "THOU SHALT SURELY DIE," from which grace had now reprieved the whole race; but the sentence, "dust thou art, and unto dust shalt thou return." This is not spoken of the soul, but of the body only; and yet it is *the only sentence*, with some of its connections, which God has ever pronounced on the whole human race. This sentence, including other temporal evils, instead of shrouding a sinful world in despair, was obviously designed as a part of a wise system of moral discipline, to restrain the wickedness of men, and to reclaim them to God under the proffers of his mercy. Thus manifest is it from the historical record, that all the descendants of Adam were to come into being and assume the relation of moral beings, not merely under a system of law, but also under an economy of grace; that all were to become sinners, and to die or return to dust, *on account of sin*, *indirectly* as a consequence of his sin, and directly as a consequence of their own sin. Such was the sovereign constitution of the wise and benignant Creator of the human race, as described in the very records of his creation, and as it has ever been unfolded in the events of his providence.*

* The act of dooming men to temporal death, and thus subjecting them to so great an evil *for sin* as a part of a system of moral discipline to restrain them from wickedness and to reclaim them to duty, would be as decisive *a proof* of their sin, as to threaten the same evil as a legal penalty. Nor would it manifest displeasure toward sin less really in the one case than in the other, since the magnitude of the evil inflicted would be the same in either. That the prospective certainty of temporal death has a reclaiming tendency and influence in this state of moral probation, and that it was designed to have such tendency and influence cannot be doubted. To say nothing of the impossibility, on account of the inadequacy of temporal death as a legal penalty or sanction of the divine law, without the sure prospect of this death, what check on human wickedness or what hope of human reformation would remain? Who, though expecting by repentance to escape the full legal penalty of sin, expects to escape temporal death?

With these facts in view, it cannot, we think, be difficult to understand the language of the apostle in the passage under consideration.

Verse 12: He says, "By one man sin entered into the world." This is simply affirming, in accordance with the acknowledged historic record, that the sin which there is in the world came into it by the sin of Adam, that is, was in some mode of connection a consequence of his sin. It is not saying, that the sin which is in the world is either universal or not, nor in what *way* or *mode* it is connected with the sin of Adam.* The apostle next asserts, that temporal death entered the world by sin—"and death by sin." This is not saying any thing concerning the mode in which death is connected with sin, whether in the mode of judicial retribution, or in the way of moral discipline under a gracious economy, or in some other way which human ingenuity may devise; it is simply the general affirmation, authorized by the original record of the fact, that the death which is *in the world*, be it more or less, is the consequence of sin. Thus two facts are very plainly asserted, *that the sin which is in the world is a consequence of Adam's sin;* and *that the death which is in the world is a consequence of sin.* How obvious are these truths from the narrative in Genesis!

The apostle then proceeds to the more particular assertion of the *universal* prevalence of death, and the more *direct* reason for such prevalence. "So, οὕτως, *in this manner*, death (being by sin as its consequence) hath passed upon all men, because (or whereunto, unto which) all have sinned."† Thus, still in accordance with the original narrative, the apostle asserts, that under that constitution of God, in which human nature was tried in one man, the whole race now under an economy of mercy, were to die, i. e., to return to dust, because the whole race were to be sinners, as the consequence of one man's sin.

In this 12th verse then, and according to the narrative of facts in Genesis, the apostle has unfolded the divine constitution in respect to that race of beings called men. According

* The specific *mode* of this connection the apostle seems to have left, in this passage, to be determined by the uninspired authority of polemic theologians.

† Vide Phil. iii. 12; Rom. x. 19, and xvi. 19; 1 Thess. iii. 7, and iv. 7; Gal. v. 13; Eph. i. 10; 2 Tim. ii. 14; 2 Corinth. v. 4; Phil. iv. 10.

to this sovereign constitution of the Creator, this race of moral beings were to be tried in one man; not indeed in respect to a legal retribution of all, but in respect to a subsequent and further trial, under a very different system from that of mere law: if he sinned, an economy of grace was to be at once adopted. Under this economy, not only sin and death were to come into the world—the latter as the consequence of the former—but *all* were to become sinners as the consequence of one man's sin, and thus all were to die or return to dust, *directly* for their own sin, and *indirectly* in consequence of his sin. A divine constitution so peculiar, and so aside from the common and natural mode of contemplating the subject by the human mind,—a constitution in which the more familiar principles of mere law and a strictly legal procedure with moral beings were so far dispensed with, by the Sovereign Creator and Disposer of all, might not unnaturally by some be doubted or denied, at least in two respects. To confirm therefore the view given, the apostle adds the 13th and 14th verses.

Verse 13: "For, until the law, sin was in the world; but sin is not imputed when there is no law." As if he had said,—"That sin and death should have existed and prevailed in the world as they have done, in any other supposable mode or manner of connection or consequence than that which I have described, is incredible, in view of an undeniable fact, and an incontrovertible principle. It cannot be supposed or said, in respect to sin, that it did not prevail in the world, except as the transgression of a revealed law; for it is a fact too palpable to be questioned or denied, that *before* the law given by Moses, *the only revealed law which God, after the sin of Adam, ever gave to men*, sin prevailed in the world. None surely can gainsay this *fact*.* Is it then said, that the death

* While the apostle had unequivocally laid down the principle, that "where no law is, there is no transgression," he had surely left his readers no reason to suppose that there could be no law except *a revealed* law. Vide Rom. i. 19, 20, &c.; and also ii. 12-15. Nor has he said any thing which implies, that "the law written on the heart" is without a just penalty; and still less, that temporal death, common to the righteous and the wicked, is the penalty of that law. Indeed none could suppose it to be such a penalty. It was important to guard against another error, to give no countenance to the idea that it was such a penalty.

which has prevailed in the world as common to all men, must be a legal penalty—a penalty of some law—if not of the law of Moses, then of the law given to Adam? 'But sin is not *imputed*,'—that is, sin is not visited or punished with temporal death (the only death of which he was speaking, and which in the present case, could be supposed to be a legal penalty), when there is no law with such a penalty. This *principle* is incontrovertible." Thus the apostle has plainly shown, contrary to what might be and what has been commonly supposed, that death in this world, or temporal death, does not come on all men by *imputing sin*, i. e., as the legal penalty of sin.*

Verse 14: "Nevertheless death reigned from Adam to Moses, even (κάι) over them that had not sinned after the similitude of Adam's transgression." As if he said—"Notwithstanding the incontrovertible principle just stated—that sin is not *imputed*, is not punished with temporal death as a legal penalty, when there is no revealed law having such a penalty, still death universally prevailed from Adam to Moses, and of course over them who had not, like Adam, sinned against a revealed law. Death therefore, as an event common to all men, does not come on them, by *imputing sin*, or as the legal penalty of sin—it does not come upon them in the way of a merely legal procedure; but under an economy of mercy, under a redemptive system,—comes upon them therefore as a system of means and influences designed to reclaim and save from sin and its just penalty. And yet *death* with other evils, according to God's peculiar constitution of things, *coming by sin*,—being connected with it as its consequence in the manner stated—*indirectly* with the sin of Adam, and *directly* with the sin of each individual,—is a decisive proof of what I proposed to prove,—that both Jews and Gentiles—all the descendants of Adam, in consequence of his sin, are sinners, and justly exposed to final condemnation."

Such then is the conclusion which the apostle establishes in the 12th, 13th, and 14th verses. Thus not by authorizing, but by expressly *contradicting* the common opinion, that the sentence in Genesis iii. 19, or any other sentence, doomed all men to bear the legal penalty of the law, in this world of mercy,—in this world, where so many are delivered from that

* What it is to *impute sin*, I have before shown, and may be easily understood by comparing 2 Sam. xix. 19; Ps. xxxii. 12; 2 Cor. v. 19.

penalty, and where God is "not imputing unto men their trespasses,"—he has shown from undeniable and acknowledged facts of history, that all the posterity of Adam, as a consequence of his sin, and according to God's sovereign constitution, became sinners; that "by one man's disobedience, many were made sinners" (verse 19).*

Having thus spoken of the evils which come upon all men, and the manner in which they come by one man, the apostle does not forget the promise, that "the seed of the woman shall bruise the serpent's head." He adds without a pause, "who (Adam) is the *figure* of him that was to come." The glorious promise of a Redeemer of the race *immediately followed* the sin of Adam, and *preceded the sentence* of temporal death, and

---

* It was essential to the apostle's argument to show that death was an event common to all mankind—that it could and did come upon them in this world, in another mode of connection than that of the legal penalty of sin. Otherwise, he would have exhibited this world as a state of exact and full retribution, and the grand object of writing this epistle would have been defeated. For with what pretense could he have asserted and proved the doctrine of Justification by grace through faith, under a system of mere law, involving the full and just retribution of sin? Temporal death had come to all who "died in faith," and who of course were delivered from the legal penalty of sin. Surely to the righteous—to the justified—to those who are blessed, because to them God does *not impute* sin (Ps. xxxii. 2; Rom. iv. 6), temporal death is not the legal penalty of sin. How then can temporal death as an event common to all men, be viewed *as the legal penalty of sin*, and *as such* be alleged as a proof of universal sin? Plainly, if it proves universal sin, it must prove it under some other relation than that of being the legal penalty of sin. If temporal death is the legal penalty of sin, then who are saved from this penalty? Were Enoch and Elijah the only men delivered from it? Did Abel, and Noah, and Abraham, and all the patriarchs who died, and to whom God did *not impute* sin, bear the penalty of the law? How could this apostle himself say, "for me—to die is gain?" What too becomes of the great doctrine of his Epistle, —the *articulus stantis*, &c.,—how are we saved from wrath—in a word, how is Christ a Saviour? Paul, as a reasoner, obviously saw the vital importance of guarding his argument on this point. Not to have done this as he has in the 13th and 14th verses, would have ruined his argument as one designed to show that all men are sinners, in consequence of Adam's sin. The answer might have been, according to a probable Jewish notion, "they die as the legal penalty of Adam's sin, or in some other supposed mode of legal procedure." If any ask, why are all men doomed to temporal death, if temporal death is not the legal penalty of sin? I answer, *to prove* the sin of all—to manifest God's displeasure for their sin, though not in that high degree which is essential to, and involved in, the legal penalty of sin, and especially that, in this way, death as an event of prospective certainty to all, while yet under a gracious system of moral discipline and trial, with the judgment to follow it, and the retribution of eternal life or eternal death, as men accept or reject proffered mercy, may serve to reclaim them from sin and bring them to Him who saves from the wrath to come.

other temporal evils, pronounced on him and his posterity. This promise from the moment in which it was announced,—how august the fact! how great the change!—was fulfilled; fulfilled so far as, that along with the evils by Adam, the blessings of redemption by Christ co-existed. Under this redemptive system, every child of Adam was to come, and did come into existence,—a condition of being, whatever other evils may belong to it, which is widely different from one which involves a full and hopeless retribution in the legal penalty of sin. The apostle was thus led to advert, in the briefest manner, to the fact of a general resemblance between Adam and Christ. As if he had said, "*As there are certain consequences of the act of one, which come upon all men; so there are other certain consequences never to be lost sight of, of the act of the other, which come upon all men.* This is the resemblance. The rest is contrast and dissimilitude." Hence the apostle hastens, as if through impatience, to contrast the consequences in the one case with those in the other, that it may appear how much the evils as evils, in the one, are surpassed by the blessings as blessings in the other. Thus he proceeds to say generally in

Verse 15: "But not as the offense so also is the free (gracious) gift (χάρισμα); for if through the offense of one many have died, much more the grace of God, and the gift by grace (δωρεὰ ἐν χάριτι), which is by one man Jesus Christ, hath abounded unto many." This was to say, immensely great (as we must suppose) is the difference between the consequences of the one offense, and what must be the results of the grace of God and of the gift by grace. For if by the offense of one many die (i. e., if many return to dust as the consequence of one sin resulting in their own sin, and of course in their just and actual exposure to final condemnation), great as the evil is, still the grace of God, and the gift by grace, which is by one man Jesus Christ, is much greater in its abounding riches as a blessing, than is the evil as an evil. The one as a blessing is so great, it so far as a blessing surpasses the other as an evil, that we may well be satisfied and grateful under a system of such overflowing grace.

Verse 16: And not as *the sentence was* by one that sinned, so is the gift, (δώρημα) for the sentence (κρίμα) was of one offense (εἰς κατάκριμα) unto condemnation, but the gracious gift (χάρισμα) is of many offenses (εἰς δικαίωμα) unto a provision or ordinance for righteousness or Justification.* As if he had said, there is yet another important difference; for according to the sentence as already explained, although all men directly for their own sin, and indirectly for Adam's sin, became justly exposed to final condemnation by one offense, yet the gracious gift is unto a provision for righteousness for many offenses. Or thus the sentence (κρίμα) of death, "dust thou art," &c.—the only sentence which God ever pronounced on the whole race; the sentence which implies and proves the sin and just condemnation of all men—was in the manner explained by one offense, but the gracious gift (χάρισμα) involves one *δικαίωμα*, an instituted provision for righteousness or Justification from many offenses.†

---

* This δικαίωμα the apostle speaks of in the 18th verse as *one δικαίωμα*. The most general meaning of δικαίωμα seems to be, that which is ordained or appointed by authority for righteousness or Justification. (Vide all the instances of its use in the New Testament, and particularly in Rom. viii. 4. Vide also McKnight *in loc.*) Where the δικαίωμα τοῦ νόμου cannot be '*the righteousness of the law*' as the end of Christ's sacrifice for sin; that is, perfect personal obedience to law, nor the δικαιοσύνη ἐκ νόμου in Phil. iii. 9, nor the δικαιοσύνη ἐν νόμῳ in verse 6th. (See P. S. on p. 305.)

† Most theologians seem not to enter into the apostle's conception of the superabundance of the grace of God in giving the posterity of Adam existence under a system of redemption. Indeed, I cannot but think that very inadequate and low views on this subject extensively prevail. That it should be so with those who believe that man is born with concreated or propagated sinful depravity, or with imputed sin, or under a necessity from some cause of sinning from the first, or that in any way he deserves the wrath of God prior to all free, responsible, moral action on his part, is not to be wondered at. But there are some who profess to maintain simply *the certainty* of his sinning in his first moral act, who still regard him as not placed in a state of fair trial. My object in this note is, briefly to advert to this last view of the subject. I remark that the very nature and condition of a moral being are essentially such—his intellect, his susceptibilities, his elective power of will, and the reasons, motives, known to him are such—that nothing can excuse the guilt of morally wrong action on his part, either in the first instance or in any other; while the mere previous certainty (involving the most perfect moral liberty conceivable), of his acting morally wrong in the first instance, can no more lessen or increase the moral turpitude of his acting morally wrong, than the mere certainty of his acting morally right would lessen or increase the moral rectitude of his acting morally right. Besides, if the mere certainty of his acting morally wrong is inconsistent with a fair trial, then no moral being in a state of fair trial can ever act morally wrong; since in every such case there would be a prior certainty of his so acting, and a reason for it. Of course no creature of God ever has sinned or can sin, except as the result of a fair trial. And further, how can the trial of a moral being, having, as he must have, perfect moral liberty, be otherwise than fair? Be temptation what it may in its nature and its circumstances, still what is it when compared

Verse 17: "For if by the offense of one, death reigned by one, much more they who receive abundance of grace and of the gift of righteousness (*τῆς δωρεᾶς τῆς δικαιοσύνης*) shall reign in life by one Jesus Christ." Here the apostle advances another step. Comprising the evils by the one offense of one man in the prevalence of temporal death, and assuming what he had just asserted, a provision of righteousness for Justification from many offenses, he unfolds in contrast the actual result of this gracious gift to those who receive abundance of grace and of the gift of righteousness (vide chap. iii. 22, and Phil. iii. 9), as reigning in life through Jesus Christ. He thus contrasts the actual and unavoidable evils in the one case with the actual blessings in the other when fully secured; and shows how immeasurably the actual evils by Adam are surpassed by the blessings actually secured through Christ by all who are willing to accept them.

Verse 18: "Therefore as by one offense (*δι' ἑνὸς παραπτώματος*) the sentence (*κρίμα*) came upon all men unto condemnation (*εἰς κατάκριμα*), even so by one provision for righteousness (*δι' ἑνὸς δικαιώματος*) the gracious gift (*χάρισμα*) came upon all men unto Justification (*δικαίωσιν*) of life." Here the one *παραπτώμα*, and the one *δικαίωμα*, are in respect to their tendencies placed in obvious contrast. The one, in the manner already explained in verse 12th, leads to condemnation; the other, in the manner explained in the three preceding verses, leads to Justification. As if he had said, As through one *παραπτώμα*, there was a sentence upon all men unto condemnation, so through one *δικαίωμα*, there is a gracious gift to all men unto Justification of life. The preposition *εἰς* is plainly *telic*, or else the apostle teaches the Justification and salvation of all men

---

with the known reasons for acting morally right? If we would form this only just view of man as a moral being,—as one so perfectly qualified for right moral action, that on *a priori* grounds it would be cause for astonishment to heaven and earth that he should ever act morally wrong (Isa. i. 2, and Mark vi. 6), and especially if we suppose that all should actually accept as they can, the offered blessings of salvation, then we should be prepared to enter into the apostle's conception of the abundance of God's goodness and grace in the economy of redemption, and to pronounce it as he does "the exceeding riches of his grace in his kindness toward us through Christ Jesus." But as our acceptance of that grace would not enhance, neither does our rejection of it diminish its abundance. Goodness to us—goodness in the forms of grace and mercy—aims at our good, and while our perversions of it evince its nature, they may instead of obscuring, only serve to augment its splendors.

contrary to verse 17; for if the sentence was one of actual condemnation, the gracious gift is one of actual Justification. Nor is this all. The two propositions amount to a palpable contradiction; for the one asserts the *actual* condemnation of all men to eternal death; the other, their actual Justification to eternal life. By failing to see the meaning of *κρίμα εἰς κατάκριμα*, and of *χάρισμα εἰς δικαίωμα*, in verse 16, and consequently that of *εἰς δικαίωσιν* in verse 18, Prof. Stuart has made the apostle assert the actual Justification of all men as truly as the Universalist could desire. The Professor probably would not admit this. But on this point he must be judged by his readers.

Verse 19: "For as by one man's disobedience (*παρακοῆς*) many were made sinners, so by the obedience (*ὑπακοῆς*) of one shall many be made righteous." As if he had said, I have thus shown how obvious it is from well-known history and all acknowledged facts, that according to the sovereign constitution of God, by one man's sin all men became sinners, as such were exposed to a just condemnation to bear the full penalty of sin, and were, as the evidence and proof of this, actually doomed to temporal death. I have also shown in the preceding part of the epistle, that by the obedience (unto death) of one man,—of him that was to come, and actually promised (Gen. iii. 15) before, and therefore virtually cotemporaneously with the sentence (*κρίμα εἰς κατάκριμα*) not only an abundant provision of grace was made for the Justification of all men, but that many shall become righteous* and reign in life. (Vide from the first verse to the twelfth of this chapter.)

Verse 20: "Moreover the law entered that the offense might abound. But where sin abounded, grace did much more abound." As if, in confirmation of his views already expressed, he had said, Justification is not by the law, for the law (meaning the Mosaic or national law, which I have before shown, comprises the first and great commandment) *entered* (*παρεισῆλθεν*) (had a limited entrance compared with that of sin, vide Doddridge *in loc.*), that sin might appear in its degree and extent, or how much there was of it. And yet abundant as sin was with its evils, grace was much more abundant; so that it

---

* The *δικαίοι* of the Scriptures are the *δικαίοι ἐκ πίστεως*, those who by faith or personal holiness are justified, and so stand right in relation to the sanctions of law.

might never be forgotten or lost sight of, that sin with all its evils in this world considered as an evil, was by no means to be compared with redeeming grace in its results as a blessing insomuch—

Verse 21: "That as sin has reigned unto death, even so might grace reign through righteousness unto eternal life, by Jesus Christ our Lord." As if he had said, while therefore there is a certain similitude between Adam and Christ in their respective relations to all men, there is a great dissimilitude. The resemblance is, that both sustained an important relation of connection with all men in respect to consequences or effects. But the dissimilitude is, that in the one case the consequences of the connection were evils, and in the other blessings,—a connection in both cases to be resolved into God's wise and benignant sovereignty, and yet capable of the most complete and honorable vindication. For if Adam injured us, it cannot be shown that it was in a greater degree than we in some other necessary condition of existence should have injured ourselves; while Christ has greatly profited us far, very far more than Adam injured us. If we compare the constitution (δίαθήκη) of God with Adam and the human race as his descendants, great as the resulting evils are, with the constitution (διàθήκη) of God in Christ as the Redeemer of the world; if we view the latter in all its provisions of grace and mercy, and judge of it aside from our perversions of it, and especially as availing ourselves of its blessings as we may, how transcendent the good compared with the evil! Who would not prefer to receive existence as an accountable and immortal being under that system of law and mercy under which he does receive it, to being placed under one of mere law, where his eternal destiny in bliss must depend on his sinless obedience, or indeed under any other system than the present, which he can pronounce possible or worthy of the Creator of all?

P. S.—The just interpretation of the passage under consideration depends much on the import of the words δικαίωμα, δικαιοσύνη, and δικαίωσις, especially as they are used by the apostle on the subject of Justification. That these words are not used by him as synonyms to denote *Justification*, as Prof. Stuart supposes, and that neither δικαίωμα, nor δικαιοσύνη can be properly rendered *Justification*, nor δικαίωμα, *righteousness*, must be obvious by comparing the use of these words in verses 16th and 18th of this chapter, and from Rom. iii. 22, and Phil. iii. 9, and Rom. viii. 4. In Rom. viii. 4, our translators absurdly represent the design of Christ's sacrifice to be *the fulfilling of the righteousness of the law on our part.* The true rendering of δικαίωμα would correct the error.

That the words referred to are always used in the Scriptures in one precise meaning, I do not here assert. What I maintain is, that they are used with great precision, and in a plain and familiar meaning by this apostle, when treating of the subject of Justification.

What I propose in this note is, to illustrate my own view of the diversity of meaning, by considering some of the obvious and prominent facts in the case of a subject of law who should be justified by the deeds of law. The case implies a trial or an investigation in respect to his relation to the sanctions of law, as that which is to be determined. It implies next his perfect obedience to law, which sustains two relations to law: one is, that it is the fulfillment of the claim of law as an act or doing, required of the subject; and the other is, that it is the ordained, or instituted ground by which the subject might stand right in relation to the sanctions of law; and this in two respects,—first, as it renders such standing consistent with justice, and secondly with all the other interests or ends of benevolence. As the fulfilling of the claim of law, it would be called τὰ ἔργα τõυ νόμου. As the ordained or instituted ground of merely rendering it consistent with justice, or with the authority of law, it would be called τὸ δικαίωμα τοῦ νόμου (Rom. viii. 4.)* As a δικαίωμα, and yet not merely as such;

* Vide Calvin, Instit., Book III. Chap. 11, S. 9, and Chap. 17, S. 7. It is obvious that δικαίωμα is here used (Rom. viii. 4) in this sense; since there is no other in which the design of Christ's sacrifice for sin can be said to be, "that the righteousness of the law might be fulfilled in us," who have broken the law. Besides, if it be understood to mean the same as δικαιοσύνη ἐκ νόμου, in Phil. iii. 9, then the apostle in the latter passage expresses a strong desire that the design of Christ's sacrifice for sin may not be accomplished in respect to himself. It is neither desirable nor necessary perhaps to change the translation of Rom. viii. 4, since the English word *righteousness* will bear perhaps the meaning, which the connection so clearly shows to be the meaning of δικαίωμα. Beza was so struck with the incongruity of understanding δικαίωμα as synonymous with δικαιοσύνη, that he translates the passage, "Ut jus illud legis," *that that right of the law*, viz.,

but also as being received by faith, rendering it consistent with *all* the ends of benevolence, that the subject stand right in relation to the sanctions of law, it would be called *ἡ δικαιοσύνη ἐκ νόμου* (Phil. iii. 9); and thus the sure and complete ground of Justification. Yet another thing is implied,—the act of Justification itself;—the act of the judge which authoritatively determines the main question,—that the subject does actually stand right in relation to the sanctions of law so far as treatment is concerned. This is called *ἡ δικαίωσις*. (Vide A. Clarke on Rom. v. 18.)

Thus in the supposed case of Justification under law, we find three prominent things, which are necessarily, easily, and familiarly distinguished;—so much so, that, as I claim, it is incredible, that the apostle, adhering as he does to the use of forensic phraseology, should not clearly and strongly distinguish them in unfolding the divine plan for the gratuitous Justification of sinners, in its consistency with the great principles of law and Moral Government. In respect to obedience to law, as fulfilling the claim of law, this, under the plan of grace, is out of the question; "for all have sinned." But if law is to be established in its authority, or the justice of God to be vindicated, and sinners are to be justified, then it would seem, that some ground or means of establishing the authority of law, or vindicating the justice of the Lawgiver, would be imperiously demanded and prominently presented; that is, some *δικαίωμα*, equivalent to that which would be furnished by the perfect obedience of the subject. I need not say how fully the apostle has shown this to be true in the third chapter of this epistle, by the clearest implication; nor how obvious it is, that the word *δικαίωμα* will bear no other than this precise import in the 16th and 18th verses of this chapter, and also in chapter viii. 4. But further, and for the same imperious reason, we should expect the apostle to exhibit, not merely a *δικαίωμα*, or ground on which the justified sinner could stand right in relation to the sanctions of law, consistently with the authority of law or with the justice of the Lawgiver, but a *δικαιοσύνη*, which,

---

to perfect obedience as the ground of acceptance might, &c.—thus, as I think, conforming to the meaning of the apostle, by distinguishing *the right of the law* to be upheld in its authority by obedience, from its claim to obedience as action or conduct on the part of the subject.

without excluding but including the *δικαίωμα*, should also render it consistent with all the other ends of benevolence, that the sinner should stand right in relation to the sanctions of law;—a *δικαιοσύνη*, which in those respects shall be equivalent to a *δικαιοσύνη ἐκ νόμου*, and so become a sure and complete ground of Justification. And now what do we find? In this chapter, "those who receive abundance of the gift of righteousness"—(*δικαιοσύνη*)—"grace reigning through *righteousness* unto eternal life;" the same thing which the apostle had called and often calls "the righteousness of God by faith of Jesus Christ, unto all and upon all them that believe." (Vide chap. iii. 22, 25, 26; x. 4; Phil. iii. 9, *et al.*) Now this righteousness of God by faith is not the *δικαίωμα* merely. The Atonement, as we have seen, simply supports the authority of law, and so far renders it consistent with that authority, that the sinner should stand right in relation to legal sanctions. It does not of itself actually place any sinner in this relation to these sanctions. For this purpose something more, as we have seen, according to a strictly legal procedure, would be necessary even in the perfect obedience of the subject of law. To become *a righteousness*, it must, as it would, render it consistent with all the ends of benevolence, that the obedient *subject* should on this ground stand right in relation to legal sanctions. So in the case of the *sinner* there must be in both respects an equivalent righteousness or *δικαιοσύνη*. This is "righteousness of God by faith"—the righteousness of God's providing; and is a righteousness, inasmuch as by the Atonement the sinner's standing right in relation to the sanctions of law is consistent with the authority of law, and by his faith (his personal holiness), his so standing is consistent with all the other ends of benevolence. Thus we find not merely a *δικαίωμα* (*ἑνὸς δικαιώματος*), but also a *δικαιοσύνη*, a *δικαιοσύνη θεοῦ διὰ πίστεως*, as sure and complete a ground of Justification for sinners, as would be their own perfect obedience to law, had they received such an obedience. Thus "Christ is the end of the law for righteousness" (*δικαιοσύνη*)—to whom, not to all men, for whom there is one *δικαίωμα*; but "to every one that believeth."

I will only add here, that it is not the *δικαίωμα*, as such, or as merely sustaining the authority of law, which becomes *a righteousness*, or the *δικαιοσύνη τοῦ θεοῦ*; nor is it the faith of the sinner as rendering it consistent with other ends of benevolence, that the sinner should stand right in relation to legal sanction, much less as meritorious, which becomes a *righteousness;* but it is both the *δικαίωμα* and *πίστεως*, as having together the same twofold relation, which perfect obedience would have, viz., as rendering it consistent with the authority of law or with the justice of the Lawgiver, and also with all other ends of benevolence, that the sinner should stand right, i. e., be regarded as if he stood right in relation to the sanctions of law; and so be justified, i. e., be pronounced and authoritatively determined, thus to stand, in respect to treatment—by the act of the judge, the *δικαίωσις*, or act of Justification. Or thus: The one *δικαίωμα* is *the Atonement of Christ* as a provision or an ordinance of God to be received by faith, and as that from which, *when thus received*, results the consistency between all the ends of perfect benevolence, and the Justification of the believing sinner. Thus viewed, the Atonement or propitiation of Christ,—not merely as such; for as merely such, it only supports the authority of law—as a provision, which is appointed of God—to be received by faith, i. e., to be *taken hold of* with all the truths involved in it,—to be embraced *as it is* by the mind with just, intellectual apprehension, and with *a holy heart*, for practical results;*—thus received, the Atonement is the one *δικαίωμα*, of which the apostle speaks in verses 16 and 18. This *δικαίωμα*, *when thus received by faith* on the part of the sinner, renders it not only consistent with justice, or the authority of law, but with all the ends of general benevolence, and thus demands of perfect benevolence, that the believing sinner *be justified.* It thus becomes to him, *in this one respect*, what his own perfect obedience to law would be under mere law,—*a righteousness*, a *δικαιοσύνη*—and being wholly from God, and not from himself—being a *δωρεὰ ἐν χάριτι* of God—a free or gracious gift—a *χάρισμα*, a provision of grace,—and so through abundance of grace it becomes to believers the gift of righteousness,—*ἡ δωρεὰ τῆς δικαιοσύνης*,—and is called by the apostle, *the righteousness of God.*

---

* What truths, and how much truth, is included in such apprehension, will scarcely be understood and duly estimated, without much reflection. It is all the truth of God's testimony in the law and in the gospel, except one in the law, the impossibility under mere law that the transgressor should escape its penalty; and yet the whole influence of law is preserved unimpaired,—law is established.

III.

JUSTIFICATION.

I.—PRELIMINARY OBSERVATIONS.—ROMISH DOCTRINE.—JUSTIFICATION NOT SANCTIFICATION.

Signification of *right, morally right, right in relation to Moral Government*, &c.—Views of the ancients in respect to justice and moral rectitude.—Righteousness under Moral Government.—Importance of understanding the Romish doctrine.—Doctrine before the Reformation.—First and second Justification.—Relation of Faith to the first, and of Works to the second.—Romish view controverted, particularly in respect to the nature of Faith.—Justification not the infusion of a principle of holiness. The Hebrew and Greek words translated *to justify*, do not admit this interpretation.—The conception unknown to heathen nations.—Scriptural usage of the word discussed.

THE word Justification in Theology, denotes an act of God in respect to men as the subjects of his Moral Government. This act of God, in its nature, in its ground, and in its condition, as presented in the Scriptures, is now the subject of inquiry. Its *nature*—in other words—*what is the act of Justification on the part of God as the Moral Governor of men*, will first claim our attention.

Before however, I enter directly on thé investigation of this topic, I deem it important to offer some preliminary remarks respecting the use and meaning of some prominent words; and also to examine as briefly as may be, the Roman Catholic doctrine of Justification, which in one essential part stands so directly opposed to the Protestant doctrine, as, if true, to supersede further discussion. I proceed—

1. To make some preliminary remarks on important words.

It is obvious that the Justification of an obedient subject of law under a system of mere law, müst in some respects be a different thing from the Justification of a disobedient subject of law under a system of law and grace combined. Now the Moral Government which God administers over this world, is not a system of mere law, as we use the word, but a system of law and grace—a system, which compared with every other system of Moral Government, except that of the Jewish Theocracy as its representative shadow or type—is entirely peculiar. This being true, a peculiarity in the use of language is required, especially in forensic terms, which under any other would be unintelligible or false in their meaning. It is this grand peculiarity in the use of scriptural language, which it is believed has occasioned much of the controversy on the subject of Justification. The use of forensic words, modified as their meaning must be under a system of law and grace, compared with their meaning under a system of mere law, demands a careful and thorough investigation.

It will be admitted, that in the Hebrew, Greek, and Latin languages, there is a word, which, with at least some circumstantial qualification, is equivalent to our English word *justify*. This word is derived from the Latin *justifico*, or *justum facere*, literally, *to make right*. I propose to examine the use and meaning of this word, or rather this word and its equivalent in each of the languages mentioned, before I enter directly on the leading inquiry before us.

The general or generic idea of the word *right*, first claims consideration. This idea or conception, we may say, is common in all languages; in which also we find a class or family of words, of whose meaning this abstract and general idea is an essential element. The primary idea is that of *straight*, or straight to, straight forward,—*right*, as in the phrase *straight or right line*. This idea by metaphorical modification, and generalization, is the idea of *fitness*,—adaptation,—tendency, stretching to. The resemblance between the primary and secondary idea is at once obvious, and accounts for the latter.

The most important application of this word, is to moral beings, their action and its ends. My own views of such action, and of its ends as *right*, and of such action as predominant and subordinate, I have already given. We have seen that *predominant* action in the form of benevolence as an elective preference of the highest good of all sentient being, and as distinguished from all other, is the only morally right action. If we conceive of subordinate action as the expression and proof of this kind, and so conceive and speak, as we often do, of the whole as one action, still the *morally* right element of the combination is the *predominant action*—the act of the heart and will—an elective preference of the highest good of all. This is not only *right*, but *morally* right in all circumstances, *semper et ubique*, being fitted, and the only one which is fitted, *in all circumstances*, to secure the great end of all action on the part of a moral being. But subordinate action is *right* or otherwise, only according to certain variable circumstances; as it is, or is not, necessary to some limited result which is essential to the great ulterior result of morally right action; or it is *right*, as it is the expression or going forth of morally right predominant action or principle. These remarks are sufficient to show that the word *right*, as a general term, is applicable to both the specific kinds of action now described, while in all cases of proper use, some epithet, or the connection and manner of use, determines the precise meaning of the writer or speaker.

Thus one kind of moral action, which may be called *benevolent action*, including the predominant action or benevolent principle, and its appropriate expression in subordinate action, is truly and properly said to be *morally right;* or to be *right*, provided the connection shows the meaning to be its fitness to the true end or right end of action on the part of a moral being, in the given case. The same kind of action of a moral being, viewed irrespectively of his sustaining any other relation than that of a moral being,—e. g., that of a parent or child, lawgiver or subject,—would be called not only *right* or *morally right*, but also, virtue, goodness, moral goodness, moral rectitude, &c. In each case, the language would designate the fitness of the action to the great end of action on the part of a moral being—the highest good of all—of the agent and of all sentient being. This complex idea, or these elementary ideas combined in one, are expressed in the manner described, by the word *right* or *morally right* as applied to the action of a moral being, without the recognition of any other relation on his part, than the great, comprehensive relation of a moral being.

But the same kind of action must be contemplated under other and more specific relations, especially under those which arise from and pertain to *Moral Government*. The moral relations of men, and of all moral beings, are their relations to themselves and to others, as sentient beings, capable of happiness and misery. These are superior to all others, and can never be superseded. On the contrary, in that system of fitnesses in which they exist, all others are subordinate and subservient. A moral being can never cease to sustain moral relations, nor cease to act, or to be acting morally. He may however, when acting morally in his moral relations, be viewed also as acting in those which may be distinguished from such as are moral. Thus in the social relations subsisting merely between himself and his fellow-beings, as in his domestic and political relations, all his action may be viewed as subordinate, in which in principle and in practice he aims at the temporal and earthly well-being of himself and of others, without deciding whether he acts from any other, either higher or lower principle. Thus conceived, action has no *moral* quality. Contemplated merely in relation to his fellow-men, to his family, or to the State, or to all these, his subordinate action may be *right*, and yet he may act not *morally* right, but morally wrong. Indeed, he acts morally right, only as he acts morally right in predominant action; i. e., in the exercise of morally right principle. Otherwise, in all moral action, he acts in the exercise of the morally wrong principle, and acts morally wrong.

I have already had occasion to show what low and inadequate ideas of the nature of *morally right action* are formed by the human mind when uninstructed by divine revelation. The most enlightened of heathen philosophers seem to have formed no higher conception than that of the εξίς του δεόντος of Pythagoras, the habit of doing that which is fit to be done, or ought to be done. Nor had this definition of virtue, which Dugald Stuart speaks of as the best given by any philosopher, ancient or modern, been so objectionable, had it not been confined in its meaning to the habit of the particular social virtues among men, as beings of earth and time. *Justice* as distinguished from *benevolence*, as the latter is required in the first and great commandment of the divine law, seems to have been regarded as the predominant action—the sum and source of the whole train of the social, domestic, and political virtues.*

* With this view, it is believed that Aristides was signalized by the surname of THE JUST, as comprising the sum of moral excellence. In Justinian's definition of *justice*, we find no recognition of benevolence, i. e., of good will, or an habitual elective preference of the highest good of all sentient being, or an habitual will to render to sentient being *what is due;* but such a will to render to every one *his due*, as if there were no morally good action on the part of man but what is comprised in *justice*. Cicero says, "*Ex justitia viri boni appellantur* (*De Offic.* ii. 11). Aristotle gives this view of justice in his Ethics, B. V. vii. 3: "We are accustomed," he says, "to cite the proverb, 'In justice is included every virtue,' and it is pre-eminently complete virtue, because it is the exercise of the perfection of virtue. Wherefore this same justice is not a part of virtue, but is virtue in its universal aspect; nor is its contrary, *injustice*, a part of vice, but vice itself."

These conceptions would of course constitute and determine the meaning of language; and in view of this fact, we see at once how inadequate must be the meaning of the word *right*, and of kindred words, as applied to the action of moral beings; and how low the conception formed of the nature of such beings viewed in their relation to God and his sentient creation, or only in the inferior relation to fellow-beings. How different also must be the conceptions which would exist in respect to the same kind of action on the part of men when viewed simply as moral beings, and also as moral beings under a Moral Government. Now whatever be the conception of *moral action*, whether that which the mind forms under the light and guidance of divine revelation, and in the true use of its reflective faculties, or that low and inadequate idea which men have actually formed without revelation, it is obvious that the action conceived not simply as *moral action*, but either as the moral action of one sustaining the relation of a Moral Governor, or as the moral action of one sustaining the relation of a subject of Moral Government, must possess other and important relations. As the action of either governor or subject, it would be conceived as *moral action*, or as morally right action. But as action *common* to both, it could not be conceived as *obedience*, for it plainly is not obedience; i. e., it is not submission to authority on the part of the ruler. And yet as common to both in a subordinate generic import of the word, it is *righteousness* or *right-wiseness*, inasmuch as it is action, which in the different relations of ruler and subject, is in accordance with the principles of Moral Government—action which is demanded by the nature and principles of a legal system, according to the relations of the one who governs, and of the other who is governed. Without here more particularly unfolding what it is as righteousness or *right-wiseness* in a Moral Governor, it requires in this discussion, as the action of the subject of Moral Government, to be considered in its more prominent particular relations. Thus considered, morally right action, instead of being conceived simply as fitted to secure the great and true end of action on the part of a moral being as such, sustains also the following important relations. One is, that *it fulfills the claim of the law or of the lawgiver.* Another is, *that as a testimony or proof, it recognizes and so upholds the authority of the lawgiver.* Another is, *that it is the ordained and necessary ground of the subject's standing right in relation to the sanctions of law, so far as any thing on his part can be the ground of his so standing.* And another is, *that as sustaining these relations, it is the ground of the authoritative act of the Judge by which the subject is determined, caused, or made so to stand in relation to legal sanctions, that he is not to be punished but rewarded.* Now for the purposes of speech on this most important of all subjects, men have frequent occasion in practical life to express these different relations of this one kind of action, and to give prominence to some one or more of them in the use of single words or phrases. Thus one and the same kind of action on the part of a moral being, as common to both ruler and subject, would be called *morally right action*, or *virtue*, or *goodness*, or *moral rectitude*, &c., to denote its relation as fitted to the great end of all action on the part of such a being in all circumstances, viz., the highest well-being of all. To denote a more particular relation of the same action to the principles of Moral Government, and still as common to both ruler and subject, and conformed to these, it would be called *righteousness*. In application to the ruler, this word would denote his perfect conformity to all those principles of right which arise from his peculiar relation as a ruler. In the case of a moral being under law to another, the same action done in submission to authority would be called *obedience*, or ἔργον νόμου, to denote its relation as fulfilling the claim of law. For yet another purpose the same action would be called *righteousness*, to denote its comprehensive relation as the ordained and necessary ground of the standing right of the subject in respect to the sanctions of law in the broadest sense of the language, according to principles of justice and benevolence. I say in the broadest sense, for while the obedience of a subject fulfills the demand and sustains the authority of law on his part, and so becomes the ground of his standing right in relation to the sanctions of law, as far as any thing on his part can be the ground of his so standing, still he does not in the broadest sense of the language so stand, without the authoritative act of the Judge determining that he so stands, and is to be rewarded. Thus his obedience to law, as *his righteousness*, has a twofold relation; it is the ground of his standing right in relation to the sanctions of law according to the principles of justice and all other principles of benevolence; and as such, it is also the ground of the authoritative act of the Judge, which determines in such a respect that he so stands—that he is not to be punished but rewarded. The obedience of a subject of law must obviously sustain all these relations, since otherwise the authoritative act of the Judge would be wholly groundless and unauthorized. If it did not fulfill the claim of law and so uphold its authority, it could not become the ground of his standing right in relation to the sanctions of law according to the principles of justice and benevolence, so far as such standing depends on the subject himself. If it did not sustain this last relation, it could not become the ground of the authoritative act of a righteous Judge, which alone determines or causes him so to stand that he can be actually rewarded; and of course, this act of the Judge could have no sufficient ground, and the subject could not be rewarded according to the principles of law or of Moral Government.

Here it may be well to remark, that of a Moral Governor reigning in rightful authority—for example, of God acting in this relation—*obedience* could not be properly and truly predicated; while both moral goodness or right moral action, and righteousness might be;—the former having its ordinary general import, and the latter a meaning modified by his peculiar relation to his subjects as their Lawgiver and Judge. In the case however of a moral being, under a system of mere law, the true predicate of either *moral goodness*, or of *obedience*, or of *righteousness*, would necessarily *imply*, but not formally express both the other predicates. From the true predicate of moral goodness of a moral being, we could not infer, either that he is or is not a subject of law, nor be authorized to predicate either obedience or righteousness of him as such. Nor would the predicates of obedience or of righteousness of a subject of law be strictly synonymous, since his righteousness at most is an inference. He is obedient, and therefore is righteous,—or, he fulfills the claim of law, and therefore is righteous so far as his righteousness depends on himself. But he is not made righteous (i. e., is not justified), so far as his righteousness depends on the authoritative act of the Judge. Nor can it be inferred that he will be made righteous in this respect, without assuming the justice of the Judge as a further premise. Nor yet can we, merely from the true predicate of righteousness of the subject of a perfect law (vide Phil. iii. 9, and Rom.

iii. 22), infer his *obedience* to law; since he may be said, in an important sense, to *have*, so far as it is possible in the nature of things he should have, another righteousness than *his own*, even that which the apostle so earnestly desired. Nor from the *Justification* of the subject of law can we infer his personal obedience to law; for under a system of grace, or wickedly under a system of mere law, he may be as fully justified by the authoritative act of the Judge, though disobedient, as were he obedient to law.

What has now been said will serve to show that important forensic terms must be greatly modified in their meaning when referring to a system of law and grace, compared with that in which they would be used in referring to a system of mere law. It will enable us, it is believed, to understand with more precision than is usual, the scriptural terms, *δικαίος δικαίοσυνη*, *δικαίωμα*, *δικαίοω*, and other important words and phrases, as employed by the sacred writers in different connections, and thus greatly aid us in the investigation of the comprehensive subject of Justification, as an act of God in relation to men as the subjects of his Moral Government. I now proceed as I proposed—

2. Briefly to state and examine the Roman Catholic doctrine of Justification.

This doctrine in one prominent and essential element, confounds what Protestants regard as distinct acts—that of Justification, and that of Sanctification; thus representing both as one and the same act—that of *making just*, or *personally righteous*. In this view, the Catholic and Protestant forms of the doctrine stand opposed, in respect to the very *nature* of Justification. It is on this account that I am led to introduce the consideration of the Romish doctrine in this connection; and though I shall present it with some particularity and fullness, and notice in my examination some of its particular elements, and hereafter still other parts, I shall now confine myself chiefly to the inquiry, whether Justification includes Sanctification? This I do now, because otherwise the way is not well prepared, in my view, to show the nature of this act as presented in the Scriptures. There is also a strong reason for noticing this doctrine, arising from its prevalence in our own country,—a fact, which, imperiously demands a more thorough examination and exposure of its errors, than it has hitherto received. If the scriptural doctrine of Justification is what the Reformers pronounced it—the *articulus stantis vel cadentis ecclesiæ*, why are not Protestants more engrossed in guarding this main pillar of the edifice, than in conflicts among themselves, or in assailing the mere scaffoldings of Romanism? It is pre-eminently by opening the batteries of truth on the strongholds of sin through the doctrine of Justification by faith, that the weapons of this warfare must become mighty through God. Besides, it is my conviction, that the broad distinction which the Scriptures make between Justification and Sanctification, was not fully unfolded by the earlier Fathers of the Church; and that even modern Protestants, though some of them, like our New England divines and the late Dr. Chalmers, have strenuously insisted on a broad distinction, have failed fully to exhibit it, through the want of accurate views of scriptural Sanctification. Into this part of the subject however I cannot here enter. What I propose in respect to the Romish doctrine of Justification is, for the reasons given, to call your attention to the subject with some increased interest, by attempting to show, though imperfectly, how entirely groundless it is, as well as directly opposed to the plainest teachings of the word of God.

I shall attempt *in the first place*, to give a fair and just statement of this doctrine; and *in the second place*, to show how entirely unscriptural it is in some of its essential parts or elements.

In the first place, *I shall attempt to give a fair and just view of the Roman Catholic doctrine of Justification.*

Here I am not led back to those scriptural forms of controversy which respect chiefly, not to say wholly the ground and condition of Justification, rather than the *nature* of the act; for the sacred writers seem ever to assume that in respect to this, there was no occasion for discussion. Controversy on this part of the subject had a later origin than in the time of the apostles. To find its commencement, we need go no further back than the rise of the Romish Church, nor much beyond the time of the Reformation. Even the early controversies of the first Christian Fathers had at this time so far ceased, and their flagrant errors had been so abandoned and modified, that we may regard the question concerning *the nature* of Justification, as embodied in that form of the doctrine in which the Roman

Church found itself confronted by Protestantism. The Council of Trent (1545–1563) had to defend the doctrine of the Catholic Church, and in so doing, solemnly to sanction to a great extent the system developed by the more eminent scholastics of the preceding period. The Canons of this Council, the Catechismus Romanus based upon them, and the views of many of the scholastic divines, as explained and vindicated by Bellarmine, Vasquez, and others, are therefore to be regarded as the true symbols of the Romish Church.

In giving a statement of the doctrine of Justification which shall shut off all plausible contradiction, there is the serious difficulty which arises from the want of consistency in the views and statements of Roman Catholic authorities. I shall be careful however, to impute nothing to them which they do not plainly teach, presuming that they are responsible for what they assert in one instance, however they may contradict it in another.

This doctrine then, as I understand it from the authorities now referred to, comprises two parts, which some have called a first and a second Justification. The first is the act of God infusing into the soul an inherent principle of grace and charity, i. e., of personal holiness, by which, original sin and all habits of sin, are extinguished. This Justification is by faith with baptism as its condition, and is called Justification by faith. Of this, Christ is said to be the meritorious cause. The principle of grace thus infused is a preparation of mind for receiving a habit of grace—*gratiam gratum facientem*—rendering the subject acceptable (not accepted) to God.* This is a speculative or historical faith, which, as involving submission to the authority of the Church, is *meritorious;* and as attended with contrition, repentance, and love, renders it congruous with the wisdom and goodness of God (what the schoolmen call *meritum de congruo*) to justify the believer. This first Justification is said to be that of which Paul so fully treats, in distinction from Justification *by works of law.*† The second part of Justification is a consequence of the first. Of this, good

* Three kinds of grace are spoken of,—*gratia gratis dans*, *gratia gratis data*, and *gratia gratum faciens;* the last being divided into *gratia operans* and *gratia co-operans*, *præveniens* and *concomitans*. (Hagenbach, vol. ii. p. 49.)

† They understand *by works of law*, works done without the influence of the Holy Spirit.

works, proceeding from the principle of grace and love, especially works of beneficence, alms-giving, and presents to cloisters and churches, are the *formal ground and procuring cause.* They are meritorious; and their merit consists in this, that the righteousness is increased by the performance of good works. Still it is maintained that the merits of men will not throw those of Christ into the shade; they are rather themselves the effects of the merits of Christ, and serve to manifest his glory among men. It is also said, that Justification is not only the remission of sins, but also the Sanctification and Renovation *of the inner man* by the voluntary *susception* of grace and gifts, whence man from unrighteous becomes righteous, and from an enemy a friend, that so he may be an heir of eternal life. It is further said, that we are justified by faith, because *faith* is the beginning and foundation of human salvation, and the root (*radix*) of all Justification; but that if any say that the wicked are justified *by faith only*, so that it be understood that nothing else is required which co-operates to obtain the grace of Justification, let him be anathema. By this twofold Justification, it is claimed that Paul and James are reconciled,—Paul treating of the first, which is without works, and by faith only, and James of the second, which is by good works; both the first and the second being necessary to and constituting the full or complete Justification of the Gospel.

This view of the Romish doctrine of Justification, may be further unfolded and better understood by adverting to some of the leading topics of controversy between the Catholics and Protestants. The parties agreed in speaking of Justification as *the act of God;* but differed in this,—that the Catholics often confounded *Justification* with Renovation and Sanctification; maintaining in some cases, that they are one and the same thing, the act of making subjectively righteous, and in other cases, implying and plainly affirming, that with this act of God is included another—that of the remission of sins and receiving to favor. Protestants on the contrary maintained a broad distinction between them, insisting that Justification is *a forensic term*, denoting the act of God as Judge, remitting sin and receiving the guilty to favor and reward, and that Renovation and Sanctification denote the act of God in making man in an imperfect degree subjectively holy, or holy in heart. Differing thus as to the nature of Justification, both admitted that it is *by faith*, but still differed widely also as to the nature of this faith; the Catholic maintaining that it is merely a speculative or historical assent or faith, which exists as the antecedent and condition of God's act of producing the principle of holiness or grace in the heart, and that this compound state of faith and principle of grace, as it expels sin, and is connected with repentance and love, renders us so far *acceptable*, though not fully *accepted*, of God. This is *the first* Justification, but not complete Justification. The second is the consequence of the first, the proper *formal cause* of which is good works proceeding from the principle of grace and love. Thus the good works and the principle from which they proceed, are the righteousness wherewith believers are righteous before God, and deserve, by the merit of condignity, eternal life. This is complete Justification, or the Justification by works which they understand the apostle James to teach. They imagine that Paul, in denying Justification by deeds or works of law, denies only that it is by works done without the grace of the Holy Spirit. (Vide Council of Trent, Sess. 6. chap. 10; and Davenant, p. 348.)

Protestants, on the other hand, maintained that we are in a sense *justified* by a merely speculative faith, but by that *faith* which they characterize as uniting us to Christ, as receiving, or relying on and embracing his righteousness—a faith which makes us one with Christ *by a mystical union*, and by which the righteousness of Christ (of God) becomes ours by Imputation. They maintain that this faith is believing with the heart, that it implies the Renovation or Regeneration, repentance, personal holiness, though in an imperfect degree; and by this faith *only—per fidem solam, sed non per fidem solitariam*—we are justified;—that no other grace, duty, or work can be associated with it, or be of any consideration in justifying us; that faith does not derive its power to justify, or its connection with our Justification, as being itself a good work, or by the love associated with it; that it is not the *formal* but merely the *instrumental* cause of our Justification, and that the righteousness of Christ, made ours by Imputation when we believe, is *the formal cause;** and that there is no proper sense of the

* I doubt whether either Catholics or Protestants always use the phrase *formal cause* in one precise meaning. Sometimes, the Catholics seem to mean by it, the

language in which it can be said, that a man is justified by works, or by good works. Thus they maintain, that a man is justified before God—to the exclusion of all works of law, and all good works—by faith only as *the instrumental* cause; and by the righteousness of Christ, as the *formal* cause. Both parties, with the modern exception of some of our New England theologians, seem to proceed on the assumption that there is and must be a perfect righteousness sustaining all the relations to our Justification under grace, which our own perfect righteousness under mere law, would sustain. That Protestants with the exception just referred to, have maintained this view of what they call *the righteousness of Christ*, more properly, if we follow the apostle, called "*the righteousness of God*," I need not attempt to show. The Catholics teach, that the formal cause of our Justification is our own inherent righteousness; that this infused habit or quality of righteousness and sanctity, by its own nature, renders us immaculate, innocent, accepted of God, and worthy (*dignos*) of eternal life; that this inherent righteousness is that which is permanent, produced and impressed by the Holy Spirit in the justified, and is presumed to be in those who cannot work, or furnish an actual righteousness, equally in infants and those who are asleep, as in adults who are awake. According to Bellarmine, this habit of grace is maintained by the Tridentine Fathers, under an anathema, to be *the formal cause* of Justification. He maintains, that it is so perfect, that by it we are *absolutely* righteous (*justi*) and are so called, and though it is imperfect by some venial admixture, and needs daily remission, yet it does not cease to be true righteousness, and in a certain sense perfect. It is true that Vasquez, another Romish authority, tells us that the doctors (*pontificios*) are not agreed whether Justification in adults is *by act* or by habit as to form.* Thus though nothing seems to be settled in the Romish Church in respect to the formal cause of Justification as consisting *in actu* or *habitu*, yet it is clearly maintained, that the formal cause is one or both, and sustains the same relation to Justification, as would sinless obedience under a system of mere law. Yet they obtrude upon Protestants

---

constituting cause of Justification; at other times both evidently mean the same *determining or procuring* cause which sinless obedience on our part would be under a merely legal system, which is impossible.

* Vide Davenant on Justification, p. 346, *sqq.*

this *formal cause* of Justification, which they themselves admit to be undecided as a matter of divine faith.*

Here I might show in detail, how entirely gratuitous and absurd it is, in its several parts, and how impossible therefore that it should be true,—I might show, as I have done, that there is no such thing as *original sin* in the sense intended; that is, that there is no such thing in man as a created or propagated property of the mind, which is sin; nor any original sin by the Imputation of Adam's first sin to his posterity; nor any other original sin, or any thing which can be called such, except "the transgression of the law" by him whose sin it is, as his own act, done in his own person. Of course there is no such thing, in the sense intended, as original sin which is extinguished by a principle of grace and charity. Nor can any sin in the mind or heart of man, in the nature of things, be extinguished by a principle of grace and charity; for the sin in the mind must cease, before the principle of grace and charity can exist, and therefore the latter, though it may follow and thus exclude, can never destroy or extinguish, the former. Nor can any principle of grace and charity (i. e., of holy love) be infused into the mind prior to or distinct from the love itself; for this, though the effect of divine grace, is the only holy or morally right principle. Nor can the supposed principle of grace and love, nor the extinction of original sin, being in the nature of things incapable of existence, be caused or produced *by faith;* and of course, there can be no *Justification*, as an act of God producing things which are not, and which cannot be. Nor can things which are not and cannot be, constitute a subjective state of Justification, of which the obedience of Christ is the meritorious cause. Nor can things which are not and cannot be, result in a preparation of mind for receiving a habit of grace; nor can any habit of grace result from them, rendering us *acceptable* to God; for, how can nothing produce something? Or if it be said, that the so-called principle of grace and charity is itself holy *love*, how can it be *by faith*, when it is also alleged that this faith is *attended* with contrition, repentance, and love? How can an *antecedent*

* For the foregoing view of the Romish doctrine of Justification, I refer to the Decrees of the Council of Trent; to Hagenbach's Hist. of Doctrine, vol. ii. pp. 39, 59, 63, 189, 191, 267, 268; to Bishop Davenant on Justification, and to Owen on Justification, &c.

cause or condition be truly said to be *attended* with its consequent or effect, especially when the two are things so distinct that they do not constitute one thing? If they actually coexist, as alleged in the present case, then why is not the love the cause or condition of the faith, as well as the faith the cause or condition of the love? Besides, as we shall presently see, the faith described often exists without love, and therefore does not imply or involve its existence. And further: what are these two Justifications? The first is the act or operation of God, producing in man the specified effect of personal holiness,—and in this sense *justifying* or making just,—and thus rendering it consistent with the wisdom and goodness of God to *justify* the believer. Here then are already two Justifications spoken of, one which is Sanctification, conditioned on faith, and another on this personal holiness, or Sanctification;—*a first* Justification, which is Sanctification, or the act of making the subject personally holy; and *a second*, which being by the first and its effect, is rendered congruous with the wisdom and goodness of God! And now what is this second Justification, if not an act of God making the subject to stand right in relation to the sanctions of law, or acquitting the subject of sin and accepting him as righteous? What else can it be imagined to be? And if it is this, and simply this authoritative act of God—the act of accepting the subject—then how can this act of *accepting* be the same as that which by its effect only makes him *acceptable?* But then again: besides these two acts of Justification, which are so palpably different, we have another *second* act of Justification, of which meritorious good works, consequent on all that has preceded, are the formal ground and procuring cause. These two Justifications, or rather these three, to say nothing of any more, constitute complete Justification. What is this? Not the act of God making the subject personally and subjectively holy or righteous or just; for this act with its effect has already taken place, and constitutes the first Justification—which is not a complete Justification—a thing which it is not. And yet this Justification which is not a Justification, is part and parcel of another. But what is complete Justification? Not good works, nor yet the act of God securing good works; but an act of God consequent on all these antecedents, and which therefore is not and cannot be any of them nor all of them together. What then is it but *a fourth* Justification?—and what is this, but an act of God acquitting the subject of the penalty of sin, and accepting him as righteous? What else can it be? What else can it be conceived to be? And what is all this but denying, and then conceding and maintaining, that Justification is an act of God placing the subject right in relation to the sanctions of his law? I ask, whether saying that Justification is one thing and not another, and then asserting it to be the latter,—whether confounding things that differ, causes with effects, antecedents with consequents, in a medley of contradictions and absurdities, is the scriptural doctrine of Justification?

Without however dwelling longer on these and other absurdities so plainly involved in the Romish doctrine of Justification, there are some things so prominent and so much insisted on in the authorized statements of it, that they must be regarded as its grand and peculiar elements. Among these the following at least must be included:—1. *That a merely speculative assent or historical belief in Christianity is a meritorious condition of Justification.* 2. *That Justification essentially consists of or includes Sanctification, or the infusion of a principle of holiness or habit of grace;* and, 3. *That works done from this principle are meritorious, and necessary to a complete Justification.*

This last proposition respects *the ground or condition* of Justification rather than its *nature*, and will therefore be examined in another connection hereafter. I say it respects the ground or condition of Justification, for this second part of Justification presupposes the first—the infusion of a principle of holiness and the performance of good works as antecedent and necessary to it. The word *Justification* in this connection must be used as we have intimated above, if used in the Protestant meaning; i. e., to denote an authoritative act of God determining the subject of his law to stand right in relation to its sanctions. Whether good works, or works done from morally right principle, are a *meritorious* condition or ground of Justification in this sense of it, will therefore be more properly considered when we come to inquire what the scriptural ground or condition of Justification is.

Without proposing fully to examine these propositions, I shall as briefly as may be, attempt to show how entirely unscriptural they are. I remark then—

(1.) *That a merely speculative or historical faith is not the condition of Justification.* That the Scriptures strongly distinguish a merely intellectual assent or historical belief in the Gospel from believing with the heart, is plainly conceded in the very statement of the doctrine now opposed; for it exhibits *faith* as the condition, and of course as the *antecedent* of the principle of grace infused. It is therefore a kind of faith which is prior to a right act or state of the heart. But how plainly and abundantly do the Scriptures teach that man is not justified by such a faith! Thus John tells us, that "among the chief rulers many *believed* on him, but because of the Pharisees they did not confess him, lest they should be put out of the synagogue." (John xii. 42; and compare Mark viii. 38. Vide John ii. 23; Luke xviii. 13; Acts viii. 13.) Were these more justified? Or were they of those who deny Christ, and whom Christ will deny? "With the heart," says Paul, "man believeth unto righteousness" (Romans x. 10). And again: "For in Christ Jesus, neither circumcision availeth any thing nor uncircumcision, but faith which worketh by love" (Gal. v. 6.) Jude calls it "your most holy faith" (Jude, verse 20). How explicit is the apostle James in showing that there is a faith which is to no profit; a faith *only*, which has no heart, no love, no principle, or spirit of obedience in it. He denounces it as *a dead* faith, καθ'ἑαυτήν, according to itself, its very nature. He compares *it*, the faith itself, to the body without the spirit. He ascribes it to infernal spirits. "The devils also believed and trembled." Surely such a faith,—a faith which they who refuse to confess, and who therefore deny Christ before men, may possess; a faith which necessarily implies an unholy heart; a heart without love; a faith which devils possess,—instead of being the means or condition of *Justification* in any sense, must leave the sinner still under the power and condemnation of sin. I admit that an intellectual belief is necessary, as is also the *truth* to be believed, or a *mind* to believe, to a change of heart or to a principle of holiness in man through grace. But the question now is, whether such a faith is certainly connected with this moral change in all cases; or has by promise connected with it the infusion of a principle of grace or holy love? This, we have seen, the Scriptures plainly deny. Nor is this all. John expressly asserts that true or saving faith, instead of an antecedent is a consequent of Regeneration, or of what the Romanist calls a principle of grace. "Whosoever believeth that Jesus is the Christ (γεγέννηται ἐκ τοῦ θεοῦ), is born of God." (1 John v. 1. Compare Acts viii. 37, and Rom. x. 10.) I am aware that it is maintained, "that the faith by which a man is justified is attended with contrition, and repentance, and love." But is this true of all that can be properly called *faith?* How can that faith which is the antecedent condition of personal holiness, i. e., of contrition, repentance, and love—a principle of grace be *attended* with its consequent, except indeed as a cause in loose language may be said to be *attended*, i. e., *followed*, with its effect, and is distinct from it, as every cause is from its effect? How can this be said in all cases of what is properly called faith? Was the faith of some of the Jewish rulers, who believed and refused to confess Christ, attended with these Christian graces? Is it true of the dead faith which James describes, or of the faith of devils, that it is attended with contrition, repentance, and love? Can there be repentance, or contrition, or love, without Regeneration, or a change of heart? As to repentance or contrition, it is itself a change of heart, a principle of holiness or grace. As to love, the apostle says, "Love is of God, and every one that loveth (his brother) is born of God" (1 John iv. 7). How could the Romish doctrine of *Justification*, in one essential element, be more plainly contradicted by Divine authority than it is? And yet this error in some form,—the error of making something on the part of sinful man the sure means or condition of Regeneration, or of that moral change for which man is dependent on the Spirit of God,—the error of making something prior to personal holiness, the condition of personal holiness—something which will secure converting grace, something done without grace, the sure antecedent and condition of Regeneration, Sanctification, Justification, and thus of final salvation,—has, in my view, been one of the most common and worst errors of the Church of God. It has marred and corrupted, if not Protestant creeds, much Protestant theology—not to say nearly all Protestant preaching; while it may be regarded in its various forms of exhibition, as the grand comprehensive error of the Roman Catholic Church. The specific form of this error, which connects with a mere speculative faith on the part of man what the Scriptures call *Justification*, or, as its advocates explain it, a principle of grace and holiness, is plainly nothing less than changing and thus falsifying the very terms of salvation which God has revealed and fixed beyond all change. I remark—

(2.) *That scriptural Justification does not consist of, nor include, the infusion of a principle of holiness or habit of grace.* That scriptural Justification does not consist of the infusion of personal holiness, though the contrary is often asserted by some prominent Papists, has been conceded by others. Thus Naclantus says, "that to some there appears to be an inconsistency between the theological teachers and the sacred Scriptures, inasmuch as the former maintain that to justify is *to make* (subjectively) *righteous*, and the latter, that it is to pronounce righteous." He adds that this is not so, and confesses that "*the forensic* signification of the word is more familiar and more obvious in the Scriptures than the other;" although he still maintains, "that the faithful are not only pronounced, but constituted righteous before God." Now what is this but a full concession, that the act of God in justifying men, as more familiarly and obviously exhibited in the Scriptures, is a forensic act? What if it be also true, that believers are sanctified by another act of God, or constituted righteous by Imputation, or in any mode, as the ground of the forensic act, or as in some way connected with the forensic act, neither of these acts is the forensic act itself; nor does the forensic meaning of *justify* cease to be obvious in the Scriptures. And what is more, nothing appears to show that *the forensic* meaning so familiar and obvious, is not the only scriptural meaning of the word. What is this view of the subject, but plainly mistaking the *ground* of Justification for the act itself?

Again: it is maintained by Papistical writers, that their view of Justification as including a principle of holiness, derives decisive confirmation from the two words of which the Latin word is compounded—*justum facere;* as if these words could have no other sense than to make *subjectively righteous*, or to make one *the subject of personal holiness.* It happens however, that the Latin words *justifico* and *justificatio* are not to be found in any classic writer, and probably have no higher authority than Tertullian or some other Latin Father, who coined the Latin word to express a scriptural idea which was wholly unknown in heathen use,—that of *justifying* in any sense a disobedient subject of law. But especially, the idea of infusing a principle of grace or holiness into the mind of man, and thus changing his moral character, is unknown in any language, except so far as the idea has been derived from revelation. From the very nature of the case therefore, this idea or meaning of *facere justum* were impossible in classic Latin, and the word *justifico* or *justificatio* could not be used by any good author in the supposed meaning. The idea denoted by this modern Latin word, would be expressed in classic Latin, by *aliquem a culpa liberare*, or *innocentem pronuntiare*, an idea or a conception of an act which one man in the capacity of a judge can perform in respect to another, and whose effect in respect to the latter is such as can in the nature of things be thus produced. But the effect of such an act cannot be conceived to be either in the nature or the moral character of the subject. How is it possible to suppose that this as a mere word, which, *de usu*, is applicable alike to an act of man as well as to an act of God, can denote the making one subjectively holy? Can man, as well as God, *renew and sanctify* the heart of his fellow-man? What then can it be, except an act of *jurisdiction*, *prerogative*, or *authority*, making, determining, or causing some effect, which in the nature of things depends on such an act? To explain somewhat further: There is an obvious difference in many cases between the *absolute* existence of a fact and its *relative* existence, or its existence in relation to those who are to regard it, and act upon it, as a fact. Thus to *verify* a fact by testimony, does not give *absolute* but relative existence to the fact,—makes or determines it to be a fact in relation to those who are to act upon it as a fact. Thus property, the ownership of which is litigated in court, may or may not in truth or in fact belong to him who has it not in possession; and yet the authoritative decision of the judge makes it *his* in an important sense in which it was not before, that is, relatively to the possession and use of it. So, *justum facere*, *to justify*, under a system of law does not give absolute but relative existence to the righteousness of one justified—an existence to be regarded and acted upon as real;—decides that he is to be treated as righteous.

Without here more particularly unfolding the nature of the act of Justification and its effect, what I have now said is sufficient to show in one respect what *the act* is not, and what *its effect* is not,—in other words, to show, so far as the etymology of the word is concerned, that the act of Justification is not that of making another subjectively righteous, or personally holy in moral character. Indeed, the act, as described by the Latin words of which the word *justify* is compounded, is from the very nature of the case, one in which the subjective character of the object of the act is, and must be presupposed, ascertained, and proceeded upon, as the basis and warrant of the act. Nor is this all. The advocates of the doctrine now opposed, have in their very statement of it, distinctly and expressly maintained all that I now assert. Thus, they tell us, that by faith, a principle or habit of grace and love is infused into the mind of the believer, and that this faith, attended with contrition and love, renders him *acceptable* to God, or renders it congruous with the wisdom and goodness of God to *justify* the believer! Now in all this, the act of God and its effect on the subject in personal holiness is described, but still it is not the act of Justification; for it is an act of God, which by its effects in personal character, only renders the subject *acceptable* to God, and prepares the way for *the act of accepting him as righteous*, i. e., *for the act of Justification.* So we are told that good works proceeding from the principle of grace and love, are the formal ground and procuring cause of the second Justification,—are the righteousness with which the believer secures complete Justification before God. What then, according to this scheme, is *Justification;* what, viewed either as a first or a second, or a complete Justification; what but an act of God, consequent on the personal holiness or character of the object of the act? Surely, the act of God by which, or by the effects of which, he merely *prepares* the believer to be *justified*, or for the act of Justification, is not the act of Justification itself.

Further: neither the Hebrew nor Greek word properly rendered by the word *justify* in our English version, ever denotes or includes the act or operation of God by his Holy Spirit producing in man subjective holiness. That the Scriptures teach this doctrine of Sanctification, as described in these general terms, I have already attempted to prove. This is also abundantly admitted and maintained by both Papists and Protestants. If the views which I have given of this work of the

Holy Spirit, and of the nature of the change in man produced by it, be scriptural, then it is not too much to say, that the views of this act or work of God, and of its effect in man, maintained and inculcated by both Papists and Protestants, at least with exceptions which need not be noticed, are neither scriptural nor true. According to both, it consists in producing some change, even some so-called *moral* change, diverse from the use of his moral powers in right moral action; some *moral change* anterior to, and distinct from, the act or exercise of supreme love to God, or of an elective preference of God. But if the view which both Papists and Protestants maintain is unscriptural and false, then it is not inculcated in the use of any scriptural term or language, either Hebrew or Greek. And further still, the scriptural idea or conception of the work of God in producing holiness in the human heart—in other words, what is commonly called the doctrine of Regeneration or Sanctification—was certainly unknown to the heathen nations, and of course cannot be found in their languages,—a fact which shows how vain must be every attempt to find a word either in classic Greek or Latin which shall express the Romish doctrine of Justification. Nor is this all. It can scarcely be pretended that the idea or conception of the work of God in Renovation or Sanctification, was imparted to men in the Hebrew language until the time of David and the later prophets. Prior to this however, the Hebrew word rendered by the Greek word *δικαιόω* in the Septuagint, and by the English word *justify* in our version, is obviously a familiar term with a definite and fixed meaning, which excludes that given it by the Romanists. There is nothing therefore in God's revelation, throughout the patriarchal or Mosaic dispensations, which authorizes the doctrine or the idea of the work of God's Spirit in producing holiness in the human heart, as it is taught in the time of David and of the later prophets. Nor is it taught at this period in any such particular form as that in which it is revealed in the New Testament, especially by the apostles. That there are some passages in the Old Testament which ascribe the change in man's moral character from sin to holiness to the supernatural interposition of God, is in my view undeniable. Still I find nothing in these passages which necessarily teaches any thing beyond that supernatural interposition and influence of God, which consists in the revelation of truth in a course of miraculous manifestation and confirmation of its divine authority, and in this way, or by these means, becomes the author of this moral change in man; nothing, which like some passages in the New Testament in the form of *explicit and absolute negation*, assert the vanity and inefficacy of even the fullest revelation and exhibition of truth in this moral change, without another and a further influence from God. So far from this, there is not the slightest evidence that the New Testament doctrine of Renovation or Sanctification was, up to the time we have specified, ever revealed to the human mind, or ever thought of by man. At the same time, the proof is decisive, that the Hebrew word rendered δικαιόω by the Seventy, and *justify* by our translators, had not such a meaning, since it was applied in a general and common meaning to the act of God and the act of man as a judge. It is therefore plainly impossible that the Hebrew word should ever have been used to denote or to include, i. e., to express the idea of the act of God in Renovation or Sanctification, as this act is unfolded in the New Testament, or as it is believed by either Papists and Protestants. How utterly incredible it is, that our English word *justify*, applied as it is to denote the act of a civil tribunal or judge in relation to a subject of law, should ever be used to denote some act or influence of a judge in producing the repentance or renovation of a culprit, when such an act was unknown and unthought of, or if thought of, utterly disbelieved! For the same reason, such a meaning of the Hebrew צָדַק, and the Greek δικαιόω, applied to an act of God, must from the time of man's apostasy to the time of the apostles, or at least to the time of David, be regarded as wholly impossible and incredible. How the Hebrew or Greek word ever acquired such a meaning, or that it ever did or ever could, has not been shown, nor could it be; for the fact is one which, in the circumstances of the case, could not exist, and therefore cannot be proved.

Again: no passage of Scripture is or can be adduced, for which such a meaning as that now opposed, can be claimed with the slightest plausibility. To be satisfied of this, we need only refer to some in which the word occurs. Luke x. 29: "He willing to justify himself." Does this mean willing to *sanctify* himself? Luke xvi. 15: "Ye are they which justify yourselves." Does this mean ye are they which *sanctify* yourselves? Matt. xii. 37: "For by thy words thou shalt be *justified*, and by thy words thou shalt be condemned." If *justified* here means *sanctified* or made *subjectively holy*, then *condemned*, its opposite, means made *subjectively wicked*. Are such to be the results of words on the judgment-day? Prov. xvii. 15: "He that *justifieth* the wicked, and he that condemneth the righteous, even they both are an abomination to the Lord." Shall we then suppose that one who should make the wicked inherently righteous, would be an abomination to the Lord? Rom. ii. 13: "The doers of the law shall be *justified*." One would suppose such to be subjectively holy or righteous already without Justification. Rom. iii. 20: "Therefore by the deeds of the law there shall no flesh be justified in his sight." Does this mean that by perfect sinless obedience to the law; or, according to Catholic interpretation, that by mere external conformity to the law, none shall be made subjectively holy by the Holy Spirit? Rom. iv. 2: "If Abraham were justified by works, he hath whereof to glory." Does this mean, that if he were made subjectively holy by the grace of the Divine Spirit, or as Catholics must interpret, *sanctified by merely external* works, he hath whereof to glory? Here I might refer to numerous other passages to show how groundless is the supposition, that to *justify* means *to sanctify;* but a few will suffice. And first, to those in which Justification is said to be not by works of law, and is said *to be by faith*. In all these, one and the same thing is said *not* to be by works of law, which is said *to be* by faith. Unless then we understand the former to assert the inept and nonsensical proposition that none are sanctified by perfect obedience to law, we cannot understand the latter to teach that we are sanctified by faith, or that we are *sanctified* at all.

In another class of passages, Justification is clearly shown to be *the opposite of condemnation* (Isa. i. 8, 9; Prov. xvii. 15; Rom. v. 18, and viii. 33, 34). If then Justification is or includes Sanctification, or the infusion of inherent righteousness by the Holy Spirit, then its opposite, *condemnation* denotes the infusion of inherent wickedness by the Holy Spirit. If this, revolting and false as it is, be not the meaning of *condemnation*, then Justification cannot denote or imply *Sanctification*.

In another class of texts, great prominence is given to the

act of God called *the forgiveness* of sin. We are taught to pray that he would forgive our trespasses as we forgive those who trespass against us. (Vide also Mark, iii. 29.) Does this act of God include the act of Sanctification?

The Scriptures very clearly and abundantly teach, that a perfectly obedient subject of law, were there any such, should be *justified.* But how can such a subject of law either be sanctified or need to be sanctified by the Holy Spirit?

In other instances, the same thing is described by other language; as imputing righteousness without works of law, as "covering sins," as "not remembering sins," as "the remission of sins which are past," or the passing over of sins before committed, as "saving and delivering from wrath," "redemption from the curse of the law," by Christ's "being made a curse for us," &c., &c. Now I ask, does this language denote or imply Sanctification? The question is not, whether according to other Scriptures those who are *justified* are also *sanctified*, but whether the Scriptures do not exhibit Justification and Sanctification as distinct acts of God; and particularly whether in the passages now cited, the language conveys or expresses in the remotest manner the idea of Sanctification. Whether the work of *Renovation* or *Sanctification* by the Spirit of God, by any just interpretation of the numerous passages referred to, could be derived or even conjectured.

Again: I might add, that the formal, essential, or real act of Justification takes place on the judgment-day and not till then. I am aware that the question, *when is the believer justified*, has often been discussed by theologians. One thing however, is undeniable,—that the Scriptures unequivocally teach *an act of Justification* on the part of God which takes place on the last great day of account, when all nations shall be assembled before him. Here then at least is one act of Justification on the part of God, which is not, and does not include the act of Sanctification, unless indeed we suppose it deferred till after the resurrection of believers from the dead. I am aware that the Scriptures often speak of believers as justified in the present tense, or in the present life, or when they believe. This however, is necessarily to be understood as nothing more than the language of anticipation,—a common and natural mode of speaking in analogous cases. Were I to propose to you to obtain from the governor of the State the pardon of another, our mutual acquaintance, and were you by making the supposed application, to obtain his assurance that he should be pardoned on some future day appointed for a public formal doing of all such acts, in announcing the fact to me or others, what more natural than for me to say, in the present time, "he is pardoned." Indeed, if this is not the usage of the Scriptures on this subject, how is it that the future tense is so often used to describe the time of the act, as, "*hath everlasting life* and shall not come into condemnation?" (John v. 24.) Other familiar examples need not be given. Be this as it may, there is one act of God entirely distinct from Sanctification, called Justification, to take place on the great day of *the revelation* of the righteous judgment of God.

I would here remark, that I know of no attempt on the part of any Catholic author to prove that the word *justify*, *denotes* or includes Sanctification, except from an assumed etymological meaning of the word—which, as I claim to have shown, neither the Latin *justifico*, nor the Greek *δικαιόω*, nor the Hebrew צדק, can in any case possibly bear. With what reason, or rather, with what decisive proof to the contrary, is it pretended that Justification in the Scriptures is, or includes Sanctification?

Here however, it ought to be stated, that a Protestant writer, Ludovicus De Blanc, in an attempt to reconcile the opinions of Catholics and Protestants on this important subject, concedes to the former, that the word *δικαιόω*, in several instances in the New Testament denotes the act of *Sanctification.* A bare inspection of these passages would, in my view, be quite sufficient to show this construction of the passages referred to, to be entirely groundless, and even to prove the contrary. And with this remark, I should be satisfied to leave them without examination, had not Beza, Osiander, and some other Protestant theologians of distinction maintained, and were there not some even among us, who hold the same opinion.

There are two assumptions on this subject, which demand a more thorough examination than, so far as I know, they have received. One respects the scriptural use of the word *ἁγιάζω* (to sanctify); the other the words *ἁγνίζω* and *καθαρίζω*. It is often assumed by both Protestants and Catholics, that these denote in certain connections, the work of God in producing holiness of heart either in its beginning or in its progress, or in both. If this be conceded in some sense of the language, I have already said enough to show, that the subjective change in the mind is not what Protestants and Catholics most commonly maintain, viz., some change other than that which consists essentially in the morally right exercise of the heart or affections. And further: I cannot but think that what may be called the Augustinian, as distinguished from the Pelagian view of the New Testament use of the word ἁγιάζω, deserves a more thorough investigation than it has had from modern critics and theologians. I will only say on this topic, that the generic meaning of the word is evidently, to consecrate, and that to obtain from the mere word itself, or even from its connection, the meaning of an act of God producing personal holiness, is more difficult than is commonly supposed. The other assumption to which I refer is, that redemption or deliverance from sin (σώζειν ἀπὸ τῶν ἁμαρτιῶν, Matt. i. 21; καθαρίζειν ἀπὸ πάσης ἁμαρτίας, 1 John, i. 7, 9; compare Titus ii. 14; 1 Pet. i. 18, and others) by the blood of Christ, is, as Socinians maintain, or at least, includes, the act of God in delivering from the power of sin. While I admit that the work of the Holy Spirit in delivering us from the dominion of sin is through Christ, I do not understand, as many do, those passages which ascribe cleansing from sin, redeeming from iniquity, *to the blood of Christ*, as including this work of the Holy Spirit. *To take away sin*, was with the Hebrews one and the same thing as *to take away punishment* (vide Isa. liii.); the idea of delivering from sin, taking it away, &c., being uniformly assumed on the ground of repentance and reformation; that is, on the antecedent *condition* of personal holiness. But I cannot here dwell on this part of the subject, and proceed to consider some of the principal texts which are relied on to show that Justification is the same thing as Sanctification. These I shall examine as briefly as may be.

Rom. viii. 30: "Moreover, whom he did predestinate, them he also called, and whom he called, them he also justified, and whom he justified, them he also glorified." It is claimed to be incredible, that the apostle in this enumeration of blessings, should omit that of personal holiness; and that he has done so, unless he used the word *justified*, to denote it. I answer first, that no one is competent to decide what the apostle would or would not omit in such an enumeration; and secondly, that he has not omitted, but fully expressed the blessing of personal holiness, in the phrase, "them he called." This calling is evidently what divines have termed *effectual calling*. (Vide Rom. i. 7; and compare 1 Cor. i. 2; Rom. viii. 28; Eph. iv. 1, 4, &c.)

1 Cor. vi. 11: "And such were some of you; but ye are washed, but ye are sanctified, but ye are justified, in the name of the Lord Jesus, and by the Spirit of our God." If being *washed, sanctified, justified*, are not here distinguished as different things by the form of expression, especially by the repetition of ἀλλά (*but* ye are, &c.), it would be difficult to say how they could be at all. But it is said that *Justification* is here ascribed to the Spirit of God, whose work it is to renew and sanctify; and must therefore mean Sanctification. One would suppose that *the washing* and *the sanctifying*, including nothing less than moral Renovation or personal holiness by the Holy Spirit, and the known condition of Justification, and all being in the name of Christ, would be quite sufficient to authorize the apostle's form of speaking; since all the specified blessings come only in the name of Christ, and are directly or indirectly by the Holy Spirit.

Tit. iii. 5, 6, 7: "Not by works of righteousness which we have done, but according to his mercy he saved us by the washing of Regeneration, and renewing of the Holy Ghost, which he shed on us abundantly through Jesus Christ our Saviour; that being justified by his grace, we should be made heirs according to the hope of eternal life." It is said that according to this passage, our Justification includes our Sanctification. If by this be meant, that Justification by grace *implies* Renovation or Sanctification, this is admitted. But how does this prove that it *is* Sanctification? How directly opposed this declaration of the apostle is to the Romanist view of Justification, is obvious from a very brief exposition of it. The apostle then expressly asserts that we are saved not by works (τῶν ἐν δικαιοσύνῃ) which are in righteousness, i. e., constitute a righteousness which we have done, but according to his mercy, by the moral purification and Renovation of the Holy Ghost; that we, being justified by his grace, i. e., that being saved by the moral purification and Renovation of the Holy Spirit, should be made heirs, &c. Now, is being justified by his grace, the same thing as being morally purified and renovated by the Holy Ghost? Such tautology is not after the manner of this apostle; while the phrase "justified freely by his grace," in Rom. iii. 24, will admit of no such meaning, as some, and even Rosenmüller, have given it in this passage in Titus.

Rev. xxii. 11: "And he that is righteous, let him be righteous still; and he that is holy, let him be holy still." In respect to the first clause in this passage, the readings are various; and one which is preferred by many is, for *δικαιοθήτω ἔτι*, to read *δικαιοσύνην ποιησάτω ἔτι—work righteousness still.* Retaining the common reading the question is, what is the *ὁ δικαίος*? I answer, he who on any ground stands right in relation to legal sanctions; in other words, is accepted of God. Hence the declaration is, that he who is in this state of acceptance and favor with God shall continue in it. But whether we adopt this meaning or change the reading for another, one thing is clear, this clause does not respect subjective personal righteousness in the sense of personal holiness produced by Sanctification; for how then could the apostle repeat the same thought in the next clause, "and he that is holy, let him be holy still?" To work righteousness is to do good works, with which Justification is connected.

These are the only passages in the New Testament which are relied on for that view of the doctrine of Justification now opposed, while the words *δικαιόω* and *δικαιόομαι* are used it is said, thirty-six times. If we have rightly interpreted the four passages, they not only will not bear the meaning opposed, but exclude it, and require another, as they plainly do in all other instances.

Again: in proof that Justification is not and does not include Sanctification, I appeal to the scriptural exhibition of the Moral Government of God. If Moral Government is any thing, it implies a Moral Governor, a law with its requisite sanctions, subjects, a holding and calling to account, a judgment and a retribution. And if in the Scriptures God has revealed himself to men in any relation, it is the prominent, grand, and most august; that to which all things else are subservient—the relation of a Moral Ruler and Judge. What else is presented to us but God in his administration of a system of law and grace? Consider his works of creation, his ways of providence, his varied and wonderful dispensations; man created in his image, his law given, and at first obeyed amid the beauties of paradise, and with the joys of communion with his

Maker, and then disobeyed with the curse in exile, and in the sorrows and groans and death of a sinful world; the promised redemption, with its superabounding grace to retain and bless; the patriarchal altars with their victims, and their holocaust fires kindled from heaven; the calling of Abraham and its covenant of grace and life anew, and more fully unfolded in the seed promised to bless all nations; Egyptian bondage, with its task-masters and years of oppression and cruelty; and then its deliverance by the outstretched arm of Omnipotence; sojourners in a strange land; heaven and earth shaken to reclaim them from idolatry to the service of the only living and true God; the desert, with its cloud by day and pillar of fire by night, its famine of food and drink, its smitten rock and gushing waters; Sinai with its terrors; Israel in the promised land flowing with milk and honey; God, their national king and tutelary Deity; their captivities and redemptions; the fullness of time, the harbinger to prepare the way of the Lord calling to repentance; the Messiah, God manifest in the flesh; the Gospel, its teachings, its glad tidings of great joy to all people; its Atonement, its miracles, its mission of the Holy Ghost in the Renovation and Sanctification of men, its resurrection of the dead, its immortality brought to light; its progress, its actual and predicted triumphs, its millennium of holiness and happiness in a new heavens and new earth, its final judgment announced with the archangel's voice and the trump of God, the melting elements and a burning world, the great white throne, the Son of man thereon, the dead, small and great, standing before him, the deeds of all laid open, every heart searched, every secret thing revealed; and now the final resistless decree, the authoritative act of the Judge, placing those already sanctified by grace, the righteous, on his right hand, and the wicked on his left. And has the former of these, the final act of God, that by which he consummates all his other acts, and accomplishes his highest and greatest design toward the children of men, no name? While the Scriptures call his authoritative act in respect to the wicked, *condemnation*, do they make so little account of his authoritative act toward the righteous as not to name it?

I only add, that the Romanists, in holding that inherent righteousness, Sanctification, and good works are the formal cause, the meritorious ground of Justification, fully concede in respect to *the nature of Justification*, all that Protestants maintain.

The Romanist fully admits the act of the remission of sin on the part of God. But no mind which can thus distinguish the act of Renovation or Sanctification from that of remission, can at the same time not regard them as distinct; nor can it conceive of the remission of sins as an act of God, except in the capacity of lawgiver and judge, nor without connecting with it the act of placing the subject right in relation to sanctions of law, or in a state of acceptance with the offended lawgiver.

JUSTIFICATION.

II.—CLASSICAL AND SCRIPTURAL MEANING OF THE VERB ΔΙΚΑΙΟΩ. JUSTIFICATION AS AN ACT OF GOD TO MAN DEFINED.

1. General classical meaning of δικαιόω.—Justice as conceived by the ancients.—Definition of the verb in question.—Authority of Lexicographers.—The derivation of the word.—The conception of the production of holiness unknown to the ancients.—2. Its forensic meaning in classical use. —Absolute and relative condition of a subject of law.—Classical forensic use not synonymous with English use of *justify*.

Scriptural sense.—1. The most general meaning.—2. Its forensic meaning in the Scriptures.—Adapted to a peculiar system of things.—Man cannot be justified under mere law.—Actual usage of the term in the Scriptures.—Justification not synonymous with pardon.—Man prone to regard Justification as meritorious.—Influence of sacrifices.—Mistake of the Romish Church.—Criteria for deciding what is the scriptural meaning.—Conclusion.

Having shown that Justification as an act of God in respect to men, is not nor does include that of Sanctification, or of making the heart morally right, I have set aside the view of *the nature* of Justification which has been most directly and chiefly opposed to what I deem the scriptural one. The question in its positive form still remains to be answered, viz., *What is the Scriptural view of the nature of this act of God?* The answer to this question will not only reveal more fully the error which I have already attempted to expose in respect to the *nature*, but will serve to correct others in regard to the condition and the ground of the act. I proceed then to say, that

Justification as an act of God in the relation of Lawgiver and Judge of men is authoritative—making, or causing, or determining a disobedient subject of his law to stand relatively right in respect to its sanctions; not according to the principles of distributive justice, but according to the principles of general justice and of general benevolence.

This view of the nature of this act of God I propose to illustrate and confirm by examining the various uses and applications of the word *Justification* or *Justify*, with the equivalent word in Hebrew, Greek, and Latin, as applied in the different circumstances of men by different nations, and also by them in different connections. I propose to consider—

I. The use and meaning of the word δικαιόω, as a classic word employed in a heathen sense; and—

II. As a scriptural word, employed in a biblical sense, or under a system of grace.

I. The use and meaning of the word δικαιόω as a *classic word employed in a heathen sense.*

The reason for giving particular attention to this word, is its use both by the Seventy and by the New Testament writers as equivalent to the Hebrew word צָדַק, both of which in Latin are rendered by *justifico*, and in English by *justify*. The Hebrew word being exclusively used under a system of facts and truths peculiar to a revelation from God, and the Greek word used in a classic heathen sense, could not otherwise be exact synonyms. The Hebrew word then must control, modify, and determine the meaning of the Greek word when used by the Seventy, and also by the New Testament writers; so that the Greek word if correctly used, must in biblical usage (and the same must be true of the Latin) be employed in a meaning equivalent to that of the Hebrew. The Greek δικαιόω as a classic word, used in a heathen and forensic sense, was employed in relation to a system of mere law; whereas the Hebrew word צָדַק, was used only in relation to a system of law and grace combined. The Greek word δικαιόω when used by the Seventy, or by the New Testament writers, if properly employed must be Hebraized, and mean the same as the Hebrew word צָדַק; for neither can be used in the Scriptures to denote an act of God, except in a system of law and grace combined. This use of the Greek word by the New Testament writers is, as we may see hereafter, undeniable. Hence it becomes highly important to ascertain the meaning of δικαιόω as a classic word used in a heathen, especially in a *forensic* sense, under a system of mere law, that we may determine the changes in its meanings, if such exist, from classic to Hellenistic use, or as Greek conformed to Hebrew ideas. I proceed then, to consider—

I. The use and meaning of the word δικαιόω, a classic word employed in a heathen sense.

Here its most general meaning in this use will first deserve attention, and then its general *forensic* meaning.

1. *Its general meaning in classic use.*—In this, the word δικαιόω denotes *to make relatively right;* or thus, it denotes the act, either personal or impersonal, of making, causing, determining, either a person or thing to be *relatively* right.

This act like every other, has an object on which or in respect to which, it produces its own peculiar effect or change, and which otherwise neither would nor could be effected. This effect or change is not in the character, nature, or qualities of the object of the act, but only in the relation of the object to *the manner* in which it is to be practically regarded and treated, as this is consequent upon and determined by the act.

This view of the general meaning of the word δικαιόω, may be confirmed by some observations on the derivation and formation of the word.

The word δίκη is the original root of a family of words compounded of it, with various terminations. Hence δίκαιος; and hence again, δικαιόω. The adjective from which the verb seems to be more directly derived, appears to be equivalent to our English word *just.* The great Christian idea of *benevolence, universal, disinterested love*, was not known to the heathen. In the conceptions of the wisest heathen philosophers, *justice* appears to have been the comprehensive virtue—the element and essence of all virtue. Piety was inculcated chiefly, if not wholly, to prevent crimes hostile to the peace and prosperity of the State, and consisted not in the love, but in that servile fear of the gods which sought to appease their anger and to propitiate their favor. Hence justice, as the great cardinal virtue as related to the welfare of civil society—justice to individuals and justice to the State—justice viewed as conformity to those established usages and customs which had the force of law, as well as to law itself—was among the heathen nations, and especially among the Greeks and Romans, the pre-eminent and comprehensive virtue—the sum and perfection of moral excellence, which secured the favor of gods and of men, and so of the government of the nation.

Justice as the comprehensive virtue, "a constant will or disposition to render to every one his due," would exist and necessarily be spoken of under a great variety of specific forms, among which what we call the administration of justice, or doing justly by the civil magistrate or judge, would be peculiarly prominent. This act of the judge, causes, makes, determines, not the character or subjective relation of the object of the act as obedient or disobedient to law, for he is in every respect one or the other before the act of the judge,—but this as an authoritative act, causes, makes, determines, only *the relation* of the object of the act to *the manner in which he is to be practically regarded and treated*, as this wholly depends on and is determined by it. It is essential to the very nature and design of civil government, that in certain cases there should be such an authoritative act; and that it be the only ground, cause, or determining antecedent of the relation of subjects of law to *the manner* in which they are to be practically regarded and treated by the State.

Besides this particular act of justice, or making relatively just or right, there would be many others both toward persons and things, which would more or less resemble and yet also differ from it. Hence all such, including the act of the judge, having a common nature, would have a common name, denoting the common idea of making *relatively* just or right. This would of course be a generic term in relation to all the species included under it, and the species under it, if determined at all, must be determined, not by the general word, which is equally applicable to all the species, but by the known nature of the subject or logical connection.

It may be well to say here, that the idea we are now defining, that of *making relatively right*, is not the same as that of *doing right*. The act may be one *particular form* of doing right. But then there are many others, e. g., feeding the hungry, clothing the naked, &c., which cannot be denoted by the word *δικαιόω*. Especially is it to be noticed, that this word cannot be used to denote the act of making its object right or just *subjectively or inherently*, but only *relatively*, or in relation to the manner in which the object is to be regarded for practical purposes, or in which he or it is to be treated.

Having made these explanatory remarks, I proceed to show that in its most general classic meaning, the word *δικαιόω* denotes *the act*, *either personal or impersonal*, *of making*, *causing*, *determining*, *either a person or thing to be relatively just or right; or just* or *right in relation to the manner in which he or it is to be regarded for practical purposes*, *or in which he or it is to be treated*. In support of this definition I allege,

In the first place, the authority of lexicographers. This kind of evidence is of course not demonstrative; but, as it must be in all such cases, probable or moral evidence, or evidence by induction. Lexicographers for the most part unfortunately attempt to give, not the most general meanings of even important words; but *some*, *many*, or *most* of their particular or specific meanings, as these are determined by the logical connection in actual usage. Now it is only from these specific meanings of a word, that its generic or general one can be ascertained, for this is common to all the specific meanings. So far then as the induction or bringing together of these specific meanings approximates perfection,—for on no subject can it be assumed to be known to be absolutely perfect,—and results in one which is common, the evidence is reliable; in other words, while it is the only kind of which the nature of the case admits, it is *prima facie* evidence, or that which is to be relied on, in the absence of all evidence to the contrary. The facts,—the instances of the specific meanings of the word δικαιόω in its classic use, given in good lexicons,—are not all that might be given, and yet are in such variety as to render it highly probable that the meaning which is common to them all, is the common and generic meaning of the word. Assuming then, as I am authorized to do, that this is true, until some evidence to the contrary is furnished, I maintain that the meaning which I have specified is that which is common to all these cases, and is therefore general or generic. No one who will look into a good Greek lexicon will deny that the meaning which I have specified is common to all these cases. Until then he adduces at least one instance of its use in a specific meaning which shall furnish an exception to the common one now claimed, he is bound to admit this to be the common and of course the general meaning of the word. In support of the present definition, I allege,

In the second place, the derivation and formation of the word δικαιόω. All, or nearly all the Greek verbs formed in the same manner as this, denote the act of making, causing, determining, not a subjective or intrinsic effect or change in the absolute nature of the subject, but a *relative* effect or change. Take as examples the following: θεμελιόω, ἀξιόω, ὁμοιόω, τελειόω, υἱόω, ἁγιόω, παλαιόω. A like mode of compounding words, is found in the Latin language, as in *glorifico*, *verifico*, &c., and in English, as in *glorify*, *verify*, &c., to denote an act, making, or causing a *relative* effect or change. But what is *making* or *causing* an effect in such cases? Not making or causing an effect which it is impossible and inconceivable should be made or caused. To illustrate by some examples will show that the effects in the cases now referred to are merely *relative.* In what sense then of making or causing a foundation, can the verb θεμελιόω be used? Not surely in that of making or causing an effect in the intrinsic nature of the material, e. g., of a rock or other substance, but in the sense of making or causing it to sustain the new and peculiar relation specified. So the verb υἱόω, is not to cause the object of the act to be a son in every respect, but to make or cause him to be a son in every respect in which he can be, as having the relation and place, and receiving the treatment of a son. I might illustrate the same thing by Latin words of like composition, as *glorifico* when applied to God, and by English words, as I have already done in respect to the word *verify.* It admits perhaps of a question, whether the words *mortify*, *vivify*, and perhaps some few others, which have been regarded as exceptions to the rule now stated, are real exceptions.

I do not affirm that none of this class of words denote in any case the making or causing of a *subjective* effect or change, as distinguished from that which is *relative.* If however there be any such, which I doubt, they must be decisively shown to be such by the nature of the case, or by other equally decisive proof. This however, can impart no doubt to those in which this class of words must at least, have the meaning of causing a *relative* effect or change, and in which there is no evidence of any other. Such, as I claim, is the fact in respect to all or nearly all the class of words now under consideration. Hence arises a strong presumption from the mere formation of such a word, that it denotes the making or causing *only* of a *relative* effect, and this is *prima facie* evidence—evidence decisive that such is its only meaning, until proof to the contrary is adduced. These remarks are strikingly applicable to the word δικαιόω. It is confessedly used to denote the act of making, causing, *a relative* effect, or change; and until it be shown that it has also some other or further meaning, the proof is decisive that such is the only one. I allege,

In the third place, that the idea of the production of virtue or holiness in the human heart, is entirely foreign to the heathen mind. This fact has been fully proved in another place. Unless then we can suppose men to express in words, ideas which they have not in their minds, it is absolutely incredible and impossible, that the word δικαιόω in classic use, should denote the act of making or causing the object of the act to be subjectively *just*, or *right*, or *righteous*. It confessedly denotes the act of making *relatively* just or right,—just or right in *relation* to the manner in which the object of the act is to be regarded for practical purposes, and of course to be treated. This therefore, so far as the main thing at issue is concerned, is the whole general classic meaning of the word δικαιόω.

With this view of the general meaning of δικαιόω, as a classic word, it is obvious that in its classic use it must have, as we commonly speak, many particular meanings, for it is applied like our word *justify* to both persons and things. It is not necessary to my present purpose to trace these in detail, but only to say what will not be questioned, that among them a *forensic* meaning is both prominent and common. To this particular use of the word I now call attention, with the design to ascertain as proposed—

2. *Its general forensic meaning in classic use.*—In this meaning and use, the word being employed of course in a heathen sense and under a system of mere law, denotes

An authoritative act of a judge, making, causing, determining a particular relation of a subject of law to its sanctions, as one to be actually rewarded or actually punished, according to merely legal principles.

To explain my meaning more fully, I remark, that the condition of a subject of mere law, whether obedient or disobedient, may be viewed as absolute *and relative.* His subjective act of obedience as fulfilling the claim of law and entitling to its reward, and his subjective act of disobedience as violating the claim of law and exposing to its penalty, may each be considered as an absolute condition resulting necessarily from the subject's own act and the nature of law. But this condition of the subject of law is changed by the authoritative act of the judge, which makes, causes, or determines the existence of a new relation to the sanctions of law, viz., that the subject is to be actually rewarded or punished. This relation depends on, and is made or caused solely by the act of the judge, and may be called a relative condition. These things, the condition of a subject of law as it depends on his own act, and as it is changed by the act of the judge in its relation to legal sanctions, differ so widely and essentially that they demand a careful consideration.

There is an obvious and important difference between giving an *absolute* existence to a fact or thing in many cases, and giving it a *relative* existence, especially in relation to its being practically regarded and acted upon as real. Thus in cases innumerable, the fact depends for this *relative* existence on a different cause or act from that which gives it its absolute existence. To verify a fact by testimony does not give *absolute* existence or truth to it, but makes, causes, or determines it to be a fact for practical purposes, or to be acted upon as such when otherwise it could not be. The authoritative act of a judge makes the litigated property of its owner *his* property in one respect, in which otherwise it is not *his* property relatively to his possession and use of it. In like manner the authoritative judgment of the supreme tribunal of the land in respect to one on trial for a crime, does not give *absolute* existence to his standing in respect to the sanctions of law, but only a *relative* existence, or an existence to be regarded and acted upon as real. Accordingly, I maintain that the Greek word δικαιόω when used as now supposed, denotes an authoritative act of a judge, making, causing, determining the condition or standing of a subject of law in respect to its sanctions, not *absolutely*, for this is already done either by his obedience or disobedience, but *relatively*, and so far as it can determine it, which is so far as it is to be acted upon.

Further: this word as classic Greek, used in the manner now supposed, whatever it may be as Hellenistic Greek, is not synonymous with our English word justify. As a general forensic term in classic use, it denotes *simply a just or right judgment, either in acquitting or condemning*. From the mere act of the judge nothing could be inferred concerning the innocence or guilt of the object. This act simply determines the standing or relation of the subject in regard to the sanctions of law in that respect in which it depends, and in some respect it does depend on such an act. The *absolute* fact is, either that the subject is obedient and ought to be rewarded, or he is disobedient and ought to be punished. But which of these is the fact, and the one to be acted upon in retribution, is in one most important respect undetermined, and must remain so until the act of the judge decides it. In other words, it must *in this respect* remain non-existent until there be an act of authority and jurisdiction determining the fact, and so giving it existence as one to be acted upon in conferring the reward for obedience or inflicting the penalty for disobedience. This act of authority and jurisdiction under a merely legal system, must be assumed in practical life to be right or just in the broad sense of being in accordance with the principles of distributive and general justice, and also with those of general benevolence. These under an equitable system of mere law are ever in harmony, for what is demanded in such a case by any is demanded by all of them.*

According to what has now been said in the way of explanation, we find the facts and the proof of them. We find that the Greek word under consideration was used by the classic Greek writers in the general forensic meaning now specified; i. e., to denote a just or right judgment, either in acquitting or condemning. Suidas in his lexicon, referring only to classic authority, says "that the word was used to denote a right or just judgment either in acquitting or condemning." The same thing will appear by referring to any good Greek lexicon, classical or biblical. Dr. Owen cites an instance of this use of the English word *justify*, from a treaty between the English and Scotch in the time of Edward VI., in the clause, "that if any one committed a crime he should be justified on trial." That such was the general forensic meaning of the word *δικαιόω* as a classic word, is confirmed by another consideration, that it is used as the opposite of *αδίκεω*, to act unjustly, and in a forensic sense to judge unjustly. Thus it appears, that as a classic word it was not used as a forensic term in the same as its Hellenistic meaning, nor as that of our English word *justify*. However, its most *general* classic meaning may have been, as we shall see it was, perpetuated, viz., *to make relatively right or just;* yet its general *forensic* meaning under a merely legal system, was not and could not be perpetuated under a system of grace. The act of the judge in the former sense would be impossible, there being no obedient subject to be acquitted, and none of course to whom the word could, with the least truth or propriety, be applied to an obedient subject.

---

* It may be well to say here what I claim to have before shown, that while distributive justice *requires* the obedient subject to be rewarded in all circumstances, it does not require that the disobedient subject should be punished in all circumstances.

Having thus attempted to ascertain the *general* and also the *general forensic* meaning of the Greek word δικαιόω as a classic word, and as used in a heathen sense under a system of mere law, I now proceed to consider it—

II. As a scriptural word, or as employed in a biblical sense.

Here, if I mistake not, we shall find that the word is greatly modified and changed when compared with its classic use, as it is employed under a system of grace; and that while it retains, as we might be sure it would, its most general classic meaning, it is not used in its general *forensic* meaning as a classic word. As these things may need confirmation, I proceed to show—

1. That the most general meaning of the word as used in the Scriptures, is the same as its most general meaning in its classic use, which is *the act of making, causing, or determining either a person or thing to be relatively right or just.*

The difference between what I have called the *absolute* and the *relative* existence of a fact, has been already sufficiently illustrated. This, as accurately recognized in the use of language, especially in the use of that class of active verbs which are applied *only* to the production of *relative* effects, cannot be denied, and ought not to be overlooked, it being easily and surely, and I may say *necessarily* determined, by the known nature of the subject. This is manifest beyond all contradiction in respect to many words, and as we now maintain, in respect to δικαιόω in Greek, צָדַק in Hebrew, *justifico* in Latin, and *justify* in English. These words, in their most general meaning, are strict synonyms; and in this, the word whether that of one language or another, is that of which I now speak, when I say it denotes, not the act of making, causing, or determining an *absolute*, but only a *relative* effect, an act done in respect to a person or thing, making or causing not *a subjective* effect or change in the object of the act, but only a relative effect designated by the word *right*, or *just.*

To *justify* or make right another, as the act of a judge—to *justify* one's self—to justify a doubtful particular action—to justify a proposition or assertion questioned or denied—to justify a crime, is to make *right* or *just* in different modes of making right or just. In the one case, the act is done by authority; in another, by assertion or proof, or by both; in another, by reasoning; in another, by sophistry. The rightness of one accused made by the act of the judge, is different from the rightness made and determined in every other case. And yet in neither of these instances is the thing said to be made right *absolutely*, but only *relatively*, or in relation to the manner in which it is to be regarded for practical purposes.

What is thus obvious from the statement of familiar examples of common life, is equally so from the scriptural use of the word. In proof of this, I appeal to a sufficient number of examples from the Scriptures, of the particular application of the word to persons and things. First to persons: "It is God that justifieth" (Rom. viii. 3). "And all the people justified God" (Luke vii. 29). "Speak, for I desire to justify thee" (Job xxxiii. 32). "He willing (choosing) to justify himself" (Luke x. 29). "God was manifested in the flesh, justified in the Spirit" (1 Tim. iii. 16). "They (the judges) shall justify the righteous, and condemn the wicked" (Deut. xxv. 1). "Which justify the wicked for a reward" (Isa. v. 23). "That justifieth the ungodly" (Rom. iv. 5). Secondly, to things: "But wisdom is justified of all her children" (Luke vii. 35; Matt. xi. 19). "The sanctuary shall be justified" (Dan. viii. 14). Now there must be one general meaning of the word *justify* (δικαιόω, צַדֵּק· *justifico*), which is common to all these different cases. It is equally obvious that they cannot all have the same specific or particular meaning. None will pretend that God is said to justify the ungodly in the same particular meaning in which all the people are said to have justified God, or in which God manifest in the flesh was justified in the Spirit, or in which a human judge is required to justify the righteous, or in which wisdom is justified of all her children, or in which it is said the sanctuary shall be *justified*. Nor will it be pretended, that in any two of the instances referred to, the word *justify* is used in the same, nor denied that in each instance it is used in a different specific meaning. The question then is, what is the *general* meaning of the word, or the one common to all these cases? Is it that of *making right* in the sense of doing strict justice? But does God in justifying the elect, do them strict justice? or is the lawyer in Luke x. 29, said to be willing to do himself strict justice? or can they be said to do strict justice, who *justify* the wicked for a reward? Is the meaning then which is common to all these cases, that of making the object of the act *subjectively holy* even in any degree,—is this the sense in which all the people *justified* God? or in which the lawyer was willing to *justify* himself? or the judges are required to *justify* the righteous? or august judges *justify* the wicked? or wisdom is *justified* of her children? or the sanctuary was to be justified? It will not I think be pretended, that either of those now specified is the meaning common to all these cases of the use of the word *justify*, nor of course its general one. But it is at once obvious that what I have specified as the general meaning of the word is common to all these cases, and that nothing more specific is or can be common to them all. This is decided at once by taking either of them as an example: thus, "the people *justified* God." It is manifest, that the word denotes at least the act of making right, *not absolutely*, but *relatively*, or in relation to his being practically regarded, treated, as right, and that it cannot denote any thing more, and still have a meaning common to all the other cases; viz., to *justifying* the elect, the righteous, the wicked, wisdom, and the sanctuary. This is as obvious and certain, as that the general meaning of the word triangle is a three-sided figure, and nothing more, whether we speak of an isosceles, equilateral, acute-angled, or a right-angled triangle.

Once more: if the general meaning of the word δικαιόω is not that now given, then the word as used in the Scriptures is falsely translated by the English word *justify*. Nothing is more undeniable than that the general meaning now maintained, is the general meaning of the English word *justify*. I venture to say, nothing would be more hopeless than to attempt to show that the mere English word *justify* is ever used in any other general meaning. If this be so (and who that at all understands the English language will pretend the contrary), then if δικαιόω has another and a different general meaning, it follows that in our English Bible it is falsely translated in every instance. I admit that it has different specific meanings, as we commonly speak in different applications; i. e., that the whole meaning of the writer as determined by the connection, is in many cases something more than the general meaning of the mere word. But I maintain, that the word as such, denotes nothing more and nothing less than what I have said is its general meaning. If it does, then our translators have sadly blundered in rendering it by the English word justify.* Had our translators the remotest suspicion that the Greek or Hebrew word meant to *sanctify;* or that as a general term it meant to do strict justice? Could they have so understood it in Daniel viii. 14; or in Luke x. 29; or in Romans iv. 5? Is it in the lowest degree credible that they understood the Hebrew or Greek word in either of these as its general meaning? Had they so understood it, nothing is more certain than that they would have rendered it by the English word *sanctify*, or by the phrase *do justice to;* and that in rendering it by the word *justify*, they have intentionally given a false translation of the word. There is then, all the evidence that the word has the general meaning now given it, which there is that these men were honest and skillful translators of the sacred writings. If they have mistranslated the word, let the error be corrected, and let it henceforth be understood, that the self-righteous Pharisee was willing to *sanctify* himself, that judges were required to *sanctify* the righteous, and that wicked judges for a reward did *sanctify* the wicked.

There are other considerations which strongly confirm this view of the general meaning of the word. I add only one, viz., the coincidence between *the general classic meaning* and what is now maintained to be *its general scriptural meaning*. The *primary* meaning of words is always changed by generalization, but the general meaning never can change, unless there is an imperious necessity for some alteration in their specific meaning arising from a change of particular facts or ideas of such facts. Every one at all acquainted with the process of generalization, must see how incredible, or rather impossible it is, that the general terms *animal* and *tree*, should become each a general term in whose meaning that of the other should be included. The same impossibility must have existed in respect to the general words rendered *justify* and *sanctify*. Notwithstanding the changes and differences in the specific meanings, as they are called, of the word δικαιόω under its general classic meaning, and especially in the Scriptures, it cannot be shown that its general classic meaning, compared with its general scriptural meaning, has been changed at all, nor that there

---

* The same thing is true of the Vulgate, as rendering the Greek and the Hebrew by the Latin word *justifico*.

was in the scriptural use of it, as a general term, the slightest necessity or reason for changing it. On the contrary, we have seen that the general meaning of the word is the same in both uses, viz., *to make right relatively* in the sense already explained. What pretense then can there be for asserting a change in the general meaning of the word, so that under this shall be included the specific meaning of *making right absolutely* or *intrinsically?* To suppose this, is, as we have already shown, not only without the least warrant and wholly gratuitous, but against decisive proof to the contrary, arising in the present case from the total absence of all such ideas of things. In addition to this, we now see that the supposition is forbidden by one of those established laws of language which must regulate all such changes.

2. That the word δικαιόω in its general, scriptural, forensic meaning, denotes an authoritative act of a judge, making, causing, determining a subject of law, to stand right in relation to the sanctions of law.

In the Scriptures, the word is used in a forensic meaning, as a common term applicable to an act of God, and of man as a judge. This is its *general forensic* meaning in the Scriptures, and is that for which we now inquire.

In this forensic use it retains its most general meaning, which, as we have seen, is the same in both its classic and scriptural use,—denoting *the act of making or determining a person or thing to be relatively right.* But, as we shall see, the general forensic *classic* meaning differs widely from the general forensic *scriptural* meaning. The former is *the authoritative act of a judge making or determining the relation of a subject of law to its sanctions, as one to be rewarded or punished according to merely legal principles;* or simply, *a just or right act of a judge, either in acquitting or condemning according to merely legal principles.* The latter is *the act of a judge, making or determining the relation of a subject of law to the sanctions of law as one to be rewarded;* or, *determining the subject of law to stand right in relation to the sanctions of law.* These statements are deemed sufficient to show the difference between the general forensic *classic* meaning of the word δικαιόω, and its general forensic *scriptural* meaning; showing the act of the judge to be the same, and the word to have the same general forensic *scriptural* meaning, whether the object of the act be obedient or disobedient to law. All that can be meant by the *mere word* in this use is, simply that by the authoritative act of the judge, the subject of the law, the object of the act, *is made or determined to stand right in relation to legal sanctions.* From the mere word, aside from the known character of the judge and the logical connection, nothing can be inferred concerning the character or conduct of the subject as obedient or disobedient to law; and nothing in respect to the act of the judge as right or wrong, just or unjust, according to legal principles. An unjust judge may actually *justify* the disobedient subject under a system of mere law. A just judge may, or rather will, *justify* the obedient subject under a system of mere law; and a just judge may, and in certain cases will, justify the disobedient subject under a system of law and grace combined. Yet in these three different particular cases, the mere word *justify* (δικαιόω) has one and the same meaning, in which it can be *truly* and properly applied to them all. In this sense the word cannot denote the act of the judge making the subject of law inherently, subjectively, and absolutely obedient or righteous. This would be palpably false in two, not to say in all the supposed instances. To say that it must be *true* in the third case, or there can be no act of *justifying*, is to affirm that there cannot be a common meaning of the word in which it can be truly applied to the three cases, which is palpably false. The only true and proper use of the word *justify* (δικαιόω) therefore, as a general forensic term in the Scriptures, is to denote an *authoritative act of a judge*, whether he be God or man, whether he be just or unjust, or whether the subject be obedient or disobedient to law, *making or determining a subject of law to stand right in relation to the sanctions of law.*

That this view of the use and meaning of the word δικαιόω may be further confirmed, the peculiar system of things under which the word has ever been used in the Scriptures, must be explained.

This system was not one of mere law, but one of law and grace combined,—one which the Lawgiver and Judge of men adopted, and revealed to our first parents in the hour of their apostasy (Gen. iii. 15), afterward to Abraham (Gen. xvii. 1–9; Gal. iii. 8), then to some of his descendants by Moses and the prophets (Rom. iii. 21), and finally, in its fullness by

Christ and his apostles. In this system there was a grand peculiarity of things, which by controlling the ideas of men must have extended an influence to language wherever the things of this revelation have been known. Nor could it be otherwise, even in respect to that class of words which had acquired a prior established use and meaning, when it should become necessary to employ them to express the peculiar and momentous things of God's Moral Government over men, as exhibited by his revelation. Words, as I have often had occasion to say, necessarily change their meaning with the ideas and knowledge of men respecting the things they signify. If, for example, some word which in its prior or heathen use had been employed on some subject to denote the act of one man toward another, should be found employed in divine revelation on the same subject to denote an act of God, and if the word in the former use would admit of or had acquired a broader application than it would consistently with truth, admit of in the latter, still it would be applied to the latter, and of course in a new and limited meaning, so far as the exigencies of truth and the nature of facts would allow and require.

Now under that peculiar system of law and grace which God has revealed, and under which, since the fall of man, he administers his Moral Government over men, no word could, in accordance with the truths or things of this revelation, come into use in that forensic sense in which the Greeks had used the word *δικαιόω*, and other nations some synonymous word or phrase, in application to obedient subjects under a system of mere law. The reason is, that none of the facts or things which are the only possible basis of such a use of the word, exist under God's moral administration over men. Before the apostasy of man, such a use of language under God's Moral Government as it then was, may be supposed possible. But from the time of that event, this government of God over men has been administered only over *disobedient* subjects. There being no obedient subject, there could be no act of God acquitting such a subject of the legal penalty, and giving him a title to a legal reward *de merito*, or as an obedient subject. No word therefore could with truth be used to denote such an act on the part of God. There neither was nor could be, a right or just judgment *de merito* of obedient subjects of the law of his Moral Government, for there were no such subjects. If then the Greek δικαιόω, or any other word, was applied to denote the act of God in determining a subject of his law to stand right in relation to its sanctions, it must be in a very different sense from that of its classic or heathen import. In its classic forensic use, it could be applied either to the act of acquitting an *obedient* subject of law, or of condemning a disobedient subject. But under God's moral administration it could not be applied to either: to the former, because there was no such subject and no such act; to the latter, for it could not be forensically applied as it is in the Scriptures, exclusively to the act of God in placing the *disobedient* subject of law right in relation to its sanctions.

Further: there is no act of God as a judge under the revealed system of grace, directly determining the relation of men to the sanctions of law, according to the principles of mere law. It is the doctrine of Paul, that the whole world will be judged according to the Gospel. I shall have occasion to treat more extensively of this topic in another connection. I only say here, that none of the human race will be judged on the last day, nor of course in this life, according to merely legal principles. Even the heathen may know "that God is, and is a rewarder of them that diligently seek him," and therefore may and will be judged substantially according to the Gospel; i. e., for having disobeyed what the apostle calls "the law of faith," as the great rule of final judgment. There was indeed a great fact assumed and acted upon on the part of God in the very act of providing an economy of grace, viz., that Adam and all his descendants were viewed as sinners, and as such, would and must, according to the principles of mere law or of strict justice under a system of mere law, be condemned to bear the legal penalty of sin. The case was hopeless without an economy of grace. But instead of pronouncing the sentence of law, or dooming the race as they under this view deserved to bear the penalty of the law, that so none could be redeemed and saved, God at once introduced an economy of grace, arresting both the sentence of the làw and the execution of its penalty. It is true, that under this economy of grace there was another sentence than that of law; not of course condemning all to bear the legal penalty of sin, but a sentence εἰς κατακρίμα, implying and proving the sin of all men, and thus the justice of their condemnation according to law. In this import and bearing of this sentence, though it cannot with even the show of propriety or truth be called a sentence *of condemnation*, it is with exact precision and truth called by the apostle a sentence *unto condemnation*. Nothing could be more remote from his mind than the idea of a sentence of God—one too, fully executed—dooming the whole race of men to bear the legal penalty of sin under an economy of grace. If then there is and can be no act of God as a Judge under the revealed system of grace, determining, that is, unchangeably fixing the relation of any of our race to sanctions of law according to the principles of mere law or of strict justice, then how could the word *δικαιόω*, or any other in the full forensic sense of its classic or heathen use, be applied in the Scriptures to denote such an act of God?

No word then, having the same general forensic meaning under a merely legal system which the Greek word *δικαιόω* had under such a system, could in such a meaning find a place in the Scriptures to denote any act of God, especially that which acquits men of the penalty of his law. The meaning in such an application would be plainly false. God actually *justifies* only disobedient subjects of his law.

As then the word *δικαιόω* is actually used in the Scriptures to denote the act of God placing only disobedient subjects of his law right in relation to its sanctions, it must either be falsely applied, or it must lose much of its general forensic meaning as a classic word, and refers to this act of God in another and a very different sense. The word in this application, as in similar cases, would retain its most general classic, and some of its general forensic classic meaning, as the connecting link between its antecedent and subsequent meaning and use. It would however, unavoidably lose so much of its general forensic classic meaning as would be inapplicable and false, and yet retain so much of it as would be true in its new application. This meaning would become the general forensic meaning of the word in the Scriptures, whether applied to the act of God or to the act of a human judge. As applied to the act of God, the particular act would respect a disobedient subject of law; as applied to the act of a just human judge, the particular act would respect an obedient subject of law. Either of these would be called an act of *justifying* as a general forensic term, as truly and properly as the other. The only meaning of the word common to both cases, is of course that of *an authoritative act of a judge, making or causing a subject of law to stand right in relation to the sanctions of law.*

If, as I claim to have shown, the Greek word δικαιόω in a heathen sense cannot be employed under a system of law and grace, and of course never in the Scriptures, then the way is prepared as I proposed,

To ascertain the general forensic meaning of the word when used under the system of law and grace which the Scriptures reveal.

I have said, that the word in this use and meaning denotes *the authoritative act of a judge, making or causing a subject of law to stand right in relation to its sanctions.*

I remark then, that the classic in becoming a scriptural word, would lose so much of its general forensic meaning as a classic word as would be inapplicable and false, and yet retain so much of that meaning as would be true in its new application. The general forensic meaning in its new application would be that which would be *common* to all cases of its actual use. It would be actually employed to denote the act of God as a judge, and also to denote an act of man as a judge. As applied to the act of God, it would respect his act done to a *disobedient* subject of his law; as applied to that of a human judge, it would respect his act as done to an *obedient* or to a disobedient subject of law. Either of these would in this use be called an act of *justifying* a subject of law as a general forensic term, and of course without denoting their specific difference, as truly and properly as the other. There is no avoiding this change in the meaning of the word in its new application, unless we suppose the coining of a new one, which is wholly unsupposable, or that no word is used to denote this act of God. But no sooner is the use of the classic word sanctioned by usage in application to this, than it acquires as we commonly speak, a new specific meaning, even that of placing *a disobedient* subject of law right in relation to its sanctions. But the word, for the reasons just given, will be applied also to the act of a human judge, one which places an *obedient* and even a disobedient subject of law right in relation to its sanctions. Thus the classic word δικαιόω, to *justify*, would unavoidably be applied in common to both of these, and either be as properly called an act of *justifying* as the other. But what meaning is common to both? Plainly each is *an authoritative act of a judge*, and is such by *making or determining a subject of law to stand right in relation to its sanctions;* and it is just as plain that it is nothing more.

This view of the subject may be confirmed under another aspect. There is then, and there ever has been since the Scriptures were written, a prominent fact in God's moral administration over men, which some word would, or rather must be used in the Scriptures to denote; viz., an authoritative act of God determining some of the disobedient subjects of his law to stand right in relation to its sanctions. This it will be admitted is the Hebrew word, which in the original writings of the Old Testament, and the Greek word, which in the Septuagint and in the New Testament, is rendered in our translation by the word *justify*. As this then would not be applied to any act of God in the general forensic sense of heathen usage, neither to that of condemning a disobedient subject of his law, nor yet to one determining an obedient subject to stand right in relation to its sanctions, there being no such subject; the word would be unavoidably and exclusively applied to his authoritative act, which determines that *a disobedient* subject of his law stands right in relation to its sanctions. So the word, when applied as it would be to the act of a human judge, would not refer to his condemning a disobedient subject, any more than to the same act of God; but to some act of a human judge to which it could be applied in a meaning common to both him and God. There would be a common nature in these acts which would be denoted by a common term; but the only meaning in which it could be thus used, is that of an authoritative act of a judge, determining the subject of law to stand right in relation to its sanctions.

Further: actual usage fully accords with and thus confirms this view of the subject. This is not only too obvious to be controverted in respect to the English word *justify* when used as a forensic term, but it is believed that the same thing is true respecting the equivalent word of every language which has been modified by and conformed to Scriptural usage. But it is important to our purpose only, to show that there is no other forensic use of it in the Scriptures. We say then, that the Hebrew word when used forensically, will admit of no other generic meaning than that now maintained, for it is applied not only to the authoritative act of God in respect to *disobe-*

dient subjects of his law, but to the authoritative act of human judges in respect to both obedient and disobedient subjects of civil law, in one and the same general meaning. Thus we read in Deut. xxv. 1: "Then shall they (the judges) justify the righteous and condemn the wicked;" in Prov. xvii. 15: "He that justifieth the wicked, and he that condemneth the righteous;" and in Isaiah v. 23: "Who justify the wicked for a reward." Here it is plain that the word *justify* has a meaning common to both cases, to the righteous and the wicked. The word therefore denotes the same act in respect to both—the authoritative act of a judge, determining that a subject of law stands right in relation to its sanctions.

In further confirmation of what has been said, we now refer to the use of the Greek word δικαιόω by the Seventy, in their translation of the Hebrew Scriptures. When they undertook this work, they found no such act on the part of God in respect to obedient subjects of his law, as a right or just judgment *de merito*, or according to the principles of distributive justice. Of course they found no Hebrew word strictly synonymous with the Greek word δικαιόω as a classic word—no Hebrew word used to denote an act of God as the Lawgiver and Judge of men, determining *obedient* subjects of his law to stand right in relation to its sanctions. Yet they found a prominent and peculiar fact in divine revelation, and also a word for it; and one which, had the facts been the same, would have been used as strictly synonymous with the Greek word. This fact is the authoritative act of God determining some of *the disobedient* subjects of his law to stand right in relation to its sanctions; to denote which, the Greek word in some of its Greek meanings would, according to the laws of usage which regulate such changes, be used by the translators. For the universal law of usage in such cases is, not to coin a new word to denote the difference in things, but to use an old one which had already been applied to that which in some essential respects is the same thing as that to be designated, and in such a modified or restricted meaning as the exigency requires. By this law of usage, the Greek translators of the Old Testament were led in the present and many other cases to employ Greek words in so much and only so much of their Greek meaning as would express Hebrew ideas or conceptions, on substantially the same or similar subjects. This use of words by the Seventy, is the principal source of the Hebrew idiom of the Greek language, or of Hellenistic Greek, which so prevails in the New Testament. Accordingly, the Hebrew fact and conception of the fact in the case under consideration, being as we have stated, these translators instead of using the word δικαιόω in its full generic forensic meaning in which the Greeks had used it, were unavoidably led by the law of usage to employ the word in a meaning conformed to the Hebrew fact and Hebrew conception of the fact. They found the Hebrew word corresponding with the Greek word when used forensically, so applied to an authoritative act of God and to certain authoritative acts of men, as to show that it was used in a very different meaning as a general term from the classic meaning of the Greek word. They were not only under the necessity of translating the Hebrew by its corresponding Greek word, but of conforming to the Hebrew meaning in this use; i. e., they were under the necessity of using the Greek word δικαιόω, to denote in its general forensic meaning, *the authoritative act of a judge, determining the subject of law to stand right in relation to the sanctions of law.*

What has been said is deemed sufficient to show, not only in what meaning the Hebrew word in the Old Testament and the Greek word in the Septuagint which we translated by the word *justify*, are employed when used forensically, but also in what meaning the Greek word when thus employed is used in the New Testament. No one doubts that the Greek of the New Testament is Hellenistic; that is, classic Greek so modified in the use of important words as to express Hebrew ideas or conceptions. From this it follows that the Greek word δικαιόω when used by Christ and his apostles forensically, denotes nothing more and nothing less in its generic import, than *the authoritative act of a judge, determining that a subject of law stands right in relation to the sanctions of law.*

The same thing will follow from admitting that the Greek word δικαιόω is correctly translated by the English word *justify*. This is indeed an argument only with those who admit the correctness of this translation. And yet there are so many even among Protestants, who deny or doubt on this point, that the argument for our purpose ought not to be omitted. Assuming then the correctness of the translation of the Greek word by the English word *justify*, the only question is, what is its generic forensic meaning? And it will not be pretended that it does not include all that which I have said constitutes this, viz., the authoritative act of a judge determining a subject of law to stand right in relation to the sanctions of law. Does it then include any thing more? Does it denote and so determine the personal character of the subject? This cannot be true. For the act of Justification, as every one knows, under mere law, and according to the strict principles of law, supposes a previous trial and decision or judgment respecting the personal character of the subject. On this the act of Justification is, and must in the case supposed, be founded. It is true that in a known case of *equitable judgment* under mere law, the Justification of the subject is proof of his personal obedience to law. One fact implies the other as the effect implies its cause. But the one is as distinct from the other, as the trial is from the judgment founded upon it. Nor is the inference respecting personal character authorized by the mere fact of Justification. Other facts, viz., that the judgment is made under mere law and that it is a just judgment, must be known to authorize the inference respecting the personal character of the subject. Besides, as we have seen, there may be a full and perfect Justification, whatever be the personal character of the subject. Prov. xvii. 15: "He that justifieth the wicked," &c. In short, as the word is properly applied to the act of God justifying the disobedient, and to that of the human judge in justifying both the obedient and disobedient, it is plain that the word can not denote an act of a judge done according to the personal deserts of the subject, nor according to the principles of either distributive or general justice, but only an authoritative act of a judge determining a subject of law to stand right in relation to the sanctions of law.

The same thing may be abundantly shown from the usage of the New Testament. It is sufficient to refer to the epistles of Paul, who so largely treats the subject, especially in his Epistle to the Romans and that to the Galatians. The prominent design of the apostle is, to deny that any are justified by works of law, and to assert that some are justified by faith; or that disobedient subjects (sinners) and none others who believe, are justified. He thus with the most studious precision of language denies one and the self-same thing (actual Justification) in connection with works of law, or with obedience to law, which he asserts in connection with faith without works. The word *Justification*, when he asserts Justification not to be by works of law, cannot be specifically Justification according to the principles of distributive justice, or the personal deserts of the subject; for he asserts the self-same thing to be by faith without works, or without obedience to law; which of course cannot be according to the principles of distributive justice. Nor can the word Justification be used in any more specific meaning so far as the mere word is concerned, than that which might be predicated of a human though unjust judge, whatever it might be *inferred* to mean from the character of God, had the apostle actually predicated of God what he denies, viz., the act of justifying the obedient. He had no occasion to use the word in this connection in any other than its generic forensic sense, since to deny the act in this, is virtually to deny it in every subordinate specific sense. Nor could he employ it in any other with truth, for he uses it in a common meaning in two cases, denying Justification by works of law, and asserting Justification by faith. If therefore he intends either more or less by *Justification* in one case than in the other, then the meaning of his language properly interpreted cannot be true. He could not be understood to mean in the former case a *meritorious* Justification, without being understood to intend it in the latter, which is plainly absurd and impossible. He could not be understood to mean, as some suppose, merely pardon in the latter, without being understood to intend merely pardon in the former, which would also be plainly absurd and impossible. What then must he be understood to mean by the word in both cases, except an act of the judge which is common to both,—an authoritative act of the judge, determining the subject of law to stand relatively right in respect to its sanctions?

Inference.—From this view of the general forensic meaning of the word Justification, I infer, contrary to the opinion of some, that Justification is not exactly synonymous with *pardon* or *forgiveness.* Justification, as we have seen, designates nothing in regard to the personal character of the subject; while the words pardon and forgiveness expressly recognize his previous sin. It is true indeed, that in most instances in the New Testament, the term *Justification* when applied to men is used in such a connection as distinctly shows their previous sin. Thus *Justification by faith, justified by grace, justified without the deeds of the law, justifieth the ungodly*, are phrases which recognize the sin of the subject,—a necessary combination of terms for the purpose, which clearly shows that the mere word *justify* does not designate and is not intended to designate the same fact. By this however, I do not intend to say that the mere word asserts or implies that the subject is *not* a sinner; but simply that the term itself does not decide either that he is or that he is not. To say *that one is justified*, merely expresses his right relation to the sanctions of law, as this results from and is determined by the authoritative act of the Judge.

But while the term *Justification* does not express or imply the particular idea of pardon or forgiveness, either of these terms under a perfect moral administration, implies all that Justification denotes. Under the imperfect governments of men, pardons, as terms are used, are mere arbitrary acts—acts often of mere State policy or of favoritism, as opposed to every principle of justice or equity. The prerogative to pardon is the result only of the fallibility of the supreme tribunal, and proceeds entirely, when unperverted, on the assumed innocence of the pardoned subject, and is only, in this view of it, placing the subject right in relation to legal sanctions; i. e., justifying him as an obedient subject. Human governments however, in their palpable violations of the principles of Moral Government, furnish neither precise examples of things, nor of words, under a perfect moral administration. In these violations, for which they must have names to conceal their nature, they may remit penalty without regarding the remission as restoring the subject to the fullness of that relation to the sanctions of law which is secured by obedience, and this may be called *a pardon*. The offender may be a prime minister, or a military commander whose influence and power may render his punishment inexpedient, but who, though *pardoned*, is nevertheless not considered as justified; i. e., as standing in the same relation to legal sanctions in which he would have stood without transgression. He is restored to some or many of the immunities of an obedient subject.* But he cannot be *properly* said to be *justified;* certainly not, merely as *pardoned*. The reason that he cannot, is, that the terms are not

* We have an illustration in the permission given to Absalom to return to Jerusalem, but not to see the king's face (2 Samuel xiv. 32).

strictly synonymous. He is not considered as sustaining the same relation to the sanctions of law as had he not violated it. He is not *justified* in any proper sense of the word. He is partially or wholly exempted from punishment, while every principle of law or of justice demands it. There is a dispensation which provides a middle state for a subject of law between punishment and reward—a dispensation which abandons law by recognizing the subject as sustaining in fact no legal relation; for it neither restores him to the standing of an obedient subject, nor treats him as a transgressor. It simply exempts him from punishment as one who is lawless by privilege. This may be called a pardon for want of a better term; but to identify it with a pardon granted under a perfect moral administration, is a burlesque. Such an anomaly of legal procedure in heaven's judicatory, and such looseness in the use of language resulting from it, are unknown. Under a perfect Moral Government no transgressor can be pardoned without a full recognition of his relation to law as its subject, and a full manifestation of its sustained authority in the grant. God's law knows no middle ground on which its subject can stand between condemnation and Justification—no intervening allotment or condition at last, but the endurance of its penalty or the enjoyment of its immunities. There is therefore no redemption from punishment to him, who is not, with all the principles of law, supported in a state of acceptance with God, —no pardon without Justification. The act of God which pardons, also justifies, and the act of God which justifies, also pardons.

With this view of the generic forensic meaning of the word Justification, which as a juridical act is alike applicable to God and to man, I now propose to show more particularly what is this act of God as the Moral Ruler and Judge of men. In giving this general forensic definition of the word, I have perhaps defined it with sufficient particularity for most speculative and practical purposes. And yet in my view, it is highly important to describe it with more of that fullness of import in which it is constantly presented to us in the Scriptures, that by giving it greater precision we may exclude those errors from the whole subject, which since the early ages of the Christian Church have been, and still are, more or less connected with it.

The human mind is ever prone to view forensic Justification, i. e., Justification in which the full authority of law is recognized, as a strictly legal act; an act according to the mere principles of law; an act *de merito*. The earliest sacrifices, which had their origin evidently in divine institution, were sacrifices for sin. I need not say how difficult to prevent their perversion, even under the light of divine revelation. These rites were perpetuated *by tradition* among the earliest heathen nations, and were thus perpetuated, though not to the utter exclusion of all ideas of sin, or of sin in the conscience, yet as an equivalent for the obedience not rendered to law; or the sin committed, and as such an equivalent were supposed to invest the offerer with the same legal claim—the same claim *de merito*, as had he not sinned. This was the view of the people of Israel when delivered from Egypt, which was ineffectually corrected under the Mosaic dispensation, and which, when this dispensation was done away by the Messiah, had become almost universally prevalent. Since the establishment of Christianity in this dark world, this error in its essential nature or principle, as representing or viewing Justification before God as a strictly *legal* act—an act *de merito*, or according to the legal merit of the subject—is scarcely less apparent. In this false principle men are confirmed, not only by their pride and self-gratulation, but by its early and familiar application in civil, and to a great extent in parental government. Hence to distinguish the forensic act of God in justifying, from that of a human judge, and to familiarize the difference to the minds of men, is important in proportion as it is difficult and unusual. Perhaps every other serious error on the general subject might be traced to that to which we have now adverted, as its true source. Thus in the Romish doctrine, the principle *de merito* is formally avowed. To what extent it has been made practical by the Romish hierarchy need not be said. Or if we examine closely the doctrine of the Reformation, which is claimed to be so directly opposed to the principle of merit or to the strict principles of law, the doctrine of Justification by faith only, what is it as fully unfolded in its more prevalent form of the *Imputation* of Christ's righteousness—of what is called his active and passive obedience to the believer, and made *his* righteousness by *a mystical union* with Christ, so that it becomes as really *his* righteousness, as would be his own personal perfect obedience to law in heart and life, and as *his* invests *him* in every respect in which such obedience would invest him with a claim *de merito*—what is this but a claim to Justification solely according to the principles of law, not only those of general but also of *distributive* justice? But without dwelling on these or other reasons for so doing, I now proceed to confirm the answer already given to our leading inquiry, or to show that

Justification as the act of God in the relation of the Lawgiver and Judge of men is an authoritative act—making, causing, determining a disobedient subject of his law to stand relatively right in respect to its sanctions; not according to the principles of distributive justice, but according to the principles of general justice and of general benevolence.

When I speak of the meaning of the word in this particular application to God, I would guard against one misapprehension. In all such cases, it is to be remembered that what in the common way of speaking is called the particular meaning of a general term, is not strictly speaking the meaning of the mere word; but rather that of the writer or speaker, as this is shown by the connection and manner of use in each case. Hence what is commonly called the particular meaning of the word *justify*, when applied to God as the Judge of men, is that which is the meaning of the writer as shown by the word and by its connection, by the nature of the subject, or by any thing else which is good evidence of his meaning. With this remark in mind, and according to the only principles or laws of interpretation applicable to the case, I now propose to establish the view above given of the act of God under consideration.

The controlling principle or law of usage and interpretation in all cases like the present, and the one on which I rely is, that whether a general term is to be understood in any meaning other than the most general, depends on evidence furnished by the known nature of the subject, the connection and manner of use, and that the particular meaning is to be determined by such evidence in each particular case.

According to this principle, the following things are deemed undeniable and incontrovertible:

First—If we could suppose the word justify, or Justification, or any equivalent word, to be so used in the Scriptures that we could not decide it to be employed in one meaning rather than another, then we must understand it in its most general meaning, as this has ever been controlled and determined in all languages, when referring to a system of law and grace. According to what has been said, there would in this case be decisive evidence of this, and of no further or other meaning. Its classic use would be changed, as already explained.

Secondly—If we suppose the word to be so employed that we can decide nothing more than that it is used *forensically*, then we can decide nothing to be meant beyond an authoritative act of a judge, determining that a subject of law stands right in relation to its sanctions; or that he is to be exempted from the legal penalty and secured in a legal reward. But in such a case we could not decide whether the judge were God or man; whether the subject were obedient or disobedient to law; whether the act of Justification were strictly conformed to a system of mere law, or were modified by a system of grace; whether it were according to the principles of distributive and general justice and of general benevolence, or whether some or all of those principles were not dispensed with or violated. Any one of these questions must be decided, if at all, on other grounds than the mere *forensic* use of the word *justify*.

Thirdly—If we suppose the evidence to require the assumption of the perfect character of the judge, and that the act of justifying is under a system of mere law, then we must understand the act to respect an obedient subject of law, and to be according to the principles of distributive and general justice, and also of general benevolence.

Fourthly—If we have no authorized belief respecting the character of the judge, and suppose the act of justifying to be under a system of mere law, then we cannot decide whether the subject be obedient or disobedient to law, nor whether the act be in accordance with the above principles, or in violation of them.

Fifthly—If we suppose the facts in the last case, with this difference only, that the subject is *disobedient* to law, then the act of justifying is in violation of the foregoing principles.

Sixthly—And without supposing all the variety of cases which are supposable, if we have proof that the Lawgiver and Judge is perfect in moral character, that he administers his Moral Government under a system of law and grace (and through an Atonement), and justifies a *disobedient* subject of his law, then we are bound to regard the act as done, not indeed according to the principles of distributive justice, but consistently with the principles of general justice and of general benevolence. I say, *not according to the principles of distributive justice.* That a *disobedient* subject of law should be justified, and at the same time be treated according to the principles of distributive justice, is impossible in the nature of things. To treat him according to the principles of distributive justice, or according to his personal deserts, is to punish him by the infliction of the full legal penalty. To suppose him at the same time to be justified, is to suppose him to be exempted from the legal penalty. To suppose both, is to suppose him to be punished and not punished by the infliction of the penalty. That such a conception or notion of the fact is expressed by any language of the sacred writers is incredible. No theory of *Imputation* or of *Putation*, nor any other theory, hypothesis, or supposition, involving this idea or conception of truth or fact on their part, can ever be made to consist with their common sense or with their use of language, and what is more, with their inspiration. Nor is there any thing in the case supposed, which requires that the act of *justifying a disobedient subject* should be according to *the principles of distributive justice;* nor even to give the faintest plausibility to this conception of it. Distributive justice as we have before shown, is not an *essential* attribute of a perfect moral ruler and judge *in all cases;* but *only* under a system of *mere law.* Or thus, while it is necessary that such a Ruler should treat his subjects according to the principles of distributive justice in all cases under a system of mere law, it is not necessary that he should so treat them under a system of law and grace combined in one by a complete Atonement. Justice as an essential attribute in such a Ruler, *in all cases* is *general justice*, or an immutable disposition or purpose prompted by benevolence, to uphold the authority of law as indispensable to the general good. This is the only attribute which, under the name of *justice*, is essentially involved in the perfect character of a perfect Ruler and Judge.* For his perfect character allows, and even demands, so far as the good of his kingdom is concerned, the dispensing with acts of distributive justice, in all cases in which the good of his kingdom will in this way sustain no injury, and be on the whole increased. Under a system of grace through a perfect Atonement, the act of justifying the disobedient subject becomes consistent with his authority; that is, consistent with justice as an attribute essential to his honor and glory, and becomes, on condition of the faith or personal holiness of the subject, consistent with and dictated by general benevolence toward his kingdom. Thus it appears that in the case now supposed, we are bound to regard *the act of justifying a disobedient subject* on the part of a Moral Ruler and Judge, as done, not according to the principles of distributive justice, but those of general justice and general benevolence.

The facts in God's moral administration are in entire coincidence with those supposed in this last case. In view of what has been said in former lectures, we are bound on the authority of reason and of revelation to assume, that God is the Lawgiver and Judge of men; that he is a being of absolute natural and moral perfection; that he administers his Moral Government over men under an economy of law and of grace—i. e., through an Atonement which fully sustains his authority as a Lawgiver, establishes his law as a rule of action on the part of his subjects, and thus meets all the demands of general justice; that he makes personal holiness, or what, as could easily be shown, is in the Scriptures called Faith, the condition of justifying the disobedient; and that thus dispensing with the principles of distributive justice—that is, without treating his disobedient subjects according to their personal deserts—he fully manifests and honors his justice as an essential attribute of a perfect Moral Governor through an Atonement; and by making personal holiness or faith the condition of Justification of the disobedient, alike manifests his perfect benevolence in preventing evil in the form of sin and its penalty, and securing good in the holiness and happiness of a redeemed kingdom.

Such are the views of God, of his character, and of his moral

---

* Both *distributive* and *commutative* justice are *circumstantial* rather than *essential* attributes; the one depending on a system of mere law, the other on gratuitous promise (1 John i. 9).

administration over men, which they are not only authorized but required by abundant proofs to entertain, and by which they are bound to be governed in deciding *what is the act of God in justifying men as the subjects of his law.*

We have seen that it must be *not an act of Sanctification*, but an act of God as a Judge, or a forensic act, determining a subject of his law to stand right in relation to its sanctions. It cannot be less than this, and must, in view of what has been said, be more. What more? It cannot be such an act of God, determining *an obedient* subject of his law to stand right in relation to its sanctions, for there is no such subject of his law among men. It cannot be such an act of God done in accordance with the principles of *distributive justice*, but must necessarily involve the entire dispensing with these principles; for according to them, *the disobedient* subject of law must be condemned. But as an act of a perfect God, it must be done consistently with general justice; for this is an essential and unchangeable attribute of God as a perfect Moral Ruler and Judge. It must also, as the act of such a being, be done according to the principles of general benevolence, for in this consists the moral perfection of his character.

Thus it appears *that Justification as an act of God in the relation of Lawgiver and Judge of men, is an authoritative act—making, causing, or determining a disobedient subject of his law to stand relatively right in respect to its sanctions; not according to the principles of distributive justice, but according to the principles of general justice and of general benevolence.*

IV.

ELECTION.

I.—EXPLANATION OF THE DOCTRINE.

"But the election hath obtained it."—*Romans* xi. 7.

It is conceded by all Christians, that the Bible contains a doctrine of Election. What this doctrine is, however, is a question which has occasioned much diversity of opinion, and none too little of the bitterness of controversy, even among the sincere disciples of Christ. And here I must be permitted to say, that writers and preachers, not content to state simply *the plain matter of fact* as the Bible does, have often incorporated with their statements of this doctrine what does not belong to it, and is inconsistent with the plainest truths of the Bible, as well as with the dictates of common sense.

The true scriptural doctrine of Election may be presented so as to be free from all difficulties and absurdities. Not only so, it may be shown to be a doctrine of the most salutary practical tendency; directly fitted to augment the power of other truths; adapted to sanctify, to strengthen, to comfort and perfect the saints, and to rouse the sinner to instant, direct, and decisive effort in the work of his salvation; and therefore, both the saint and sinner, if they have any wise regard to their highest, best interests, will believe and welcome it.

I do not indeed suppose, that any exhibition of this doctrine, however clear and consistent it may be, will be sufficient in actual fact to put an end to all caviling and objection. This were too much to hope for in respect to any doctrine which so humbles man and exalts God. Still it can not be denied, that in some minds there are real difficulties on this subject; and that many things are often said on both sides, which ought with becoming firmness to be denied and exploded, as false and of evil tendency. We preachers are not infallible, nor yet our hearers; and in respect to the field of theological difficulties, not unfrequently "fools rush in where angels fear to tread." Still, the Scriptures contain a doctrine of Election, and all

Scripture is profitable, and he who bears God's commission must not keep back God's counsel. We fear the lightning of his indignation if we do this.

My object in the present discourse is explanation chiefly, believing that this is needed more than labored and protracted argument, and that I can so present this doctrine in its connection with other scriptural truths, that we shall be of one mind respecting it.

For this purpose I shall consider the doctrine—

I. As comprising a simple matter of fact, in which I think all Christians will agree; and—

II. As it is related to, or connected with, other doctrines or truths.

I. The simple *matter of fact* which I would state, and which constitutes the entire doctrine of Election, is this: THAT GOD HAS ETERNALLY PURPOSED TO RENEW, AND SANCTIFY, AND SAVE A PART ONLY OF MANKIND.

Here it may be well to distinguish this statement of the doctrine of Election, from some other forms of presenting it.

First—It is palpably distinct from the doctrine of *a national election*, or an election of certain nations or communities to peculiar external privileges. That the Scriptures teach such a doctrine is admitted. But it is maintained that this is not the only doctrine of Election which they teach. Pelagians, Arminians, and indeed all who oppose the Orthodox doctrine, maintain that a national election, particularly the election of the Jewish nation to peculiar external privileges, is the only scriptural doctrine of Election which has any relation to, or connection with the salvation of men. That which the Orthodox maintain is a very different doctrine.

Secondly—The Orthodox doctrine is not an Election to salvation, or a purpose of God to save *on condition of repentance and faith, as uncertain and unknown events*, as maintained by some Pelagian and Arminian writers.

Thirdly—The Orthodox doctrine is not, that God has purposed to save a part of mankind *on condition of foreseen repentance and faith.* Though it is not inconsistent with it to maintain this doctrine in some sense of the language—though it is undeniably true that God has determined or purposed to save all those who he foresees will repent and believe, yet this is not the Orthodox doctrine of Election properly so called; nor by any means all that they believe respecting God's purpose to save a part of mankind. This is not merely a purpose to *save*, or a purpose to give eternal life on condition of faith and repentance, that is, of personal holiness. It is, if spoken of in relation to salvation, as it commonly is, a more comprehensive doctrine, viz., a purpose to *renew*, *sanctify*, and save a part only of mankind.

Leaving all other points for the present as being no part of the doctrine, I only state in this place *a matter of fact*, and one in which all who are not Universalists, and who believe in the necessity of God's grace to renew the heart, must agree. For if we are not Universalists, we believe that a part only of mankind will be saved. If we believe in the necessity of divine influence to change the heart, in other words, that holiness in man is the gift of God, we must believe that God *purposes* to give a new heart or holiness to all to whom he does give it; and that if he begins the work, and carries it on, and finishes it in eternal glory, he *designed* to do what he does. For who will say that God ever acts without design; that he does any thing without intending to do it? Is that grace of the Holy Spirit which is to produce, perpetuate, and bless God's redeemed kingdom, directed by chance? Does ignorance or fate sit at the helm of the universe and sway its destinies? Are we to look forward only to its results, in darkness, terror, and dismay? or is there a designing God on the throne?

Nor will any one who believes that there is a God, hesitate to admit that he is omniscient and immutable. God then knows all his works from the beginning. The purposes of the eternal God are eternal purposes. If God actually renews, sanctifies, and saves a part only of mankind, he always knew that he should, and always designed to do it.

Now I am happy, as I am confident, in the conviction that no one will deny this matter of fact. Whatever diversity of opinion may exist on other parts of this subject, in this plain matter of fact we must agree. We believe that a part only of mankind will be saved. We believe that their hearts will be changed by God's grace, and therefore must believe *that God designs, and has from eternity designed, to change every heart which he does change.*

I need say no more on this point. We all know, and we

all believe, that if God has made us Christians he meant to do it; or in the language of the apostle, "of his *own will* begat he us." Without a feeling or a note of discord, Presbyterians, Episcopalians, Baptists, Methodists, are ready to join in the song, "Not unto us, O Lord, not unto us, but unto thy name give glory."

I now proceed to consider—

II. The doctrine of Election in its connection with some other doctrines or truths. Among these are the following:

1. That *Christ died for all men.* He died as truly for one as for another; for the non-elect as for the elect. "He gave himself a ransom for all." "He is a propitiation for our sins; and not for ours only, but for the sins of the whole world." The sacrifice on Calvary has done this. There, on that hill, the Son of God dies; and as he bows his head and exclaims, "It is finished," on earth and in heaven there is nothing great beside. Thus this world's Atonement is made. And now the message of divine mercy is sent forth to every dweller on the face of the whole earth, and its generous annunciation is, "The spirit and the bride say, come; and let him that heareth say, come; and let him that is athirst, come; and whosoever will, let him take the water of life freely." Abundant provision then is made for the salvation of every human being.

2. *All will be saved, if they will repent and believe the Gospel.* The promise of life and the threatening of death are not made to men as elect or non-elect, but as penitent or impenitent, believing or unbelieving. To all who will repent and believe, the promise of life is sure. They have the oath of God for this.

3. *All men can repent and believe.* All are free moral agents, as fully qualified to choose right as to choose wrong. Nothing therefore can prevent their compliance with the terms of life, but their own free, voluntary perverseness in sin. Neither the want of renewing grace, nor the purpose of God not to give it, can prevent, for they are fully qualified to comply without grace. Suppose a servant will not obey his master unless he gives him his estate in addition to his wages; whose fault is it? Who would say that the not giving of the estate prevented the servant's obedience? Plainly he could, and therefore ought to have obeyed without the gift. So the want of grace does not prevent the sinner's repentance, for this

plain reason, he can repent without grace. Let him do what he can and he performs all his duty, for God requires him to love only with all his strength. Let him do what he can, and a universe cannot prevent his repentance. Whether there is any grace for him or not, he is a moral agent, and let him not blame God because he himself will not do what he can and ought to do, even his whole duty.

4. It is the will of God, or his unqualified preference, that *all men should comply with the terms of life rather than continue in sin.* He is "not willing," saith the apostle, "that any should perish, but that all should come to repentance." By the same authority we are told, that he "will have all men to be saved and come to the knowledge of the truth." And again by the mouth of his prophet: "As I live, saith the Lord, I have no pleasure in the death of the wicked, but that the wicked turn from his way and live." And yet again: "Have I *any* pleasure *at all* that the wicked should die, saith the Lord God, and not that he should return from his ways and live?" Now observe here, that we are not told what *God will do* or *will not do*, but what he would that *men should do.* It is not said that God WILL BRING all men to repentance, but that it is his will that they SHOULD COME to repentance; not that *he will turn* the wicked from his way, but that it is his pleasure that the wicked himself *should turn*, rather than go on in sin and die. This is what he says when he could swear by no greater, swearing by himself. Can there be any mistake here? Is the language ambiguous? Is the oath of God false? No. God would that all men, elect or non-elect, should turn and live, rather than sin and die.

I am not saying *that God will change the appointed system of influence*, or in other words, do those things which may be necessary to secure the repentance of the non-elect sinner. To do this, to change in the least the influence which he in his wisdom has appointed to be used with each, would be worse than to leave the sinner to his choice under the influence appointed. It would result in more evil than good. This principle is distinctly laid down and applied by our Lord to this very subject, when he teaches us that it were better to leave the tares among the wheat rather than to destroy the wheat by pulling up the tares. So a kind father may most sincerely and earnestly desire the return of a disobedient son to his duty and his home. But it by no means follows that he will, or that he ought to do all that he can, and all that may be necessary, to secure the return of the prodigal. This might occasion the disobedience and ruin of all his other children, or occasion some other evil that would be worse than to leave the prodigal to his own perverseness. So God will not change the degree of influence which his wisdom has appointed, for the sake of bringing sinners to repentance; he will not occasion a greater evil to prevent a less. Still God does all that he can wisely do to bring every sinner to repentance; he does this at every moment of his probation; he does it with the yearnings of the tenderest father, yea with the compassion of a God; he desires, he longs, that under the influence he uses, every sinner should repent and live, rather than sin another moment.

5. *Not a human being will comply with the terms of life without divine grace.* Abundant as is the provision for the salvation of all, unqualified as are the overtures of pardon and life, free as men are from all preventing influence from God, abundantly able as they are as moral agents to comply with the terms of salvation, and willing, yea solicitous as God is that they should comply and be saved, not one will do it. Left to themselves, each and all of them will persist in rejecting Christ, and by their own choice plunge into perdition. I wish you to look at this world of sinners in this condition. Nothing but voluntary, willful perverseness can ruin one of them. Yet with all that eternal mercy has done, with the same powers and faculties in kind which angels possess, yea, made in this respect in the very image of God (Jas. iii. 9), and invited and allured by all the entreaties and proffers of redeeming grace—in defiance of all the motives a universe can furnish—they will go down to hell, if the interposing grace of God does not prevent.

6. In the midst of all this darkness, with no prospect before the whole race but that of self-ruin, *God interposes with the purpose of Election.* He not only prefers that all should repent and be saved rather than sin and die, but he purposes that some *shall repent and be saved.* He is not willing that his beloved Son should die in vain, and see no reward for his agonies and death; nor can he consent that all these creatures of his power and objects of his love, perverse as they are, should remain in eternal alienation and exile from his friendship. He

who knew how to create mind, knows how to influence it in a way that accords with its nature, and with the nature of free moral action. He resolves therefore to interpose, so far as he wisely can, with such an influence—one which is over, and above, and distinct from the influence of truth and motives, even the power of his Spirit, and by this to overcome the perverseness of a part of our guilty race. His purpose is not to save them from any physical necessity—from any compulsory power that pushes them onward to perdition against their will; but to save them from going down to the pit by their own free choice, and by an influence which he knows exactly how to use for the purpose, to bring them to choose life just as freely as they now choose death. And this he resolves to do, after having done every thing in the form of motive, persuasion, and entreaty worthy of God, to prevent their ruin, and done it in vain.

There is one thing more in respect to this purpose of God, to which I request particular attention, as constituting the key to all the difficulties on the subject.

7. *God purposes to secure the holiness of as many of his moral creatures as it is possible in the nature of things that he should secure.*

That we may see this clearly, I remark that *a moral system is the best conceivable system.* No other creative act could so unfold the wisdom and power of God as that which gives existence to moral beings. No other creatures could so resemble God himself. Without them, the ascending scale of being from mere animal existence toward God himself had been a chasm; the universe a solitary waste, exhibiting only the barren magnificence of rocks and deserts. Moral beings alone can contrive, design, and produce good to any extent worthy of notice. How imperfect would be a system in which mere animal sensation should take the place of holy affections and holy activity, with all their blessedness; in which there should be no acts of intelligent communion between the Creator and his creatures; no acts of kindness done by God to intelligent recipients; no song of praise returning the testimonies of gratitude to a divine benefactor; no oneness of purpose nor acts of mutual co-operation; no beings with capacities to discern between right and wrong—between God and other objects of affection; none to admire, to adore, to love, to trust, to enjoy God; and God sitting on his throne the solitary spectator of the laws of matter and of the acts of instinct. But what magnificence is there in a moral system! Here are beings which no man can number created in God's image; fit to correspond with God; meet for immortality; qualified to be workers together with God to advance his designs, and to be one with him amid the scenes and grandeurs of eternity. We say that such a system is the best, and that infinite benevolence must adopt it.

Again: *No beings can be so happy as perfectly holy beings*, and of course, no kingdom so happy as that in which should reign the purity and the joys of perfect and universal holiness. This we know. We know from the nature of the mind, that holiness and not sin is the necessary means of the highest conceivable happiness. A perfectly holy mind is perfectly blessed. We know it from the character of God. To be like God in character, is to be like God in blessedness. We know it from the nature of his law. God's law requires the best kind of moral action, and perfect obedience to it is perfection in character and in happiness. We know it from the nature of sin. Sin is evil in itself, in its nature; evil in all its tendencies, wholly evil. Sin is hell. God therefore, as a benevolent God, must purpose to produce the greatest amount of holiness which he can. For who will say that a benevolent God will not do all the good possible for him to do?

Besides, *What is the law of God if it is not an expression of his will*, i. e., of his preference of holiness to sin? God give a law, and not prefer that his subjects should obey rather than disobey! It were an imposition and a mockery,—a burlesque on all legislation. But it is said "he prefers holiness to sin in itself considered, but sin to holiness all things considered." And what is this? I will tell you what it is. It is as if a father should say to his child, "Be honest, and true, and sober, this is my law—this the rule by which you shall be judged;" but then adds, "I prefer on the whole, all things considered, that you should cheat, and lie, and get drunk, rather than be honest, and true, and sober." Such is God as some would have us believe! He would rather, so they tell us, that men, all things considered, should do wrong than do right! God himself the minister of sin! No. God prefers, all things considered, that men should do right; fully obey his perfect law rather than sin once. Will he not then do all that is possible for him to do, to secure the entire holiness of the greatest number of moral subjects? Hear his own declaration: "What could have been done more to my vineyard that I have not done in it?" Deny this, and you make God the friend, approver, and patron of sin.

But we are told that "*sin is the necessary means of the greatest good.*" And can this be so? Sin the best kind of moral action! To rebel against God the best thing a man can do! To hate God, and angels, and men, and to act accordingly! This the best way to bless the universe! Must some men become devils, to glorify God and make his creation happy? But it is said, "If there had been no sin, God could never have glorified his mercy in redemption." It is true indeed that God could never have redeemed from sin if there had been no sin. But what kind of mercy is that which produces evil merely for the sake of putting an end to it? Does a kind father push his children into a pit, or down a precipice, for the sake of showing how merciful he can be in bringing deliverance and in healing their broken bones? Does a benevolent God design, and so order his providence, that our whole race shall fall into the gulf of sin and ruin, for the sake of showing his mercy in their rescue; and this when he could as well have preserved them and all other beings in the purity and joys of perfect holiness forever? Or does it better accord with God's character to suppose, that when men have freely plunged themselves into this ruin, against his law and against his will, God *then* comes in the glory of his mercy to redeem and save? This were indeed work for mercy—for God's mercy; and what else deserves the name? Push your children over the precipice; then fly to their relief, and tell them that you have broken their bones and mangled their flesh for the sake of showing them how merciful you could be in restoring them again to health and soundness! Call this mercy if you will; but Oh, ascribe not such mercy to our God!

It is also said, that "*the sin and sufferings of the lost are necessary to the highest happiness of the saved.*" But can it be? God doom some of his creatures to everlasting sin and everlasting fire, as the necessary means of higher happiness to another portion, which otherwise they could not possess! Are celestial spirits made happier by the smoke of the torment of the damned, than they possibly could have been had there been no sin? Do they actually praise and thank God for that peculiar delight—those higher and exquisite raptures which they derive from the sins and agonies of others in everlasting burnings? Would not these benevolent spirits—would not God, think you, have gladly dispensed with these peculiar joys, and been satisfied with the perfect holiness and perfect happiness of his moral creation? Or must there be sin, with all its turpitude, and groans, and anguish, that God and other holy beings may be perfectly happy? Who shall prove, that were the moral universe a heaven of perfect holiness—and of course of perfect blessedness—it would not be a happier universe than one with a hell in it? Look up to the paradise of God, and then down on the lake of fire, and say, had there been no sin, and no necessity for punishment—had all been like God in character, whether the universe had not been perfectly happy? Who then shall say that God could secure such a result, and secure it for eternity, and yet would not?

But I shall be told that this is *denying God's omnipotence*—limiting his power. I reply, that it is not limiting the power of God to say that he cannot accomplish impossibilities. Omnipotence is not power to make a thing to be and not to be at the same time. The question then is, not whether God is omnipotent, but whether there is not an impossibility in the very nature of things, that God should secure universal holiness in his moral kingdom? Every subject of such a kingdom must be a free agent; i. e., he must possess the power to sin, and to continue in sin, in defiance of all that God can do to prevent him. If God destroys this power, he destroys his moral agency, and then even God cannot make him holy. With this power, he can set at defiance all influence from truth and motives—from the spirit and power of God, and go on in sin. How do you know, how can you prove that he will not do this—that he will *not* do what he *can* do? If he should do what he can do, God could not prevent his sinning. This would be to suppose that he should sin, and be prevented from sinning, which is a contradiction. But it will be said, "*God does prevent some from sinning; why can he not prevent all?*" I grant God prevents some, and will prevent very many; yea, I will grant that he could have prevented all sin that has existed, and that now exists, and will exist for myriads of ages to come. But suppose this to be done. God must do something which he has not done; something which he has determined not to do; he must change the appointed system of influence (for all the sin that has ever existed would certainly take place under the present system); he must resort, in order to prevent any sin, to some further interpositions than those determined on, and who then could tell the results in eternity? Who can say that the interposition requisite to remove the tares will not destroy the wheat; that if he prevents rebellion in one place, or at one time, it will not break out in worse forms in another? Who can say, that if God were to change his appointed system of influence in one iota; if he were to bring to repentance one sinner whom he has determined not to bring to repentance, that the result would not be the hopeless, and, to him, the irretrievable revolt of the whole moral creation? No one. God knows how to govern better than we can tell him. He can not govern moral beings by physical power, nor by machinery. Moral government is the government of free, uncompelled, voluntary moral agents, and God, if he adopts it, is restricted by its nature and its principles as truly as man is. God knows, as does every wise human legislator, that by securing the loyalty of one, or of a few, he may occasion the hopeless and eternal rebellion of many. Had God used any more influence, or brought one more sinner to repentance than he has, the standard of revolt might be seen waving on the very hills of salvation, and the cry of rebellion be heard triumphant from one end of heaven to the other.

Will it still be said that *I limit God?* No. It is the objector who does this, and in a manner the most dishonorable. He supposes that God can produce more holiness (and as holiness is the best kind of moral action, it follows that he can produce more happiness) than he does or will produce. God, then, does not produce all the good he can. He is not perfectly benevolent; not good enough to bless the universe to the extent of his power. I love and adore a God more who does all the good he can. None else is worthy of my love. Or if you say that *holiness is not, but sin is the best kind of moral action*, still you limit God, for then God can not secure the greatest good without sin as the means of it. And is not this limiting God? God, you say, *can not* secure the greatest good by means of universal holiness. Without sin, and sin enough for the purpose, this great end can not be accomplished. God has not power, in the language of the objector, to do it. Omnipotence itself is weakness here, without sin as the necessary means of this end! Should all perform their duty perfectly and forever, God could not accomplish this high end! If all should do the very thing which God commands them to do, the great end of his creation would be defeated! He must have sin as the means of this end, or the end must fail! He therefore dooms multitudes to endless sin and its miseries, that he may have wherewithal to make the universe perfectly blessed! Such, we are told by some, is the glory of God's omnipotence. He is dependent on the wickedness of men and devils as the only means of accomplishing his purposes. These creatures of God are brought into existence that they may commit all that sin, and bear all that misery which are necessary, that an omnipotent God may bless in the highest degree his moral creation. Is this a basis for confidence and joy under his government, or cause for consternation and dismay?

But to come to the turning-point of this great question—*why is there, why will there be forever, sin and misery under the government of a perfect God?* And here it must be agreed by all who would vindicate the ways of God to man, that there is some limitation in the nature of things, in respect to the production, on the part of the Creator, of perfect unmingled happiness. An infinitely benevolent God would secure such a result were there no such impossibility. To deny such impossibility is to say that God might produce more happiness than he does produce, and this is to deny his benevolence. Here then we must rest. Here all do rest who believe that evil exists and that God is good. The question then is simply this, *where does this impossibility lie; in the nature of sin*, or in *the nature of a moral system?* Is sin so good a thing that God can not produce the greatest good without it? Is that which is wholly an evil—evil in all its tendencies and relations—the best thing as the means of good—even the necessary means of the greatest good? Or is moral agency such a thing that some moral beings who can sin, will sin in despite of all that can be done to prevent them? Which is the most rational; to suppose that what cannot be, is, or to suppose that what can be, should be? Which is the most rational; to suppose that sin, which can not be a good thing, is a good thing, or to suppose that moral agents who can sin, should sin?

God, according to this view of the subject, has adopted *a moral system as the only and the best means of accomplishing the high ends of infinite goodness;* he has adopted it notwithstanding he foresaw that some moral agents would pervert their high powers of moral agency, and that sin and suffering would follow; he purposed these results rather than not adopt the best system, still determining to secure the greatest good in his power, and knowing that the results would make the fullest, brightest manifestation of his attributes in the production of good, which he could make; doing all which was possible, to secure the perfect holiness and happiness of each and of all, consistently with securing the perfect holiness of the greatest number; and doing it with the most unqualified preference of the holiness and happiness of all, to the sin and misery of any; giving to all the strong confirmation of his oath that so it is; calling them to his friendship and favor with all the tenderness of redeeming love, even to brokenness of heart in view of that perverseness which forces upon him the necessity of punishment; and at last giving up the incorrigible to their merited doom, with the sorrows of parental bereavement, because in despite of every effort which his wisdom, and goodness, and grace could make to save them, they would sin and die.

REMARKS.

1. In the view of our subject now taken, *how illustrious an exhibition of the goodness of God is made in the creation and government of moral beings!* The true and just criterion of goodness is the good designed, and not that which is produced. It is no impeachment of a father's kindness, that its results are impaired or prevented by the child's perverseness. The question is, what was the good designed, aimed at, sought? What was the result intended? By this criterion let the goodness of God be estimated. What are the beings created? The most like God which God could make; made in God's image and destined to immortality.

> "Oh, what a patrimony this! a being
> Of such inherent strength and majesty,
> Not worlds possess'd can raise it; worlds destroy'd
> Can't injure; which holds on its glorious course,
> When thine, O Nature, ends."

"There is but one thing," says Augustine, "greater than a

soul, and that one is its Creator." Such in dignity and grandeur are all the myriads of moral beings to whom God has given and will give existence. What now is the real, actual design of God in their creation? To render them one and all like himself in character, and like himself in blessedness. Such is the result designed; such, uncounteracted, had been the actual result; such is the measure of the Creator's goodness. Read, if you would read it aright, read the goodness of God in a moral creation thus holy, thus happy; read it in the purity and joys of universal holiness, and thus answering the "great idea" of Him who made it.

But this world revolted—strange alienation of the thing formed from him who formed it—this world revolted from its Maker. Still, has he relinquished or changed the great design of his goodness toward it? Is it a justly incensed Creator taking vengeance on his revolted creation that we see? No; it is a redeeming God. It is God in Christ reconciling the world to himself. The great design in man's creation is not abandoned. Like the sun it still pours forth its light and warmth on this dark world; counteracted in its results, but still unobscured in its splendors. Resistance only gives new intensity and new luster to its beams. Read this design of God in his unspeakable gift, in the sacrifice that atones for every particle of guilt in this sinful world; read it in the terms of life,—"whosoever will, let him take the water of life freely." Read it in those high powers of yours by which heaven and hell are placed at your own disposal; in those accents of entreaty more tender than angels use. Read it in his oath, that he has no pleasure at all in your death; in that purpose of electing love, formed in view of man's perverseness, to renew and save all that he wisely can; in those proofs of love, those intimations of grace and glory that gladden every moment of life. Read it in the song of angels,—"glory to God in the highest, and on earth peace, good-will—good-will toward men;" in the commission of the swift messenger who bears these glad tidings to all. Read it in the tears of mercy with which Jesus points you to the crown of life; in the stilled tempest of God's wrath and the smiles of his inviting love. Read, Oh, read the design of a redeeming God as you would, were it uncounteracted by sin, and fully accomplished in the everlasting life and glory of all earth's millions. Such, such is God's design, counteracted by sin, but unobscured. Such his goodness, shining still in all its brightness amid the darkness of sin; the heart of infinite love fixed in all its fullness and intensity, and longings of desire on you, O sinner! Sin has not diminished the compassion, the kindness, the love of thy God. Will you not yield to love like this? How could the God who made you, love you more? Can you still resist such a design of God, thy Maker? Is he not good? Is he not sincere? Does he not now desire and long to bless and save you? Sinner, sinner, falling into hell as you are, trust thy God to save thee.

2. With the view given of the doctrine of Election in this discourse, *how overwhelming must be the reflections of the lost sinner!* Why did God elect others to holiness and everlasting life, and not him? Not because God did not as really and as much prefer his repentance and salvation to his impenitence and perdition, as he did theirs. When these things are compared in the case of every sinner, elect or non-elect; when the question is, what God would that sinners should do, his preference is absolute, unqualified; the same in respect to all. "Not willing that any should perish, but that all should come to repentance." Why then elect others, and not him? Not because God desires his sin or his death as the necessary means of good. God has no pleasure that he die, but that he turn and live. Why then elect others, and not him? Not because God cannot bring many sinners, or any individual sinner to repentance, who will be finally lost. Why then elect others, and not him? Because, according to the view that has been given, there is nothing which God can do to bring him to repentance more than he has determined to do, without producing more evil than good; lest in rooting up the tares he should root up the wheat also. Because when God, in the true and proper import of the language, has done all he could to save him, i. e., all he could to save him consistently with securing the greatest number of perfectly holy beings in his moral kingdom, that sinner would persist in sin and die. The purpose of God to save others, has not touched him. God desired not his death, but his repentance and life. God aimed at this, designed it, sought it with the overflowings of infinite love; doing all that infinite love guided by infinite wisdom, could do to reclaim and save the giant rebel. Such are the circumstances, such the condition of every sinner who shall be finally lost;

God doing at every hour and moment of his probation, all that infinite love guided by infinite wisdom, can do to reclaim and save him; God ever ready to welcome him to the embrace of everlasting mercy.

And what is it to persist in sin and perish eternally in circumstances like these? What agonizing reflections await such a self-destroyer! To know, and feel, and say forever, "God made me, that I might be happy. He redeemed me, that I might be happy. He invited and entreated reconciliation, that I might be happy. He opened heaven; he pointed me to that crown of life; he showed me that throne of glory, that I might be happy. He told me of the songs and joys of those ransomed spirits whom I see in the heavens of his glory; he took me as it were in the arms of his love; he held me to the bosom of his mercy; he mourned over me. I saw his heart turn within him, and his repentings kindle together. I heard the sounding of his bowels as he said, 'How shall I give thee up, Ephraim?' But I broke away from the embrace of his mercy and plunged into hell. Yonder in the distance is the paradise of God. I see its holy, happy, acclaiming throng. There I might have been. There God desired I should be. But the great gulf is fixed. Time is no longer. Eternity has begun its ceaseless, rolling ages. In hell I am ruined, self-ruined."

ELECTION.

II.—THE MODE OF EXECUTING THE PURPOSE OF ELECTION.

"Seeing ye have purified your souls, in obeying the truth, through the Spirit."—1 *Pet.* i. 22.

In a former discourse I presented the doctrine of Election, as consisting in this simple matter of fact; viz., that *God has eternally purposed to renew, sanctify, and save a part only of mankind.* I trace the connection of this doctrine with the following scriptural truths; that God, by the Atonement, has made abundant provision for the salvation of every human being; that all will be saved if they comply with the terms of salvation; that all, considered as free moral agents, *can* comply with these terms; that it is the will or purpose of God that all should do so rather than continue in sin; that not a human being will comply without divine grace; that it is in view of this fact of universal self-ruin, that God interposes with the purpose of Election; and that God purposes to secure ultimately the perfect holiness of as many of his moral creatures as it is possible, in the nature of things, he should secure.

The subject now proposed for consideration, is *the manner in which God executes the purpose of Election.*

I know of no single passage of Scripture which so fully exhibits in one combination the material facts on this subject, as the text: "Ye have purified your souls, in obeying the truth through the Spirit." These are the four following:—1. That the change produced in the sinner is his own act: "*Ye have purified your souls.*" 2. That this change is the act of obedience, or right moral action: "Ye have purified your souls in obeying." 3. That the act is in conformity to truth: "Ye have purified your souls in obeying *the truth.*" 4. That the Spirit of God is the author of this change: "Ye have purified your souls in obeying the truth *through the Spirit.*"

I propose briefly to consider these four facts, and by them to test several opinions on the subject before us. The last-mentioned, claims according to the order of things, the first consideration.

1. *The Spirit of God is the author of the change in Regeneration.* I cannot suppose it necessary to dwell on this fact in opposition to Pelagian error, or the proud self-sufficiency of the human heart. The *fact* of divine influence in the production of holiness in the heart of man, meets us as it were on almost every page of the sacred record. What the fact is however, or what it involves in some respects, demands consideration. The necessity of this influence, as we have already said, arises solely from the sinner's perverseness in sin.

Again: *This influence of the Spirit when effectual, is unresisted.* Obedience to truth cannot be produced by compulsory power. Dr. Dwight says of this influence: "It is of such a nature that their wills, instead of attempting any resistance to it, coincide with it readily and cheerfully, without any force or constraint on his part, or any opposition on their own." President Edwards says: "The dispute about grace's being resistible or irresistible is perfect nonsense. For the effect of grace is on the will; so that it is nonsense, unless a man with his will can resist his own will." The Synod of Dort says: "This divine grace of Regeneration does not act upon man like stocks and trees, nor take away the properties of the will, or violently compel it while unwilling; but it spiritually vivifies, heals, corrects, and sweetly and at the same time powerfully inclines it." We have still higher authority. "Except," says the Saviour, "the Father who hath sent me, *draw* him." Mark the language. It is an influence that draws, not compels; which attracts, not forces to duty.

Again: *This influence of the Spirit is distinct from the natural influence of the truth; and though not miraculous, is supernatural.* This fact is asserted in the text and in many other passages of the Scriptures. The change is in view of truth, by the word of truth, and also through the Spirit. The text thus clearly teaches, that by the mere influence of truth and motives, the sinner will not be persuaded to the performance of his duty. The powers of moral suasion, truth, motives, persuasions, warnings, promises, threatenings, eloquence, tears, the hope of heaven and the fear of hell, will not make him yield. "Paul may plant and Apollos water, but God giveth the increase. So then neither is he that planteth, any thing, nor he that watereth, but God who giveth the increase." Every Christian will say, and exult to sing in eternal song, "By the grace of God I am what I am."

2. *The change in Regeneration is the sinner's own act.* "Ye have purified your souls." Could it be said in plainer terms that the act of moral purification was their own? "Ye have purified." Could it be said in plainer terms, ye have done it? If the Bible tells us any thing, if human language can say it, this book tells us that religion in the human heart consists in repenting of sin; in believing on the Lord Jesus Christ. It is breaking off our sins by righteousness; it is making a new heart and a new spirit; it is doing the will of God from the heart; it is ceasing to do evil and learning to do well; it is amending, reforming our ways; it is doing righteousness; it is choosing whom we will serve. In a word, it is loving God; and love is the fulfilling of the law. Can there be a doubt whether this language is a literal description of true religion in the soul of man? Can any better religion, any better change, be conceived of than these? Does this language not describe mental action; the right exercises of the heart? Most undeniably. It ought then to settle this point finally and forever.

But this is not all. How careful are the sacred writers to show us the same fact, even when they describe this change in the strong language of metaphor—the language which is so commonly perverted. It is a *creation;* but it is being created *unto good works.* If there can be a remaining doubt on this point, one text will remove it. "That ye put off the old man, and that ye put on the new man, which after God is created *in righteousness* and true holiness." It is a creation in righteousness and true holiness. And not only so, but Christians are said *to put on the new man;* i. e., *to do* the thing which is said to be created. The thing produced by the power of God is their own act—*the act of putting on the new man.*

To show you that there is nothing novel or peculiar in this sort of theology, I give you the statement of President Edwards on this point. He says, speaking of this change, "God produces all, and we act all. For that is what he produces, viz., OUR OWN ACTS."

3. *The change in Regeneration is a change from wrong to right moral action; it is the act of obedience.* "Ye have purified

your souls in obeying." But as an act of obedience, it is one which God has commanded, and which the sinner is required and bound to perform. The change then in Regeneration is not a physical change; not a change in any of the properties or powers of the soul, but a moral change. It is a change from wrong to right moral action. It is simply the sinner *doing* that identical thing which God requires him to do. But can sinners actually *do* that which God requires, when they do nothing? Can duty consist in merely being acted upon? If God produces any other change in the mind than right moral action—if he produces any effect in which the mind is wholly passive, is this doing any thing on the part of the sinner? Is this obeying God? You may as well say that we obey the moral law of God in being created out of nothing! Nor does this change consist in any thing more than, or in any thing different from, the act of obedience. Look into the Bible. There you will see that what God produces by his Spirit is the very thing which he requires in his commands. God gives a new heart. But his command to sinners is, "Make you a new heart." God works in them to will and to do. But his command is, that they work out their own salvation in willing and doing. God gives repentance. But his command is, "Repent and be converted." Love is the fruit of the Spirit. But the law is, "Thou shalt love the Lord thy God with all thy heart." Thus what God produces in the sinner by his Spirit, is the very thing which he requires in his commands. In giving a new heart, he brings the sinner to exercise those holy, right affections in which a new heart consists. The powers *proximately* exercised in these affections, are the mental powers or faculties of the sinner. It is not God who exercises these affections. A sinner loving God is surely not God loving himself. A sinner repenting of his sins is not God repenting of sin. The sinner must, from the very nature of the case, do all the loving and all the repenting. These moral acts are, and must be the sinner's own moral powers in exercise. Nothing can be moral acts, but moral powers in exercise. The right exercise or act is all his own. In the words of President Edwards, "What God produces are our own acts. It is our act and our duty." The sinner does that through grace which he is competent to do and ought to do without grace. Through grace he does his duty.

4. The fourth fact which I mention as presented in the text is, that the change in Regeneration is *conformity to truth.* "Ye have purified your souls in obeying THE TRUTH." "Of his own will," saith another apostle, "begat he us with the word of truth." And another, "Being born again by the word of God." "The law of the Lord," saith the Psalmist, "is perfect, converting the soul." Such is the testimony of the sacred writers on this point, and there is not a word or a fact in the Scriptures to show that the change in Regeneration ever did or ever will take place, except *through the truth.*

When I say that the change in Regeneration is through the truth, I mean that the mind acts or exercises right affections in view of truth, or of the objects which truth presents. Truth presents the things to be done; the objects, the motives, the reasons, in view of which the mind must act. It tells us what God is, what Christ is, what sin is, what heaven and hell are, what the terms of life are, what man is, and what he must be. It is the light which shows God to the mind in his excellence and glory, as the object of supreme affection, that we may love him. It shows the Lord Jesus mighty to save, and willing, yea solicitous, to save every soul for which he died; and this to call forth a fearless, unfaltering, delightful confidence in him as our Saviour. It shows sin to us in all its turpitude and odiousness, as the governing principle of conduct in our own hearts, that we may abhor and renounce it. It shows us the principle of holiness, in its beauty, dignity, and excellence, that we may assume it as our own and act from it henceforth and forever. It shows us in the man Christ Jesus a perfect model; the most attractive, lovely object in the created universe; a perfect moral character, that we may be like him. It shows us the bright path of duty and the joyous field of holy activity, in which we may do the perfect will of God, live under the light of his countenance, and as workers together with him, advance his designs. It points us to the dark precipice of damnation; it lifts up the everlasting doors that we may flee from the wrath to come and lay hold on eternal life. Thus the sinner in Regeneration acts through the truth. In its light he sees what God is, and loves him; sees what Christ is, and trusts his lost soul to his keeping; sees what sin is, and hates and renounces it; sees what the service of God is, and chooses it. Thus the sinner "purifies his soul in obeying the truth."

I have thus briefly presented the four great facts on the subject before us. They amount to this, that in Regeneration, the sinner, in view of truth and through the influence of the Holy Spirit, does his duty. Through grace, the sinner, as a free, voluntary, accountable subject of God, obeys him. This is the great change, the glorious transformation of moral beings in moral character. This is that work of God, which tames, and softens, and subdues the spirit of rebellion, and changes it into the spirit of obedience—the spirit of heaven; transforms what would become the unquenched hate and malice of an infernal, into what will become a seraph's love. This is that new creation, compared with which "the former shall not be remembered nor come into mind."

If any should be curious to inquire how can these things be, or what is the *precise mode* of the Spirit's operation beyond what is involved in the facts now stated, I answer, no man knows, no man can tell what it is. To any one who says it must be this or that particular mode and can be no other, I should say, "There are more things in heaven and earth than your philosophy has dreamt of." He who knew how to create a mind, may know many ways in which he can influence mind, —ways in which *he can secure mental action in perfect accordance with its nature as mental action.* We have one class of facts which furnish an illustration. By that influence of the Spirit of God which we call *inspiration*, he produced in the minds of the sacred writers and the first preachers of Christianity, intellectual acts—thoughts, acts of memory and of reasoning, views of truth, which otherwise would not have existed in their minds. Still, these were as truly their own mental acts as any other. THEY thought, THEY remembered, THEY reasoned. So in Regeneration, God can produce *moral* acts or exercises in the mind which otherwise would not exist, and which shall be as truly moral acts, and the acts or exercises of the sinner's own powers and his own acts, as were they to take place without divine influence. Without creating new powers, God can bring the sinner to use aright those he already possesses. He can bring the sinner to love him and to repent of sin, and yet the sinner do all the loving and all the repenting. The reality of this divine influence is known by the *results*, not by *the mode* of their production. "The wind bloweth where it listeth, and thou hearest the sound thereof, but canst not tell whence it cometh nor whither it goeth. So is every one that is born of the Spirit." The omniscient God knows how to produce, and does produce by his word and by his Spirit, right moral acts or exercises in the mind, in a way perfectly consistent with their nature. This is enough for us to know.

Having thus attempted to explain and establish the four great facts stated in the text, I now propose to test *by these facts* certain opinions respecting the manner in which God executes the purpose of Election; proceeding on this principle, that whatever is involved in these facts is true, and whatever is inconsistent with them is false. I remark—

1. That the manner in which God executes the purpose of Election, involves an *earnest, serious attention to truth on the part of the sinner.* By this I intend that thoughtfulness, that sober, solemn thinking of the objects which truth presents; that wakeful sensibility to these objects which are necessary to secure their effect on the mind in right moral exercises or action. It is easy to see, that neither the truth nor the Spirit of God can influence the mind through the truth, if the truth be not thought of. It is easy to see also, that it may be reflected on, and yet the sensibilities may be so held back, checked, restrained, or so engrossed with other objects, that its influence shall be wholly counteracted. In this way it may fall as the rain and distill as the dew, but it falls on the cold rock. On the other hand, truth may be so thought of, especially God's truth, that it shall bear on the spirit like the pressure of great mountains, and so that the sinner can not rest in sin; so that thought, feeling, emotion, shall be occupied with what eternal truth tells him; so that he shall even tremble like a dying immortal falling into damnation; so that the world shall lose its attractions and its charms in view of the ruin that awaits him; and so that he shall put himself with the earnestness of such a condition to instant compliance with the terms of mercy. Let it not be forgotten however, that no duty is done—no duty is or can be done, until the supreme affections of the heart are fixed on God. Attention to truth is an indispensable preliminary to a right act of the heart. But no sinner is the better merely for his attention or thoughtfulness, nor for his anxieties and trembling, nor for any attempts to love God until he does love him. Nor is there, so far as we know, any attention to truth

which the sinner will in fact give, which creates any certainty that the heart will be changed. On this question we can neither affirm nor deny. God has not told us that there is a certain connection between any preliminary acts of the sinner and his conversion. The soul is never safe until the heart is right. We see sinners, so far as the human eye can judge, returning to sin from every degree of anxiety and earnestness, and can not therefore assert any certain connection between preliminary acts and a new heart; nor yet can we assert the contrary.

Two things however we can say. Many who give attention to the subject are converted; and none are converted who do not. So it was in the days of Christ and his apostles. So it has been in the revivals of later days. Many, not to say most of those who think, and feel, and are in earnest on the subject of religion, become Christians. But I speak of those only who take up the subject and enter on the work, as one which is to be done because heaven and hell depend on the doing of it. Look the world over, and you never knew or heard of the conversion of an unconcerned, heedless sinner. The conversion of the jailer, of Lydia, of Matthew, of the woman of Samaria, of the Ethiopian eunuch, of three thousand on the day of Pentecost—of each, of all, was through the truth and attention to truth. Even the conversion of Saul of Tarsus was not achieved till he was an awakened, distressed sinner. The Bible, as we have seen, affirms that Regeneration is through the truth. It is impossible, in the nature of things, that it should be otherwise. A sinner love God without thinking of him, without feeling his obligations to love him, without attempting to love him! Believe in Christ without a thought of Christ! Repent of sin without a thought of it! Never. The Holy Spirit will not convert a sinner while remaining thoughtless of his God, of his Saviour, and of his own soul. I care not what else is true of him, be he who he may, while he sleeps in sin, God will not convert him. Elect or non-elect, 'tis death. Elect or non-elect, so sure as there is a hell, he who remains careless in his sins is the victim of its woes.

On the contrary, let the sinner awake to the great concern of his salvation, and there is, we do not say an infallible certainty of his conversion, but there is all the hope which he can have, while there is nothing but despair without his so doing. Let him under the pressure of his necessities as a guilty, lost, perishing sinner, bring himself to the point of complying with the terms of mercy, to the point of giving his heart at once to God in view of what God is, and his soul to Christ in view of what Christ is. Let him take it up as a concern now on hand, and put himself to it with the urgency of a present achievement, as that which may be done, which must be done, and which may as well be done now as ever; as that which, if it can not be done now, there is decisive proof that it never can be done; and more than all, as that which must never be abandoned. Let him thus put himself, the whole man, to the point of duty; to the very act of giving his heart to God, and who shall say, that by the grace of God it will not be done? Peradventure, God will give him repentance. Neither man nor angel can say, that in that same moment such a sinner will not, by the grace of God, become a child of God, and an heir of his glory.

2. The manner in which God executes the purpose of Election, requires that *the sinner should act in performing his duty in precisely the same manner as he would were he not dependent on God.* Some there are who suppose that the sinner has nothing to do in this work; that he is to take the attitude of a mere recipient; that he is to regard himself simply as the subject of an effect; a being not to act, but to be acted upon, and at most, as one who, by his unholy prayers, is to induce God, if he can, to change his heart. But let us remember the facts. The change in Regeneration is a change from wrong to right moral action; and right moral action is the right exercise of moral powers. There is no necessity for the creation of any new powers, and no necessity for any other act than the right exercise of powers already existing. No new or other duty devolves on the sinner, because he, by his perverseness in sin, is dependent on God. The self-same thing is still his duty; the self-same thing is to be done, and to be done in precisely the same manner or mode of acting as were he not dependent. But can the sinner perform right moral action without even a thought or suspicion that right moral action is what he has to do? The thing to be done, and the only thing in his view, is not the right use of moral powers already possessed, but the actual creation of such powers by God. Will he then attempt to use powers aright which are yet to be created? Believing that he has no soul, or at best only a part of a soul, will

he ever exercise, or attempt to exercise that repentance, or faith, or love, for which as yet he supposes he has no capacity? He will never think of it. He will stand there till he dies, waiting for God to do what, in his view, God only can do. And now, is this the impression which ought to be made, which the Bible is designed to make? No. The sinner must take the attitude of an agent, the attitude of a doer. Something is to be done on the part of the sinner. And the thing, and the only thing to be done on his part, as a moral agent, is right moral action, and he must put himself directly to its performance. And be it remembered, that if God ever changes a sinner's heart, it will be, not when the sinner is trying to make God give him a new heart, but when he is trying to give his heart to God. Every thing that God does in this work is to bring the sinner to act right; to exercise right moral affections. Every thing in the Bible is designed and intended to put the sinner to the performance of right action. Every command, call, entreaty; every promise and every threatening, shuts the sinner up to the act of duty. God and his Son, prophets and apostles, call the sinner to the act of duty. This is required, and every thing but this is prohibited on pain of endless death. "Thou shalt love the Lord thy God." "Make you a new heart." "Believe on the Lord Jesus Christ." "Except ye repent, ye shall all likewise perish." The most distinct and loudest summons from the throne of the Eternal: "My son, give me thine heart;" and every voice of truth, every accent of mercy, every denunciation of wrath, heaven, earth, judgment, hell, echo the call, Do it! do it!

Do you say that *the sinner has no power to change his heart?* You contradict one of the facts. A new heart is the right exercise of moral powers. Without the power in the sinner, how can even God give him a new heart; how cause powers to act which do not exist? Or, if you say that God gives the power, still new power is not a new heart; is not a holy heart. The possession of moral powers is not the right use of moral powers. These may all exist and still be perverted. Surely it is no proof that a being will do right because he has the power to do so, nor yet is the fact that he does wrong, any proof that he has not power to do right.

No power! Have you ever read the law of God? and if you have, do you not know that what God requires, and all he requires is, that the sinner love with all *his* heart, all *his* mind, all *his* soul, all *his* strength? Do you not know that if the sinner were thus to love God with all his powers, he would be a perfectly holy man? And if God were to bring him to do this without giving him any new powers, would not this be Regeneration? Would not this be a holy heart? And does the sinner then need any new powers? Has the sinner *no* power, when he would be absolutely and perfectly holy, would he love God with all the power he has? Away with this Antinomian license to sin; this plea for legalized rebellion against the living God! My Hearers, if a man were to tell me under the solemnity of an oath, that he has no power to obey God, I would not charge him with willful perjury, but I should fearlessly say, *You know better.* What, not know better than to say that you have not ability to love God with all your power; cannot do what you can do!

But it may be said, *the grace of God is irresistible grace;* so that when this grace is given, the sinner is converted whether he acts or does not act. Nothing depends on what he shall do or shall not do. I appeal again to the facts. The change in Regeneration is moral action. And can such action be compelled action? According to this scheme, the sinner would be a volunteer *dragged* to his duty. Would this be holy obedience to God? God, by the mere force of omnipotence, crushes the moral agency of the sinner in producing moral action; makes the sinner willing against his will, and actually secures moral action by rendering moral action impossible! And can these things be?—the sinner will choose both ways at once! Choose right, and at the same time choose not to choose right! Love God with a heart wholly averse to God! Love and hate at the same time! Is such the absurd achievement of the grace of God in the conversion of the sinner? True, sinners are dependent on the grace of God. They come to Christ only when the Father draws them. Mark the word—when the Father *draws* them. It is an influence that draws, not compels; that attracts, not forces to duty; an influence which perfectly accords with the free, unconstrained, voluntary nature of moral action; an influence as attractive as the glories of his own Godhead; moving upon, softening, melting the rebel's heart like the love of Jesus, and persuasive as the accents of his mercy. It never violates the freedom of the sinner's act; never crosses the laws of voluntary action; never dispenses with the true and proper exercise of every moral power of the moral agent. It is an influence which the sinner can, and often does resist; an influence to which *he himself* must yield, and yielding to which, he would be drawn by its mysterious, heavenly attractions to the bosom of his God.

Thus every thing conspires to show you that the sinner is to put himself to the act of duty exactly as he would, as to the manner of doing it, were he not dependent. The influence of the Spirit of God modifies nothing, changes nothing *in the manner* of performing right action. It is still, though done through the Spirit, the self-same thing on the part of the sinner; the same free, voluntary, moral act which it would be, and done *in the same manner* in which it would be, were it to be done without a divine influence. This influence, though distinct from that of truth and motives, is yet in perfect harmony with it, and both combine and bear in the same direction and tend to the same result, viz., to produce right moral action. In a manner unknown to us, God, by his truth and by his Spirit, aims to enlist all the moral powers of the soul in the performance of right moral action. What the sinner has to do, is to accord with this design, by putting himself—all his powers—directly to the act of duty. His understanding, in the form of solemn thought, must be exercised in apprehending, knowing, seeing what the objects of right affection are. Sensibility must wake up, and feeling and emotion must associate with thought,—feeling in all the forms of hope, and fear, and desire, and a sense of obligation and duty. The heart must be applied to right objects in the form of love and preference, softening in contrition and godly sorrow for sin; the will must be fixed in the form of choice, of full purpose, in one resolve, immutable, to serve the living God. This is right moral action. To this, God by his truth, through his Spirit, would bring the sinner. Let the sinner then who would not resist God and his grace, yield himself, heart and soul, to these influences. Let him do it, as to the manner of doing it, just as he would had he never heard whether there be any Holy Ghost. Let him think of God, his character, his relations. Let him look thoughtfully on that Being whose glories enrapture all heaven. Let him yield his heart in supreme and everlasting love to that perfect Being; and when he loves, when he can say, "Whom have I in heaven but thee, and there is none upon the earth that I desire beside thee;" then let him add, in grateful praise, "By the grace of God I am what I am."

3. The manner in which God executes the purpose of Election, shows, that *the sinner under the call to duty, should begin the work of duty without waiting for God to do more than he is now doing.* Appeal again to the facts. The change in Regeneration is "obeying the truth through the Spirit;" and God's call to duty is truth. Truth brought to the mind of the sinner is always felt. And nothing prevents him, when truth is in his thoughts, from becoming at once a convicted and a converted sinner, but his own voluntary resistance of the truth. Do you say *the effect in conviction, however slight, is to be ascribed to a divine influence attending the truth?* Be it so, and God forbid that I should authorize a doubt on that point. But ought the sinner now to resist this combined influence of truth and the Holy Spirit, or to yield to it? Ought he to say, and ought you to confirm him in the opinion, that God must do more for him than he is now doing, in order that he may put himself at once to the performance of his duty? Ought he to make light of God's commands and God's grace, and say all this is nothing, something more must be done, and thus remain in the firmest attitude of resistance, aggravating his guilt and endangering his soul?

But you say, *the sinner resists what God is now doing, and he will resist unless God does more.* Yes, the sinner resists what God is now doing; and what is worse, he always will resist it in every future moment of his probation, if you preach and he believes that he must and will resist it. Your own doctrine believed, infallibly produces this effect. It annihilates thought of any thing else; it paralyzes all attempt at any thing but resistance, by the assurance and belief that he shall do nothing but resist; for when was such a thing heard of, that a man ever attempted to do what he fully believed that he should not do? Never. And thus it is that this unauthorized doctrine, that God must do more than he is now doing, in order that the sinner may begin the work of his salvation, will account for the fatal resistance of truth and of the Holy Ghost, and the final ruin of the soul in the case of thousands. *God,* you say, *must do more for the sinner than he is now doing.* I do not deny it; but I affirm that you have no warrant for the assertion.

What more? Will he turn the sinner to holiness from a state of absolute stupidity in sin, change his heart when he sleeps in his iniquity, or cause him to love him while he resists and shuts out the light which reveals the glories to be loved? Do you say, *he must awaken the mind and impress and convict the conscience, and so at least as to give some intimation that he is ready to convert him?* But how does this appear? The true and only reason that the sinner is not now awakened, and does not now give his heart to God, is not that God must do more, but that the sinner resists what God is now doing. Truth without the Spirit would be enough if the sinner did not resist it. But this is not all. How do you know that the sinner would not, by the power of the Holy Ghost, perform his duty, when called to it, did he not resist the Holy Ghost? Indeed, where is the sin of resisting it, if his influence could produce no salutary result were it unresisted? And who shall say, that under every call to duty from God, there is not (we do not say that there is, but who shall say there is not) an influence from the Holy Ghost that would conduct the sinner to holiness and heaven, did he not freely and perversely resist it?

We may view this subject with advantage in another light. Why has God revealed the doctrine of the sinner's dependence? Is it to prevent him from doing his duty when God commands him to do it? From doing it at once, even with the very first thought of it? Does God call sinners to instant duty in every command; does he in every call and every entreaty do this; does he in every promise and every threatening suspend the eternal life or death of the soul on immediate duty, and yet by the doctrine of divine influence, tell them to sit still and wait for him to do something more than he is now doing? What says common sense? It says, that if, when God calls the sinner to repentance, it is truth known to the sinner that God must do more than he is now doing, or is ready to do, that the sinner may repent, let the sinner wait till God does more. Is there any reason why a man should now attempt to do what he knows he shall not now do? Is there any more reason why a man should attempt to become wise, or rich, or honorable, when he knows that he shall not succeed, than why he should try to visit the moon by flying thither? It matters not, *as to this point*, what the ground of the certainty is, whether it is want of power or of inclination, so long as there is a known certainty that the sinner will not attempt to perform his duty, there is a good reason why he should not attempt it. If it be known truth that he will not act without a further influence, reason says, common sense says, wait for the influence; let the sinner sleep on, and sleep away the hours of his probation, waiting for God to do more. But is this the message that eternal mercy sounds in the ears of sleeping guilt? Oh no, my hearers. The sinner under the call to duty must perform it. God tells him to begin, and begin in earnest. He tells him in every command of his authority, and in every entreaty of his love. Every voice that speaketh from heaven says, "Strive to enter in at the strait gate;" and every voice that speaketh truth on earth repeats the summons. And you may be sure that while God thus urges the sinner to move and stir himself in this work at once, he does not paralyze every effort by assuring him that he will not act until something more is done for him than is now doing.

Why then has God revealed the sinner's dependence on his Spirit? Pre-eminently—I had almost said solely—to prevent utter despair, and consequent inaction. If it were not true, that God by his Spirit can and may overcome the perverseness of the sinner's heart, what could the sinner hope for? 'Tis all the hope that one of our lost race will ever see heaven. Without it, we should, and well we might, sit down in inaction, despair. But here it is in this book of God's grace and mercy; and here it is for the purpose of saving us from the hopelessness and horrors of the state into which sin has brought us. Here it is, as the arm of the Almighty revealed for our deliverance; as the hand of eternal mercy which has taken hold of us to raise us from the pit, and to convince us that heaven may be obtained. And shall the sinner sit still and do nothing, because God may be willing to help? Shall we thus pervert this hope from God's own arm; break away from the grasp of omnipotent love and plunge into hell, because God has undertaken to save? Oh, what a perversion of the grace of God were this!

But it will be said, *there are some sinners who never will attempt the work of their salvation, and that God knows they will not.* True. But still, is there no good reason why they should? The question here is not what God knows, but what the sinner knows. Is there no reason why a drowning man should make an effort to escape impending death, because God may know that he will not escape? Do you say that if he knew what God knows, there would be a reason why he should not try to escape? That is exactly what I say. If God has revealed the certainty that there is no escape, and that no effort will be made, then there is a reason for not making an effort. But the fact that the sinner does not know but that by effort he may be saved, or rather the known fact that by it he may be saved, is surely reason enough for effort. If it were a revealed truth, that under the calls of God to duty, there is no hope of compliance, that the sinner will not attempt it, then all efforts are as preposterous as if the sinner were a corpse.

If God has revealed such a doctrine, we ought to preach it, and when we carry to sinners the moving message of wrath and mercy, tell them that they will not move; that they may with entire propriety remain quiet and undisturbed; for after all they will lie as dead, and hopelessly dead, till God, by some new and higher influence, shall move them, as if a word had not been uttered. But Oh, what another Gospel would that be, which should read to this thoughtless world such a warrant for sloth, or such a message of despair! It might indeed tell us, and tell us with propriety, that we ought to repent. But if it told us that unless God should do something more than he is now doing, we never should even attempt it, not even make a beginning by having a thought about it, how would the conviction of the uselessness of effort paralyze us! Then would the tenfold slumbers of moral death take hold of this fallen world, and the shadows of the second death come up over the face of it; and this region of hope, this theater of divine mercy, where the kingdom of God now suffereth violence, and the violent take it by force, be changed into the pathway to hell, and every human being, in the gloom or frenzy of despair, take his solitary way down to everlasting burnings!

But such is not the world we live in. Such is not the Gospel its God hath sent to it. Hear the song of angels when its Redeemer came: "Glory to God in the highest, and on earth peace, good-will toward men." Hear the Saviour who bled and died for it: "God sent not his Son into the world to condemn the world, but that the world through him might be saved." Consider God's purpose of electing grace, executed in such perfect accordance with the free, unconstrained, voluntary action of the mind, as not to hinder the salvation of one, and that none can perish but by his own choice. Look abroad too at the work of this world's redemption going on. You see Zion's rising glories in every land, and in anticipation, her converts multiplying as the drops of the morning; you hear their songs of deliverance, and you see this redeemed company, all of them sinners who have waked up and begun the work of their salvation, while not a man of all earth's thoughtless millions is to be found among them. And, My Hearers, if *you* would be saved, *you* must begin. Under the mandate of the living God, you must act. You must think of something beside mere vanities. You must think of and feel something beside these nothings of earth and time. You must think of the things that belong to your everlasting peace; you must feel the powers of the world to come; you must ply the whole energy of the inner man to the point of duty, the single point of giving God your heart. You must begin the work as one which may be done, which ought to be done, which must be done; or, under God's condemnation, you must soon be plunged into the realities of eternity.

Such is the manner then, in which God executes his purpose of Election. God you see, has no purpose of Election to bring any sinners to repentance who sleep away their probation in the stupidity and sloth of sin. He has no purpose to bring any to repentance, except through their own wakeful, free, voluntary activity, under the influence of his Spirit. Dependent then as sinners are on God for a new heart, it rests also in a most vital respect on themselves whether they have a new heart or not. If they sleep in sin, God will not give them a new heart. If they awake to their duty, he may. Yea, listen. No voice of truth throughout the universe says he will not. You see then that such is the manner in which God executes the purpose of Election, that your salvation so depends on what you do, as to create all the propriety, and all the importance, and all the necessity for these efforts, that can be conceived of. Without them, elect or non-elect, God will never convert you. With them the work may be done. It is then with you to say, whether you will be saved or lost. If you yield to God as you can, you will be saved; if you resist God as you can, you will be lost. You must go to hell, if you go there at all, as a voluntary self-destroyer, with this conviction of the fact, as the never dying worm, the quenchless fire in your own guilty bosom, *I am self-destroyed, self-destroyed for eternity.*

When therefore, Fellow-Sinner, the question comes up in your thoughts,—for it will come whether you will do any thing or not, whether you will begin, or wait for God to begin by doing more than God is now doing,—remember that if you do not begin, God will never convert you, and if you delay a little longer, there is a fearful probability that God will give you up to determined sin and final ruin. And now think of this; let it ring in your ears and thunder in your conscience, that nothing less than heaven or hell depends on what you do, and do soon. Perhaps your present purpose will decide it. Perhaps while celestial eyes are now beaming with tenderness upon you, and the bosom of eternal love swells with solicitude for you, you are making in your own heart the decision which God from the throne of final judgment will ratify; a decision of your own heart, whose result will be heaven with its eternal joys, or hell with its everlasting woes. Think of this. God the Father, God the Son, and God the Holy Ghost, are not unconcerned for you. Even malignant spirits beneath think of you, and their moanings of despair may have ceased, and the clanking of their chains may be stilled, intent to know your decision. The blessed above may have stopped their songs, ay, and some hovering angel may have paused on another errand of mercy, and be resting on his broad wings over this assembly, to witness and report in heaven a decision of your heart, on which heaven or hell depends.

ELECTION.

III.—OBJECTIONS TO THE DOCTRINE OF ELECTION.

"And say, We are delivered to do all these abominations."—*Jeremiah* vii. 10.

THE design of the present discourse is, to answer the principal objections alleged against the doctrine of Election. For this purpose I recall to your minds the view of the subject as it has been given in two former discourses. This I will attempt to do in the form of an example. Let us suppose that several subjects of an earthly king have revolted from his government. The prince, the king's son, endures in view of the assembled empire, a degree of suffering which renders it consistent with the honor of the king, and the authority of his law, to pardon all, on condition that they will return to their duty. On this condition pardon is proffered, with the assurance that they who comply with the terms shall be exalted to distinguished honors in the empire. To these proffers of mercy the reply of the rebels is, "Accept of pardon on such terms?—we had rather die; we dislike you and your laws as much as when we determined on rebellion; we will not submit to such tyranny." Some however, on hearing these offers urged upon their acceptance, are more thoughtful of the matter than others. They dread the hour of execution; their conscience feels the power of obligation; they think of the mercy that provides and proffers deliverance. They soberly consider the question, whether they will comply with this overture of mercy. Still however, the spirit of rebellion keeps its hold on the heart; their real feeling is, we can not, will not submit to the authority of one whose laws we so much dislike. Thus all in heart are rebels still. Who now will hesitate to say, that all deserve to die; and deserve it more than had no mercy been offered and rejected?

We will now suppose that the king, by some extraordinary influence—by a peculiar power he has of reaching the heart through the motives he presents—which perfectly accords with the freedom of action, can cause these rebels to fall in cheerful, humble submission, at his feet. The question now is, will he do this for any; and if so, *for how many*, and *for whom?* In determining these questions, the king sees and knows that to bring all to submit, would perhaps result in greater evil than not to do it; he sees that it might be made the occasion of, and even prove a direct encouragement to rebellion; that many of these would rebel again, and that hopelessly, and still greater multitudes with them. They might reason in this way: "There is nothing to fear from our indulgent sovereign; rebel as we may, he will not punish." Thus a universal, hopeless revolt might ensue. All this we will suppose the king foresees, and therefore determines not to bring all these rebels by this peculiar influence to submission. Shall he then bring a part? This he can do consistently with wisdom and goodness. This he can do, and secure the loyalty and happiness of a greater number of his subjects than by not doing it. But who shall be the favored subjects? Not those who persisted in treating the offered mercy with scorn—who, in the spirit of rebellion, turned from the message of grace only to meditate treason, and who would scarcely give it a hearing. Not one of these shall partake of the blessing. He determines then, to confer the favor on some of those who treat the message with more apparent respect; not because they are the better for this, or for their upbraidings of conscience, or for their tremblings at approaching death; but because it may be, that there is less that is provoking and offensive, or because he can do more for them without injury to others, or because he knows that when reclaimed, they will prove useful in the administration of his government, or for some other wise and good reason. These he thus brings to submission, and gives them the promised rewards. The rest, though he sincerely desires their repentance under the influence he uses, and while he has used all the influence to secure it which he wisely can, he orders, as they deserve and as the public good demands, to be executed. Supposing now the king to have foreseen all that we have supposed, and in view of it to have done all he has; has he not done right, and in every respect what wisdom and benevolence would dictate? And if so, was it not right to *determine* to do it?

This I give as an exact illustration of the doctrine of Election in its connection with other truths, as it has been stated and explained in two preceding discourses.

I now proceed to the inquiry, whether there be any valid objection to this doctrine? I remark—

1. That the doctrine of Election is consistent *with the free moral agency of man.* Here I readily admit, that if men are not free agents without grace, then if they are not elected, they neither are, nor will they ever be, free agents. But, as we have shown, men are free moral agents without grace. God does not give, nor purpose to give, converting grace to men because they are not moral agents without it; but because they are, and because without it they will only pervert their moral agency to sin and death. Indeed, grace (the grace of the Gospel) can not make man a moral agent. This is a matter of equity or goodness, not of grace. The grace of the Gospel is favor to those and those only who are already moral agents, and sinful moral agents. Otherwise, "grace is no more grace." The object then of God's purpose of Election, is not to produce moral agency, but to prevent the abuse of it; it is to prevent the wrong and secure the right use of moral powers already possessed. God has never formed a purpose to give converting grace to stocks, or to animals, or to machines. God can produce holiness in no beings except moral agents, and of course can purpose to produce it in no other. The doctrine of Election then, instead of proving that men are not free, proves most decisively and unanswerably that they are.

View this topic in another light. *The mere purpose of God to renew the heart of sinners can not of itself, while unexecuted, destroy their free-agency.* The purpose is formed before they exist, and therefore as a mere purpose it can not touch them. Not the purpose then, but its execution, if any thing, must destroy their free agency. The present objection therefore, does not lie against the purpose, but against the execution of the purpose; i. e., not against the doctrine of Election, but against the doctrine of Regeneration. The question then is, whether the execution of the purpose destroys free agency? If it does, it must have this effect on those only on whom it is executed; i. e., only on the elect. The purpose respects no others; it touches none but the elect, either in design or execution. The elect then, who are renewed, sanctified, and made heirs of glory, are the men to be pitied, and to complain, if any, because their free agency is destroyed. As to them however, we have already shown that in their Regeneration they act as freely as in any act of their lives; that the change in them consists in freely "obeying the truth through the Spirit;" that the thing, the very thing which God produces in Regeneration, is the right exercise of free agency. As to the other class, the non-elect, their free agency can not be impaired by a purpose which has nothing to do with them. If they would be free without such a purpose, they are also free with it, for it never comes nigh them.

But it will here be said, "*What God purposes shall take place, will take place; and if the actions of men are decreed, how can they be free?*" I readily admit that what God purposes shall take place, will take place. But the same thing would be true respecting every event, if we suppose God to have no purpose respecting it. The proposition concerning any actual event that it will take place, made before its occurrence, would be as true as the proposition made after its occurrence, that it has taken place. The previous certainty of every action and every event must be admitted, decree or no decree, election or no election, the contrary—uncertainty in the case—being impossible and inconceivable. But how can the simple certainty of an action impair its freedom? Was it not certain that God would create the world before he did create it; and did this certainty impair the freedom of this act? Was it not certain that you would come to the house of God this evening, and did this certainty impair your freeedom; did it destroy your power to have done otherwise? What can be plainer, than that a man may have power to do many things which he certainly will not do, or power to do otherwise than he certainly will do? If any two things are consistent, *certainty of action* and *freedom of action* are consistent. But you say, "the action is decreed or purposed of God." True; but what is this? An action is purposed by God when it is in accordance with his providential will; when it is what he for some reason designs shall take place. Can not one being act in accordance with the will, the pleasure, the designs of another, and still be free? Can not a friend, a child, a servant, act according to the will of his friend, parent, or master, and still be free? If all the world had acted according to the will of God as expressed in his law, would they have ever thought of doubting their own freedom? The fact that the action of one accords with the will of another, is no more inconsistent with its freedom, than if it were contrary to his will. Besides, God in purposing the moral actions of men, purposes none but free actions. He purposes not merely that they shall take place, but that they shall be free. How then can his purpose destroy their freedom? Do you say, that "according to our doctrine, God purposes that some men shall sin, and ask how this can be consistent with God's sincerity in forbidding sin as a Lawgiver?" This question I will shortly answer, but that *now* before us is, how is it consistent with man's free agency? And we say, that it is one of the plainest and most certain of all truths, that one being may act according to the will of another and yet act freely.

But the sinner still replies, "*I can not change my own heart, and if I am not elected, I must continue in sin and die.*" Here the precise question is, what does the sinner mean when he says "*I must,*" "*I can not?*" Does he mean that he is compelled to sin; that he has not the powers of a complete moral agent—powers which fully qualify him to love God and to make himself a new heart? This plea is false; contradicted by the obvious consistency between the existence of these powers in man and God's purposes; contradicted, as we have seen, by the law of God, which expressly recognizes in man every power of moral agency; contradicted by his own consciousness, for every man knows that he has these powers; contradicted too by the doctrine of Election itself, and by the manner in which God executes this purpose; for this is nothing but a purpose to secure the right use of the powers of moral agency. Besides, if the sinner has not these powers, his election of God would not help the matter; for it is not God's design to give them to a single human being, but rather to secure the right use of those already possessed.

What then do you mean when you say, "I *can not* change my own heart?" Do you mean that you are so determined, so desperate in your purpose of rebellion, that you will not give it up; that no truth, motives, commands, entreaties, will persuade you to submit to God; that nothing but the power of God will ever overcome the obduracy of your heart; that without this you will persist in sin, and freely, and with your eyes open, go on to everlasting ruin? Do you mean that you have such a heart as this? True, you have just such a heart, and it can belong to no other than a free agent. Can a mere stock, or stone, a machine, a mere passive being, form such a purpose as this? What being, or creature, or thing, can form such a purpose of rebellion against the Most High, except a free agent? And has it come to this, that beings who can choose one way, can not choose the other when every possible motive exists to induce them to do it; that beings who have power to reject and to resist every degree of moral influence which a universe affords, and who could not but choose otherwise if they did not resist it to the uttermost, should not be free? Surely, surely here is no lack of power. If there can be a free agent, such a rebel against God is a free agent. The same powers employed in resisting sin in the same manner as they are in resisting God, would make the sinner like "an archangel strong" in the service of God. Thus it is that the provisions of the Gospel are for man as a free moral agent. The Atonement of the Lord Jesus has cleared the path of his return to God of every obstacle; his prison doors are thrown open; his chains are knocked off; an inviting God, proffering heaven's glories, calls him to life, and he freely, by his own act and deed, rejects the offer; and in faithfulness to his soul, we must add, *he knows it*, and if he dies in his sins, will have it to reflect on for eternity.

2. The doctrine of Election is perfectly consistent with *the sincerity of the divine invitations.* Here I would say, that things have been said on this subject which are palpably *inconsistent* with God's sincerity. It has been maintained by some, that sin is the necessary means of the greatest good, and that on this account God prefers sin to holiness in every instance in which sin exists; and that God's purposes would be painfully crossed, were men in every instance in which they sin, to do their duty instead. But you will remember, My Hearers, that I have taught no such doctrine as this; but on the contrary, that if all men, elect and non-elect, would, under the influences which God uses to bring them to repentance, actually repent, i. e., do their duty as they are able and ought to do it, it would be what God prefers they should do. When God says that he is not willing that any should perish, but that *all* should come to repentance, he means exactly what he says. Compliance on their part, on the part of every sinner, would be the consummation of the strongest desires of eternal love toward him.

But it will be said, that "*God knew that some would reject his invitations, and continue in sin and die.*" Be it so. May not the tenderest earthly parent regard the reformation of a froward, abandoned son as hopeless, and still most sincerely and ardently desire his reformation? Even if he knew his continued profligacy to be absolutely certain, would he not still sincerely desire his return to duty, rather than his continuance in crime and wretchedness? Ay, and his heart break with grief at the thought that all is thus hopeless in respect to this object of his love? And, My Hearers, it is God, who in view of the known perverseness of sinners, and at the thought of abandoning them to their chosen way,—it is God who says, "How shall I give thee up, Ephraim; how shall I set thee as Admah, and make thee as Zeboim? My heart is turned within me, my repentings are kindled together." 'Tis the Saviour who says, "O Jerusalem, Jerusalem, how often would I have gathered" (think of this image, for did you ever witness the solicitude of the parent-bird to protect her young, and doubt her sincerity?)—"how often would I have gathered thy children together, even as a hen gathereth her chickens under her wings, and ye would not!" There is no mockery—no mistake here. 'Tis the overflowing of divine compassion—the very heart-breaking of bereaved and disconsolate love. God does not desire the life of the sinner the less because he knows he will die.

But you will ask, "*If God thus sincerely desires that all should come to repentance, why does he not bring all to repentance?*" I answer by asking why should he? This would be to change the system of influence which infinite wisdom and goodness have resolved on in respect to each, as best fitted to secure the greatest amount of holiness and happiness which God can secure. To change this influence in a single and in the least degree, might occasion ultimately more sin than it would prevent, even a hopeless revolt of his whole moral kingdom. No man can say, that if God were to bring one non-elect sinner to repentance, it would not be an act of unkindness to that sinner himself, since he might apostatize and perish under a more aggravated doom than now awaits him. You see then, how with all the ardor of infinite benevolence, God may prefer that all men should repent, rather than go on in sin, and yet not purpose to bring them to repentance. If they would do as he invites them to do, if all would come to repentance under the influence he actually uses and which is all he can wisely use to save them, he would rejoice over them with paternal love and gladness. Is he not sincere then in his invitations?

But I have another thing to say. God's purpose of Election in the manner in which it is executed, instead of being inconsistent with the sincerity of his invitations to all, *is one of the decisive proofs of their sincerity.* If I make a rich, abundant provision for the entertainment of my neighbors, and send forth unqualified, urgent, warm-hearted invitations to them to come and partake, and they all refuse to accept them, am I to be reproached with insincerity because I do not now resort to some extraordinary influence, because I do not give a thousand dollars to each to induce him to come? Is *their* refusal a proof of the insincerity of my invitation? Suppose now that I resort to this extra influence, and actually use it with as many as I can consistently with other and higher interests, and by large sums of money prevail on a part to come, does not this show that I was sincere in my invitations to all? Am I not doing all that I can, in the proper sense of the language, to induce the greatest number to come? In what conceivable way—by what possible act or deed, could I evince my sincerity if this does not? Precisely like this is the proof of God's sincerity which is furnished by the doctrine of Election. It is a purpose to give effect to his invitations of mercy to the utmost possible extent, in which as a wise and benevolent God he can do it. In this view of the subject we see God thwarted indeed in his gracious design toward all by their perverseness—perverseness which no urgency of entreaty can overcome—still repeating his invitations, assuring one and all that he has no pleasure in their death, but would rather that they turn and live; that he has made all things ready by the sacrifice of his Son as a ransom, entreating the acceptance of all with more than paternal tenderness, declaring that there is room enough in the mansions of eternal love and bliss, that there is a crown of life and a throne of glory for each and for all; coming to them with the supplications and tears of a bereaved and broken-hearted father, and exclaiming in the anguish of his grief, "How can I permit these creatures of my power and love to lie down in everlasting fire?" and now because he can not consent to leave them thus, he sends the Holy Ghost with his transforming influence to save, in the true import of the language, as many as he can save! And is not this sincerity? Could God, as the Redeemer of this perverse and guilty world, have shown the sincerity of his desires, these longings of heart for its salvation as he now does, had he never formed the purposes of electing grace? Thus this doctrine, the one that has been so confidently alleged as inconsistent with God's sincerity, becomes the most decisive proof of it; revealing as it does, a love stronger than death and that passeth knowledge—love never to be satisfied till it has done all that it can do to save and bless a self-ruined world.

One thing more ought to be said on this topic. Whatever any sinner may think of the sincerity of God's invitations as addressed to others, he can never know that they are not sincerely addressed to him. He can never know in this life, but that in the high counsels of God they are associated with an eternal purpose of grace to bring him to repentance. It may be so. Would he set himself in earnest to comply with the invitation of his God, the event may prove that that invitation was addressed to him, that God might accomplish in him his eternal purpose of grace and salvation. How then can he stand there in all the stupidity and sullenness of determined sin, reproaching God with insincerity? Why, Fellow-Sinner, you know not but you are elected. You never can know it until you have put the sincerity of God to the test. Make then the experiment; put the sincerity of a redeeming God to the trial by some degree of earnestness—some sincerity on your own part. Do what you can, *clear yourslf in this matter*, and be sure you have done it, and then if all is in vain, doubt or deny God's sincerity; but never, never doubt it till you *know* that you are not resisting and grieving the sincerest love of thy God for thy salvation.

3. The doctrine of Election *does not involve God in the imputation of partiality*. By partiality here, must be meant some injustice through favoritism, or the conferring of blessings on one when there are equal or stronger reasons for conferring them on another. As to the question of injustice, that must be put to rest forever by the consideration that all deserve death. If there be injustice in the case, it must respect the non-elect. But how are they the less guilty, because God who would that all should come to repentance, does all that he

wisely can to bring all, and so actually brings some to repentance? They who are left lose nothing by Election. Their perdition is no more certain with Election than it would be without it; and if God shows favor to the elect, it is not at the expense of any rights of the non-elect.

But it may be said, "*There are as good reasons why God should confer his grace on all as on a part.*" I reply, that in respect to moral character, there is no reason why the blessing should be conferred on any. But the question is, when all deserve death, whether infinite wisdom may not see reasons for making a discrimination? What being of yesterday is competent to decide the contrary? These are high matters. When the law of God's kingdom has been trampled under the feet of rebellion, is man qualified to decide what ought to be done? When the very throne and dominion of the Eternal are thus put in jeopardy, it becomes a question worthy of God's counsels whether any of the rebels can be forgiven with safety to his kingdom; and if so, how many, and who? God has a moral kingdom to govern. He can not bring to repentance by dint of power, nor yet by physical causes. He can not convert his subjects into machines and preserve that kingdom. They must still be moral agents, with powers to rebel as well as to obey, and this under any influence which he can use to prevent rebellion. Their rebellion or loyalty will and must depend on the course he takes. How much and what influence can be used to secure the greatest amount of obedience is the question, the decision of which of all others, requires the wisdom of him who occupies the throne of legislation. When God sees, as he may, that he can not bring all mankind to repentance without injury to his universal kingdom, perhaps without subverting his throne, then the question assumes a new aspect. Has God good reasons for sanctifying only a part? What is the dictate of wisdom and goodness? Plainly, to sanctify not all, but as many as he can consistently with securing the greatest number of perfectly holy and happy beings which he can secure. This God will do, and as we have explained the doctrine of Election, this he has purposed to do. And now, when all may justly be left to perish, and when God has devised a way in which he can save some, and will save as many as the greatest good possible to him permits—when he saves as many as he can consistently with infinite wisdom and goodness, is it a reproach that he does not save all? Is it a reproach that he does not by his own act occasion revolt, and spread dismay and wretchedness throughout his dominions? Surely, with this view of the subject, we must see that God may have good reasons for saving only a part. My Hearers, when God is willing to save you and to save all—willing, yea desirous, that all should turn and live rather than sin and die, and when you will go down to hell by your own free choice—for be it remembered this is the only way in which you can go—will you reproach God because he does not prevent you by sacrificing the whole moral universe? Is this your objection, that God saves as many as he wisely can? Is this your philanthropy, your charity, which complains and murmurs when God saves as many of your miserable associates in sin as he wisely can, that he does not damn them as well as you? Is this the dictate of benevolence?

Further: as God may see that it is best to bring only a part to repentance, so he may have good reasons for bringing to repentance the very individuals whom he has selected. Those restored to loyalty may be more useful than others in promoting his designs. There may be reasons for enlisting in the work of an apostle him who was brought up at the feet of Gamaliel, rather than such a traitor as Judas, though the former was the most guilty. There may be reasons in the individuals themselves; for although none who are brought to repentance will apostatize, yet if others were, they might apostatize and perish under a more aggravated doom. Nay more, should we expect that God, when he can wisely bring to repentance only a part, would select those who treat the overtures of his mercy with the most deliberate contempt and pointed scorn—those who will not compliment the message of his grace so much as to think of it? True indeed it is, that they who think of and tremble at the coming wrath, and are serious and outwardly respectful in hearing the calls of mercy, are no better for this while they cherish hearts of rebellion. But which class of sinners should we expect God to bless with the gift of his transforming grace—those who are thus thoughtful and respectful, or those who treat the message of eternal mercy, even when sounded in their ears by the voice of the living God, with as much indifference and contempt as they do the whistling of the breeze? Save these rather than the others! Would not this look like favoritism? Save the worst, the most contemptuous and hardened! Would this be the way to avoid the reproach of partiality? Thus you see, that God may have good reasons for saving only a part of mankind; and that the general interest, the public good may forbid that he should do any more than he does for the lost sinner. If he saved all, it would be dishonorable, disgraceful partiality. It would be sacrificing the good of the whole from favoritism to a part—the well-being of his universal kingdom for the sake of the well-being of individuals. So he may have good reasons for saving the very individuals whom he does save; and nothing but undue partiality, nothing but dishonorable favoritism could save others instead of these. God therefore, instead of meriting the reproach of partiality for what he does, would deserve it were he to do otherwise. What rash inconsideration! What reckless presumption it is, that charges God with partiality in the dispensations of his grace!

4. The doctrine of Election is *consistent with the propriety of immediate action on the part of the sinner.* It is a standing objection to the doctrine of Election, that, if it be true, there is nothing for sinners to do. Now, I readily concede, that if the sinner in Regeneration were the mere passive subject of an effect; if he is merely to be acted upon; if the change can, and is as likely to be produced when he is asleep, as when he is awake; if nothing, in any sense or manner, depends on his acting more than on his not acting, then the present objection is valid; there is, as he says, nothing for him to do. Such however, is not the doctrine of Election. God's purpose of Election is to bring the sinner to the performance of right moral action; to bring him, voluntarily, freely, to "obey the truth, through the Spirit." This involves, as we have seen, direct action on the part of the sinner, not less than were this moral change to be accomplished by the mere influence of truth and motives. He must think of God as he is, and love him; of the Saviour as he is, and trust his lost soul to his mercy; of sin as it is, and abhor and renounce it with contrition, and a sincere purpose of holy obedience. In this manner he must apply his mind, his understanding, his conscience, his heart, to the point of duty. In this way, through the grace of God, duty may be done, and it can be done in no other. Is this the manner in which God executes the purpose

of Election, and is there no good reason why the sinner should act? May he become a child of God, and be saved *by acting?* Will he remain a sinner, and be damned *without* acting, and is there no reason for acting? Can a better, a more decisive reason for acting, be assigned for any action ever done by a human being? Take any conceivable case. You are sinking in the waves of the sea; *by effort* you *may* escape; without it you will infallibly perish. This is all you know; and is there no reason for making effort? A falling rock is descending from the precipice that overhangs your head; by effort you may escape; without it you will be crushed in almost instant death. Is there no reason why you should stir? Like this, Fellow-Sinner, is your condition. You are condemned already. Now, of a long time, your judgment lingereth not, and your damnation slumbereth not. Sleep on, if you will; sleep away your probation, dreaming that you may be elected; but remember, that in this course, not the grace of God, but the fires that shall never be quenched, will first rouse you from these slumbers.

But you say, "*If I am elected, God will interpose and prompt me to begin this work, and I may therefore safely wait for his interposition.*" Now the question is not, whether the sinner ever begins even to think of his salvation without that influence which we call the strivings of the Divine Spirit,—we believe that he never will,—but the question is this: whether, under the present call to duty, and under such influence of the Spirit as may attend it, it is not indispensable to any salutary result that the sinner begin on his part. Suppose what degree of divine influence you will, does not the result depend, in a vital respect, on what the sinner does? This is the real question, and the answer depends entirely on what is the kind and mode of this divine influence. If it be a physical, a mechanical, or a literally creative influence,—i. e., one which secures its results in spite of all resistance, and when the sinner is doing all that he can to resist it, just as the power of steam carries the boat through the resisting waters,—then you are right; and to call on the sinner to act, on the ground that any thing depends on his acting, were as absurd and useless as to call on the waters to make way for the boat. For in such a case the sinner yields to an influence which he can not resist. But such is not, as we have seen, the true doctrine. Converting grace is not *irresistible*, but *unresisted* grace—grace that *draws*, not *compels;* that *attracts*, not *forces.* It can be resisted by the sinner. On whom then does it truly depend, whether the result be secured or not? Suppose the waters could convert themselves into solid granite, as well as remain in a liquid state, on what would the passage of the boat through them depend? Somewhat on the force applied; but also on what the water should do. Now, if you will indulge the figure, the sinner, under any measure of divine influence, can make his heart solid granite, yea, as adamant and the nether millstone. Suppose what influence of truth and of the Spirit you will, the sinner, as a moral agent, *can* resist it. The change to be produced is from wrong, to free, voluntary, right moral action. If this change take place, the sinner must make it. It depends therefore as truly on what the sinner does, as on what the Spirit of God does. Do you say, that God does more for one sinner than for another? Be it so. But the sinner who is brought to repentance by God's doing more for him than for others, could have resisted all that God has done; and, had he done so, had perished in his sins; while, for the other who actually dies in his sins, God has done enough and more than enough to save him, had he not resisted God. But you will say, "*God does more at one time to awaken and convert the same sinner than at another.*" We admit it, but still ask on whom does the result depend? You say, on God. Right. But does it not also depend on what the sinner does? Could he not have resisted even this influence, and made it the occasion of greater hardness of heart than ever? If not, then he was not a moral agent, nor was the result right moral action. But if he could have resisted it, and did not, but yielded to it in voluntary right moral action, then the change depended as truly on what he did as on what God did. Hence you see, take what view of the subject you will, when God does all that he ever does for any sinner, whether the moral change takes place or not, depends on what the sinner does. Whatever the influence be, it is one whose result is, in a material respect, at the sinner's own disposal. It is for him to say, whether by the grace of God he will be saved or lost. Though he be an elect sinner, still it is immutable truth, that if he does not relax his resistance to the grace of God—if he does not yield to this influence in voluntary right moral action, he will continue in sin and die in sin. But there is one thing more, which is all the sinner can say on this point. If God has determined to bring me to act right, I shall act right, and therefore I need give myself no concern on the subject. It is true indeed, that if God has determined to bring you to act right, you will act right. But it is just as true, that *if* you give yourself no concern on the subject, and dismiss all thought of acting, God will never bring you to act. If God has determined that you shall leave this house to-night, or that you shall go to such a place, or that you shall read such a book, it is true that you will do it. But it is just as true, that if you do not think what you shall do, and decide upon the act, God will never bring you to do it; it will never be done. So, Fellow-Sinner, presume on God's purpose of Election to bring you to act right, without any thought on your own part; never put yourself to the performance of right action, and you will never perform right action. God bring you to act right without a thought of acting right? Impossible! God can not execute his purpose of Election in behalf of such a sinner. Do you now say, "If I am elected, I *shall think* of acting right?" Your objection then amounts to this—"If I am elected, I shall think of acting right; therefore I will not think of acting right." What sort of reasoning is this? It may be certain that I shall think of doing a given action, therefore I will not think of doing it. It may be certain that I shall eat and drink, and think of so doing as necessary to the preservation of life; therefore I will dismiss all thought of either eating or drinking, and take the consequence. I only say, maintain this opinion, believe and act on this principle in regard to the life of your soul, and you will soon find that you are given up to "strong delusion, to believe a lie, that you may be damned."

But the present objection often proceeds on the opposite supposition.

It is said, "If I am not elected, my heart will never be changed, do what I may. I shall never give my heart to God even IF I attempt it." This is not true. You say IF I attempt it. Take a case exactly in point. Suppose that it is a matter of absolutely certainty, that God knows that you will die in a few days by voluntary starvation, and solely by this means. Now IF you should eat and drink as usual, would you die by starvation—would you not live? The error in such reasoning lies in overlooking the fact that the hypothetical proposition is just as true as the absolute. Suppose the latter, that you will die by voluntary starvation, to be true; still the conditional proposition, IF you eat and drink you will not die by voluntary starvation, is just as true. So, IF the non-elect sinner were to make the same efforts to give his heart to God which the elect sinner makes, there is no reason to believe, nor warrant to assert, that by the grace of God he would not do it. It may be so. If then you are in fact a non-elect sinner, and you do not make these efforts, never make an attempt to give God your heart, and so die in your sins; and if it shall appear that had you made the attempt you had been converted and saved, whom will you reproach as your destroyer? God may have purposed that you shall die by voluntary starvation. If then, on the ground of such a possibility, you should actually starve yourself to death, who would be the murderer?

But you still say, "If I am *not* elected I shall not make these efforts, and therefore there is no reason why I should." Do you, can you believe this? No reason why you should do a thing which you can do, and on which your everlasting all may depend, because it *may be* certain that you shall not do it? Then there is no reason for performing any future act of your life; for which act of futurity do you know to be certain? Carry out your reasoning then, and say that God may know that I shall never either eat or drink again, but shall soon die by voluntary starvation, and therefore there is no reason why I should eat or drink: or, God may know that I shall never leave the seat I now occupy, and therefore there is no reason why I should move, or even think of so doing. Is this sound reasoning and common sense; or is it folly too great to be reasoned with, and fit only to be ridiculed? Why then do you say, if the doctrine of Election be true there is no reason why I should make an effort for my salvation? No, my hearers. The true, practical principle which governs all but madmen is, not what God knows to be certain, or what is in fact certain, but *what we know and what we do not know*. And if we do know that without some given act all that is dear to us will be lost forever, and if we do not know that we shall not do that act, then reason, and conscience, and God says DO IT; nor until we are omniscient can we act on any other principle. What, perform no action without first knowing that we shall perform it; or at least, until we know that no previous certainty pertains to human actions even in the Omniscient mind? Then should we never act at all. The activity of this world's busy population would be changed into the stillness of the grave. Admit then the principle, and the only principle of reason, of philosophy, of common sense, of the Bible, that certainty of action is consistent with freedom of action. The mere certainty of human action forces no one, compels no one. It leaves freedom, the power of choice, power to the opposite action, unimpaired. Apply now the only practical principle which ever did, or ever can move to a single human effort or action in all the business of life. You do not know but that you shall make the requisite effort to give your wicked heart to God in holy love; you do know that if you never attempt it you will die in your sins—die eternally. Can there be a better, a more imperious reason for instant effort in the performance of duty? Who is a fool or a madman, he that makes it or he that does not?

I have one thing more to say on this point. The doctrine of Election *is not only consistent with the propriety of action on the part of the sinner, but it is in one respect the only ground of such propriety.* Take it away, deny it, and see. Suppose that God has formed no purpose to change one human heart, then surely no human heart will ever be changed. Go then, and preach, and prove to this world of hopeless rebellion—publish it to these sinful, dying immortals, that God has formed no purpose to change one human heart, and that not a human being will ever change his own heart without grace. And Oh, how would despair, like a cloud from the bottomless pit, come up over the whole earth! NOT A HUMAN BEING WILL BE SAVED! There is no hope. Man will not change his own heart—God will not change it. A created universe can not change it. Every arm is palsied. Every face of man and of angel is pale with despair; and that cloud from beneath only thickens, and darkens, and thunders damnation. But look again. The doctrine of Election sets a bow on that cloud. God's purpose to renew, and sanctify, and save some, wakens hope in these guilty bosoms. God has purposed to save some, and some, even a great multitude which no man can number, will be saved. God's purpose is to save none but those who will wake up from their death-like slumbers in sin, and begin the work of salvation in earnest. All, all are lost—lost forever, who do not. Who then can wish the doctrine of Election to be false? Who of this guilty, ruined race, would oppose and annihilate this only ground of human hope? Who, while this beam of mercy falls on him from the throne of God, will sleep in sin another moment?

To conclude. If we have not erred in our reasonings, the doctrines of Election, of man's free agency, of God's sincerity, and the necessity of action on the part of sinners, are true, and are consistent truths. They are solemn and awful truths, too, to the determined sinner. Let him look at them and see, while deliberately adhering to his purposes of sin, what darkness and terror they shed on his path; what a prospect of pain and woe they open before him in an approaching eternity. Could he change one of these truths into falsehood, he might find the quietness and consolation in his chosen way which he covets. Could he deny his accountability to his Maker, he could still those agitations of conscious guilt which now tell him of the worm that never dies; then he might hope, if not to escape, at least to brave the final sentence of his Judge with the plea of innocence. Could he deny the sincerity of a redeeming God calling him to eternal life, he might hope to palliate the guilt, and to mitigate or avert the doom of a despiser of God's great salvation. Could he deny the doctrine of Election, he might defer the work of turning to God with the presumption of self-reliance; the security of one that holds the destiny of his soul in his own hands, in proud independence of the God he so fearlessly offends. Or could he persuade himself of the uselessness of effort or action on his own part, he might tread his quiet way onward to death and hell, undisturbed by the conviction that he is a self-destroyer. But no; these truths are all immutable. As a sinner and a free moral agent, he deserves the wrath of God. As a sinner who despises the sincerest proffers of life from his God and Saviour, he deserves the still deeper damnation of a rejected Gospel. As a sinner who cherishes an unconquerable perverseness of heart, he has placed his soul at the sovereign disposal of an incensed God, who may save or destroy as seemeth good in his sight. As a sinner, in the chosen, willful insensibility and death of sin, he sleeps on the verge of the eternal pit, and sleeping a little longer, will fall into hell.

There, Fellow-Sinner, not one token of grace and salvation distinguishes you from those who will perish forever. Every cause which has destroyed thousands exerts its full and uncounteracted power on you. Not one ray of hope from God's high sanctuary falls on your dark and cheerless way. No hand of mercy will ever reach you to reclaim and save. There God, the Saviour, the Sanctifier, will abandon you to your own choice of eternal sin and eternal sorrow.

And now believing as I do these things, with some portion, as I trust, of the compassion and love for your souls, of him who died to save, I come with thy aid, Divine Saviour, to speak to these sinners. Now, when death and judgment are so near, heaven so glorious, hell so dreadful; when these things are so certain and are coming on so fast, is it not time to awake and take care of your never-dying soul; that soul, that being of eternity, yourself? Is it unworthy of a thought? Now, when the God that made you, implores, when the Son of God weeps as a suppliant at your feet, when new joys would gladden every heavenly bosom, and every heavenly hill break forth in new songs of rapture, when angels invite you to their eternal fellowship, when saints supplicate God to be gracious, when the paradise of God throws open its gates, and its thrones of glory and crowns of life attract; now, when you are solemn and serious and know these things are so; now, when the Holy Ghost touches your heart, and makes you feel the attractions of Jesus' love; now will you not give yourself to that Almighty, perfect Saviour? Oh, will you never awake, until the voice of mercy is heard no more? Will you never ask for mercy, till God shall answer only from the secret place of thunder, and the eternal fires kindle upon you?

ELECTION.

IV.—REFLECTIONS AND APPLICATION.

"All scripture is given by inspiration of God, and is profitable."—2 *Tim.* iii. 16.

It has often been said, that if the doctrine of Election be true, and contained in the Bible, still it ought not to be preached. To this objection, thus stated, there is one general answer, viz.: that ministers of the Gospel are bound to declare the whole counsel of God. When it is once admitted that a doctrine is contained in the Bible, we must say, either that it ought to be preached, or that we are wiser than God, and that what he has revealed, and declared to be profitable, ought not to be taught. Here, this very common objection to the doctrine of Election might be left. It may be well, however, to trace its salutary practical tendency, and show those who hear us, that a wise regard to their own best interests will lead them to desire it to have its place in the ministrations of the pulpit.

I remark then—

1. That the doctrine of Election is a plain doctrine, though it has been pronounced mysterious, and hard to be understood and difficult to be explained. Now, if what has been said on this subject in former discourses be just, the supposed mystery and difficulties do not respect the doctrine, i. e., the simple matter of fact which constitutes it; but certain theories, or modes of explanation, which have been incorporated with the doctrine, and which, instead of being any part of it, are merely matters of human speculation. Theories are one thing, facts are another. Various theories have been devised to account for the fact that the sea ebbs and flows. But whether these are all consistent or inconsistent with the fact, that remains—the sea still ebbs and flows. So the matter of fact—the doctrine—that God has purposed to renew, and sanctify, and save a part of mankind, remains unaltered and unalterable by any theories devised by men to explain its

consistency with other truths. Not only so, but these theories have created all the mystery and difficulties which have ever embarrassed the subject. The two assumptions, that God on the whole prefers that men should do wrong rather than right, and that there is no impossibility that God should secure the universal holiness of his moral creation, involve the doctrine of Election, and I may say the whole system of Theology, not merely in unintelligible mystery, but in the most palpable absurdity. But here I appeal to my audience, whether I have not extricated this doctrine from these absurd and monstrous theories. Has it not been shown, that it is not only not inconsistent with man's free moral agency, but that it necessarily implies it, inasmuch as the very object of the purpose of Election is the right use of moral agency; that it is not only consistent with God's sincerity in his invitations to all, but the most decisive proof of it, inasmuch as it exhibits God as most earnestly desiring the repentance of all, rather than the impenitence of any, by what he does to secure the repentance of some; that it is not only consistent with impartiality in God, but actually implies the best reasons for the discriminations which it makes; and that it is not only consistent with the propriety of acting on the part of the sinner, but is the only ground of hope that he will act successfully? If I have shown these things, the supposed difficulty of seeing the consistency between the doctrine of Election and other scriptural doctrines, is imaginary.

Let us now appeal to the doctrine itself, which is, that God from eternity has determined to renew, and sanctify, and save a part only of mankind. Is this proposition in the least degree dark or obscure? Do you not at least understand my meaning, when I say that God has formed such a purpose, as well as you understand your own meaning, when you say he has not formed such a purpose? Surely, the mere negative particle *not* can add nothing to the clearness of the other terms of the proposition, and if yours is intelligible with it, mine is also without it.

But let us examine the proposition in its several parts. *God has purposed.* If you do not understand this, you do not know what it is for God to will; what it is for God to give a law, or to design, or purpose his own actions; nor indeed any thing of God which is of any importance; for the purposes of God are the true and only index of his character. *God has purposed from eternity.* If you do not understand this, you do not understand the truth that God is an eternal Being, for the eternity of God's purposes are as easy to comprehend as the eternity of his existence. *God from eternity has purposed to renew, and sanctify, and save.* If you do not understand this, the doctrines of Regeneration, Sanctification, and of the whole Gospel are unintelligible to you. And as to that part of the proposition which confines the purpose *to a part only* of mankind, there can be no difficulty, except to understand that a part is less than the whole. Pardon, My Hearers, what in these remarks may seem to imply some disparagement of your intellectual capacity. My object is to show that a plainer proposition in theology is scarcely conceivable, than that which is so loudly denounced as unintelligible mystery.

But you say, the doctrine is plainly inconsistent with man's free agency, and other acknowledged truths, and that therefore, after all that is said, you can not understand it. Be it so. If you can pronounce this doctrine inconsistent with any other, then you understand the doctrine itself; for how else can you decide on its inconsistency with another? Thus you concede the very point in debate. Besides, to say, because you do not understand its consistency with another doctrine, that therefore you do not understand the doctrine itself, is like saying, that because you do not comprehend *how* your soul and body are united, that you do not understand the assertion that you have either a soul or a body. So far then as plainness—the obvious meaning of a doctrine is requisite to its utility—the doctrine of Election is sufficiently distinguished by this characteristic.

2. The doctrine of Election has no injurious, but a highly useful, practical tendency. This will appear from the following considerations:

First—It tends *not to produce, but to prevent despair.* It has been often said, that the doctrine tends directly to produce this state of mind. If it be so, then truly it is a serious objection to the utility of preaching it. Despair is fatal to all effort. Despair, even in presence of the greatest good, or most appalling evil, sinks the spirit of man into sullen inaction. Man will never act, so long as he despairs either of acting, or of obtaining his object. Is it then the tendency of the doctrine to produce this state of mind? Has it in fact ever produced it? I do not say, that some false view of the subject, something which, by a gross misnomer, may have been called the doctrine of Election, has not, in some instances, had this effect; but has it ever been true of the doctrine, as stated and explained in these discourses? This I fearlessly deny. The thing is impossible. Can I believe that God will renew, and sanctify, and save some, even many of this guilty world, and legitimately infer from this that my perdition is sealed? Did I know that God would hereafter save but one human being, I could not justly infer that I should not be saved, for I might be the individual whom the purpose respects. Can I believe that many will be saved, and infer, by legitimate deduction, that none will be saved? If not, then plainly as an individual, I can not infer that I shall not be saved. We believe that many in this assembly will live till to-morrow. Can any one hence infer that he shall not live till another morning?

But further: the doctrine of Election is an infallible preventive of despair. Can I believe that thousands and millions of my fellow-creatures, who have no better prospects of life than I have, will live another year or day, without also believing that I may live? Can I as a rational man avoid this conviction? In like manner, can you and I believe that God has purposed to save a great multitude from among men—a multitude which no man can number—and at the same time avoid believing that you and I may be of that happy company? No. In view of the doctrine of Election, no sinner can despair of eternal life.

Again: this doctrine of Election not only prevents despair, it is *the only thing* indispensable to its prevention. Not a human being will ever turn to God and be saved, unless God by his grace turn him. Deny then the doctrine of Election: preach to beings thus desperate in rebellion against the Most High, that God has formed no purpose to sanctify and save one of them, and what could they hope for? Will the unchangeable God form new purposes? No. Can they hope to convert themselves? No. Can they find a created arm throughout the universe to help? No. There is no hope. Hide then from human vision the purpose of God's electing grace, and heaven's gate is shut, and barred, and bolted. Not a ray of light from the upper sanctuary falls on this midnight of sin; a cloud deep and thick as the blackness of darkness covers the world, and you see how beings hastening to God's judgment-seat sit down in the sullenness and gloom of despair, or rage and howl in its frenzies. Oh, who can deny and reproach the doctrine of God's electing grace! Who can wish to extinguish this only beam of hope from the throne of eternal mercy!

Secondly—The doctrine of Election tends to *destroy presumption in sin.* If sinners cherish an unreasonable and groundless confidence of final salvation, it were immeasurably desirable that it should be taken away from them. In its true tendency it is as fatal as death. Now every stupid sinner does cherish such a confidence. Throughout Christendom, there is not a man living quietly in sin, who is not venturing on in the path to ruin with the rashness and madness of a maniac. What violence to reason more gross and shocking than that a sinner under God's present condemnation, and liable every moment to death and endless perdition, should quietly defer repentance another moment? And yet how almost universal is the fact, even under the full conviction of its necessity? Now what is the reliance of such men? It is either directly or indirectly on their own strength, and their own acts, associated with a purpose of future repentance. Do you doubt it? Throw away every such hope from futurity. Suppose that you knew that you were to stand before God's judgment-seat this very hour, and that your preparation was in his hands and at his disposal, could you sleep in sin, quietly relying on what you intend to do hereafter? How then shall we break up this delusion; how restore such infatuation to sense and reason? Shall we tell these sleepers on the brink of ruin that life is uncertain, and death always near? You may throw the deepest and most chilling shade on the prospect of life, but when health and strength return, how they still believe that death is remote, and with a confidence that frequent and sudden deaths, and deaths in sin all around them, scarcely agitate! Others may die without preparation, but they shall not. Thus thousands are going on to their last account. And can we only repeat that life is frail, and death is near? Do you say, we must destroy this self-confidence, this presumptuous reliance on themselves, this trusting to their own heart, by telling them that repentance is the gift of God, and that it is only by his grace that they will ever be prepared to meet him in judgment? True, this doctrine thus stated, is of great, of indispensable importance. But then they already believe it, while they also believe that this necessary grace is ready for them whenever they shall be ready and condescend to use it. They do not, they will not believe, that the God of mercy may withhold his grace, even though they slight it till their last hour. Determined on present quietness in sin, they will practically believe, either that they can save themselves without grace, or that the requisite grace is always, even to the last, at their own disposal. And this, My Hearers, is the very presumption that holds these guilty thousands under the light of salvation in such death-like slumbers, that no accents of mercy, no, nor the notes of the second death, while this expectation remains, will ever move them. It is a presumption and a hope that must be torn away from the sinner, or he dies. And the case calls for all that truth can utter. He loves his sins, he loves the world, he is averse to God and his service, and he will persist in his chosen way till these hopes of salvation in such a course are cut off. If then you would rouse him from his lethargy, and suffer him to have no peace in his sins (and the God of mercy declares there is no peace to the wicked); if you would throw over his prospect the gloom and the forebodings in which truth invests it, preach the doctrine of Election. Point the thoughtless man to the eternal counsels of the Most High. Show him a sovereign God. There he will read, that by his own perverseness of heart he has rendered his salvation hopeless, without the grace which is his gift,—has put his salvation into the hands of an incensed God,—and that in view of that perverseness, God has decided respecting the gift of his grace, in those counsels that never change. Thus will he see that God who can, and may save him, and yet who can and may destroy, and will destroy if he has formed no purpose to save him. With such a view of the living God, can the sinner rest in his sins? Can he now presumptuously rely on what he intends to do hereafter; or even on the grace of God, as that which will always be ready whenever he shall choose to accept it. No; instead of regarding his own salvation as a contingency to be made certain by what he shall do, or may intend to do, he would wake up to a restless solicitude, and to a laborious earnestness of effort, that he may ascertain how this great question is decided in heaven's high counsels, and, if it may be, that it is decided well for him. Contingency, as opposed to certainty, in respect to the salvation of the soul, is truly a consoling thought to the determined sinner. On this scheme, nothing is in fact certain in his future being. But who is the man that can think of the eternal life or death of the soul, as already certain in the counsels of an unchangeable God; that in his present state all the evidence in his own case is, that he is one who shall die eternally; and that there is one way, and only one, in which the terrors of his condition can be alleviated,—one way, and only one in which he can ascertain that he is the object of God's electing love;—I say, who is the man that can think of these things and not feel himself, as it were, compelled to adopt the only method by which this unknown certainty shall be divested of its appalling aspect? Oh, the terrors of even the possible truth, that I am not included in God's purpose of electing grace! Who does not feel himself almost forced by such a thought to renounce sin and the world at once, that thus he may obtain the authorized and joyful assurance that he is chosen of God as an heir of all things? Can there be a doubt whether such is the true practical tendency of the doctrine of Election. Suppose yourself to have been tried before a human tribunal on a question of life and death; that you knew that the question was decided, but that the decision was still kept in profound secrecy, could you avoid a restlessness and an overwhelming solicitude in regard to it? When the sinner thinks of God's purpose of Election, a painful uncertainty respecting what is certain in God's mind—an oppressive, agitating anxiety, will be felt. The doctrine will fasten itself on his thoughts, and excite emotion. It will be like hearing that the final decision is made, without being told what it is; and instead of the peaceful reliance of sinners on what they intend to do hereafter, they will see, as they think of the counsels of an omniscient and immutable God, that their destiny is known but concealed. Perhaps it is life, perhaps death—perhaps heaven, perhaps hell! The feeling will be, not so much as if the final sentence were yet to be formed, as if it were soon to be pronounced,—as if but another moment were left for ascertaining by instant repentance the joyous truth, that in God's eternal counsels he is an heir of everlasting life.

And here I can not but remark is the very influence of the doctrine of Election which leads sinners to say, "It destroys all hope and drives to despair." It does destroy all *their* hopes of safety in determined sin. It does destroy these hopes, for they are false, deceitful, ruinous, and the sooner they are destroyed the better. God would destroy them and we would destroy them, not to produce despair, but that we may show them exactly what truth warrants them to hope for. This brings me to remark—

Thirdly—That the doctrine of Election furnishes to the sinner *all desirable encouragement.* By this I intend that degree which is best fitted to prompt the sinner to instant direct effort in the work of turning to God.

When an object is one of difficult attainment, and when also it has engaged the strongest affections of the heart, then confidence of success will give strenuousness to effort. But how is it when the heart is on the object opposite; when the very effort requisite to secure the one proposed is revolting to the heart, and when the only reason for effort is a painful, odious necessity, and when of course the whole tendency of the mind is to regard even this necessity as remote, and to defer acting? Is it not certain that the mind will defer acting as long as in its own view it can with safety; and will it not deem it safe to defer just in proportion to the probability that efforts when made will prove successful? To come then to the question—

How much probability of success as pertaining to those imperfect efforts which sinners make in turning to God, is best adapted to prompt them to immediate action? One thing is certain, there is no promise of God that his grace shall attend these attempts of the sinner. So far from it that for aught we can say to him, he may be already given up to hardness of heart. Not only is there no certainty of success in these attempts, but in proportion to the probability of it, and the facility of performing the unwelcome task, the danger of delay is diminished, and with it the pressure of the motive to present effort. Nor is this all. If there is a high probability of success from present attempts, then there is a higher degree of such probability than would otherwise exist from future attempts; and it is this belief, it is this false persuasion, that the work can be easily done now, and easily done at any future time, that is the solace of the sinner in procrastinating his duty to his God. To influence him then most powerfully to present action in duty, the prospect of success must be viewed as doubtful. It must be lowered down to what the apostle calls *a* "*peradventure* that God will give repentance." True it is this degree of probability may be very diverse in different cases. Still it is always so low in degree that if the sinner lessens it, as he inevitably must by delay, if he procrastinates *now*, he may well-nigh despair for the future. God in his Word confines all hope to the present hour, crowds the concerns of eternity as it were into the passing moment, throwing darkness over futurity, and converting the very thought of procrastination into "a fearful looking for of judgment and fiery indignation." That an almost absolute necessity of present action may be felt, and that the pressure of it may overpower all temptation to present inaction, "the Holy Ghost saith, To-day if ye will hear his voice, harden not your hearts."

Now that this degree of encouragement is that which is altogether most useful to the sinner, the best fitted to move him to immediate action in the performance of duty, may be shown by an example. Suppose then you were in a prison where continuance is so desirable (for to make out a parallel case we must suppose madness in the heart), that nothing but the loss of life would even make you ever think of leaving the place. Suppose now the prison to be on fire, but that having the key in your own possession, you can with entire safety remain in the enjoyments you love still longer. Would you be in haste to escape? Not at all. You would still linger and still delight yourself in pleasure, and let the flames come nigh, for escape is easy, and this is all your concern. But suppose that the key is in the hands of another; that he is your enemy, one whom you have greatly provoked to withhold every favor, and to leave you to perish. Suppose however, that you know that he has delivered others in the same fearful condition; that some of those, not all, who have waked up to a sense of their danger and addressed themselves to strenuous efforts to escape have succeeded; that if you do so, you through his interposition may escape; while every moment's delay is a moment of provocation to final abandonment to the flames. You see that the moment you were apprised of your danger would be the moment for effort—the moment in which you would wake up in agony to secure the interposition of that arm from which alone deliverance can come.

Now like this, is the case of every unconverted sinner in respect to the work of turning to God. The service of God has no attractions to his heart. Instead of love he feels aversion. The necessity of repentance to avoid future punishment is all the influence he feels. He loves the world, he loves his sins; he would firmly resolve always to live in sin were sin not to be punished; he abominates the necessity of renouncing it; and so long as he believes that he can safely continue in sin, so long he will do it, and with fearful probability, till the fires of the pit take hold of him. And now how much encouragement would you give him that success will crown his efforts to turn to God and escape perdition? Would you raise it to a high degree of probability? But this is the very presumption which he cherishes, and which emboldens him to go on in his iniquity. In this way you encourage procrastination, and brighten with hope the path which God darkens with the frowns and the terrors of his exhausted patience. No, if you would rouse him to attempt his conversion at all, preach to him *the peradventure* of the doctrine of Election. For while this is an immutable purpose of God, it is the sinner's only hope. Though it is formed in eternity, it is rightly viewed only in relation to what sinners shall do or shall not do in time. Accordingly it tells them with a plainness and power peculiar to itself, that stupidity in sin is death in sin. It tells them that all reliance on futurity, even for a moment, is the presumption of one walking on slippery places, where fiery billows roll beneath him. And yet it also tells every sinner that there is an attention of mind, an earnestness of effort, a plying of the moral powers to the act of duty, which in many cases does, and which even now in his case MAY, by the grace of God, result in the performance of duty and the salvation of the soul.

Thus the doctrine, while it shows him that the work may be done, brings upon him what sober reason would regard as the pressure of a present absolute necessity of doing it, with an almost insupportable weight, showing him that it must be done soon; bringing upon him the conviction that it must be done now, or with fearful probability it never will be done. It shows him that many, not to say most of those, who under this pressure put themselves to instant effort, with the fixed decision never to abandon it while life lasts, do in fact succeed. It shows him to himself sinking in the great waters, where without a struggle he is lost, but where by instant effort he may escape. If there be any condition conceivable which can wake and rouse the sinner to such effort, it is such as this. And thus to show him his condition, is all the encouragement that friendship, human or divine, would give him. Increase it if you will, but every addition is false and delusive. Increase the probability that a being who loves sin, and who will continue in sin so long as he thinks he can with safety, will be converted and saved, and in that proportion you allay his fears, confirm his presumption, and embolden him in rebellion against God. Tell him that the Spirit is now ready, and will always be ready, and you tell him just what he wishes to be true to comfort him in his sins. You tell him what you have no warrant to say, that God may already have abandoned him to hardness of heart. You tell him what has been hitherto his solace in sin, that God will still wait and still consult his convenience and his wishes; and so doing, you add your own strength to push him from the precipice where he stands, into everlasting burnings. Give him then the encouragement, *the peradventure* of success which pertains to a present effort. Balance the probabilities of failure and success, so as to give the death-blow to all thought of a moment's procrastination. Bring upon him all the urgency of the crisis, NOW OR NEVER. Give him any other counsel, and while he follows it, his breath may stop, his soul may be lost, and his blood may be on you, his treacherous counsellor.

Fourthly—The doctrine of Election brings upon the sinner *the entire power of moral obligation.* God's purpose of Election respects not machines or stocks, mere passive subjects of an influence, but intelligent, free moral agents, who are to live and act under the Moral Government of God forever. God can not make, nor purpose by grace to make, a creature holy who is not a complete moral agent; that is, one having every power qualifying him to become holy without grace. Nor can I conceive how any man should be weak enough to think, or to imagine that others should think, that this purpose of eternal grace should respect any other beings than accountable immortals. Surely the mission of the Holy Ghost, purposed and planned in these high counsels, must have an object worthy of such an embassy. If the creation of a world for man's probationary residence—if the law of God, coming forth with the authority of his throne—if the work of redemption by the blood of his Son—if the preparing of heavenly mansions in his temple on high, bespeak the exalted nature and relations of man as an accountable being, not less does God's eternal purpose of love and grace. Accordingly, no man can look at this great purpose of grace and mercy, without feeling that so it is and so it must be. When God is seen to make so much of man, man must make something of himself, instead of shrinking away from his obligations to his Maker and his Maker's government; sinking in his own estimation into the insignificance of a creature whose conduct touches no interests but those of time; of an insect who may be crushed and not missed from God's creation. God's purpose of Election does not thus make light of him. It tells him what the soul is, in the price paid for it, in the death of God's own Son; it tells him that he is capable of God's moral image, for to this it proposes to restore him; it tells him that he is formed to be a co-worker with God in accomplishing his designs, for thus it proposes to employ him forever. It brings him out upon the broad theater of accountable existence, and shows him that his character, his moral principle, his every action, reach the designs, the works, the glory of God in this and other worlds, and are to react upon himself also, either in a far more exceeding and eternal weight of glory, or in the endless agonies of God's condemnation. Thus it shows man to himself in his nature and relations, as an accountable subject of the Eternal King, living and acting for God or against him, amid the glories and grandeurs of eternity.

More than this. The doctrine of Election reveals the superadded obligations of an economy of redemption. It is man redeemed from the curse of a law which he is qualified and bound to obey, to whom the great salvation purchased by blood is proffered; manfully qualified to embrace the offer, is the being to whom it is made. It proceeds wholly on the ground that the purchased inheritance is proffered with the sincerity of a God who does not lie—who does not mock his creatures with delusive offers; on the ground therefore that man is a moral agent without grace; that he can and ought without grace to accept the offer. Is not the purpose of Election a purpose of God to bring men to accept of his great salvation already offered? Yes, I say offered. And can God offer salvation to the trees of the forest, or a statue, or a corpse? No. God's offers are made to free moral agents, and the purpose of Election proceeds entirely on the sincerity with which they are made to each and to all—offers urged by command, and entreaty, and love, and mercy, and every motive the universe can furnish; influences perfectly adapted, in view of the moral powers of man, to secure the acceptance of the offers. Is man then under no obligation to accept them? Does not the purpose of Election distinctly, unanswerably announce this amazing fact; coming before the mind as it does, simply as a purpose of God to bring men by his grace to fulfill these high obligations which exist without grace? And can man admit the purpose, and deny his obligations? No man can believe this in the clear, unperverted light of the doctrine of Election. If any doctrine combines in one view every thing that creates and enhances man's duty, if any thing can put the unyielding grasp of obligation on his conscience to do what God's law and gospel require, it is this. He must see himself under all the obligations of a law which has been bought off from its curse by God's mercy and a Saviour's blood; and he must see them recognized and set forth in all their length, and breadth, and height, and depth, by the doctrine of Election. Had not these obligations existed, God's purpose of electing grace had never been known, nor heaven ever heard one song it has inspired. Let any man then, attempt to fly from his obligations and find a refuge in the doctrine of Election if he can. Let him retreat to this hiding-place, and attempt to throw off his obligations from himself upon his Maker; but if he will listen, even there he will hear the voice to duty sounding in his ears its most distinct and solemn language, and the summons of obligation be to his soul like the trump of God. Go if you will, but even there shall you hear that God's purpose of Election seeks its objects in a world of rebels—rebels against law, rebels against grace, of giant rebels, of whom you are one.

Finally—The doctrine of Election discloses to sinners *just views of their guilt and danger*. It rests on the basis of this fact, that men under the immeasurable obligations just described are under all the guilt and the fearful exposure to eternal condemnation of their violation. Otherwise the purpose of Election could have no object and could never have been formed; it were an absurdity and a solecism. God purpose to renew and sanctify, and save from sin and condemnation, beings who are not sinners! to save from hell those who are not exposed to it! Think what the doctrine is, and say, is not man's character that of a sinner, a rebel against God, and is not exposure to hell, while he is impenitent and unforgiven, his fearful condition?

But this is not all. For why this purpose of electing grace? The answer to this question discloses an overwhelming fact; I mean *that perverseness of the sinner's heart which nothing but the purposed grace will ever subdue.* Can there be a doubt of this? Inquire then into the reasons for this purpose of God. Is it because man is a sinner and exposed to endless ruin? Not simply that. Is it because he is not redeemed by an all-sufficient Atonement? Not at all. Is it because the sincerest offers of life are not made to him? Plainly not. Is it because he is not as truly able to accept these offers as he is to reject them? Nothing can be further from the truth. Is it because he is not under every conceivable obligation to accept of these offers? Surely not. Why then this purpose of renewing grace? Because the sinner will *perversely and infallibly reject these offers without this grace.* Here is the true reason, the tremendous fact, and the doctrine of Election reveals it, pouring the daylight of truth on all its guilt and all its terrors. Calls and invitations, entreaties and warnings, are to no purpose. Urged by the sincerest love of a redeeming God, awed by the frowns and denunciations of his wrath, amid Bibles and Sabbaths, the voice of men and angels, the wooings and the tears of compassion, human and divine, under the strivings of the Holy Spirit, with all the light of truth and all the motives in the universe concentrated and poured burning and blazing on his heart; Oh, how he still plants the firm footstep of rebellion on Jesus' blood; how, as a reckless, ruined, damned spirit, he rushes on the thick bosses of Jehovah's buckler, and hastens his infatuated way to hell! Nor is there a sinner on earth who can look at the doctrine of Election, and not see himself as in a glass to be just such a rebel as this. None other can the purpose of Election respect.

Why then will not the sinner actually perish under all this guilt? Let him look at the doctrine of Election, and see what is the measure of guilt it discloses in the perverseness of his own heart; how he has hated and perhaps vilified this purpose of God, and despised and slighted its gifts; how he has to this hour refused all accordance with God's mode of dispensing grace, and habitually grieved the Holy Spirit. Let him look at the doctrine of Election, and see that the sovereignty of that God who hath mercy on whom he will have mercy, hangs a fearful uncertainty over all his prospects, and that the holiness of God must abhor a character of such moral deformity as his, and that it might be expected to revolt from all intercourse of love with him forever. Let him look at the purpose of Election, and see how it has hitherto left the broad way to destruction thronged with fellow-beings, and how it still leaves the multitudes of living men treading on with thoughtless footstep the same road to death,—how many no worse than himself, with no more to provoke final rejection, and with the same hopes from futurity, are falling every day into perdition. Let him look at this purpose of Election, and in its actual development what a field of observation this world spreads out before him; how it mocks human hopes, and trifles with the schemes and plans of salvation of human devising; how it hurries away by death, amid the joyous anticipations of health and strength, unpardoned and unsanctified men; how with the lightning's flash it wakes up from the fondest dreams of salvation to the agonies of eternal disappointment and woe, and how through human perverseness it renders the prayers of God's secret ones, and all the instituted means of his grace, the occasion of exhausted patience and of an aggravated doom; how at the last consummation it will fix all destiny, shutting the gates of death and hell that they be opened no more, forbidding all mercy and excluding all hope. Let him look at the doctrine of Election, and see up to the present hour of this world's history how few—Oh, how few! of all its myriads are saved; let him look at himself, what he is, where he is, and whither he is going, and let him say if he feels no alarm. As he thinks of these high counsels of the Great Disposer of all, and sees how they are in fact unfolded in this sinful world, let him say if no salutary dread takes hold of his thoughtless, guilty spirit. He is, he must be afraid. He does not, he can not think of that throne of a sovereign and yet offended God, and not fear him; he can not see that rising cloud of wrath, and not hear those thunders roll, which so fearfully forebode the coming tempest of God's indignation upon every stupid sinner, and not tremble. Hark! how it murmurs damnation to thy soul!

REMARKS.

1. According to the views given of the doctrine of Election, *it can be opposed only by the determined sinner.* As the doctrine which, in one respect, is the only basis of hope to a guilty, lost world, surely none can oppose it. If then it be opposed at all on the ground of its practical tendencies, it must be on account of its tendency to destroy all presumption in sin; as furnishing no more encouragement to seek salvation than what prompts to immediate and strenuous effort to obtain it; as bringing upon the conscience of the sinner the full power and pressure of his obligations, and unfolding the measure of his guilt and danger. And now I ask, who is the man that is unwilling that a doctrine should actually produce these effects on himself? Who is the man that wishes to go on in sin, with the false and fatal presumption that all will be safe in the end? Who is the man that wishes for that encouragement in respect to the salvation of his soul, that supersedes and prevents all present solicitude and all present effort? Who is the man that refuses to feel his obligations to his God and Saviour, and thoughtless of his guilt and unrelenting for it, chooses to walk quietly and unmolested on the brink of damnation? The determined sinner, and he alone. Well may he oppose, and deny, and pervert the doctrine of Election. Otherwise, it would break up his present quiet in sin. It would come in like the strong man armed, upon his firm purpose of rebellion against God; it would bind that purpose, and spoil and demolish all his hopes and comforts, and scatter them to the winds. And, My Hearers, it is not worth while to conceal this plain matter of fact, to palliate and excuse, when we have God's message to deliver and your souls to save. A sinner at ease, while he thinks of God's purpose of Election; while he thinks of his soul forfeited already to God's justice, and through his own perverseness at the disposal of God's sovereignty; at ease, while he thinks that he may be passed by in the unchangeable counsels of electing grace! He can not be. Does he say, this is a hard doctrine, he can not bear it. Yes, very hard to the

determined sinner. But true, and very useful even to him is the doctrine which benevolence, the sincerest kindness, if it can gain a hearing, would preach to every such self-destroying soul. Eternal grace and mercy first preached it. And shall we not repeat it, lest the sinner should be disturbed; lest he should not go down to hell without annoyance? Would to God that the doctrine of Election might have its proper influence on each sinner in this assembly. Then would he fear the justice of that God whom he so boldly defies, and yet is not without hope from his grace. Then would he for once look to that God who may show him mercy; then would he ask, what must I do to be saved; then would he have no rest till he found it in the everlasting arms.

2. Sinners who oppose the doctrine of Election, *oppose their own best interests.* They oppose those very truths which, in some form, must come home to their conscience and their heart, or they must be damned. In some form or another they must see the mad presumption of stupidity in sin; that there is a fearful uncertainty that they will ever repent and secure their salvation; that they are under a weight of violated obligation, and a measure of guilt which are enough to sink them to the lowest abyss of ruin; and have a perverseness of heart and stubbornness of will which tells only of inevitable destruction. I say, they must consent to see and feel this. God will not convert a sinner who denies his dependence on his grace, nor take him to heaven who is unprepared to thank his deliverer. These are the truths embodied and held forth in the doctrine of Election with peculiar clearness and force. Fellow-Sinner, I wish you to remember this—believe this doctrine. Let it come to your mind as it is. It will show you on the one hand all the hope there is for you; and on the other, that you are in the hands of an incensed God, who may indeed save you, and yet may justly destroy you. This is what we wish you to see and to feel, and we can not in kindness to you but try to make you feel it. Look then at this doctrine, and you will not sleep in sin another moment. You can no more face it with stupidity and unconcern, than you can look into the burning lake without emotion. If then you would be saved, if you have not resolved to perish, I charge you not to resist the heart-searching, conscience-troubling doctrine of Election. You are fighting against your highest, your eternal interests—

taking one of those fearful steps toward everlasting perdition, which in the case of thousands, have taken hold on hell.

3. To conclude, the condition of sinners as disclosed by the doctrine of Election is solemn and affecting. So the great apostle viewed it. Paul's preface to this doctrine was, "I say the truth in Christ, I lie not, my conscience bearing me witness in the Holy Ghost, that I have great heaviness and continual sorrow of heart, for my brethren, my kinsmen, according to the flesh." Life is rapidly passing away. These hours in which God will renew and sanctify the souls of sinful men will soon be gone. Their speedy termination will bring you, continuing as you are, to the bar of God, not to arraign his justice in your condemnation, not to impeach his grace by casting the guilt of your impenitence on any decree of his, not to lighten your final doom by the conviction that the guilt is not all your own, but to penetrate your inmost soul with the conscious, agonizing truth that you are self-destroyers. You will come to the judgment with the remorseful conviction, that God, with more than a father's love, desired and sought your salvation; that it was his unqualified purpose that you should repent and live, rather than sin and die; that you freely and deliberately defeated this purpose of his love. You will remember that when he revealed his purpose to save some by his grace from going down to ruin by their own choice; when he told you that he did all that he wisely could to save you, that you never devoted one week, or day, or even hour of your probation to this great concern; never made one honest effort to give your heart to him in love; were never for one moment willing that the Son of God should save you, but met and requited all his love, and entreaties, and grace, his blood, his agonies, his death, his authority, his pity, his wrath; met them all with firm, unyielding, desperate resistance. Oh, what must it be to stand at God's judgment-seat with such upbraidings riving the conscience, and thundering in the soul the sentence of doom!

And are there not those in this assembly whom such an appearance at the final bar awaits? My soul can weep in secret places for you. I could fall at your feet and with tears entreat you. For whose perdition is certain, who will lie down in the devouring fire, if not some of you who yet remain stupid in your sins? Reflect, ye who are thus wasting your probation, how long you have lived in sin, what means of grace and salvation you have perverted; reflect how you have persevered in sin amid the outpourings of God's Spirit; how you have stood aside from all the peculiar influences of such seasons, and defeated all the efforts of eternal love and mercy to save you. Think too, that the number of God's elect from this generation may be well-nigh completed, and that the influences of the Spirit to convert and save may here be given no more till you shall have gone into eternity. And now say, My Dear Friends, are there no reasons to fear that you will never see life? Are there no marks of that reprobation of God upon you, which abandons sinners to strong delusions, that they may be damned? There may at least be one such. Fellow-Sinner, it may be you. I fear it, and with trembling, and compassion, and love for your never-dying soul, I call on you to sleep no longer. Take, Oh take the hope which God's purpose of grace imparts, for he may yet save; and take also its terrors and flee from the wrath to come, and lay hold on eternal life. From such an attempt there is hope. Set yourself to it then, as a work to be done before another sun shall rise; yea, this hour, this moment. Cheer the dark hours that shall intervene before another morning, by reconciliation with God and hope in his mercy. Oh, the blessed hope that now beams upon you from the counsels of eternal grace; the glad assurance that even now you may become a child and an heir of God! But venture on in the way of determined sin, and what can you hope for? In that path stands death, with which you have made no covenant; on that way an angry God pours only the darkness, and the tempest, and the fire of his indignation; ay, at the next step in it, a reprobating God may meet you, saying, "He is joined to his idols, let him alone." Let him alone, ye embassadors of the great salvation; let him alone, ye angels of mercy; thou only Saviour of the lost, let him alone; Spirit of all grace, let him alone.

V.

PERSEVERANCE.

"Being confident of this very thing, that he who hath begun a good work in you will perform it until the day of Jesus Christ."—*Phil.* i. 6.

PAUL wrote this Epistle to the Philippians when he was a prisoner at Rome. He tells them that he never thought of them without gratitude to God for their fellowship in the Gospel; and that he felt such lively emotions of joy in their behalf, as greatly to solace him under the trials of imprisonment. Nor did the joy of the apostle on account of these converts to the faith, result *merely* from the fact that God had *begun* a good work in them,—a good work which after all there was much reason to fear would never be finished, but terminate at last in sin and perdition. It was alike his confidence and his consolation, that he who had *begun* this good work would perform it; would carry it on toward perfection till it should be completed at the final day, being confident of this *very thing*, "that he which hath begun a good work in you will perform it until the day of Jesus Christ."

My object in the present discourse, is to show that the same thing is true of every real Christian; in other words, to establish the doctrine, as it is called, of the Saints' Perseverance.

I. I propose to explain this doctrine.

For this purpose I remark—

1. That by the doctrine of the Saints' Perseverance, we do not mean that true saints never fall into sin. They do. "There is not a just man on earth that doeth good and sinneth not." David committed adultery and murder. Peter denied his Saviour with oaths and execrations. Real Christians then are sometimes left to the commission of the grossest crimes.

2. The doctrine is *not*, that real Christians, if they fall into sin, will be saved without repentance. I say this because almost all who deny it, represent us as holding, that all real Christians will be saved, whether they persevere in holiness to the end or not. We wish it then to be distinctly understood

that we hold no such doctrine. No doubt if any real Christian falls into sin and dies without repentance, he will be damned.

3. Our doctrine is not, that Christians CANNOT fall into sin and finally perish. They can. The Christian has the same power to sin, considered as a moral agent, which he always had, and left of God, would fall away and perish. The question does not at all respect what Christians can do, or what they have power to do. They have power to commit sin, and to go on in sin till death and perdition overtake them. But the question is, whether *they will in fact* die in sin and perish eternally. We maintain the negative of this question. I therefore remark—

4. That *the real Christian will never be left so to fall away as finally to perish.* We maintain that God will so keep his own children, so sanctify them through the truth, so invigorate their faith and love, so revive their graces when they languish and decay, so reclaim them from their backslidings, so perform the good work begun in them, that they will at last be found in the way of holiness and obtain eternal life.

That there may be no mistake on this subject, allow that one real Christian will in fact so persevere in holiness as to be saved; allow that there is no absurdity in the warnings and cautions against apostasy as addressed to that one; allow the necessity of constant watchfulness and vigorous effort on his part; say that he can fall away; that if he falls into sin and dies impenitent he will perish;—say all this and whatever else you please, but only allow that one Christian will so persevere in fact as to reach heaven, and I add, this is precisely our doctrine, with this only difference, that what you affirm of one we affirm of every real Christian.

II. I shall offer some direct *proof* of the doctrine.

The doctrine of the Saints' Perseverance I regard as taught by revelation, and its truth or falsehood to be wholly decided by what the Bible teaches.

I can not in one discourse bring together but a small part of this proof. I shall aim only to give you some of the various forms in which the Scriptures teach the doctrine, citing under each, only one or two passages from many which are equally conclusive.

1. The promise of the Father to the Son of his reward. The promise was, that the Redeemer should see a seed who should

prolong their days,—see of the travail of his soul and be satisfied. Christ further unfolds the import of this promise thus: "All that the Father giveth me shall come to me, and him that cometh to me I will in no wise cast out." "And this is the Father's will, that of all which he hath given me, I should lose nothing, but should raise it up at the last day." Now if all who were given to Christ shall come to him, and if no one of these shall be cast out; if nothing shall be lost, will not every such person persevere in holiness and be saved?

2. From the intercession of Christ. Having prayed that they may be one with him as he is one with the Father, he adds: "Neither pray I for these alone, but for them also *who shall believe on me* through their word, that they all may be one, as thou, Father, art in me and I in thee, that they may be one in us." Now here is a prayer offered for every Christian to the end of time. It has been offered by the Son of God, him "whom the Father always heareth."

3. From the covenant which God hath made with his people. This covenant is virtually the whole Gospel. It may be contemplated in its general comprehensive promise, and in its particular promises. First—Its comprehensive promise. This is nothing less than this: "I will be their God, and they shall be my people." Could more be promised, even by God himself? Will the blessing of sanctifying and saving grace, the richest, best gift of God to man, be wanting? Will even the least real blessing be withheld? We are at no loss on this point, for he hath told us that he "will give *grace* and *glory*, and withhold no good thing from them that walk uprightly." And again, "*All things* are yours." Will any to whom God hath made such promises as these, perish eternally?

Secondly. Let us contemplate this covenant in some of its particular promises. Here a wide field opens before us; I can only glance at some of them. Here consider the specific development of this covenant. "Behold the days come, saith the Lord, that I will make a new covenant with the house of Israel; not *according* to the covenant that I made with their fathers in the day I took them by the hand to bring them out of Egypt, which covenant they broke,"—[this covenant was *conditional*, and they broke it, and the new one now made, as the apostle says, is founded in better promises,]—"but this shall be the covenant that I will make with the house of Israel;

after those days, saith the Lord, I will put my law in their inward parts, and write it in their hearts, and I will be their God, and they shall be my people. ' And I will give them one heart and one way, that they may fear me *forever;* and I will make an everlasting covenant with them, that I will not turn away from them to do them good; but I will put my fear within their hearts, that THEY SHALL NOT DEPART FROM ME." But say our opponents, some will depart from him. Which will stand, their speculation or the covenant of God? But let us contemplate still further these particular promises as they occur, I may almost say, on every page of the Bible. Consider those which connect salvation with holiness once begun in the heart. "He that believeth on the Son, *hath* everlasting life." "This is the will of him that sent me, that every one that seeth the Son and believeth on him, may have everlasting life, and I will raise him up at the last day." "Mary hath chosen that good part which shall not be taken away from her."

Consider those which secure the Christian's growth in grace. "The righteous shall hold on his way, and he that hath clean hands shall wax stronger and stronger." "Every branch that beareth fruit, he purgeth it, that it may bring forth more fruit." The path of the just is as "a shining light, which shineth more and more unto the perfect day."

Consider those which secure him against the fatal power of all temptation. "But God is faithful, who will not suffer you to be tempted above that ye are able, but will with the temptation make a way of escape that ye may be able to bear it."

Those which secure recovery from falls into sin. "The steps of a good man are ordered by the Lord; though he fall, he shall not be utterly cast down, for the Lord upholdeth him with his hand." "A just man though he fall seven times, yet shall he rise again."

Those which promise no further remembrance of his sins. Saith the Lord, "I will put my law in their hearts," &c., "and their sins and iniquities I will remember no more."

Those which secure deliverance from condemnation. "He that believeth on Him that sent me, hath everlasting life, and *shall not come into condemnation*, but is passed from death unto life." "There is now no condemnation to them which are in Christ Jesus."

Those which secure confirmation in holiness to the end.

"Who shall confirm you unto the end, that ye may be blameless in the day of the Lord Jesus." "The Lord is faithful, who shall establish you and keep you from evil."

Those in which this confidence is expressed in respect to others. "Being confident of this very thing, that he which hath begun a good work in you will perform it until the day of Jesus Christ." "And we have confidence in the Lord touching you, that ye both do and *will do* the things which we command you." "We are persuaded better things of you, and things which accompany salvation."

Those in which good men have expressed this assurance themselves. Saith Asaph: "Thou shalt guide me with thy counsel, and afterward receive me to glory." "I know," saith Job, "that my Redeemer liveth," &c., "whom I shall see for myself." Paul says: "I am persuaded that he is able to keep that which I have committed unto him." "Henceforth there is laid up for me a crown of glory."

Those which assert the enduring nature of real religion. "The fear of the Lord is clean, enduring forever." "Blessed is the man that feareth the Lord, his righteousness endureth forever." "Surely, he shall not be moved forever; his heart is fixed, trusting in the Lord." "His righteousness endureth forever."

Those which exclude all disappointment. "When thou hast found her [wisdom] then there shall be a reward, and thy expectation shall not be cut off." "For whoso findeth me [wisdom] findeth life, and shall obtain favor of the Lord." "A hope that maketh not ashamed." "Whosoever drinketh of the water that I shall give him, shall *never* thirst; but the water that I shall give him shall be in him a well of water springing up into everlasting life."

Those which assert their union with Christ. "They are members of his body, of his flesh, and of his bones." "They are one with him, as he is one with the Father."

Those which base the assurance of God's perfections *on his immutability*. "I, the Lord, change not, therefore ye sons of Jacob are not consumed." "Having loved his own which were in the world, he loved them to the end." *On his faithfulness.* "The very God of peace sanctify you wholly; and I pray God your whole spirit, and soul, and body be preserved blameless unto the coming of our Lord Jesus Christ." "Faithful is he that calleth you, who also will do it." *In his truth.* "God willing more abundantly to show unto the heirs of promise the immutability of his counsel, confirmed it by an oath, that by two immutable things in which it was impossible for God to lie, we might have strong consolation, who have fled for refuge to the hope set before us, which hope we have as an anchor to the soul." *On his power.* "Who are kept by the power of God through faith unto salvation." "My sheep hear my voice, and I know them and they follow me." *His omniscience and eternal purpose.* "Whom he did foreknow he also did predestinate to be conformed to the image of his Son." I add but one passage more, the bold and triumphant challenge of the apostle, in which, with God and Christ engaged in behalf of believers, he bids defiance to the universe beside. "What shall we then say to these things? If God be for us, who can be against us? He that spared not his own Son, but delivered him up for us all, how shall he not with him also freely give us all things? Who shall lay any thing to the charge of God's elect? It is God that justifieth. Who is he that condemneth? It is Christ that died; yea, rather that is risen again, who is even at the right hand of God, who also maketh intercession for us. Who shall separate us from the love of Christ? Shall tribulation, or distress, or persecution, or famine, or nakedness, or peril, or sword? Nay, in all these things we are more than conquerors, through him that loved us. For I am persuaded that neither death, nor life, nor angels, nor principalities, nor powers, nor things present, nor things to come, nor height, nor depth, nor any other creature shall be able to separate us from the love of God which is in Christ Jesus our Lord." Here is the triumph of the saints, triumph in God their Saviour. A universe is boldly challenged and defied. Nothing, nothing shall separate from Christ these members of his body, of his flesh, and of his bones. They are safe. An omnipotent God will keep them.

III. I shall briefly consider the objections to our doctrine. These, so far as they demand consideration, may be reduced to three or four.

1. It is said that the Scriptures record instances of actual apostasy from real religion. I reply, no such instance can be found in the record. Let us examine one of the most plausible, the case of Judas. The passage relied on is this: "Those

whom thou gavest me I have kept, and none of them is lost but the son of perdition." This passage, to a mere English reader, seems to teach that Judas *was given* to Christ, whereas, properly translated, it implies the contrary. The true reading is this: "Those whom thou gavest me I have kept, and none *of them* is lost; but the son of perdition is lost." But allowing that Judas was in some sense said to be given to Christ, one thing is absolulely certain, viz., that he *was never a true disciple.* "Jesus answered them, Have I not chosen you twelve, and one of you *is a devil?* He spake of Judas Iscariot." On another occasion, long before the apostasy of Judas, Christ said, "But there are some of you which *believe not.* For Jesus knew from the beginning who they were that believed not, and who should betray him." But, Brethren, for an unbeliever, a devil, to betray Christ, is not falling from grace.

But I have not time, nor is it necessary to examine other particular cases. There are two passages of Scripture which remove all these objections at a stroke. "We are not of them that draw back unto perdition, but of them which believe to the saving of the soul." Now here are two classes, comprising those who do not and those who do draw back to perdition. Who are they who do not draw back? They who *believe to the saving of the soul.* Who are they who do draw back? John tells us. "They went out from us, but they were not of us; for if they had been of us, they would, no doubt, have continued with us. But they went out from us that they might be made manifest that they were not all of us."* In other words, had they been of us, i. e., real Christians, they would never have apostatized. Now this settles the question henceforth and forever in respect to all apostates. They never were real Christians. They were always hollow at heart, and their open apostasy only proves it.

2. It is said that the Scriptures exhibit the *salvation of real Christians as conditional;* for example, as in this passage: "We are made partakers with Christ, *if* we hold the beginning of our confidence steadfast unto the end." It is claimed that this class of passages prove that Christians MAY fall away, may not endure to the end, may possibly be lost. Be it so; undoubtedly they *may;* I have fully and expressly said this in

---

* Translate, "that they all were not of us."

stating the doctrine. These passages prove that they *may* fall away. But is not this all? Do they prove that they *will* fall away? This is the point. Is proving that Christians *may* fall away and perish, the same thing as proving that they *will?* Then indeed we are in an awful predicament. For this class of texts proves that all Christians *may* fall away and perish; and if this is proving that they *will*, then will every soul be lost.

How is it possible that any rational man should be imposed on by such reasoning as this? All Christians can fall away and perish, or they may fall away and perish; therefore all, or at least some, will do so! All in this assembly can go without food and die by starvation, and therefore all, or at least some, will in fact die by starvation! Or, every man in this house can and may commit suicide to-day, and therefore every one, or at least some, will commit suicide to-day!

But let me illustrate in this particular the doctrine of the Saints' Perseverance by an example. During the dangerous voyage of Paul with others to Rome, an angel appeared to him from God, and assured him that not one of the company should be lost. This fact then was certain, was revealed, that no one on board should perish. But afterward, when the sailors, alarmed for their safety, were about to leave the ship in the boat, "Paul said to the centurion and the soldiers, Except these abide in the ship ye can not be saved." Now both were true. It was true that no life would be lost, for an angel from God had said it. It was also true, that if the sailors left the ship, none could be saved, for so said an apostle. And yet no life was lost. So we maintain, that while the Bible clearly asserts, that unless Christians remain faithful they can not be saved, it no less abundantly asserts that no real Christian shall be lost. When therefore, you find texts which declare that real Christians will perish, *if* they fall away, they no more prove that any will fall away, than the above declaration proved that the sailors would leave the ship.

But we shall be asked (and the objection is substantially the same as that we are considering), if none will in fact ever apostatize from real religion, why so many warnings and cautions in the Scriptures against apostasy? I answer, because real Christians *can* and *may*, and doubtless would apostatize and perish, if they were not solemnly warned against it. And now

I ask the objector, can you give any better or any other reasons for these warnings? But he says, they prove that some will in fact apostatize and draw back to perdition. But I ask, how so? What, My Brethren, because God, with all the solemnities of judgment and eternal retribution, warns his children against apostasy, does this prove that they will apostatize? Because he takes the best means to prevent apostasy, do these very means insure it? Suppose a case. Your neighbor says to you, I fully believe that all, or at least some of your children will yet prove to be liars, thieves, and robbers. Why so? you inquire. Why, says he, I heard you, the other day, giving them the most solemn warnings against these crimes. True, you reply, my object and confident expectation is, by this means, to prevent their committing these crimes. Oh, no, says he, such wise, and faithful, and solemn warnings are infallible proof that some of your children will become liars, thieves, and robbers, for no parent ever warned his children against these crimes without their committing them. Would you not think your neighbor was deranged? Yet this is the reasoning of our opponents from the warnings which God addresses to his children. They infer that some of them will certainly apostatize, because God, on pain of eternal death, has warned them against apostasy!

But it may be said that no parent warns his children against crimes which it is impossible that they should commit. True. Neither does God; for as I stated before, it is *possible* that his children should apostatize, though I maintain that *they will not*. There is the same possibility in one case as in the other; and therefore, the same propriety in warnings in the one case as in the other.

But you say, no parent would think it necessary to warn his children against crimes which he *knew* they would never commit. But does not God do this? Or do Christians in fact commit every sin against which God has warned them? Besides, suppose you knew that cautions were necessary to prevent, and would in fact prevent the crimes of your children, what would you do? Now precisely in this light are the warnings of God against the apostasy of his children to be viewed. They are necessary to prevent, and addressed to Christians for the purpose of preventing it; they are perfectly fitted and designed to secure this end. And shall we infer that the means which God adopts to secure a given end will defeat it? Is it proof that Christians will apostatize and perish, because God by the most solemn cautions and awful warnings has undertaken to prevent it? Surely the most rational inference is, that they will secure the end designed, and thus through grace prove the means of their continued holiness and final salvation. If the warnings of God therefore prove any thing, it is that none will apostatize.

3. It is said that our doctrine leads to licentiousness, tends to relax Christian watchfulness, lessens the power of motives to holiness, and even emboldens Christians to sin under the impression that they shall at last be saved. I readily admit that if the Christian had no love of holiness, or if he could be supposed to possess any evidence of his piety with the love of sin in his heart, or if our doctrine did not maintain the necessity of a faithful, diligent practice in all holy living, then it would be liable to the present objection. But it is not so. The man who does not love holiness above all things else, who finds the love of the world and of sin reigning in his heart, and who denies the necessity of faithfulness and diligence in all duty, has no warrant to rank himself among those that will be saved. All the evidence is against him. He has no reason to think that he is or ever was a Christian, or that the promise of salvation ever embraced him. The man, and the only man who can believe or hope to persevere in holiness and be saved, is the man who is holy, who loves holiness and loves heaven. And the question is, whether such a man will be led into sin by believing that he shall persevere in holiness, that he shall go on in the course in which above all others he desires to go, and obtain the end which above all others he longs to obtain? Now we can bring this question to an infallible test. Suppose then, it were revealed that all men who love good living and desire long life, shall eat when they are hungry and drink when they are thirsty, and that they will continue to do so, and that by so doing, and in no other way, they will secure the longest and happiest life possible; would the belief or the knowledge that you should continue in this course and thus secure a long and happy life, have any tendency to induce you to forego the pleasures of a single meal? Would it have any such effect, when by so doing you would only prove to yourself that you did not after all belong to the class to whom the

promise was made, and were in fact entering on a course that with fearful probability would end in starvation and death? Now this is a case exactly parallel with the one before us. The question is not whether our doctrine tends to lead hypocrites into sin, and thus to unmask their hypocrisy. It doubtless has this tendency, and so much the better. But the question is, does the doctrine tend to lead the real Christian into sin? The Christian hungers and thirsts after righteousness, and the promise is that he shall be filled; and has this promise any tendency to destroy his appetite and to lead him to love sin? Do men cease to love food and drink, because they believe that they shall always love food and drink, and actually eat and drink to the end of life? Is the man who loves holiness and delights in the service of God, likely to neglect it because he believes he shall continue to be holy, and thus obtain eternal life? Appeal to facts. Can you find a man who has truly loved the service of God, and forsaken it because he believed he should love and serve him forever? Ask the thousands and millions who have believed our doctrine, whether the heart that loves God resorts to it as a license to sin against him? Have not those who have believed this doctrine, been among the holiest men the world has ever seen? Ask them whether they felt their zeal abate, or their labor in his cause languish, because they believed that heaven would in this way become their certain inheritance? Ask the noble army of martyrs, and all the saints who have met death in triumph, whether they were less desirous to glorify God and enjoy his presence because they regarded heaven as near and certain. Ask Job, who knew that his Redeemer lived; ask Asaph, who knew he should be received to glory; ask Peter, when assured by his Saviour that his faith should not fail; ask Paul, when he looked upon his crown in the heavens as a sure possession. Ask these men whether this assurance cooled their love to Christ and put them in love with sin? Ask angels; ask the multitude before the throne who have washed their robes in the blood of the Lamb, whether their safe entrance into everlasting glory, awakens the love of sin, and tempts them to rebel against the God whom they worship? Ah! here are facts, and facts are not to be reasoned against. Surely, he who loves his God and Saviour will not be induced to sin against him by the promise of everlasting life.

REMARKS.

1. Our subject will enable us to compare the practical bearing of believing and denying the doctrine of the Saints' Perseverance. What then is the practical influence of denying it? One thing is plain; the Christian deprives himself wholly of any *peculiar* influence from the promises to animate and encourage to holy obedience. He has on this scheme no promise of preserving grace, no promise of God to secure his perseverance. His salvation, of course, is just as truly a matter of doubt and uncertainty as when he was yet in his sins. *Then* he *might* be saved, and so he *may be* now; and this is all that can be said. *All* the promises of God to the Christian it is claimed are *conditional*, as truly so as to the sinner. The results therefore, are as *uncertain* (unless he dies before *he can* fall from grace), as were he still under condemnation. And can this be? Does the Gospel open no prospects, and give no consolations to God's children, but what it also gives his enemies? Do you say, there is a hope, a probability that God will carry on the work of his grace when once begun? But I demand your warrant for these. According to your scheme you have no divine declaration, no promise of God; no, not a word in all the Bible to authorize such a hope. Every promise of God you say is *conditional.* The sum total of all that God says, is, *if* he endures to the end he shall be saved, and if he draws back he shall be lost; and this decides nothing in respect to which he will do. On what then, I ask, does your hope of the Christian's perseverance depend? Simply and *wholly* on his own *faithfulness.* And what is such a hope? Contemplate such a Christian. With grace in his heart as a grain of mustard-seed, that heart frail and wandering in its affections, fluctuating and fitful in its best resolutions, surrounded by a tempting world, ever prone to relapse into sin, often quenching the Holy Spirit and provoking God to abandon him; called to wrestle against principalities, against powers, against the rulers of the darkness of this world, against spiritual wickedness in high places (his own strength weakness), and not a particle of grace promised from God to secure that faithfulness on which all depends;—what hope of victory has he? Who would not say, there is every thing to discourage and depress, to damp the ardor of hope and to sink to the weakness of despair! *All*

you say, depends on his own faithfulness, and his faithfulness depends on what? Not on any promise of grace, for there is not a word from God to secure it; but on his own heart—a heart which like that of *Christian* Judas, as some esteem him, can and may, and for aught that appears, *will* betray the Son of God with a kiss, and sell him for thirty pieces of silver! On such faithfulness, with no better security, depends the Christian's hope of heaven! Who that knows his own heart would not expect to prove a traitor and to go to his own place?

Contemplate now for a moment the Christian who believes our doctrine. *Himself* he can not, *dare* not trust. With the conscious fickleness of his own heart, his best resolutions so often broken, his liveliest emotions so soon abated, his proneness to sin so constant, his return to God so difficult, his own faithfulness such a broken reed, so much to be done, with such a body of death to discourage, and overwhelm, how soon, without the promised grace of God to keep him, would he abandon all in despair! But with the promise of a faithful God sounding in his ears, "My grace is sufficient for thee," his heart revives, and he is filled with the inspiration of hope. He listens, and again he hears, "My strength shall be perfected in thy weakness;" "none shall pluck thee out of my hand;" and he rises as in the consciousness of the promised strength, and enters the career of obedience as with its reward insured and in sight. The otherwise insurmountable obstacle of unconquered corruption no longer appalls. This mighty barrier at the very entrance opens before him, the rough places are made smooth, every mountain is brought low, every valley is filled, and by the promises is unvailed the salvation of God. Guilt is made to hope, and weakness itself looks up with confidence, and the path of obedience up to the paradise of God, is cheered and brightened with the assurance that what God hath said, God will do.

2. By the practical use we make of this doctrine, we may be helped to determine whether we are Christians indeed. The doctrine unperverted, in its true tendency, animates the real Christian in the path of obedience. One who believes it, reasons and acts thus: "With all my imperfections, defects, and unworthiness I bear the marks of a child of God. I love holiness, I hate sin. My meat and drink is to do the will of my Father in heaven. I desire nothing so much as to be like my

Saviour, and to be freed from all sin. Remaining sin is my burden, my grief, my abhorrence. Who shall deliver me from the body of this death? I thank God, through Jesus Christ our Lord. Amid all my corruption, and inconstancy, and weakness, and vain resolutions, I do not, will not sink in discouragement, for in the Lord have I strength. His grace shall be sufficient for me; his strength shall be perfected in my weakness. Here I take courage; my desires to be like God will be realized. Weak in myself, but strong in the Lord and in the power of his might, I press toward the mark for the prize of my high calling in Christ Jesus my Lord. I shall awake in his likeness; then and not till then shall I be satisfied." This man is a Christian.

Another who believes this doctrine, turns it, by a gross and horrid perversion, to a very different purpose. "Once a Christian," he says, "always a Christian. Having once the marks of a Christian, no matter whether I possess these evidences now or not; no matter whether I desire holiness and hate sin, it is enough for me that I was once a Christian." Once a Christian! Never, never was this man a Christian. Whatever may have been his experience, whatever may have been his hopes, his joys, whatever proof he may *think* himself to have had, he is a hypocrite. He loves the world, he loves sin; it is not in his heart to love God and glorify his Saviour. In the language of the apostle, he goes out from us because he is not of us, that it may be made manifest that he is not of us. He remains to this moment in the gall of bitterness and in the bonds of iniquity. And does the doctrine that they who love holiness *will persevere in holiness*, warrant the conclusion that he who loves sin is a Christian? Does the doctrine which supports, and comforts, and animates a heart full of divine love, administer equal consolation to the heart of an enemy? Brethren, whatever such a man may hope or think, he never was a Christian. He is a hypocrite, and his hope shall be as the spider's web when God taketh away the soul.

3. The Christian may see to whom all praise is due. Not to himself, not to his own faithfulness. Faithful indeed he must be; faithful indeed he will be. But in view of his faithfulness itself, as well as all its results—in view of all that he is as a Christian, his language must be, "By the grace of God I am what I am." God begins the work, and God carries it onward.

Not indeed against the will of man, but by making him willing. Not without our co-operation we will and do; but God works in us to will and to do. We repent, we love, we give the heart to God, we return from our backslidings, we press toward the mark, we perfect holiness in the fear of God, but without God we never should; and when he begins this good work, he performs it until the day of Jesus Christ. If, Dear Brethren, you belong to the number of those who love God, he will not leave you, either to a tempting world, nor to the devil, nor to yourselves. He will cause all things, the assaults of Satan, the temptations that beset you, your very sins, to work together for your good. No part of your salvation will be neglected. In his own Almighty arms he will carry you through the opposing hosts of earth and hell; he will give you the victory and the crown of everlasting life. Give yourself therefore to him in holy love, in unfaltering trust, and wipe away every tear. As God is true, eternal life is yours. Jesus will not forget the souls cleansed in his own blood. Not one of them shall be lost. In a little time conflicts, trials, temptation, sorrow, and sin will be over and past. On Mount Zion, in the light and amid the glories of eternity, you shall retrace the care, the love, the grace that brought you to its joys. And then, Brethren, we shall not give credit to our own faithfulness, and to our own resolutions. But whatever may be our speculations here, there, without a feeling or a note of discord, shall we say together, "Not unto us, but unto thy name be all the glory." "Blessing, and honor, and glory, and power, unto Him that loved us, and washed us from our sins in his own blood."

Finally. In view of this subject I would invite those who are yet in their sins, to comply with the terms of the Gospel. I bring to you, My Dear Friends, this invitation, not without, but with the *promise* of salvation. My commission is not to say to you, Repent and believe the Gospel, and you *may be*, or perhaps you will be saved; but believe the Gospel and you shall be saved. I do not indeed say that you will be saved if you repent and then draw back to perdition; God forbid. But I say, he that believeth on the Son, hath passed from death unto life, and shall not come into condemnation. I do not say that you *can not* repent and believe, and then draw back to perdition; I do not say that watchfulness, and care, and diligence, and effort will not be necessary to secure final salvation. But I do say, Begin this work to-day, and by the grace of God it will be completed in eternal glory. Begin this work to-day, now, and the promise of God's all-sufficient grace is yours. Begin this work to-day, and you shall be kept by the power of God through faith unto salvation. This is no enterprise depending, in its results of eternal life and death, upon chance; but on the unchangeable promise of the unchangeable God. It is not an affair of accident or hap-hazard, is not a heaven which may or may not be yours, but heaven made sure by the attributes and pledged by the oath of God. Fear not, then. Believe on the Lord Jesus Christ to-day, and heaven *shall be* your eternal home, and God thy God forever and ever.

VI.

WHAT IS TRUTH?

"Pilate saith unto him, What is truth?"—*John* xviii. 38.

This Roman governor seems to have been fully initiated into the skepticism of those philosophers who admitted but one truth, viz., that nothing could be determined to be true. After hearing our Lord declare himself to have come into the world to bear witness to the truth, and that every one that is of the truth heard his voice, he contemptuously threw out the question, *What is truth?* and disdaining to wait for an answer, "went out again to the Jews."

I need not say, that modern skepticism is of the same sort. The licentious depravity of the human heart is in nothing more apparent, than in its propensity to bring all practical truth into doubt and uncertainty. This, at a stroke, breaks the bonds of moral obligation. Rebellion against the Most High, in its own imaginings, is thus emancipated from his dominion, and brought into the joyous liberty of doing as it listeth; as if truth were destroyed by being doubted,—as if the pillars of God's throne were not strong enough to stand against the doubts of disloyalty.

From the general form of the question in the text, and from the declaration of Christ which occasioned it, that he came into the world to bear witness to the truth, we are led to give to the inquiry both a general and a particular answer.

What then is truth? I answer generally—

I. Truth is the reality of things.

Truth in this sense may be distinguished from the propositions which declare it. It is asserted, for example, that the sun shines. This proposition, in common language, may be said to be *truth;* meaning that its language accords with the fact, the reality. But then, though this accordance of words with things is necessary to the truth of a proposition, yet the truth, in the sense now referred to, does in no respect depend on the assertion. The truth, the reality of things, exists, whether it be asserted or not.

Truth also may be distinguished from the knowledge and the belief of it. Contrary to a favorite conceit of all skepticism, truth exists in absolute independence of all knowledge and all belief. No doubting, no ignorance, no sincerity of unbelief can alter it. We know that two and two are four, and so it would be whether we knew it or not. We believe that the earth revolves around the sun, and so it is, believe it or disbelieve it, as we may. Things are what they are, independently of all assertion, of all evidence, of all knowledge, of all belief, and of all unbelief. Whether it be known or not, asserted or not, believed or not, there is a reality of things.

This reality of things comprises the nature, the relations, and the fitness of things. It comprises the nature of things. Every thing has a nature, or properties peculiar to itself—a nature which is essential to its existence. Matter has a nature by which it is distinguished from spirit. Animals have a nature by which they are distinguished from men; men and angels, angels and God, God and all creatures, have a nature by which they also are distinguished. This nature of things is a part of the reality of things.

The reality of things includes also their relations. These are founded in the nature of things. From the nature of God and the nature of man, result certain relations between God and man. From the nature of men and the nature of their condition, result their various relations to one another. It is perfectly obvious that so long as things are what they are, their relations must be what they are; for these relations result from the nature of things, and are determined by it, and are therefore as unchangeable as the nature of things from which they result. No opinions of our own, no exercise of the authority or power of God can alter them, while the nature of things is unaltered. They are a part of the reality of things; nor is any change conceivable, unless we can conceive things to be what they are, and not to be what they are, at the same time.

Once more: Truth, or the reality of things, comprises the fitness of things, or their adaptation to certain ends or results. This fitness of things may be contemplated as it results from their nature, considered as actual existences; and also as the ground or reason of the divine choice or will which gave them existence. In one sense, whatever God has created is what it is, because God willed that it should be what it is. This may be assigned as the reason why men are what *they* are, angels what they are; in a word, why the universe is what it is. As actual existences, all things, with their properties, relations, and fitnesses, are what God willed them to be, and because he willed them to be what they are. But it is not irreverent to ask, why did God create things as they are? The true answer honors God: because by being what they are, they are best fitted to answer the best ends. If the Most High made things as they are for this reason (and to suppose any other is to dishonor him), then there was a fitness of things by which, as a Being infinitely wise and good, he could not fail to be influenced. Thus it was right that the Creator should secure the greatest good possible to him to secure; and there was some one way in which this might be done. It was so not because he willed it to be so. God could not have prevented it, or caused it to be otherwise. To say that there was a way in which he could secure greater good than he could secure, is an absurdity; and to say that there might be *many* ways in which he could secure the same degree of good, is to say that God has chosen the way which he has chosen without a reason for his choice. There was therefore a fitness of things which was as independent of his will, as his own existence and attributes. This fitness of things is a reality which no act of the will of God, no exercise of his power, no mandate of his sovereignty could alter. It is that which makes right what it is and wrong what it is, beyond all change. This fitness of things, instead of being determined by the will of God, determines his will, and is the ground or reason why God has done what he has done, and will do what he will do throughout eternity. To ask why it is, or whence it is, is like asking why or whence is infinite space or interminable duration, or why or whence is there a self-existent God.

Nor is it dishonoring God to say this. To place God above this fitness of things, is to place him above the eternal rule of right; to suppose him to act without a reason for what he does, and therefore not to exalt but to degrade his character. It is the glory of God, not merely that he does as he pleases, but that he pleases to do that which is fit and proper to be done. This fitness of things then is independently and eternally the same; and is a part of that reality of things by which the acts and doings of God are determined, and which we call truth.

But the question in the text, as I have remarked, has a further application to that system of truth, to which our Lord came into the world to bear witness. *What then is truth* in this application of the term? I answer—

II. It is *that reality of things which the Gospel reveals.*

In other words, the great system of doctrines, of laws, of precepts, of promises, of threatenings, to which Christ has testified, is a simple declaration of things as they are. These things are what they are asserted to be, not because Christ declared them to be so, nor because his testimony is supported by signs and wonders wrought by the finger of God. They are realities just as they are declared to be, independently of all testimony. They are a part of the reality of things, as this comprises the nature, the relations, and the fitness of things.

This may be illustrated in several particulars.

1. The Lord Jesus Christ hath borne witness to the character of God. He has told us what God is, what he is in himself, and the relations which he sustains to us. His testimony is true, because in his representations he deviates not in the least from the reality. Had nothing been declared concerning him, the self-existent God had been, and been what he is. Admit the begun existence of an atom, and you admit the existence of Him who inhabiteth eternity. Admit a creation, and you admit a self-efficient Being. As an eternal, self-existent, independent Being, he must be an unchangeable and an infinite Being. As an infinite Being, he must be an all-perfect Being. He must be as wise, as powerful, as good, as true, as just, as holy as this book declares him to be. Being what he is in the infinitude of his nature and perfection of his attributes, he must sustain to his creatures the same relations which this book reveals. For example, the relations which he sustains to creatures as their Creator, can not but be what they are, for he can not cease to be their Creator. So of every other relation, it can not but be what it is, himself being what he is. What God ever has been, God will ever be; and we may as well think of causing an infringement on his Godhead in that eternity which is past, as in that which is to come. The being, the perfections, the relations of God do not depend on the testimony of revelation. There is such a God, and the testimony of this book concerning him is true, because the God whom it reveals is a reality.

2. The Bible also reveals the providential government of God. It teaches that God governs the world; that his government includes all things, even the minutest, in its plan; that it is formed, arranged, and managed according to his eternal purpose, and carried onward to its results with all the securities of omnipotence. Whatever God has purposed shall take place, will take place. Whatever does or shall take place, will, all things considered, be better than its prevention by himself. The result will show God's capacity to bless the universe of his own creation. He can not be God, if he has put the result at hazard by opening a door to the operations of chance. He can not be God, if he increase in knowledge or form new purposes. We submit the question to any one: Is this world of intelligent, sentient beings, forsaken of its Maker? Yea, is this universe of worlds and of systems abandoned to some blind, accidental, fortuitous energy? Or, is there a designing God on the throne?

3. This book also reveals the Moral Government of God. Its subjects, not the insects of a day, who through their insignificance can retreat from the responsibilities of their Maker's government, but creatures of God, made after his similitude, fitted to correspond with him and heaven, and to live and act as co-workers with God forever. And is it not so? Is it credible that there should be a perfect God, and he not give existence to such beings? A perfect God, and the universe without a creature qualified to admire, to love, to serve and to enjoy God! A universe of his making, destitute of all the moral magnificence and glories of a moral kingdom! No subjects in the purity and joys of holiness, reflecting his moral image; no sanctuary of blessed worshipers; no intelligence to see and adore Him that sitteth on the throne; no heart to bring offerings of gratitude; every song of praise still, and God, the glorious God, the mere superintendent of the laws of matter and of instinct! Such a God as Jehovah reigning over such a desert! No. If there is a God, then hath he moral and accountable subjects, and will reign over them amid the glories and grandeurs of eternity. Can we doubt it? Human consciousness attests human accountability. It attests our existence as intelligent, voluntary agents; and from this fact, the conviction of right and wrong action is inseparable. As agents we do and must act, and right and wrong are nothing but the rela-

tions, tendencies, or fitness of free, voluntary actions—relations as inseparable from actions as the properties of matter or spirit are from its existence. Can we suppose the actions of an intelligent, voluntary agent such as man is, without tendencies to good and evil? The eye of his own consciousness looking upon all the movements of the inner man, and himself ignorant of their tendencies? An intelligent being thus knowing right from wrong—knowing that the one tends to bless the universe, the other to fill it with lamentation and woe; a free, voluntary agent, qualified to choose between right and wrong, and yet under no obligation to choose right? It is no more possible that man should possess these powers and properties, and be released from moral obligation for a moment, than that he should possess and not possess them at the same time. He may deny it, he may argue against it, but he knows better. By his very nature, by the very properties of his conscious being, he is doomed to the conviction of his accountability—a conviction that ever does and ever will possess the soul with the certainty that whatever is, is.

4. The Scriptures contain the law of God. This law is true, not simply because it is God's law (though this is the highest proof of its perfection), but because man, from the nature, relations, and fitness of things, ought to love God with all his heart, and his neighbor as himself. He ought thus to love God, because there is no object so great, so excellent, so worthy of affection. Here is no mistake. For who does not know that love is the fulfilling of the law? Who does not know that *he is bound to intend to do all the good he can?* Who does not know that he is bound to act from this principle? Who that is a man does not know it, as surely as he knows that he is a man? We all know it. The whole world knows it. Atheists, deists, infidels, sinners, devils, all know it. All know that the purpose to do all the good we can, expressing itself in action, is the perfection of man in character and in happiness; the perfection of one and of all of the entire moral universe. The divine law therefore does not create obligation, merely by its promulgation. It declares that to be our duty, which is so in the nature of things. What it declares is reality. Were God to make a law forbidding us to love him with all the heart (if such a supposition may be made), it would not destroy our obligation to love him. God would still be lovely.

While God then remains what he is, and man what he is, our duty to God can never change, can never cease.

The same thing may be said of our duty to our neighbor. Nothing, no authority or command of God can make it right to hate a fellow-creature, or to exercise malevolence or cruelty. The law therefore which defines our duty to our neighbor, is not the dictate of despotic authority, but the simple declaration of what is true, what is real, what is lovely, what ought to be done were there no law.

5. The precepts of the law and the Gospel are also founded in the nature of things. It is as obvious to every one as are the tendencies of actions—and the tendencies of actions are as obvious as the tendencies of fire and water—that it can not be right to lie, to steal, to murder. Examine which moral precept of the Gospel you will, you will see that it is just what it should be, making reality the standard; that it declares that to be right which is so in the very nature, relations, and fitness of things; that let any other precept be put in its place, still that and that only would be the right, true, and best precept. The greatest enemies of Jesus have been obliged to lay this testimony at his feet.

6. The penalty of the law, and the more awful curse of the Gospel, rest on the same foundation. These, dreadful as they are, are no arbitrary denunciations. They result unavoidably from the nature, relations, and fitness of things. It is fit that God should administer a Moral Government—a government by law. It is fit that obedience to the best of laws should be secured, and disobedience prevented if possible by motives, and that these should be as weighty and powerful as may be. Obedience to the best law is the best thing, and it is fit to secure the highest possible degree of it; and it is equally right that any and every thing that shall come into competition with this result should be sacrificed. The sacrifice of the rebel's happiness, and that in any degree, may be demanded, for obedience is the best thing, and it is fit that the highest possible degree of it should be secured; and that whatever this highest, best end demands, should be done. On the certain principle then, that a less penalty would not secure as much obedience as the greater, this highest, best end, does require the penalty of God's law.

Or view the subject in another light. The greatest good

requires a moral system—a Moral Government over moral beings. This is a government by authority, whose influence and energy lie in this—*thus saith the Eternal King*. But this influence, this authority, this right to give law which imposes an obligation to obey, can not be sustained a moment unless the king show that in giving his law and punishing its violation, he acts on the principles of eternal rectitude. He must show that he esteems things as they are, and will act accordingly; that he considers his law as the necessary means of the highest good, and as of the same value therefore as the end itself—as his own perfect dominion and the highest good of his universe. Now the subject who violates this law, pronounces it unworthy of regard, tramples on the authority of the lawgiver, and virtually treads the whole system of Moral Government in the dust. If God does nothing his designs are defeated, and all that infinite wisdom and goodness have done, or ever can do to secure their high purpose, is in ruins. God then must do something, or the catastrophe is inevitable. And what? The sinner has shown how he esteems the law; God must now show his regard for it. He must show that he esteems it as the best means of the best end, and that whatever comes into competition with his authority shall be sacrificed. He must show a measure of indignation toward this act of the rebel, which shall tell how he regards his authority and his law; that he will turn a revolted world into hell, rather than subvert the principles on which his throne alone can stand. How then shall this be done? Every one answers, only by inflicting punishment on the transgressor. But what punishment? If he inflict a temporary evil, it must be either because that will show his true and real regard for his law and authority; or because he is unwilling to express that regard by the entire sacrifice of the sinner's happiness. But can any temporary evil show God's real disapprobation, his just indignation for an act that would destroy all good? Can it express his real estimate of that law which he values more than a universe beside? Would any thing less than endless punishment be a just expression of the value he puts upon it? Why then does he inflict a limited punishment? Plainly because he values the sinner's happiness so much that he is not willing to sacrifice it for any regard which he has for his authority, and for those higher interests which that authority is pledged to protect.

He values the well-being of the rebel more than he values his authority, his law, his kingdom. He is willing to sacrifice the greater to the less. He is not just to his kingdom. He no longer acts upon principle, and shows that he does not. All ground for confidence and reason for submission are gone. His authority is prostrated. He is no longer entitled to respect nor worthy of submission; but is virtually driven an insulted, degraded exile from his throne. The bands of his moral administration are broken for eternity, and nothing is to be expected but that the fires of hell burst forth unchecked, and rebellion stand triumphant on the ruins. Ought this to be done? or, will God act upon the principles of eternal righteousness? Is this the truth, the reality? or has God guarded his throne and his kingdom by the securities of a law with an eternal penalty?

View this topic in yet another light. Suppose the penalty of the divine law repealed—declared null and void. What then? Other things remaining as they are, would hell be annihilated? Sin is hell. Where is it? Wherever sin exists and reigns unsubdued and unrestrained. So it is, so it must be so long as sin is sin; and in proportion to the guilt must be the torment. To the honor of God let it be remembered that he can not make sin holiness, nor its appropriate effects aught but wretchedness. Sin is, and must be hell, as an eternal reality. As to say that he who obeys the law of God shall *live*, is declaring one of the plainest and most unalterable of all realities, viz., that he that is holy shall be happy; so, to say that he who disobeys that law shall die, is declaring a reality equally plain and unalterable, viz., that he that sins shall be wretched. Break then the everlasting chains, and put out the fires of the pit, it remaineth to the sinner against God an eternal reality, "myself am hell."

7. The great doctrines of the Gospel rest on the same foundation. The facts, the things declared, are realities.

(1.) The sinful depravity of man is a reality. The testimony of the Scriptures does not alter his character, nor make it what it is. The Scriptures only give us an account of the matter of fact. The conduct of men evinces the reality and power of the selfish principle in the human heart beyond all question, and this by three incontrovertible principles. The one is, that the conduct of unrenewed men, in its fairest forms, can all be accounted for by tracing it to this principle. Secondly, there is a total destitution of all that is decisive of the holy principle. And thirdly, there is much, very much, that is absolutely decisive of such a sinful principle. Accordingly, the conduct of men does, in all human belief, evince its existence as decisively as the burning of a house shows the property of the element that destroys it. We no more think of exempting any individual from the operation of those laws, checks, and influences that are designed to restrain this principle, than we think of kindling a fire in the midst of our dwellings. Throughout the wide world, all the laws, provisions, and methods adopted by men to regulate the conduct of mankind are simply an appeal in some form to the selfish principle. There is no hope in, no reliance upon, any other in the human bosom; and for this reason, we know that there is no other there to be relied upon. Who is willing to dispense with bonds, and deeds, and mortgages, and trust the simple naked principle of doing as we would be done by, in his fellow-men? Take away all else, all regard to law, to public opinion, to reputation, to profit, to interest in every form—suppose no security against acts of violence, but the simple abstract principle of benevolent action—consternation would possess every mind in a moment. We all know that the security that we feel in every community of human beings is, that selfishness in some form will govern selfishness in other forms. We all know that the men of this world are honest, and true, and just, and kind, just so far, and no farther than it is for their interest to be so, and the proof is, that in all the wide range of business and intercourse all act on this assumption. This is just, or it is not. If it is, the fact is established. If it is not, it is a universal slander of our fellow-men of which all are guilty. These things show what man thinks of man, or rather what he knows to be true of him. And if we look at the providence of God, how do sorrow and sickness, trials, and calamities, pain and death, tell us that God is angry with us; how does this groaning creation proclaim that man as a moral being is in ruins! Appeal also to human consciousness. Who does not know, that not the principle to impart, but the principle to obtain all the good he can, has been *his* governing principle? And this is depravity in its perfection. Oh, My Hearers, we all know our own hearts in this matter. Human depravity then, is a part of the reality of things, a fact notorious as the sun in the heavens, whether the Gospel had declared it or not. The reality existed, in all its deformity, before the picture was drawn.

(2.) This depravity of man is *by nature.* By this I do not mean, that the reason why man sins, in the first instance, is a previous sin. That the cause of all sin is itself sin, is a self-evident absurdity. Nor do I mean, that man deserves damnation for being what his Creator makes him. Nor, that man has a nature which compels him to sin; nor that man is not in his first, and in every moral affection, exercise, or act, an accountable, free moral agent. None other can do right, or do wrong. But I mean, that the universal sinfulness of mankind, free moral agents as they are, must be traced to their nature. The universality of a fact proves the universality of some cause, ground, or reason of it. The universal fact, that heavy bodies, in all circumstances, move toward the earth, is proof that the fact is *by nature.* So in the present case, the universal sinfulness of man, proves that it is by nature. For, in all circumstances, under every possible influence of light, truth, motives, example, persuasion, he exhibits, with absolute unvarying uniformity, the same moral character. Appeal to the history of all nations and all ages, when or where is the solitary exception to the fact, that selfishness is the first governing principle of human conduct; the element and substance of human character, as it first exists in every human being. Show us the exception, by showing us the man whose first moral character has not been formed by the selfish principle. Show us the instance of prevention, by the influence of truth, or motives, or the power of example, or by any influence within the appropriate limits of our earthly being. Show us the man not depraved by nature, and we will show you a stone that does not tend toward the earth by nature. We know indeed, that the phenomena in these cases differ widely. So also do the causes. One is the cause of free moral action, and consistent with the nature of such action. The other is a physical cause and appropriate only to a physical effect. Still the cases are alike in one important respect—in uniformity of result. And if the uniformity with which an unsupported body moves toward the earth proves that it is by nature heavy, so does the uniformity of human sinfulness prove that man is depraved by nature. No change of condition, no increase of light, or of motives, no instructions, nor warnings, no power of argument, or example, changes the result. Unless there be some interposition not included in these things—unless there be something above nature, the case is hopeless. Placed anywhere within the appropriate limits of his earthly being, man, an intelligent, free moral agent as he is, has also such a nature that he will be a sinner.

(3.) An Atonement, if we admit the pardon of sin, is another reality. We have seen that according to the nature of things, especially of law and Moral Government, sin must be punished. A law without sanctions, or which dispenses with its sanctions, every child knows, is no law. A law once broken must cease to be a law, or its authority must be sustained, either by the execution of penalty, or by an Atonement. The penalty must be executed, or that must be done which shall answer the end of its execution. Now these are plain principles, and regarded as no less infallible by the unperverted mind, than that food will nourish, and poison destroy the body. The conviction of their truth and infallibility results from, is coeval with, and as it were incorporated into our very being. They are among the earliest, most unhesitating convictions of the human mind; being associated with the condition of infancy itself, in its subjection and subordination to the will of a superior. Every tenant of a prison understands them, as truly as the judge that condemned him. The nature and end of law, the reasons, the *why* and the *wherefore* of its penalty, are understood and admitted as among the most necessary and infallible of all truths. No man ever did, or ever can live and act as a member of human society, without admitting and acting on these principles. Men may deny them, they may speculate themselves into perdition in defiance of them, but they can never speculate themselves wholly out of the secret and troublesome conviction of their reality. In view of a coming eternity they can never rest in the securities of infallible truth, till they rest upon these principles. What? A society of free, voluntary beings like men, living harmoniously, happily, without any rule of action! Such a world, such a God as Jehovah, and he not reigning over it! A moral kingdom without a law! Or what would be substantially the same thing, a law proffering pardon to its violator, promising rewards alike to loyalty and rebellion! The whole influence of the king inviting to one as well as to the other! His law, leaving the execution of penalty at the option of the culprit! The King of kings do this; withdraw every check and restraint from human selfishness, and throw the reins loose upon all its waywardness and violence! Think what man did in paradise,—what angels did before the eternal throne, guarded as it was by all the jealousies of the Godhead; and then say who would wish to live—who would *dare* to live in such a community, though its name were heaven? No; if sin be pardoned, law must be sustained by an Atonement. The pardon of a sinner demands an Atonement on the same immutable principle as the violation of law demands its curse. If the pardon of sin be a reality, then is an Atonement a reality.

(4.) The necessity of Regeneration is another illustration of this subject, a necessity resulting from the nature, relations, and fitness of things. "Except a man be born again, he can not see the kingdom of God," is no arbitrary decision; not a rule of exclusion from endless bliss by the prerogative of mere sovereignty. The impossibility asserted, is in the nature of things. Let this book decide as it may, there can be no heaven to a sinner without this change. What is heaven? A holy world; a world whose employment, society, joys are holy; the habitation of God's holiness, and whose rapturous song is—"Holy, holy, holy Lord God Almighty." What fitness then has the unholy for such a world as this? When removed into that eternity which is just before him, not a single object can be found to satisfy one wish of his heart. His spirit, with desires stretching onward to immortality, must remain in eternal want. He has no taste for contemplating the glory of God. He has never seen his need of a Saviour; never felt his obligations to him, nor sought redemption by his blood. How then can he adore him in the songs of the redeemed? What has an enemy of God to do with employments and joys like these? Alas, he knows not the meaning of that song, "Worthy is the Lamb." There is not a note which he can sing; its every sentiment were a lie on his tongue and anguish to his heart. Admit him then into that world, surround him with all that blesses the bright hosts of glory, and he is unable to taste one drop of that bliss with which their cup overflows.

While each redeemed celestial, with endless rapture, cries, "Worthy is the Lamb! worthy is the Lamb!" he can only say in the language of real feeling, "Oh, what a weariness is this!" In the presence of that God he hates, among heaven's acclaiming throng, he is a solitary, forsaken, wretched outcast! In the midst of all that ocean of blessedness there is not a drop for him! So sure is it, that to the unholy mind heaven itself must be an absolute desert. The solemn truth of the sinner's immortality, the living fountains from the throne of God, are to him only sources of woe, and hell must be sought as his only refuge, the only relief from torments with which heaven would overwhelm his guilty spirit.

(5.) The necessity of the Divine Spirit's influence in Regeneration is another reality. "Except a man be born of water and of the Spirit, he can not enter into the kingdom of God," is a truth, whether God had declared it or not. Not indeed that it would be truly and properly a miracle, if man as a free moral agent should make himself a new heart. Not that man has not that heart, and soul, and mind, and strength with which his Maker requires him to love Him,—powers in man, which according to the very terms of the law, limit God's demand; but that man, through his own voluntary cherished perverseness, will never use these powers as he ought, without the special, supernatural, transforming grace of God. Admit then the fact, that mankind are depraved by nature, and you admit the fact that no light, nor moral suasion by truth or motives, will ever accomplish the requisite moral transformation in his character. Let Paul reason; let Apollos persuade; they are nothing,—but it is God who giveth the increase. Let the powers of oratory—to convince, to allure, to awe, be exhausted, such is the nature of man, and such his perverseness in sin, that no power of truth, no charms of redeeming love, nor the revealed glories of heaven, nor the rising smoke of torment, will rescue a human being from the character and condemnation of a depraved sinner. This fact stands out before us, with all the obviousness and all the certainty of the ordinances of heaven. It is not the result of divine prerogative, but of human perverseness; not the result of imperfection in God's work, but of perverting the powers of a being made in the similitude of God; not in the way of God's mending his work, but in the way of a new moral creation, and according to the nature and laws of such a creation, and compared with which the former shall not be remembered nor come into mind.

I might make these illustrations more extensive and minute. Enough however has been said to show what truth is, and particularly that *the truth*, to which the Son of God bore witness, is the reality of things. In this sense of the term we are to consider the Gospel, not as making these things what they are by the testimony of its Author, or by our belief or disbelief of them, but as simply declaring what is reality. In a word, the Gospel is a glass held up before us by the Son of God, to show us these tremendous realities as eternal truth.

REMARKS.

1. This subject gives us an exalted view of the Gospel. It reveals to us realities. It exhibits the things of which it testifies just as they are. Did we know nothing more of the declarations of this book than that they are the declarations of an Almighty Being who had power to execute his will; were we obliged to regard all their importance as consisting in this, that they are *his* declarations, and to admit that any others coming from him would have the same importance, even then it would seem as if they would irresistibly claim our respect. Nay, were we satisfied that it were a mere fiction; that the God whom it reveals, in his perfections, his government, his doings; that the immense system of dispensations here unfolded; the work of redemption here portrayed; the final judgment of angels and of men, and its scenes of eternal retribution, were mere images of the fancy, still this book might reasonably excite our highest wonder. But how must our views and feelings rise, when we see and know that what we read is all reality; that what this book reveals is truth, whether we believe or disbelieve it—truth not merely as supported by the highest testimony, but truth consisting in the reality of things—truth comprising the nature of things which the unchangeable God has given them; the relations of things which are as unchangeable as the things themselves; and that fitness of things which is unchangeable by God himself. The Gospel tells us not what *might* have been, not what may be or may not be, but *what is*, what God is, what Christ is, what the divine law is, what man is, what the way of salvation is, what the judgment is, what heaven is, what hell is. It brings out and spreads

these great realities before us. It is the mirror of truth held up by the Son of God, to show us these realities. No sooner do we look into it than we behold the self-existent God in all his majesty and glory. We see his eternal and unchangeable purposes formed by infinite wisdom, and rolling onward to their complete and glorious fulfillment; we see ourselves accountable and immortal beings, under that law which is the great bond of Jehovah's empire, and fixed as his throne; we see ourselves too, the transgressors of that law, and with the amazing interests of the soul before us, condemned by it to bear its fearful penalty; we see a world in revolt, and the work of its redemption achieved by its God—a world which is the only place of our probation for the allotments of eternity—a world where the offers of pardon and everlasting life are made, and repeated to us in the midst of all our provocations and guilt—a world visited by angels, and redeemed saints, as ministering spirits—a world, in a word, in which, through the efficacy of Jesus' blood and the power of the Holy Ghost, the work of redeeming love is carried on to its glorious consummation. In a moment we see the heavens passing away, the elements melting with fervent heat, the earth and its works burned up. The throne of judgment rises to our view with all its glories and its terrors. On the one hand the bright hosts of the redeemed are ascending through the portals of glory to the throne of God and the Lamb. We behold their white robes, their palms of victory, their eternally brightening splendors, and increasing joys. On the other, the multitude of guilty, impenitent, unpardoned immortals, descending to the chains of darkness—the groans, the agonies of eternal despair. How solemn, how tremendous, that all this is no empty vision—no dream—but reality! With what holy awe should we unfold these sacred leaves, and read this book of God!

2. How safe and how happy are they who are of the truth! To be perfectly conformed to truth is to be perfectly holy. The reality of things perfectly accords with the feelings, affections, and purposes of all beings who are of the truth. Every thing is exactly as they would have it. God is just such a God as they would have him to be; his government just what they desire; Christ just what they wish him to be; the divine law, the Gospel in its provisions, exactly suits their desires and their

wishes. The vast reality of things they would not alter. Nothing in it or about it crosses their path or disturbs their quiet. The mighty whole is unspeakably lovely and glorious. With God himself they survey it and pronounce it "very good." That which pleases God pleases them; that which satisfies God satisfies them. The amazing system of realities which is and which constitutes the glory and the blessedness of God is their portion. What can annoy their peace or lessen their happiness? What if the sea rage and the heavens gather blackness? What if the hail descend, and the lightnings play, and the thunders roar, and earth shake to its centre? Still God lives, God reigns. Can God injure? No, for they are like himself. Can Christ? No, for they are one with him. Can the divine law? No; they are rescued from its curse and conformed to its demands. Can the Gospel? No; they walk in its light and are surrounded, protected, comforted, blessed by its promises of everlasting truth and grace. Can wicked men or devils hurt them? No; truth binds them in chains of everlasting darkness. Nothing, nothing can harm them. What God hath said, God will do. He will carry on his purposes to their perfect accomplishment; his kingdom will rise in all its glory; that new and brighter creation of Christian promises, the amazing reality of things, will stand an eternal monument of the wisdom, and power, and goodness of the infinite God, and they be found blessed whom God makes blessed. Learn then, Dear Brethren, the truth. Love the truth, walk in the truth, obey the truth. In this way all, all is well with you for eternity.

3. Our subject gives us an interesting view of the work of the ministry. This work consists pre-eminently in the exhibition of the truth or the reality of things. Its design, its end is to conform the character of man to this reality, and thus to bring him, in his affections, purposes, and action, into an unchangeable alliance with his God. How high and awful a function is this! The means are those realities which the Scriptures display; the God there revealed; the Saviour, his incarnation, his miracles of grace, his great sacrifice by blood, his dominion and his triumphs; the Holy Ghost, his transforming power in the Renovation and Sanctification of his people; the government of God; his law; its holiness, perfection, immutability in its demands, its penalty; man, a guilty, ruined

immortal; redemption, unvailing the triune God in all the attractions of infinite love and grace to the guilty and the lost; angels, as ministering spirits to the heirs of salvation; death, the end of probation; the resurrection of all earth's millions, a material universe on fire, judgment, heaven, hell;—these are the realities of exhibition—these are the realities to be brought to influence, through divine grace, the soul of man, to illuminate its powers by a celestial light, to expel the corrupting, enthralling control of this materialism; to establish the dominion of God in the soul, and introduce it to an intimate eternal fellowship with the Father of spirits. What an honor thus to release, under God, these prisoners from their bondage of vanity and shadows, guilt and madness, and to raise them into the regions, and place them amid the light and transforming glories of eternal realities! That labor surely can not want dignity, which associates with itself the power of the Holy Ghost, in bestowing upon man such a character and preparing him for the destinies of eternity.

What advantages too are possessed by the Christian minister for the cultivation of personal holiness. The high-priest of old occasionally entered the Holy place; the minister of the Gospel lives and acts continually in the sanctuary of divine and eternal realities. His work, though done on earth, respects the things of eternity. His message is from the God of eternity. His business is the same that employs those spirits who are sent from on high to minister to the heirs of salvation. Even in his study, he seems as it were in the council-chamber of God. In his ministrations he stands in that temple where the glory of God doth lighten it, and the Lamb is the light thereof. What a savor of heavenly things in Christ should rest on such a man! What superiority to worldly ambitions and selfish aims! What devotion to God and to the kingdom of his dear Son, and to the salvation of earth's redeemed millions should characterize a Christian minister!

It is true, My Brethren, we have cause, abundant cause to serve the Lord with humility and with many tears. Fear, and weakness, and much trembling become an apostle; much more do they become us. We ought to think little of ourselves, but we may not think lightly of our calling. As a work which so brings us in contact with the realities of God's revelation, and is designed to fit men for their eternal destiny, and is associated with the supernatural agency of God, it should lead us to stir up the gift that is in us, and to consecrate ourselves to it with unwavering purpose, and to expect through a divine blessing, results becoming God's own institution. Let such be the practical influence of this view of our office. While we draw our instructions from these oracles of God, we shall be clad with truth as with a garment. While we bow to the dictates of that truth which we preach, and yield to the power of that grace which we supplicate, we shall have strength to be faithful. Then with what emotion shall we witness, not by faith but by sight, the realities of the judgment and of eternity! To have obtained mercy ourselves, and to have imparted it to others; to recognize amid the innumerable multitude the souls of our ministry; to have given to these, under God, that far more exceeding and eternal weight of glory; to hail them as our joy and crown, in the presence of the Lord Jesus Christ at his coming;—with what rapture and praise shall we see the hand of Eternal Mercy place such a crown on such unworthy heads!

Finally: how vain it is to deny or to reject the truth! Truth is the reality of things. Object, cavil, doubt, disbelieve, deny the truth, you can not change it. Come with what weapon you will, you are in arms against the reality of things. Until right shall be wrong, sin holiness; until it can be right to hate God and to hate your neighbor; until you can make heaven hell and hell heaven, and subject to dissolution and change, the being and attributes of Him who is eternal, you can do nothing. Truth will remain. It will do all its work. It will bless its friends, it will crush its enemies.

These hills and rocks shall crumble and perish; this earth and these heavens shall pass away and have no place any more; but truth, the word of God, abideth forever. Truth, Fellow-Sinners, will still commission death to sweep on its chilling blast, and carry these bodies to their graves. Truth will seize these spirits for their last trial, blessed or unblessed with the preparation of peace. It will sound the trump of God, and with the archangel's voice call you forth for its judgment and its retribution. It will summon you to that throne whereon God sitteth, and in its own clear and cloudless day will show you to the Judge and the Judge to you. It will utter in all its fearfulness the doom of the second death, and in the revealed righteousness of this its last, unalterable and resistless decree, will stop every mouth. Truth will carry you away to her eternal prison of wailing and despair; it will forge and put on the chains of darkness, fix the impassable gulf, and light its quenchless fires. It will forbid all pity, exclude all mercy, quench all hope, and bind destiny forevermore. Oh, who will deny, who reject the truth? Ignorance may willfully refuse instruction, and unbelief, and skepticism, and a heart devoted to the world may make the fleeting phantoms of earth the only realities, and the realities of God's revelation the only phantoms. The things of truth displaced from thought, and lost in the obscurity of distance or doubt, may relinquish the whole man to these lying vanities. These may form his character, and his preparation for the scenes of his immortality shall be as if God were not; as if Christ, and heaven, and hell, and all that lies beyond this short life were not. But, Oh, when these realities shall break on the sight in eternal day—when truth shall show them to such a man—when God shall become a reality, never more to be forgotten or unthought of in the terrors of his indignation—heaven a reality never to be forgotten or unthought of as a lost inheritance, and hell a reality in the ceaseless experience of its woes—who, who then will not wish that he had received the truth in the love of it?

THE END.

www.ingramcontent.com/pod-product-compliance
Lightning Source LLC
LaVergne TN
LVHW020920110826
845150LV00004B/725

* 9 7 8 1 4 2 5 5 5 4 9 3 4 *